CULTURESHOCK!

W9-BZY-379

A Survival Guide to Customs and Etiquette

AUSTRALIA

5X12/07LT 10/07

Ilsa Sharp

GRAPHIC ARTS®
BOOKS

Marshall Cavendish
Editions

First published in1992
This edition 2005
Copyright © Ilsa Sharp

This edition published in 2005 by:

Marshall Cavendish Editions
An imprint of Marshall Cavendish International (Asia) Pte Ltd
1 New Industrial Road, Singapore 536196
Tel: (65) 6213 9300, fax: (65) 6285 4871.
Email: te@sg.marshallcavendish.com
Online bookstore: www.marshallcavendish.com/genref

and

Graphic Arts Center Publishing Company
P.O. Box 10306, Portland, Oregon 97296-0306
United States of America
Tel: (503) 226 2402
Website: www.gacpc.com

ISBN 981-261-117-7 (Asia & Rest of World)
ISBN 1-55868-925-7 (USA & Canada)
ISBN 0-462-00799-5 (Europe)

Printed in Singapore by Times Graphics Pte Ltd

ABOUT THE SERIES

Culture shock is a state of disorientation that can come over anyone who has been thrust into unknown surroundings, away from one's comfort zone. *CultureShock!* is a series of trusted and reputed guides which has, for decades, been helping expatriates and long-term visitors to cushion the impact of culture shock whenever they move to a new country.

Written by people who have lived in the country and experienced culture shock themselves, the authors share all the information necessary for anyone to cope with these feelings of disorientation more effectively. The guides are written in a style that is easy to read and covers a range of topics that will arm readers with enough advice, hints and tips to make their lives as normal as possible again.

Each book is structured in the same manner. It begins with the first impressions that visitors will have of that city or country. To understand a culture, one must first understand the people—where they came from, who they are, the values and traditions they live by, as well as their customs and etiquette. This is covered in the first half of the book

Then on with the practical aspects—how to settle in with the greatest of ease. Authors walk readers through how to find accommodation, get the utilities and telecommunications up and running, enrol the children in school and keep in the pink of health. But that's not all. Once the essentials are out of the way, venture out and try the food, enjoy more of the culture and travel to other areas. Then be immersed in the language of the country before discovering more about the business side of things.

To round off, snippets of basic information are offered before readers are 'tested' on customs and etiquette of the country. Useful words and phrases, a comprehensive resource guide and list of books for further research are also included for easy reference.

CONTENTS

PREFACE

I would like to think that this book may help explain Australia to newcomers and visitors and thus bridge any 'culture gaps', improving the chances of mutual empathy and friendship. It is my particular, personal wish that Australia and Asia should draw closer together.

I hope, too, that the book will help Australians understand themselves and what it is that makes their culture unique, by holding a mirror up to them and asking them to see themselves through outsiders' eyes.

Finally, I must beg Australia's pardon if any of my interpretations have been skewed somewhat by my own 'Sandgroper' bias, due to being located at Perth, despite my best efforts to avoid such imbalance, and for any other inadvertent 'greenhorn' errors.

This book would not have been possible without the help of the Australian people in general, or of many published writers already well established in the field of 'Australia-watching', besides numerous friends and acquaintances. If I have inadvertently omitted anyone's name, my sincere apologies.

I particularly want to acknowledge my debt to several reference works (for details of publishers, etc., refer to 'Further Reading' at the back of the book):
- *The Penguin Australian Encyclopaedia*
- *The Little Aussie Fact Book*, Margaret Nicholson
- *A Dictionary of Australian Colloquialisms*. G A Wilkes
- *The Macquarie Dictionary of Australian Quotations*
- *The Macquarie Book of Events*
- *The Lucky Country*. Donald Horne

Permissions
- *The Daily News*, Western Australia—Barry Thornton, Deputy Editor, for the meat pies picture.
- John Timbers of John Timbers Studio, London, for his photograph of Dame Edna Everage.
- Quotations from the *Macquarie Dictionary of Australian Quotations*, reprinted with permission of the publisher, The Macquarie Library Pty Ltd.

In Perth, Western Australia
- Siva Choy, for patience beyond the call of marriage, yet again.
- Dan (gardening buddy), Cally (walking buddy), Troy and Marina Nelson, for too much to list here, besides a smooth landing in Oz.
- Sandra and John Theseira, for much besides food, but the food *was* good!
- Danny and Jocelyn Stacey, also Denise and Joyce, for unfaltering mateship.
- Loyola and Eliza D'Souza, who wed in our home.
- Titus and Sandra Wumkes, our mates in the hills.
- Brian Balen, for counsel, hospitality and his photos.
- Adil Mistry, for deep thoughts, and being a 'plant buddy'.

- Sam and Winnie Davamoni, for companionship, hospitality and fun birding.
- Members of the Eurasian Club of WA Inc (now the Australian Eurasian Association of Western Australia), for fellowship and good times, especially Ivan and Veronica Fitzgerald, Harvey Fitzgerald, George Bentley, and Kay Klass, Colin Clark, Eddie and Barbara Fernandez, Uncle Ivan and the late Peter Richards, Patrick Cornelius, Priscilla and Max Clutton, Jim D'Oliveiro, Royston Sta. Maria and family, Maurice and Estelle Pestana, Teresa and Bernard Noronha, Maureen Lewis, Ivy and Harry Klass, Derek, Yvonne and Elsie Nunis.
- Brian and Vivien Ward.
- The late Herman Aroozoo.
- Len and Wilma Bridge.
- Winston and Betty.
- Dev Govindasamy, a mine of information.
- Gina Knight, for being a bright spirit.Danielle Pender, for dancing magic.
- Faridah Ali.
- Tony Shotam.
- Marilyn Hardoon .
- Herbert and Angela Teo.
- Alfonso and Pat Soosay.
- Carlos Eapon.
- Ismail and Geraldene Ahmad.
- Manjeet Kaur.
- Narinder Kaur.
- Dhevika Rani and her mother, Yasotha.
- Matthew and Joyce Chin.
- Gudrun and Edward Benjamin.
- Edmund and Janice Teo.
- Lorna Ollson
- John O'Brien.
- Hema and Claudia Peiris, and the late Lucia Peiris.
- Rudy and Chris Riduan.
- The late Roland Sharma.
- Helen Stirling, Steve Rattenbury, Sreetha Rajalingam and Roger White, our faithful house-sitters.

- Frank and Yolanda Caddy; Stephanie, Wayne, Shamone and Courtney Eade; Ashok, Neelam, Manav and Aditya Bhalla, our neighbours.
- Alastair Annandale..
- Sarjit Singh Gill, cobbler-philosopher.
- Kerryn Franklin.
- Kenny and Anne Barker.
- David Morrison, my patient boss for a while.
- Steve Quill.
- Chris Lewis and Pam Lanzell, for help and hospitality.
- Janis Hadley.
- Lorraine McMillan and Babs Lawson.
- Dr Eric Tan.
- The Chung Hwa Association.
- Dr Garry Rodan, Director, and staff of the Asia Research Centre, Murdoch University.
- Greening Australia (WA), for helping me to understand the land and the plants.
- *The Western Australian*, Syndication Department.
- Members of Birds Australia (WA) for good times outdoors.
- Committee members, Singapore-WA Network (SWAN).
- The WA Singapore Business Council (WASBC) and its President Mrs Cecilia Wee.
- Ishar Multicultural Centre for Women's Health, its Director, Shobhana Chakrabarti, and staff.

Outside Western Australia
- The Weller Family, Netherlands, for photos and fun.
- John Halliwell, UK, for photos and solid practical help.
- Hugh Mabbett, sorely missed friend and adviser.
- Christine Moulet and Ted Knez, Canberra.
- Liz Blyth, Queensland.
- David and Amanda Landers, Sydney.
- Peter and Betty Game, and Babe Mitchell-Dawson of Melbourne; the late Ian Newton of Sydney; James Osborne of Diamond Beach Casino Hotel, Darwin; Tony and Chris Lewis of Balfe's Hill Farm, Tasmania, The Australian Tourist Commission, the various State Tourism Commissions, at home and in Singapore, and

Qantas—for looking after me so well on my Australian travels 1985–1991.

- Philip Conn of Singapore, Barry Whalen of Hong Kong, David Townsend of Canberra, Jonathan Stone of Adelaide and Bruce Wilson of Melbourne, for my very first introductions to Australia, way back when.
- Iain Finlay and Trish Sheppard, Sydney, for times past.
- Angus Finney, Sydney, for showing me Tasmania, and for being himself.
- Arshak and Sophie Galstaun, Sydney.
- Kenny Minogue, Darwin, for introducing me to the sounds of Gondwanaland.
- Peter and Ree Dawson, Darwin.
- Peter Saltmarsh, Darwin, for showing me wild Australia.
- Bronwen and Gareth Solyom, Tasmania/Indonesia/Hawaii.
- Sally Taylor, USA/France, for friendship and advice.
- Zainon Ahmad, *New Straits Times*, Malaysia.

In Singapore

- Members of the Singapore Australian Business Council, and staff of the Australian High Commission and Austrade.
- Margaret and Ben Cunico.
- Beth Kennedy.
- Michael de Kretser.

This book is dedicated with respect and affection
to Australia,
a country which has had the foresight to welcome
the strangers knocking at her door,
and the courage to embark on an experiment
with multiculturalism.

MAP OF AUSTRALIA

GULF OF CARPENTARIA

PACIFIC OCEA

AUSTRALIA

INDIAN
OCEAN

GREAT
AUSTRALIAN
BIGHT

CANBERRA ●

BASS STRAIT

SOUTHERN SEA

FIRST IMPRESSIONS

CHAPTER 1

'A wilful, lavish land –
All you who have not loved her,
You will not understand.'
—Australian poet Dorothea Mackellar (1885–1968),
from 'My Country', a hymn to the Australian land that
newcomers should read in its entirety.

FIRST IMPRESSIONS ARE OFTEN CLOSER TO THE TRUTH than later, more compromised, qualified and considered views. What strikes you first about Australia may not be the whole story, but it is a good outline to fill in later. I've written about likely first impressions here in the order of the most powerful impressions made, not necessarily with any logical linkage topic-wise.

GEOGRAPHY: LAND AND LIGHT

It was April 1989. We had just made our first landfall as migrants to Australia, in grand old-fashioned style aboard a (Russian) cruise ship and carrying masses of goods and chattels including our precious fax machine, at Fremantle docks in Western Australia. An Australian customs officer was suspiciously snooping through our bags. Spotting a huge camera lens, he said, "Phew! What's that?" "Oh," says my husband, " that's a wide-angle lens." He gazed at us with dreamy sun-washed eyes, and said laconically, "Yeah, right, well, you'd certainly be needing that here, wouldn't you?"

He knew and we knew that Australia is, well, big—very big. Pretty hard to frame with most average wide-angle lens, in fact. 'A wide brown land' as it has famously been called by Aussie poet Dorothea Mackellar in her poem 'My Country' Perhaps the very first things you notice about Australia are to do with the land, and with that legendary light, that blistering sun shafting out of a brilliant blue sky immodestly naked of any white clouds at all. Everything looks bright and sharp-edged, as though you have just 'photo-shopped' the Contrast element in a photo already shot through some kind of polarising filter.

My Tamil-Malayalee (South Indian) husband comes from tiny, crowded island-nation Singapore, one of the most densely urbanised countries on the planet, so perhaps unsurprisingly (even though his idea of an 'outdoors expedition' is to drive his car through open bush without ever getting out), he says the thing he loves most about Australia is the way the horizon stretches endlessly before him, unblemished by a single skyscraper, or any other building for that matter. And indeed it does. Open 'empty' land is an enduring image of Australia.

With this comes the sense of distance—'the tyranny of distance' is another cliche often aptly applied to Australia. It's not that easy to grasp that Australia, including the offshore southern island of Tasmania, is more than seven and a half million sq km (or almost three million sq miles) in area, which means it is as big as the USA (without Alaska) and 24

The 'tyranny of distance'—the road stretches as far as the eye can see—is typical of Australia.

times the size of Great Britain. If you are in Perth, Western Australia, you don't just 'run over' to Sydney, or vice versa; it's just like going 'overseas'. You might as well 'run over' to Asia—it's closer.

So Australians are nonchalant about driving a few hours to visit the 'rellies' (relatives) for 'tea' (read 'dinner') or for a routine business meeting. And they are very car-bound. This is a land of big highways, articulated long-distance truck juggernauts and routine speeds of 110 kmph. Americans will recognise it.

PEOPLE: STRAIGHT-TALKING, EASY-GOING, APPAREL-CHALLENGED

The next most likely first impression will be of a chatty, friendly people who are also prone to straight-talking unembellished with niceties, and who don't seem to worry much about what they are wearing—or not wearing. In the neighbourhood shops, on the street or in the bus, you will be amazed at how long you have to wait for service while the counter-person has a little chat with the person in front of you in the queue, or at how easily you can strike up a friendly conversation with strangers, or get help from them. The message is 'slow down, talk to me.'

The same generous smiles are wheeled out in negative situations too. There is a general acceptance for example, that you, the customer, will not get upset just because the counter-person tells you with a sweet smile and a shrug, "Oh, sorry, we ran out of those last night/last week/last month" even though they are clearly listed on the stocklist/menu. The plumber or repair man who didn't keep his appointment but turns up two days later will beam broadly, "Yeah, sorry mate, had a few things to do." This is a recurring scenario. Why get upset?

Turning on the radio or television will give some of you a heart attack as you register some reporter savaging the Foreign Minister face to face without any respect for his position or title, referring to him as a 'you pompous dope' (true!), or witness fairly extreme nudity and lewd acts on 'Big Brother' at the relatively early hour of 9:30 pm. The language

Hotel lounge sign in Darwin suggests how naked Aussies can get.

heard all around you on the streets may seem very raw, liberally doused with the 'F...' word. Don't come to Australia for respect for authority, modesty or linguistic restraint. But sometimes, it's liberating to be as rude as you can be in Australia. Watch Parliament and enjoy a good fight.

White people without shoes, strolling the streets shirtless or virtually in their underwear are all particularly puzzling to migrants and refugees newly arrived in Australia from what used to be called 'Third World' countries. And why does one see so many incidents of sheer rage, shouting scenes, what should be private quarrels, open and public on the streets? Who knows. Some trace it to a violent history in a rugged land.

LANGUAGE

The unique 'Strine' or 'Austrayan' use of the English language is really in your face from the minute you land. From the moment you struggle with whether the restaurant dress code means a G-string-style bikini bottom or rubber ('Japanese') sandals by 'No Thongs' (the latter actually) or make a fool of yourself taking an entire dinner service of crockery to a party where you have been asked to bring 'a plate' (of food, you dummy!) to 'tea' (gotcha, it's dinner not tea!), this issue will plague you for a long time to come. No, you do not 'root' for your favourite footy team—unless you want to 'cop' an obscenity rap—instead you 'barrack' for the team. Consider the car-yard placard that says 'You Beaut Utes, Lay-Bys' and translate: 'Excellent Utility Vehicles (a small truck with a front cabin and an open back 'tray' section for carrying light loads), no-interest hire purchase deals available', is an approximation.

An Embarrassing Situation

There was this newbie refugee lady who had completed her visit to the doctor in Australia and as she left the doctor's room, the nurse said cheerily, "See you later then, love." So the woman sat and waited in the clinic to see when she would be needed later. When it came to closing time the staff asked her if she had a problem and she said, "But I thought you needed to see me later, so I'm waiting." "Oh no, dear," giggled the nurse, "That's just the Aussie way of saying goodbye!"

The poor lady was mortally embarrassed.

Another aspect of language that strikes many non-Western arrivals is Australians' extreme preoccupation with 'politically-correct' forms, for lack of a better term. Banish all thought of continuing to use terms like 'handicapped' (change to 'disabled', 'differently abled' or 'challenged'); 'blind' ('visually impaired' or 'visually challenged'); 'spastic' (just 'disabled' will do); chairman (always 'chair-person'); 'husband', 'wife', 'spouse', 'girlfriend', 'boyfriend' ('partner' works for everybody, including gays—homosexuals if you don't understand 'gay'—but leads to some confusion when you are not sure whether or not a business partner is meant!); 'natives' ('indigenous Australians', 'traditional owners' or just 'Aboriginals'); 'prostitute' ('sex worker', 'working girl').

The Irony of It All

In Western Australia, it has always given me some malicious pleasure to watch educated left-liberal leaning white Australians squirming as they try to remember what is the acceptable term for an iconic and ubiquitous local 'shaggy-haired' black-trunked plant once tagged the 'Blackboy'—in deference to Aboriginal Australians, this word has been dropped by many for its racial undertones, in favour of the more anodyne 'Grass Tree' or even the original Aboriginal word 'Balga'. But the irony is, you'll hear most Aboriginals refer to it quite happily as a 'Blackboy' because that's the European word they first learned for it and that's fine with them.

ACCENT

With the language comes the accent, quite contagious. Soon you too will be raising your voice at the ends of sentences, greeting people "G'day" ('Good-die') and asking "What toime (time) is it?" as naturally as Steve Irwin the crocodile hunter himself.

But another thing that you will notice in your first few weeks is the sheer variety of accents on the streets; multicultural Australia is right there, upfront. Your taxi-driver speaks with the thick accent of an Iraqi or maybe a one-time Yugoslav; the doctor's receptionist or the pestering telemarketer on the phone has an Indian lilt to their voice; your real estate agent has a distinct French accent, your house-cleaner or part-time 'ironing lady' is Polish, and that TV journalist, isn't he a South African? The voices of a future Australia waft across the breeze to you from behind flapping black chadar cloaks and veils on the street, from the African drums rehearsal in a community hall, the chants wafting out of the nearby Sikh *gurdwara* (temple) and the posh hotel dinner meeting hosted by prosperous local Chinese businessmen.

CUSTOMS

Every society has its hidden codes. In Asia, your gentle hosts will never criticise you for not taking your shoes off when you enter their home, but by not doing so, you separate yourself from them and their culture for ever. In Australia of course, you're considered a bit weird if you do take them off, and no Australian will voluntarily take them off on entering your home either. But Australia too has its unspoken rules and if you don't spot them, you could seem rude. When you first arrive, you will probably notice some of these little rules quite early on. Like visitors leaving not just the room, but the house itself to smoke, out in the backyard. Like picking up your cups and plates after you have eaten in someone's home and taking them to the kitchen sink at least, possibly also offering to wash them up (no maids here, see?). Like bringing a bottle of 'booze' or 'grog' (wine or beer) when you come over for dinner, maybe a 'plate' (of food) too if 'pot-luck dinner' has been suggested. Like men attending to the barbecue, women mucking around in the kitchen doing salads and things. And maybe, sometimes still, a separation of the party into men talking sport and women talking, well, yes, sigh, children and things. Like not talking money and possessions too loudly—generally, not 'spruiking' ('selling') your own achievements too much. Like splitting the bill and remembering to buy a 'shout' (round) of drinks if your mate does 'shout you'. Like remembering to check if a restaurant is solely 'BYO' (Bring Your Own) and making sure you've brought a bottle of wine along with you.

On the Flip Side

Paradoxically, in this largely helpful society, nobody bothers much nowadays about standing up for a 'lady' on the bus, or opening a door for her—a recent correspondence in the Western Australian newspaper indicated that it was now the bus company's official policy that asking anybody, including youngsters, to stand up for anybody else, even the infirm elderly, was 'discriminatory'. So you might be thought odd—or worse, on the make—if you stood up for a woman on the bus or train.

Like signalling considerately well in advance of changing lanes when driving. Like stopping to offer help to fellow motorists in distress. Or flashing your headlights to let other oncoming motorists know that there is a speed camera or a 'booze bus' (breath testing for alcohol consumption) just ahead of you. And making sure that you pass your unexpired parking coupon on to an incoming motorist as you leave the carpark—they would do the same for you.

UPSIDE-DOWN LAND: NATURE AND ENVIRONMENT

For anyone who enjoys nature and the outdoors, the first encounter with Australia is also full of wonder and delight at the extraordinary, truly unique nature of the Australian environment. First of all, for everyone from the northern hemisphere and temperate climes there is the simple oddity of being 'down under', where going south suddenly means getting colder, and where December becomes summer, July winter. A summer around 27°C or so (over 80°F), you quickly discover, is 'mild.'

You are confronted with curious fauna and magnificent flora found nowhere else in the world.

Yes, there really are Kangaroos, Wombats and Wallabies, Goannas and Blue-tongues! Only now that you are actually on 'Terra Australis' is it brought home to you that Australia's biota boasts a natural diversity and 'endemism' (uniqueness) equal to any tropical rain forest (with which Australia is also endowed) and priceless in global terms. Of Australia's more than 30,000 total plant species (including things like mosses), 90 per cent of the 18,000 'vascular' plant species are not found anywhere else (are 'endemic'), while 89 per cent of Australia's marsupial animals (like the kangaroos) and 73 per cent of other Australian animals are unique to the continent. The monotremes (platypus and echidnas) are found only in Australia and New Guinea.

It is hard to mistake the look, and resin-laden smell, of an Australian 'gum' (eucalyptus) forest, the soft-white peeling trunk of a Paperbark tree, or the nose-twitching aroma of a Lemon-scented Gum, for trees from anywhere else, any more than you would mistake the hysterical cackling of Australia's Kookaburra bird or the screech of a Cockatoo or Lorikeet for a European blackbird or a finch. Around my suburban home in Western Australia, the chortling and burbling of Magpies, the menacing cawing of big black Australian Ravens, the shrill piping of the perky Magpie Lark, the chatter of the aggressive tail-flicking black and white 'Willie Wagtail' fantail, the happy chirrups of Honey-eaters and the urgent squawking of a bevy of black Carnaby's Cockatoos overhead, all say 'Australia' to me in a very special way. And another thing that strikes you about Australia is the relative tameness of the wild birds, which will come very close to humans at times; that's mainly because almost nobody harasses them, and cagebird culture is not as developed as it is in, say, Asia.

You may be struck too by the devotion ordinary Australians show to their wildlife. Consider highway signs warning motorists to drive slowly because there may be ducks or kangaroos crossing. And the amazing spectacle of 1,000 volunteers up to their chests in bone-chilling sea water as they struggle to keep a school of 100 beached whales alive for hours on end (in Western Australia, 2005). At times like these, Australian altruism seems nothing less than noble.

An American Observation

American Nana Ollerenshaw married an Australian and moved to Australia in 1965 at the age of 22. The following piece appeared in *The Weekend Australian* in 2005. Nana concedes that Australia has changed much since the time she moved here, but many of her observations still stand nonetheless.

'My brother spelled Sydney with an 'i' and some of my parents' friends thought I would never be seen again. "Do they have supermarkets?" they asked (when I moved to Australia)...

I ardently compared Australia with the US, prefacing every statement with 'In America, we...' until a forthright family friend put a stop to it...

At parties, men and women divided as neatly as a meat cleaver separates cuts, the men talking sport and politics, the women shopping and babies. I had no one with whom to discuss Jane Austen. I laughed at words such as 'crook' and 'strides' and at expressions like 'come a cropper'. And how could 'directly' mean 'not immediately'? I learned not to say 'I'm stuffed', nor did I say 'fall on your fanny'. In the US, 'fanny' means your 'butt', but they call it, euphemistically, your seat. The Puritan heritage lingers. Other differences, apart from language, were single-storey brick houses, corner pubs, memorial statues, the hard, white merciless light (which poet John Betjeman said was 'like being inside a diamond'), the hang of gum leaves, new stars, bizarre animals.

From four seasons I changed to two. From a country of mountains and rivers I went to flatness and a place where heat and light became weapons of nature. As a teacher I was dumbfounded by the emphasis given to sport. I knew I was different. I felt serious among Australians, unable to be light-hearted. I was ruled by an internal clock but they just let the day happen... I have changed too, almost an Australian, unrecognisable to my own people. The sight of an Akubra, the sound of a dry laconic voice in an overseas airport would catch my breath... So we are turned. Like chameleons we take on the colours that surround us.'

Among your keenest first impressions will surely be the feeling that almost every Australian must be a gardening fanatic, as you stroll along suburban streets endlessly lined with flower-laden gardens and swaying trees, all clearly lovingly nurtured. You are almost certain to catch the national horticultural fever. In your garden or in the local park, and along the street verges, may be various species of red-flowered Bottlebrush or Grevillea plant, perhaps a soft green Tea tree or gracious Peppermint tree, a phallic-flowered Banksia or if you are very lucky, a Grass-tree. None of them looks like a European tree and one of the first things a new arrival may learn to his or her cost is that Australian gardening conditions are mostly utterly unlike any others. If you have been used to temperate northern-hemisphere or tropical gardening, prepare for a shock. Your rules simply do not apply. With a bit of help from the innumerable Australian TV gardening programmes, after some years, you may finally understand that native Australian plants are uniquely adapted to their own environment, meaning they may not need as much water, and may actively hate too much nitrogen-rich fertiliser (although this is over-simplifying); they may flower happily in winter and spring but disappear in summer. Beginners who get stuck with recalcitrant coastal sands such as those on the Perth plains of Western Australia will wage battle with constant loss of water during a vicious 38–40°C (100–104°F) summer, until they learn about soil wetting agents and the greatest saviour of all, mulch, mulch and more mulch (soil-coverings of wood-chips, stones etc.). In the summer, hanging baskets will grow 'crusts' on the soil surface, with water running off them as if from a duck's back, never reaching the plant's roots. The cure? Guess what, a solution of ordinary washing up liquid.

It's all an intriguing learning curve, then, but the thing is, you are in Australia and it is like nowhere else.

THE BASICS

CHAPTER 2

'One seems to ride for ever and to come to nothing,
and to relinquish at last the very idea of an object.
Nevertheless, it was very pleasant.
Of all the places that I was ever in this place
seemed to be the fittest for contemplation.'
—British novelist Anthony Trollope,
in his documentary *Australia and New Zealand*, 1873.

THE LAND OF AUSTRALIA

No matter how urban or suburban the Australian is, the land of Australia lies in his or her subconscious, whether as a sensation of joy, reverence or fear.

Nobody can live in Australia without being affected by the land, the landscape and the extraordinary ecosystem it nourishes. In his own strange way, the Australian white is linked with the land, just like the Australian Aboriginal. The land is his mother too. Only he does not articulate this half-sensed emotion as clearly in his culture as do the Aboriginals.

You see this subconscious leitmotif reflected in the landscape paintings (except for the very early colonial ones, which rather desperately rendered Australian scenery much like English pastures and oak forests), the cinema and the great literature of white Australia. In the formative early years of Australian cinema during the late 20th century, it was characteristic for movies to linger on the land, long and lyrical. Seen from the outside, particularly from the white, Western point of view, Australia's is a uniquely harsh, intimidatingly vast and seemingly empty environment, hostile to human life. But the Aboriginal would not agree.

The Basic Facts of the Land

First, let us get to grips with the immensity of Australia. It is about the size of the USA if you exclude Alaska; 24 times the size of the British Isles. In absolute figures, it is 7.7 million sq km (almost 3 million sq miles) in area. The mainland distance east-west is 3,983 km (2,475 miles), north-south, 3,138 km (1,950 miles). The Western Australian capital of Perth and the Northern Territory capital of Darwin are closer to Asia than to any other Australian city.

A continent in its own right, Australia lies across the Tropic of Capricorn in the southern hemisphere, sandwiched between the Indian and Pacific oceans. Antarctica is just 2,000 km (about 1,243 miles) to the south. 'Australia' derives from the Latin *Australis*, meaning 'southern land'. Much is made of the Southern Cross constellation as a nationalistic symbol, which features on the Australian flag, since this magnificent group of five stars can only be viewed from the most southerly positions in the southern hemisphere.

This is the driest continent on Planet Earth, with recorded temperatures of up to 53°C (127°F) in places. People still die in Australia's deserts. A year's reading of the newspapers is sure to yield a clutch of such incidents, even today. There are sad place names dotted over the continent recalling the trials of early explorers—names like Lake Disappointment for a dry lake.

Australia still remembers with respect the ill-fated Burke and Wills expedition of 1860, which attempted to cross the continent from south to north; Burke and Wills died of starvation during a terrifying journey.

But there are great variations in climate and landscape, from the lush tropical north with its end-year monsoonal 'wet', rainforests and mangrove swamps, to the chilly temperate forests of the south and the ski slopes of New South Wales and Victoria.

Rocks and Ranges

Australia was once part of a prehistoric super-continent named Gondwanaland that first started to fracture about 150 million years ago. Out of its parts were formed Australia, Antarctica, South America, Africa, India, Madagascar and New Zealand. Australia broke off from Gondwanaland between 70 and 45 million years ago. This makes Australia a very old continent indeed, with a geological history dating

The distinctive 'Three Sisters' rock formation is part of New South Wales' iconic Blue Mountains.

to the Pre-Cambrian period of 600 million years ago; the landforms of Europe and the USA, in contrast, evolved only up to 65 million years ago. With no volcanic activity or other land-forming events for the past 80 million years, the scenery you encounter in Australia is the original prehistoric landscape, undisturbed.

It is largely a flat continent, one of the flattest land areas on the globe, with major exceptions like the Great Dividing Range of the east, running from north Queensland down into Victoria in the south, which includes tablelands, alps, plateaux and mountains—the famous Atherton Tableland of Queensland, the Blue Mountains of New South Wales and the Grampians of Victoria, for example. Australia's highest peak is Mount Kosciusko in the Snowy Mountains of New South Wales, at 2,230 m (7,316 ft).

There are some very strange and dramatic excrescences on the otherwise flat Australian vistas, the most famous of these being the 335-m (1,099-ft) tall Ayers Rock monolith, rising straight out of a central plain. The vivid red Olgas, rock monoliths described by an early explorer as 'monstrous pink haystacks', are in the Northern Territory, in the same Uluru National Park as Ayers Rock.

The outdoor life, never far away; here, just outside Canberra.

Others include the Pinnacles, about 200 km (124 miles) north of Perth in Western Australia—platoons of natural limestone obelisks standing up to 2 m high (almost 7 ft)—and the ancient sandstone formations of the Bungle Bungle range in the remote Kimberley region of north-west Western Australia, rising 450 m (1,476 ft) above the grasslands.

THE COUNTRYSIDE

Close to 90 per cent of Australians live in capital cities or towns. Few live or even work in rural or outback regions such as the arid, dusty 'Red Centre' around the famous outback town of Alice Springs.

It is still possible to capture the old romance: cattle-drover 'cowboys' silhouetted through a shimmering veil of dust, marshalling great rivers of cattle over treeless bush, one-street towns and two-house stations stuck on lonely plains, the occasional cry of 'Coo-ee!', the old Aboriginal bush cry connecting humans separated by great distance, adopted by the whites.

But rural Australia is bleeding. The young are leaving for the pleasures of the city. Those who stay are battling high interest rates and the loss of overseas markets for their produce (wool is a key example), in addition to regular natural disasters like drought, fire, floods and, in the far north, cyclones. And the creeping menace of salinity, ironically caused by the white farmers' own agricultural practices, unsuited to this unique land. Depression and suicide in the countryside are the flip-side of the apparent rural idyll.

Doctor in the Air

Life in outback Australia stimulated the establishment of the world's most impressive aerial medical service, better known as The Royal Flying Doctor Service. An Australian-born Presbyterian missionary, John Flynn—'Flynn of the Inland' they called him—was the founder in 1928 of this voluntary organisation funded by government grants and other contributions. The service uses a sophisticated radio network to link outback stations with its hospitals and planes.

Children in these remote areas do their schooling over 'Schools of the Air', using the Flying Doctor's two-way radios. In times of emergency, such as floods or fires, the service helps to drop supplies, and also mounts search and rescue operations.

Fire!

The Australian ecology is built to burn. The Aboriginals have always known this and have used fire as an instrument for controlling and benefiting their environment. Fire disasters are a regular occurrence in the hot summers. The 'Black Thursday' of 1851 in Victoria, the 1939 'Black Friday' fires in Victoria and the 'Ash Wednesday' fires of 1983 in South Australia and Victoria, were terrible examples, with 70 lives lost in the last-mentioned of these. In January 2005, more than 40,000 hectares (about 99,000 acres) turned into an inferno that killed nine people, on the Eyre Peninsula of South Australia.

The worst fires often occur at times of drought. The extremely high temperatures reached in the Australian summer combine explosively with native plants like the oil-bearing eucalypts, which act much like petroleum thrown on the flames. Hot winds from the north do the rest. But fire seems also to stimulate new plant growth.

In recent years, the finger has often been pointed at arsonists, as much as at Nature—recent research suggests that as many as half of Australia's destructive bush fires may have been set deliberately. The totality of such fires cause an estimated A\$ 77 million of damage every year, quite apart from lives lost. It's frightening to note that by definition, fire-fighting is a job that attracts pyromaniacs and so unsurprisingly perhaps, many arsonists are found among fire-fighters, with a very good understanding of exactly how to set a really dangerous fire too. Among those who are not pyromaniacs, the motives cited are stunningly banal: most arsonists seek attention or recognition, excitement or relief from boredom, are expressing anger, or just fancy a spot of mindless vandalism. Arsonists' lives apparently are characterised by family relationship problems and the breakdown of normal social interactions, employment and academic performance.

Needless to say though, setting fires in the summer when the fire-risk has been declared high, is a criminal offence. This means neither a simple campfire nor even the home barbecue fire is safe, if the fire-risk is high enough. Australia has developed a magnificent network of volunteers as well as professionals to combat fire, such as the State Emergency Service established in every state—these wonderful folk will turn out of bed at night even during a bad storm, to assist householders with smashed roofs or whatever.

The Flora

The 'flagship' plants of Australian botany are of course the eucalypts, a genus classified within the Myrtle family, especially the smoother-barked versions known popularly as 'Gums'.

Eucalypts have a tall and spindly look, with foliage sparsely dispersed along scarecrow branches, that is quite distinctive. They also give off a very special resinous aroma that says 'Australia' as soon as it reaches the nose on a summer's breeze. Or, as with the Lemon-scented or Peppermint versions, their leaves may yield a wonderful perfume when crushed between the fingers.

There are also the Stringybark eucalypts of the east, with their rough barks, and the largely tropical Ironbarks. The giant Karri forests of south-west Western Australia are the second tallest in the world after the California redwoods. The Jarrah, from the same region as the Karri, has a fine

The author in bushland, a gum in the background.

red-grained timber often found as polished flooring in older Western Australian homes. In Tasmania are some the finest stands of cool temperate rainforest in the world, featuring pine and beech species as well as myrtles that largely predate the mainland gums, originating as they do in the Gondwanaland era of about 60 million years ago. Hence the constant 'greenie' protest against logging in Tasmania.

Coalseam flowers in full bloom.

One of the loveliest sights of the Perth summer is the flowering of countless Jacaranda trees (actually South American imports from way back when), clouds of lavender-blue.

My husband got quite excited one December day in Perth, telling me, 'Look, we've got our very own Christmas tree, on the front verge!' It was a Bottle-brush, ablaze with tall red flower 'candles', yet another myrtle.

In the same Myrtle family again—there are 1,300 species of myrtle in Australia—are the Paperbarks, sometimes referred to in Australia by their genus name, Melaleuca, and quite often identified by their peeling, papery bark. Other familiar myrtles are the Tea trees, which fall within the Leptospermum genus, including the Lemon-scented Tea tree.

Every Western Australian spring, about October–November, tourists and residents alike are presented with the most spectacular display of gorgeous wildflowers in the countryside and in the bush. It is literally a case of the desert blooming, in profusion.

A National Symbol

A famous national symbol, of course, is the Wattle, in the genus Acacia, part of the Mimosa family, with its familiar golden blossoms. There are 900 species of wattle in Australia.

Be aware too that there are many unwelcome 'guests' among Australia's flora—foreign plants brought by ignorant settlers, that can do great harm to Australia's unique ecology. There are dedicated self-appointed 'weed police' everywhere to lecture you on this, but if you could see the damage that imports such as the Water Hyacinth, Lantana, Patersons Curse and the Blackberry have done, to name only a few, you might have some sympathy for their concerns.

Roos and Devils

Australia's long isolation from the rest of the world has contributed to the evolution of some extraordinary life-forms unique to the continent. The existence of the ancient supercontinent of Gondwanaland can be traced from the fact that there are some related species to be found in New Guinea and in South America.

The best-known oddities in Australia are of course those egg-laying, nipple-less mammals, the monotremes—just three of them, being the Duck-billed Platypus and two species of Echidna, also known as Spiny Anteaters—and the pouched marsupials, with the Kangaroo the best-known example.

The grey kangaroo at Yanchep Park in Western Australia.

Today, the greatest threat facing the lovable koala is the loss of its natural habitat. It is believed that there are only about 100,000 koalas remaining in Australia.

A less well-known feature of some marsupials is the fact that they have bifurcated penises, nobody knows why. One Aussie zoo director experimenting with the breeding of endangered marsupials said to me, 'Well, maybe we have double the chance of success!'

There are 19 marsupial families, encompassing not only kangaroos and wallabies, but also arboreal animals like the Koala (*not* 'koala bear', please, a misnomer) and possums, various mice and rats, wombats and 'native cats' (which look more like mongooses than cats). Half of Australia's 250 species of mammals are marsupials.

The Wombat is a wondrous beast, stocky and powerfully built, like a small bear, weighing in at about 40 kg (88 lbs). Somewhat less cuddly is the Tasmanian Devil, a smallish black-and-white carnivorous marsupial endemic to Tasmania, which makes the most appalling screeching and grumbling noises, feeds on almost anything, including carrion, and is equipped with jaws that could reduce the thickest bone to shredded-wheat consistency.

Cute at a wildlife park, but the Tasmanian devil's jaws can crunch bone.

Possums are harmless but they can keep you up at night if you have one holed up in the roof space of your home.

Some of the kangaroo-type marsupials have marvellous names, like the Potoroo, the Wallaroo, the Quokka (found only on Western Australia's Rottnest Island, off Perth) and the Pademelon.

Possums you may get to know better than you would prefer. Although essentially harmless, they are the bane of many a householder's life since it is their habit to hole up in ceiling and roof spaces of ordinary homes, even in the city, scrabbling around and making an awful racket at night.

A Brace of Trivia

Just for interest: the platypus may look cute, but in fact, the male has a nasty pair of poisonous spurs on his ankles, and the name 'koala' is Aboriginal for 'He who does not drink'—the koala gets most of its moisture from the leaves it chews, although actually, it does very occasionally drink liquids. Belying their looks, koalas are not particularly cute, being bad-tempered and sullen, slow-moving animals most of the time.

All native animals are protected under federal law in Australia. However, killing of wild kangaroos, populations of which are thriving and multiplying, is licensed for 'culling' purposes from time to time. Farmers in particular treat these great macropods as vermin, because they compete with domestic livestock for grass fodder. The issue of kangaroo harvesting is charged with emotion in Australia.

Sadly, many of these unique animals are threatened by unexplained recent outbreaks of disease—one wonders if it must be something human beings have done to them or their environment. Tasmanian devils are now plagued by putrefying cancerous facial tumours, while platypus have fallen prey to a disease producing skin lesions and attacking internal organs, koalas are prone to chlamydia bacteria, possibly have been for many years, and wombats often collide with cars.

Emus and Galahs

There are 700 species of birds in Australia. When the first white settlers arrived in 1788, one of them, surgeon Arthur Bowes Smyth, remarked that as his ship hove into what was to be Sydney Harbour: 'The singing of the various birds among the trees, and the flights of the numerous parraquets, lorrequets, cockatoos and maccaws, made all around appear like an enchantment.'

Here again, you see the traces of Gondwanaland, with the Australian Emu closely related to other flightless birds like the South African ostrich and New Zealand's kiwi, for example.

Other unique avifauna include the Black Swan. This reverse-image bird, seen in northern hemispheric terms, has caused awful trouble for the Japanese, since their word for swan can only refer to a white bird.

Of course, of all the Australian birds, the 'laughing' Kookaburra is perhaps the most widely known. It is quite a cheeky bird. The few times I have been out to use the public barbecue pits in Perth's King's Park, there have always been a couple of these quite large and handsome birds sitting beside me on my log seat, hinting that they would like to be offered a few slivers of meat, please. In Western Australia, they are unwanted guests, being eastern states birds not native to the West.

Very Australian too are the 50 species of parrot, from the brightly coloured Rosella and exotically multi-hued Rainbow Lorikeet (my friend Arshak in Sydney calls these lorikeets down to his garden, to feed in psychedelic flocks perched all over his body), to the black-capped, yellow neck-

The pink and grey galah is usually found in flocks.

ringed, green 'Twenty-eight' or Ring-necked Parrot, and the familiar Cockatoo.

There are more cockatoos, however, than just the white-bodied sulphur-crested one so commonly seen in Western aviaries (protected but considered a pest by most Australians). There are, for instance, handsome black cockatoos like the palm cockatoo of Queensland and the Carnaby's cockatoo unique to Western Australia, besides the red-headed cockatoo ('Gang-Gang') and the pink-and-grey Galah (pronounce with the stress on the 'lah', quickly swallowing the first half of the word).

> The poor galah has entered Strine-talk as a synonym for idiocy—in expressions like 'Mad as a gumtree full of galahs.' If you wish to express your contempt for someone, you could refer to them as 'a silly galah'.

We must not forget the Fairy Penguin, resident on Victoria's Phillip Island; their nightly 'parade' is a big tourist draw.

Personal favourites of mine are the stately Pelican found almost everywhere, the majestic 1.5-metre tall Brolga crane, symbol of the Northern Territory, the delicate little Honey-eaters sucking nectar from the red Grevillea flowers in my garden, the cackling Wattle-bird with his dangling red neck lappets and the large crow-like black and white Magpie whose bell-like chortling always means 'home' to me when I am in Perth.

Scalies and Slimies

There are some fairly dramatic lizards in Australia—450 species, including the large dinosaur-like Goanna, or Monitor Lizard (good eating), the dragon-lizards (Agamidae) such as the histrionic Frill-necked Lizard of the north, and the much smaller, ceiling-walking house Gecko. But the reptiles which attract the most attention are snakes and crocodiles.

Snakes admittedly are more alarming in Australia than almost anywhere else: of the approximately 160 species found in the country, the poisonous ones outnumber the harmless ones. And some are among the most dangerous in the world—the Giant Brown Snake and the Taipan of the north, the Tiger Snake of the south-east, the Copperhead and various types of Sea Snake. However, there are only about 15 of these very dangerous snakes.

There are some scary tales about species like the Brown Snake or the Red-bellied Black Snake not only standing their ground against humans, but even attacking or chasing them, in the breeding season. You should certainly give any snakes sighted a wide berth.

Crocodiles are the stuff of Australian legend and a fascinating link with Earth's prehistory. Thanks to conservationist policies which have granted them complete protection in Australia since the early 1970s, their number has increased dramatically; some estimates now put the population of the Estuarine or Saltwater Crocodile at about 100,000 or more.

The focus of public fear and awe is the 'Saltie', which will take human beings if they are at hand—and has done so on several highly publicised occasions. The reality is about 15 fatal crocodile attacks in the 20 years between 1985 and 2005, although the total number of attempted killings may be greater of course. Crocs are efficient killers. The animal grips larger prey in its jaws and then takes it below water to drown it in a 'death roll', rolling over and over in the process, then stores the body underwater before eating it a few days later. The danger to humans has probably been increased by tourist operators who bait crocodiles by hanging carcasses

Daredevil feeding of crocs.

like chickens high above the water from large boat decks, thus teaching the beast to leap ever higher. The average small fisherman's boat then becomes no problem for the crocodile.

Make no mistake about it, the seemingly lumbering 'saltie' can move at an impressive speed on land. Just watch 'show-time' at some of the Northern Territory crocodile farms, when rangers feed huge specimens by offering them dead chickens at the water's edge, and see what you think after that.

If travelling the land, particularly in northern Western Australia, the Northern Territory and Queensland, you should be careful when approaching coastal inlets, swamps and even large rivers quite far inland. In fact, frankly if I were you, I would never ever try to swim anywhere in such areas. If you are camping near such a spot, I am told it may be advisable to move camp every so often and generally, never to do the same thing twice in the same place at the same time of day. The crocodile apparently is quite cunning and may stalk you for several days to determine your habits before he strikes. The next time you go down to the billabong to fill your kettle for tea, at 5:00 pm, the same time as you always do, could be your last. Better still, don't go near the water's edge at all, not to get water, not to wash vegetables, not to wash yourself. Yes, they are that dangerous and you probably won't see them until they hit you.

The Ferals, and Other Unwelcome Guests

Feral domestic animals—in other words, humankind's animals left to go wild in the bush and desert—are some of the great banes of the Australian ecology and a constant reminder of the ignorance of the early white settlers.

(By the way, as an aside, you will frequently hear the word 'feral' used in a different context in Australia: it is a derogatory term used to dismiss contemptuously all somewhat left-wing, 'hippie', unconventional people, such as 'greenies', who protest against things or live alternative lifestyles. Often the implication of this use of 'feral' is that the person referred to is also dirty, unwashed, unemployed and on welfare).

There are feral buffalo, horses and donkeys, rabbits, feral birds too, such as mynahs and starlings, and perhaps most startling of all, dogs and cats. If you are a newcomer, do not approach 'pussycats' seen in the countryside with the same affectionate trust you might offer your best friend's pet cat. It could turn out to be a snarling tiger-like thing if it is a 'feral'. The heavier ferals, such as the buffalo, which love to wallow in muddy ground, and wild ponies, do immense damage to natural bush vegetation and soils, particularly in the case of hoofed animals.

Another legacy of thoughtless white Australia is the rabbit. Rabbits came with the First Fleet in 1788 but really took off when some new arrivals were imported in the mid-19th century. Their multiplication to near-plague proportions and the damage they can do to agriculture by devouring pastureland grasses provoked the erection of thousands of kilometres of 'rabbit-fences' across the land. The disease myxomatosis was introduced after World War II and successfully controlled the rabbits for some time, although now, the animals are developing resistance to the infection. The latest strategy has been deliberate introduction of rabbit calcivirus which miraculously does not harm any other Australian animals.

Still worse than the rabbit has been the European fox, which was introduced for nothing better than the pleasure of the hunt, in the 1840s. This predator has had a disastrous impact on Australia's many unique small mammals.

Toad Tales

One notorious introduction occurred in relatively recent times, to the nation's great shame: the cane toad, also known as the giant or Queensland toad, was introduced to northern Queensland in 1935, from its South American homeland via a stopover in Hawaii. Americans will be familiar with this creature. The idea was that the toad would control beetle pests in Queensland's economically important sugar cane plantations.

The toad in fact did not do this job very well, but spread widely across the north and began to eat native animals as well. Because this noxious beast has poison glands in its skin, it is also dangerous to native predators which may take a fancy to it.

Proving that human behaviour is any time more bizarre than any animal can produce, there are reports from the USA of drug fiends actually licking live cane toads for kicks afforded by its poison glands; in Australia, it is suggested that Queenslander drug-freaks may be smoking dried toad-skin as a hallucinogen.

Certainly, there is a mass of folklore surrounding the cane toad. In fact, the cane toad has become a cult object in Australia, regarded with perverse affection. A brilliantly hilarious and surprisingly informative, award-winning documentary called Cane Toads has been made. Hire it at your local video shop in Australia; this is a 'must-see' item of really offbeat Australiana. There is even an underground political newspaper in Queensland named after the toad and political satirists regularly cartoon unpopular Queenslander politicians as cane toads. Meanwhile the toad marches on and in 2005, even remote Western Australia was nervously eyeing its northern border for signs of a cane toad invasion.

The Thylacine that Got Away

One of the great zoological puzzles of Australia is the Thylacine, also known as the Tasmanian Tiger or the Marsupial Wolf, the largest carnivorous marsupial known to the world. It is extinct—or is it?

The last known tiger died in Hobart Zoo, Tasmania, in 1936. White settlers put a bounty on surviving tigers from about 1830 and shot it to extinction when it took to hunting their sheep.

But claims of sightings are regularly made today, often in south-western Western Australia, where the Thylacine may have roamed thousands of years ago—and one of these was seriously discussed and published in the eminent British science magazine, *The New Scientist*, during the 1980s. For the moment, searching for, and reporting on, the Thylacine remains one of Australia's more delightfully silly preoccupations—you might like to join the fun and start an expedition yourself, perhaps. Or you could respond to the A$ 1.5 million bounty offered in 2005 by the national news weekly, *The Bulletin,* for a live capture (offer may be closed by the time you read this). But not content with waiting for this, the Australian Museum actually has an active programme for cloning the Thylacine from a thylacine pup it has preserved in alcohol, collected in 1866, thus bringing the creature back to life. Go to http://www.amonline.net.au/thylacine to learn all about it.

Sea, Surf, Sun

White Australians love the seas around their land even more actively than they do the land. Which is amazing, considering all the nasty things in those seas—sharks, crocodiles, jellyfish, sea snakes and so on. Unfortunately, there are also other man-made hazards nowadays: the waters off Sydney's famous Bondi Beach, for example, are badly polluted.

Australians who cannot swim are few and far between. So if you are a newcomer and cannot yet swim, start taking lessons to become one of the crowd.

Australian surf life-savers are one of the great macho images of the nation—muscled, bronzed and noble—and

Australians have a deep love for the sea. Many enjoy spending time at the beach, taking in the ocean air and the easy pace of life.

perhaps deservedly so. From 1906 up to 2002, some 500,000 people had been saved by the Surf Life Saving Association of Australia. This is vastly more than the Australian death toll in the two world wars.

The surfing fraternity in Australia has developed an elaborate subculture with its own language, publications and values. Do not let your young son get too involved in this essentially male, macho mystique if you want him to stay at school and pass exams.

Dicing with Death

Australian author John Pilger has said that it is the constant effort of peering through the sun that makes the Australian face look so 'laconic', with its lopsided smile and permanent squint. Certainly, there are a lot of glazed blue-grey eyes set in wrinkle-tracks to be seen in Australia.

Right up to the turn of the 20th century, the typical Australian exhibited a strong streak of paganism, laced with hedonism, when it came to beaches, stripping down at the slightest excuse to catch a suntan. Owning a tan has always been an essential part of the Australian Dream. There are beaches which allow women to indulge in bare-breasted 'topless' bathing, just to help the tanning process along, further bolstering the pagan image. You are not supposed to stare.

This culture survives but it is looking more and more antique as a new generation grows up that has been carefully trained at school to 'slip, slap, slop' sunblock cream liberally over their bodies, to swim in whole-body suits, and to don a large cap with a 'desert-fighter' or 'Foreign Legion' style protective flap hanging down the back of the neck. The message has got through that the sun-worshipping culture is dangerous.

And with good reason. Skin cancer is an ever-present bogey. The skin cancer rate in Australia is the highest in the world, three times that in the USA and six times that in Britain. And it is in the younger active years that the foundation for cancer apparently is laid. Older Australian men with many years' exposure to the sun behind them have shown me their arms, gouged deep with sickly white scars where cancers have been cut out. I am told that some cases are sitting in hospital with their scalp-skin rolled down to graft into new noses or foreheads. All the statistics point to a rapid increase in skin cancer cases over the past decade.

Apart from sun-block cream, it is important to wear as thick a cover of clothing as possible. Amazingly, the sight of Australian labourers toiling in the sun in bare chests and shorts, or of young boys cycling half-naked, is still commonplace. Not to mention the amount of flesh exposed on Australian beaches.

Ozone-depletion is a more threatening reality in Australia than elsewhere, because of its proximity to the ozone hole over the southern pole, and because the country's classic blue skies do nothing to filter harmful rays. You need sun-creams with an 'SPF'—Sun Protection Factor—of 15 or more to protect exposed areas of skin against cancer. The fairer your skin, the higher the SPF you need, and the shorter the time you should spend in the sun. Your cream must be water-resistant for swimming, applied to dry skin and re-applied every one to two hours.

The bad news is that it is also possible to get the worst form of skin cancer—melanoma—on parts of the body not exposed to the sun. The back is a danger spot, as few people can see what is going on there. Get a friend to check regularly for any obvious changes. The good news is that skin cancers are easily detected early—they are visible—and very curable. Simply watch out for changes in your skin. Few skin cancers are painful. The most important thing is to train children in self-protection against the sun from an early age.

At the risk of sounding sexist, women particularly should avoid the Australian sun; the drying and wrinkling effect on the skin can age them by many years. One Aussie medic's test on a 25-year-old surfing life-saver at the beach, who had spent half his life on the beach, rated the youngster's skin with a medical age of 60.

When I am in Australia, I find I need extra moisturiser. Anyone who has lived in a humid tropical climate suffers from flaky skin when at first suddenly deprived of moisture in Australia. The most uncomfortable thing is the way your lips crack up; most Australians carry a stick of lip salve about with them to deal with this.

Needless to say, you also need very 'serious' sunglasses, the sort that really do filter harmful rays such as ultra-violet (i.e. offering 100 per cent UV absorption), fully polarised, of the cool-dude 'wrap-around' design (about 35 per cent of UV light creeps in around the sides of most 'sunnies'), preferably with an endorsement sticker from the Australian Cancer Society and an 'EPF' (eye protection factor) of 10 (= 99 per cent protection). Note that there is some argument about how early and how much children should wear sunglasses though; they may need some exposure to UV in order to develop protection against it.

The fun part of sun protection is the typically Australian penchant for hats. For real protection, you need a broad-brimmed one, but within that parameter, there are so many wonderful choices, from 'dinky-di' Aussie bushranger hats, with the famous Akubra at the pinnacle of the genre, to charming straw hats with bedecked ribbons and applique flowers, and huge confections for special occasions like the Melbourne Cup race day, weddings or a classy picnic.

Atoning for Past Sins

Just as white Australia has a debt to repay to the Aboriginals, so it also has quite a bit of explaining to do about what it has done to the Australian environment. In both areas, a severe case of guilty conscience is tangible throughout the nation.

Through the combined ravages of habitat clearance, mining extraction and introduced predators and competitors, at least 20 native species of animals have been lost during the period of European settlement. About 65 species, close to a quarter of the total, are still considered under threat.

Although Australia to the casual observer seems a wild and largely untouched land, it is in fact dreadfully scarred by the hand of humankind. Groundwater has been polluted by chemicals; more than half the land requires soil-rehabilitation measures to combat salinity, acidification and erosion.

In reaction to the past, the average young Australian or schoolchild is now well versed in basic environmentalist responsibilities. Small children will lecture you on not using plastic bags, or on recycling aluminium 'tinnies'. (South Australia was the first state to announce a total ban on the use of plastic bags, operable by 2008, and the signs are that this ruling may soon spread through the whole nation, to combat the difficulties of plastic-bag disposal and the threat such bags pose to wildlife).

Supermarket shelves are crammed with 'environmentally friendly' goods, including items such as non-phosphate, biodegradable washing powders and dishwashing liquids, and recycled, unbleached toilet rolls or tissue packs. (A wry cartoon by Aussie Mark Lynch has two elderly suburban housewives peering suspiciously at the recycled-paper toilet rolls and remarking doubtfully, 'I don't think my Eric would be too keen on toilet paper that's been used before.') At the checkout counter, they will pack your purchases in paper bags if possible (others may charge for plastic bags). Many responsible shoppers now make a point of taking their own, canvas or woven, shopping bags to substitute for supermarket plastic bags.

Every neighbourhood has its sorted recycling bins for glass, cans, newspapers, old clothing, etc. Local councils arrange for sorted garbage pick-ups, gardening groups teach you how to compost organic waste. There is nothing you cannot recycle if you want to.

Australia was one of the first countries to outlaw leaded petrol and ozone-depleting chlorofluorocarbons (CFCs), and is a leader in substituting the much cleaner liquefied petroleum gas (LPG) for conventional gasoline in vehicles, over about a quarter of the transportation sector. The country is of course a major LPG producer.

Solar energy is another exciting form of alternative fuel—a fifth of Western Australian households use solar water heaters, a figure growing to almost three-quarters in the sunny Northern Territory.

However, as is well known, Australia's lack of commitment to the Kyoto greenhouse gas treaty has been lamentable, alongside that of the USA. The treaty has been signed by 141 nations, including 30 industrialised economies, but not by Australia or the USA.

A Darker Shade of Green

Over the past three decades, a vociferous, energetic and sometimes militant 'Green' movement has grown up to wield considerable political power in Australia. No Australian politician can really afford to adopt an obviously 'un-Green' position nowadays.

Almost every day, it seems, running battles are fought between environmentalists and mining companies, sawmill and plywood companies, housing and tourism developers, and so on. The 'greens' will man barricades, harass nuclear or fishing vessels in port, tie themselves to trees, bury themselves up to the neck in the ground before advancing bulldozers, you name it. They are committed, serious, and emotional. Unfortunately, the atmosphere often is one of confrontation rather than discussion.

The major conservationist players are the Australian Conservation Foundation (recently headed by singer, now Australian Labor Party Member of Parliament, Peter Garrett, leader of the top-ranking Midnight Oil, a social-conscience campaigning band), the Wilderness Society (born in Tasmania, now national), and Greenpeace, particularly active on issues like whale and dolphin protection and nuclear energy, as well as the state-based

Conservation Councils. There are myriad other groups at the state and local levels, besides many less politicised nature-rambling clubs.

Environmentalist politicians such as Tasmania's Bob Brown (briefly calling the shots in Tasmania after the 1989 state elections), cut their teeth on a number of issues, but most notably on the Franklin River controversy of the early 1980s. The federal Labor Party's support for the environmentalist position on the proposed dam on the Franklin River, one of Tasmania's most dramatic wilderness regions, swung the 'green vote' behind it at the 1983 elections which brought it to power—the dam was scotched. The green lobby also succeeded in getting the north Queensland rainforest and Kakadu National Park in the Northern Territory declared World Heritage sites. Battles are still periodically fought over the uranium mining potential in Kakadu. In 1991, in the midst of a terrible recession, the Labor government decided not to go ahead with the potentially lucrative mining of Coronation Hill in Kakadu, to the great dismay of the mining lobby.

While Australian Labor Party has long been associated with the green lobby, there were signs of cracks in this facade in 1991, with the passing of hotly-debated 'resource security' measures designed to guarantee the logging and mining industry future access to national forests, under a Labor government. In truth, today green issues rank lower on both the major parties' (Labor and Liberal) agendas than apparently more pressing concerns centering on immigration, border security and terrorism, and the economy in general.

The Australian Greens party was formed at the national, federal level in 1992, although there had been green parties at state level before this. By July 2005, the Greens had secured four seats in the federal Senate (the 'upper house' that reviews and can amend or reject bills for legislation) thus filling the very important 'keep the bastards honest' role (as Aussies traditionally put it) formerly held by the Democrats. Despite the Greens having no formal leadership, Bob Brown is universally regarded as their de facto leader.

SURVIVAL SENSE

Survival in Australia's remote outback and deserts is a skill that really needs to be learned; there are courses and many good handbooks to help you do so. Although the Australian environment is unique, basic survival techniques are much the same as those taught elsewhere, be it the USA, Canada, England or Asia. However, one or two tips may help the casual camper, driver or hiker who finds him or herself in a tight situation.

Fire

First, never go bush-walking if the newspapers, radio and television tell you there is a 'High' fire alert or a total fire-lighting ban. Leave longer walks till after summer is over.

If caught in a bush fire, do not panic, and do not run if you can avoid it—fires are anytime faster than you. Especially, do not run uphill, which is exactly the way fires love to go. Take shelter where you can to avoid radiated heat (more dangerous than flames or smoke), for instance in a depression such as a vehicle wheel-rut, and cover yourself with a blanket, or even just soil.

This may be hard to believe, but your chances of survival are far higher if you *stay* in your car or your house than if you run from them, even if fire is approaching. And that does not mean driving off in your car—the majority of the 2005 bushfire deaths in South Australia for example, were of people trying to drive away from the fire.

The evidence is that your car's petrol tank will *not* explode. You need only survive the climax of the fire passing over you—a maximum of four minutes. If you panic and run, you not only get exhausted, but radiated heat will kill you. Lie low and *cover yourself*.

Snakes

First, wear long trousers and closed shoes when hiking; second do not go near snakes or provoke them.

If bitten, do not perform the old macho ritual of slashing the bite with a razor blade to bleed it and tying a tight tourniquet between the bite and the heart. This is potentially dangerous. Tight tourniquets (which should be released every

30 minutes) are used only for funnel-web spider, blue-ringed octopus and box jellyfish cases.

The important thing is to act quickly and apply firm pressure with a crepe bandage wound extensively around the bitten area; use a piece of shirt if there is no bandage. To hold the bitten limb immobile, it should be splinted using a strong stick, binding the splint over the bandage. The patient must be kept very still.

Bush Ticks

These are common in the wetter parts of the East. Their bite is not fatal but can make you very ill.

Do not try to pull the tick out—you may create a septic wound. Just touch the tick with a hot match head, or dab it with kerosene or methylated spirit. As it backs out of your flesh, seize it with fingers or tweezers, taking care to pull the head out, not just the body.

It is possible not to know that a tick has visited you. If you have any problem walking or with body co-ordination after hiking in the bush, see your doctor. The tick may have left, but not its poison.

Leeches

Relatively harmless in themselves, leeches are bloodsuckers and may leave small open wounds which could get infected. They are found chiefly in wet areas, like rainforests. Keep bite-wounds clean. You can deter leeches with rub-on insect-repellents, but they are quite easy to remove with a touch of salt or tobacco.

Bush-Walking

You are safest if you have taken a course in map-reading. However, compasses and maps do not survival make; they can even go wrong. Ultimately, you will be thrown back on your own common sense, and whether or not you have prepared wisely.

Even in the apparently meek and mild temperate forests of the south, you must take care. For example, there is a rather horrible thing called horizontal scrub, in which vegetation has bent over and layered itself horizontally into a springy 'floor' which may in reality be several feet above the true forest floor. The unsuspecting hiker could fall through this mass and might find it very difficult to get out.

You must have with you a good water container, and preferably water too, of course. Some means of making fire should be with you. Beware of the 'I'm just going for half a day, why bother with food and water and medical kits' syndrome. If you get lost, you are really in trouble without food and water. Always carry at least some, no matter how short you intend your walk. In high temperatures, you may need about 5 litres of water a day—but do not drink unless you really need to. There is evidence that excessive drinking while walking or otherwise exercising only makes things worse. Sometimes just moistening your lips will do.

Of course, if you have studied 'bush tucker' with the Aboriginals, you may be able to live off the land in an emergency. But better play safe and carry food …

You should particularly be ready for violent weather changes, common in southern areas like Tasmania, but also encountered elsewhere. Sudden drops in temperature are the greatest threat.

Water purification tablets, salt, wool or string (to mark a path taken), a plastic groundsheet (which can be spread over a sunlit pit packed with vegetation around a centrally placed container, weighted with a stone over the container, and thus used to collect condensation water in the container overnight), a torch, a knife—these could all be useful. But don't take so much that it becomes a misery to carry your pack!

Put the essentials in a body belt, always with you. It is no good having a first-aid kit if you have left it behind in your pack at camp.

If you are lost, leave messages as you walk or at your camp if you leave it—scratched in the earth, for instance. Light a smoky fire to guide rescue aircraft. Construct an SOS message with each letter at least 2.5 metres high so aircraft can see it. But before all this, whenever you go 'off the beaten track', walking or driving, leave your intended itinerary and return date with someone, such as the local park ranger, policeman, hotelier or pub-owner and stick to

If you decide to go exploring, make sure you leave word with someone on where you are going and when you will be back.

your timetable, so that there is someone to worry when you don't get back on time.

Last of all, don't worry, it won't happen. Take no notice of all this and do go bush-walking! It is one of the best reasons for being in Australia.

A SENSE OF NATION

Australians know how to laugh at themselves, as I have said. But try laughing at them as an outsider and you will find the ground rules have suddenly shifted beneath your feet. Such sensitivity is not unusual in young nations—and white Australia's 200 years or so *is* still young in the history of nations.

Geography the shape of the land itself is one of the several pillars propping up the Australian sense of self and nation; the others include history and race/culture.

Get Wise about Gallipoli

I have said that anything is fair game when it comes to Australian humour: from cripples to Christ on the Cross. This is true. But not Gallipoli, or 'the Anzacs'…

Gallipoli? You will certainly have to get wise about Gallipoli if you wish to penetrate the Australian psyche. Anyway, you only have to stay long enough in Australia to hit the Anzac Day national holiday on 25 April to understand its importance.

No matter how small the Australian town you may chance upon on 25 April, you can be sure there will be an Anzac Day parade around the local war memorial, complete with emotional speeches, brass bands and little boys clutching their fathers' hands, both wearing the traditional cocked Digger slouch hat. ('Digger' has been the name for an Aussie soldier since World War I, but nobody seems to know for sure why, possibly because so many Aussies are miners of Australia's considerable mineral resources, including gold.)

Gallipoli was the site of a great battle during World War I, in Turkey. The only thing is, like Dunkirk, France, in World War II, it was a great defeat and retreat, not a great victory.

The British, who still remember the evacuation from the beaches of Dunkirk with pride, and perhaps the Americans, who similarly still remember non-victories like Custer's Last Stand against the Sioux Indians in the 19th century or MacArthur's retreat from the Philippines during World War II, may perhaps empathise with the Australian celebration of failure at Gallipoli.

For others, particularly 'face'-conscious Asians, it may take a little longer to get the hang of things. You may as well hear the whole story now, from me. It will save you some mystification later, when the great 25 April fuss hits you via the newspapers, television and radio. As columnist Max Harris has commented in *The Weekend Australian*: 'Australians regard an honestly won failure as the essence of success. We're a weird mob.'

Anzac Day commemorates the terrible trials of the Anzacs—the Australian and New Zealand Army Corps—in their attempts to scale and control the rugged sea-cliffs at Gallipoli, from the landing date, 25 April 1915, until their withdrawal on 19 December that year. During this time, 8,000 or so Australians (and more than 2,000 New Zealanders, as well as French soldiers and others) were killed, and 19,000 Australians were wounded. Their bravery in the face of hopeless odds won the Australian soldier an enduring reputation thereafter, to this day—one reconfirmed elsewhere, as at the battle for Singapore in 1942.

The real significance of Gallipoli lies not so much in the nobility of the Australians' dogged courage in attempting the almost impossible, nor in their legendary 'mateship' unto death, but rather in the fact that they were fighting for, and obeying orders from, the Imperial British government. This despite the fact that Australia had announced its intention to become independent of Great Britain in 1900 and had proclaimed the Commonwealth of Australia in 1901, holding the first federal elections that same year.

The sense of abandonment experienced at Gallipoli— it was all British war leader Winston Churchill's fault—saw the beginning of the end for Australian ties with the 'mother country', Britain. Australian director Peter Weir's epic film of 1981, *Gallipoli*, conveys this well: find a video of it if you can.

Underlying the Gallipoli celebration each year then, are not anti-Turkish feelings (on the contrary, the fashion nowadays is for survivors of both sides to embrace one another), but strong anti-British sentiment, and a feeling of 'To hell with all the others.'

The historic animosity for the British felt by the Irish, who formed a large part of Australia's original convict settlers, has reinforced this feeling. (Britons, beware of telling your favourite Irish joke in Australia before you ascertain your host's family origins). Gallipoli crystallised a sense of nation; hence its sacred-cow status when it comes to acceptable jokes.

The moral of the story: do not poke fun at Gallipoli and, despite his cultural ties with England, do not imagine that the Australian is just an Englishman in disguise. He is his own person. For one thing, he has learned to cope with a country about 24 times the size of the British Isles.

HISTORICAL MILESTONES

Even in the 16th century, many Western explorers were convinced that 'a Great South Land' existed. Several among

them found parts of Australia but did not recognise the significance of their discoveries: Dutchman Willem Jansz around Cape York Peninsula in 1606, his compatriot Dick Hartog off Western Australia in 1616, and another Dutchman, Abel Tasman, who discovered Tasmania in 1642. Others include Englishman William Dampier off the north-west coast in 1688, and Willem de Vlamingh, who discovered Perth's Swan River in 1696.

1770 ▪ Englishman Captain James Cook lands at Botany Bay and calls the eastern coastline New South Wales.

1788 ▪ The First Fleet arrives at Botany Bay under the command of Governor Arthur Phillip, with the first convict settlers from the British Isles—548 males, 188 females.

1793 ▪ Arrival of the first free settlers.

1828 ▪ First census shows 36,000 convicts and free settlers, as well as 2,549 soldiers.

1840 ▪ Abolition of transportation of convicts to New South Wales.

1851 ▪ First discovery of gold, New South Wales.

Eureka!

Few outsiders have heard of the 'Eureka Stockade' incident of 1854, but most Australians are well aware of its significance in their political history. The incident is an icon of the left wing and socialist Australia, and considered to be one of the sparks that lit up Australian democracy. You can compare its meaning to that of the Storming of the Bastille for the French or the Battle of the Alamo for the Americans.

'We swear by the Southern Cross to stand truly by each other and fight to defend our rights and liberties', was the oath sworn by thousands of gold diggers gathered in protest at Ballarat, Victoria, in 1854. 'It is the inalienable right of every citizen to have a voice in making the laws he is called on to obey... taxation without representation is tyranny', the diggers declared, demanding the vote they did not have and opposing property-owning qualifications for members of Parliament. The gold diggers' uprising may well be the original reason for Aussie fighters or soldiers earning the proudly boasted name 'Diggers.' But in fact, the 25,000 diggers living at Ballarat were a multicultural lot, including immigrants from America, Ireland, Europe and China, among other places, very few of them born in Australia.

It was the rebellious diggers who adopted the Southern Cross flag as their emblem and flew it for the first time in Australia; today the Southern Cross constellation of stars is a motif integral to the national flag. You can see the diggers' original flag still proudly displayed at the Ballarat Fine Art Gallery today. Protesters for various causes occasionally still coopt the simple Southern Cross flag to their cause even today.

The Eureka Stockade was a justified gold diggers' rebellion against petty and oppressive government authority and as such it stands for the tradition of Australian resistance to authority in general. The officials governing the early Victorian goldfields were cruel in their exercise of elite power and privilege, oppressive and corrupt in their arbitrary policing and farming of the gold-digging licences.

The actual process of extracting the gold was particularly gruelling and uncertain. After a series of brutal incidents between the diggers and their oppressors, thousands of diggers rose up and declared 'war'. Led by Peter Lalor, the most militant of them marched to a predominantly Irish area called 'The Eureka' and proceeded to fortify it behind a wooden stockade. But with only a few hundred men behind the stockade on 3 December 1854, government troops made short work of their flimsy defences, rounding the stockaders up, killing 20–30 diggers and quickly declaring martial law. However, the incident was seen as a turning point in the development of Australian democracy; 13 arrested stockaders were acquitted in court in 1855, a Commission of Enquiry castigated the administration of the goldfields, and in a short time most of the miners' demands were granted, including their inclusion in parliamentary democracy. Peter Lalor was even elected to Parliament.

The Round House, 1831, Fremantle, Western Australia. Old prison legacy from Britain.

1876	▪ Death of Truganini, the last full-blooded Tasmanian Aboriginal.
1883	▪ Silver discovered at Broken Hill, New South Wales.
1900	▪ The Australian states federated; Australia announces intention to become independent from Britain.
1901	▪ Census counts 3.8 million (white) population.
1902	▪ Women get the vote at federal elections.
1908	▪ Canberra chosen as the federal capital.
1914	▪ World War I declared, Australian troops embark for Europe.
1915	▪ Australian and New Zealander soldiers land at Gallipoli on 25 April but are evacuated by 18 December.
1920	▪ White population now 5.4 million, according to official figures.
1932	▪ Sydney Harbour Bridge opened.
1940	▪ Australian troops detailed for service abroad in World War II.
1942	▪ Darwin in the Northern Territory bombed by the Japanese, and Japanese submarines enter Sydney Harbour.
1947	▪ Australia's new drive for immigration begins, focusing mainly on Britain and Europe at first.

An obelisk that commemorates those who have given their lives for their country in the two World Wars.

1949 ■ Australian citizenship comes into being and is granted to all Australians.

■ Robert Menzies' Liberal government comes into power.

1952 ■ Discovery of uranium in the Northern Territory.

1956 ■ The Olympic Games held in Melbourne.

1961 ■ Iron ore deposits found at Pilbara, Western Australia.

1964 ■ Australia's first truly national newspaper, *The Australian*, is born.

■ National Service was introduced, a two-year scheme. For the first time, army conscripts could also be sent anywhere, opening up the possibility of their participation in Australia's Vietnam War commitments.

1965 ■ Australian infantry battalion sent to Vietnam.

1966 ■ Prime Minister Sir Robert Menzies, Australia's longest-serving leader (1939–1966, except for 1941–1949), retires.

■ Decimal currency is introduced and the metric system of weights and measures phased in.

1967 ■ Australians vote in a referendum to abolish all forms of discrimination against the Aboriginals.

- Convicted gambler-thief Ronald Ryan is the last person to be hanged in Australia, for stabbing a prison warder to death when trying to escape, provoking enormously emotional public protest and street demonstrations against the sentence.
- Prime Minister Harold Holt disappears at sea off Victoria.

1968
- John Gorton, Liberal Party leader, becomes prime minister of Australia.

1969
- Bob Hawke is elected president of the Australian Council of Trade Unions (ACTU).
- Women are granted equal pay for equal work.

1972
- Labor Party wins elections under the leadership of Gough Whitlam, after 23 years in opposition, riding on the public's desire for change, and the slogan 'It's Time'.
- The 'White Australia' policy is formally ended.
- Conscription for military service is abolished in favour of a small professional volunteer army.

1973
- 18-year-olds get the vote.
- Queen Elizabeth II of Great Britain to be known as 'Queen of Australia'.
- The Sydney Opera House opens, 16 years after the initial design had been selected.

1974
- Cyclone Tracy hits Darwin in the Northern Territory on Christmas Day with wind speeds of up to 300 kmph, and inflicts terrible devastation (at least 50 deaths, 30,000 evacuated), requiring complete rebuilding of the town.

1975
- Dismissal of the Whitlam government by Governor-General Sir John Kerr. Malcolm Fraser's Liberal-Country Party coalition government takes power.

1979
- Aboriginal Land Trust now has title to 144 properties, former Aboriginal reserves.
- ACTU calls second general strike in Australia's history.

1980
- Campbell Inquiry into Australian financial system.
- Nugan Hand Bank collapses.

1982
- The Franklin Dam controversy erupts in Tasmania, Australia's biggest-ever 'Green' battle.

1983 ▪ Prime Minister Malcolm Fraser is granted a double dissolution of Parliament, followed by an election for both houses. The Labor Party takes power under the leadership of Bob Hawke.

▪ 'Ash Wednesday' bush fires devastate South Australia and Victoria—75 dead, 8,000 homeless.

▪ Australia wins the America's Cup with its yacht *Australia II*.

▪ Australia's first AIDS death—since then there have been more than 1,500 reported cases and more than 800 deaths.

1984 ▪ Government, business and union leaders sign the 'Accord' on prices and income policy.

▪ Control of Ayers Rock given to the Aboriginals of the area.

1985 ▪ The Federal Treasury, as part of general financial deregulation, allows 16 foreign banks to apply for banking licences.

▪ Lionel Murphy, a High Court judge, found guilty of attempting to pervert the course of justice. Cleared at a second trial, he dies of cancer in 1986, aged 64.

1986 ▪ Queen Elizabeth II of Great Britain signs a proclamation while in Australia which finally clears the way for Australia's severance from the United Kingdom, expressed in the Australia Act of the same year.

▪ The movie *Crocodile Dundee*, starring Paul Hogan, becomes the highest-earning film in Australian history and also the highest-earning foreign film to be shown in the USA—it took more than A$ 180 million at USA box offices, and another more than A$ 110 million with its 1988 sequel.

1987 ▪ Labor retains power at federal elections.

1988 ▪ White Australians celebrate the bicentennial anniversary of the arrival of Britain's First Fleet, while Aboriginals stage a massive protest against this celebration of the white 'invasion' of Australia.

1990 ▪ Labor again retains power at the federal elections.

1991 ▪ In December, a coup in the ALP's inner circle ('Caucus') results in Bob Hawke's ouster by Paul Keating, as the government gears up for a tough fight in the 1993 federal elections.

1996 ▪ In March, the electorate ends 13 years of ALP rule and returns John Howard's liberal government.

1997 ▪ Bushfires rage across the nation.
▪ A 370-day royal commission ends its investigation into police corruption.

1998 ▪ An economic crisis in Asia and political turmoil in Indonesia adversely affect Australia's economy and psyche.

1999 ▪ Federal Parliament declares the nation's 'deep and sincere regret' over past ill treatment of Aborigines, but avoids the explicit apology many Aboriginals and other Australians expect.
▪ Historic referendum on becoming a Republic with a Parliament-appointed President replacing the Queen gets a 55 per cent 'No' vote, and the Constitutional Monarchy stays.
▪ Australia's relationship with and role in Asia changes with Australian initiation and leadership of the United Nations-mandated Interfet peacekeeping force in newly independent, formerly Indonesian territory of East Timor.

2000 ▪ On 1 July, controversial major tax reforms, including a new 10 per cent Goods and Services Tax (GST), come into force.
▪ The nation is shocked by 'cash for comment' revelations—senior commercial radio journalists and talkback showhosts, hitherto respected for their independence of thought, are shown to yield to private commercial sponsorship contracts.
▪ In February, the Australian-led Interfet force in East Timor hands over to the 'blue beret' United Nations Transitional Authority in East Timor.
▪ In September, Sydney hosts the Olympic Games.

A JIGSAW NATION

Few outsiders realise that Australia was for long no more than a collection of separately autonomous colonies. Nationhood is still a very new thing.

To make matters worse, internal communications and understanding have been hampered both by the geography of a harsh and huge terrain, almost 4,000 km (2,500 miles) from east to west, over 3,000 km (1,864 miles) north to south, and by economic stupidities such as it costing about the same to fly abroad as to air-commute internally (only recently mitigated by the advent of budget airlines such as Virgin Blue and Jetstar Airways).

The remnants of that early colonial structure, still expressed in the independence of the six state governments, are only now being broken down. For example, only in 1991 was a decision taken to form national bodies which would standardise legal procedures, electrical power, road systems, and the gauge used on railway lines across the country. But whether all of this will actually materialise is still in doubt. Inter-state differences have been a great block to economic progress, and to crime-busting too, for many years.

Different Standards

For years until 1991, sausages had differing content regulations in different states, preventing their inter-state sale. Quite often, a single product had to wear different labels and packaging in each different state. There were three definitions of bread; one state demanded that margarine be sold only in cube-shaped packages.

Protectionist measures block eastern potatoes reaching Western Australia, among many other examples of interstate quirks. There is a federal policy to increase competition but some states are only being dragged kicking and screaming towards that goal.

Electricians, plumbers, doctors and lawyers needed licences to work outside their home states. A rail cargo container sent east-west from Sydney to Perth was subject to four changes of locomotive, five safe working systems, six sizes of loading gauge and had to spend 12 hours at sidings for crew changes and inspections.

The states can raise some of their own revenue by taxation but their power to collect state-based income tax was grabbed by federal legislation in 1942; the Federal Government generally raises the equivalent of 80 per cent of all government spending. Regular 'blues' (fights') between the federal and state governments over a beast called 'horizontal fiscal equalisation' or the distribution of federal monies to the states, nowadays mostly in the shape of federal GST (Goods and Services Tax) revenue, are a routine feature of the Australian political and economic landscape.

THE SPIRITUAL AUSSIE

Adherence to formal religion, especially to the church-going brand of Christianity often claimed as the 'bedrock' of Australian society by conservatives ranging from John Howard to Pauline Hanson, is declining noticeably in Australia. About 68 per cent of the population claims to be Christian but church attendance is far lower than you would expect from that figure— and looking at some of the congregations, you could be forgiven for believing that the churches only survive by grace of a large number of devoted Christians of immigrant origin, particularly from Asia. Recruitment of the younger generation is not really happening. In 2005, the number of Catholics attending Mass at Perth churches in Western Australia had fallen to its lowest level in 25 years, with less than one third of Catholics attending Mass on weekends, while the local Anglican churches were considering holding services on days other than Sundays in order to fit in with families' social and work timetables and combat declining attendance. The Catholics in Perth even went so far as to take an advertisement in the local paper *The West Australian* to cajole believers back into church. Nationwide, the percentage of Australians professing a non-Christian religion rose from 1 per cent in 1971 to 5 per cent in 2001; the fastest growing faith is in fact Buddhism, accounting for close to 2 per cent of the population. Significantly, close to 17 per cent of Australia professes no attachment to any religion now, compared with only 7 per cent in 1971.

That 'Christian Anglo-Saxon' stereotype of Australians that even some Aussies still harbour about themselves is really wearing thin these days.

How Aussies See Themselves

When the liberal Prime Minister John Howard proposed a new Preamble to the Constitution as a secondary question with the Republic Referendum on 6 November 1999 (more on this in The British section), Australians roundly rejected it.

Nonetheless, the text of this ill-fated document offers some interesting insights into Australian perspective of themselves and their nation today. It was controversial in its incorporation of Aboriginal ties with the land and of the migrant contribution and in enshrining not only the concept of God but also that of 'mateship':

'With hope in God, the Commonwealth of Australia is constituted by the equal sovereignty of all its citizens.

The Australian nation is woven together of people from many ancestries and arrivals. Our vast island continent has helped to shape the destiny of our Commonwealth and the spirit of its people.

Since time immemorial our land had been inhabited by Aborigines and Torres Strait Islanders who are honoured for their ancient and continuing cultures.

In every generation immigrants have brought great enrichment to our nation's life.

Australians are free to be proud of their country and heritage, free to realise themselves as individuals, and free to pursue their hopes and ideals. We value excellence as well as fairness, independence as dearly as mateship.

Australia's democratic and federal system of government exists under law to preserve and protect all Australians in an equal dignity which may never be infringed by prejudice or fashion or ideology nor invoked against achievement.

In this spirit we, the Australian people, commit ourselves to this Constitution.'

HOW AUSSIES SEE SOME OF 'THE OTHERS'

Chapters One and Two touch on some stereotyped images of Australia and Australians. In their attempt to define their own identity when it comes to other nationalities, races, creeds and cultures, obviously the Australians too harbour their own stereotypes of 'the outsider'. Understanding these may help you position yourself better when relating to Australians.

The French

There has been great hostility to the French among Australians, based mainly on France's nuclear on Australia's doorstep and a general suspicion that the French are untrustworthy. Paradoxically, amid this debate, little has been said or remembered of British nuclear tests inside Australia between 1852 and 1958.

The tone can sink low at times. A heading in *The Weekend Australian* (25–28 September 1993) read simply 'The Bloody French'.

While this Francophobia is yet another legacy of Australia's British heritage, some of its stems from the famous Australian 'cultural cringe'—a feeling of inferiority when confronted with alleged European sophistication, history, culture and what-have-you. So when an Australian reviles 'the frogs', he is only getting his own back for being made to feel small because he cannot cope with a French menu. But nowadays, there is a bit of a grin behind all this abuse, and one senses that the jibing is a lot more affectionate in essence now than it used to be, that there is now more admiration for what is generally perceived as French 'style'.

The British

Better known to Australians as Poms or Pommies (believed to derive from POHM–Prisoner of Her Majesty—in reference to Britain's convict past in Australia), the British are more usually referred to as Pommy Bastards or Whingeing Poms. Aussies believe that the British specialise in the art of whingeing (which means griping, complaining or moaning) and have taken it to a high level as shop stewards dominating the Australian trade union movement.

'Australians are the most morbidly small-minded, petty, nationalistic, chippy, insecure, over-sensitive houseplants ever to find their way out of the greenhouse.'
—Anglo-Australian warfare surfaces in an editorial in England's *The Evening Standard*, reacting to Australian reports of 'Pommy whingers' in 1997

Indeed, the New South Wales Anti-Discrimination Board found in 1997 that most (22 per cent) of the complaints it received in the previous year came not from Asians, but from Poms.

Australian folklore says Pommies do not bathe enough. Hence the phrase 'as dry as a Pommy's towel (or bathmat)', apparently coined by comedian Barry Humphries' Barry McKenzie character.

Traditional ties have weakened considerably since Britain joined the European Economic Community and gradually dropped in her ranking as one of Australia's most important export markets. T-shirts have been emblazoned with such legends as 'Keep Australia Beautiful—Shoot a Pom' and 'Grow your own dope—Plant a Pom'.

One of the primary reasons many Australians make cruel and sometimes ribald jokes about the Liberal Howard government's Foreign Minister Alexander Downer is that he seems a mite too Anglicised and carries the accent to go with it, being a graduate of Oxford University, England, with his mother 'Lady Mary' by virtue of his knighted father. He is constantly portrayed by cartoonists as wearing fishnet stockings, in a sly reference to a once-revealed possible cross-dressing incident in his wayward youth; the implied stereotype here of course is the English pervert who has emerged from the alleged gay culture of elite English private schools (called 'public' schools in England).

The paradox in such attitudes, of course, is that the Queen of England 20,000 km (almost 12,500 miles) away, remains the Queen of Australia represented by the Governor-General, a position cloned in each of the Australian states. Futhermore, although the federated Commonwealth of Australia was proclaimed in 1901, only in 1986 did the Australia Act finally sever most ties with Britain by denying the British the power to make laws for Australia or to exercise any governmental responsibility and by removing the mechanism of legal appeal to the British Privy Council.

The Queen had a nasty moment on 6 November 1999 when Australia went to the polls on the Republic Referendum. However, some 55 per cent voted the Queen should stay, proving once again that there is nothing Australians detest more than change, and missing a historic opportunity to greet the new millennium and the centenary of federation with a brand new face.

To be fair to Australians though, a bit of fancy political footwork had succeeded in skewing the result somewhat. Instead of being asked to vote simply whether or not to have a Republic, voters were offered what many branded a 'politicians' republic' with a Parliament-appointed President. Most

Australians, democratic to the core, preferred direct election of the President, and therefore rejected the proposition—not necessarily because they were anti-Republic.

The Referendum question read: 'Do you approve of an Act to alter the Constitution to establish the Commonwealth of Australia as a Republic with the Queen and Governor General being replaced by a President appointed by a two-thirds majority of the members of the Commonwealth Parliament?

'No' said 55 per cent. But nobody could tell from this what the support for a Republic really was. Recent polls suggest not only a decline in support for the idea—amazing, considering the relatively unattractive conduct of the British Royal Family in recent times—but perhaps also general disinterest in the issue and a feeling that there are more important things to worry about. A second chance at a Republic may be a long time coming.

Americans

White Australians share many national traits and also historical experiences (such as gold rushes) with the Americans. The two nations are also military allies, together with New Zealand, under the ANZUS security treaty dating back to 1952. There are several somewhat mysterious American satellite surveillance and defence installations in Australia's remote heartland. A Free Trade Agreement between the two countries went into operation from 2005, raising issues for some in the pharmaceuticals, food labelling and creative services areas, but nonetheless cementing an already solid trade relationship: the two partners' 2003 two-way trade was worth A$ 40.9 billion, with Australia exporting A$ 14.2 billion in goods and services, and importing A$ 26.7 billion from the USA.

The two peoples are similarly outgoing, both preferring informality, tending to be brash, loud, and wearing their opinions and emotions on their sleeves. They have both conquered a big country (Australia and the mainland USA, excluding Alaska, are almost the same size), including quite a bit of rough terrain.

One of the similarities between white Australians and Americans is the rodeo.

White Australians too have their cowboys and, in the Aboriginals, their Indians. It is significant perhaps that one of the many delegations of helpers who have visited Australian aboriginal settlements to advise on coping with social problems like the petrol-sniffing addiction, came from America's Indian reservations, where they share the same problems. The two nations also share the passionate rhetoric of freedom, human rights and democracy.

The two people's languages and their cultures—from drive-in everything and hamburgers to country-and-western music, and of course, television imports—are drawing closer every day. One Australian newspaper columnist recently complained bitterly that somebody had changed the old English word 'torch' to the American 'flashlight' behind his back when he wasn't looking.

In general, there is a feeling of natural affinity. And it must be said, of admiration on the Australian side, despite a regular chorus of complaint against American cultural infiltration. Occasionally, the admiration takes the negative form of a 'cultural cringe' in relation to American superiority as a world power. For one thing, it is generally agreed, by Australians too, that America saved Australia from a Japanese fate worse than death during World War II.

Everybody, on both sides of the argument, was delighted at the symbolically significant union of quintessential Aussie Paul Hogan ('Crocodile Dundee') with his American leading lady (and for many, the marriage of Hogan's natural heir, 'crocodile hunter' Steve Irwin, to his Canadian wife Terri is about the same sort of thing). On the darker side, some Australians further to the left look askance at Australia's strong defence and security links with the USA, and at the alleged American penetration of the Australian political process. This paranoia has deepened with Prime Minister John Howard's dogged show of loyalty to President George Bush in post-September 11 times.

Like American Texans, Aussies like everything Australian to be the biggest.

For a fascinating exposition of this darker school of thought and many other less often discussed aspects of Australia, see London-based Australian journalist John Pilger's devastating and controversial book, *A Secret Country*.

Italians and Greeks

Most jokes about the Italians or Greeks are quite good-humoured. After all, an awful lot of Australians can claim Italian or Greek ancestry (more than 4 per cent and 2 per cent respectively), and Melbourne in the state of Victoria is accounted the world's second biggest Greek city. The Italian accent is often caricatured publicly, as on a one-time popular advertisement on Perth television, where 'Luigi' genially instructed the viewer on how to 'Sava-Dava-Moni'. The SBS TV sitcom series *Pizza*, set in a pizza shop, is enormously popular for its somewhat politically incorrect depiction of various ethnic types from Mediterranean 'wogs' (almost a term of affection in Australia now) to a Lebanese rapper, a white Aussie 'bogan' (yob, lout), a Maori 'Kiwi' (New Zealander), a Chinese, and others. It is generally agreed that any Australian houses sporting neo-classical porticoes, pillars, columns, statues, lions and the like usually prove to belong to, or have been designed by, nostalgic Italian-Australians—from my own observation, they really do!

New Zealanders

You might imagine that Australians would feel some affinity with the 'Kiwis' of New Zealand, by virtue of being close neighbours, as well as military of allies.

Not so. As far as Aussies are concerned, Kiwis are pinching Australian jobs—their passports allow them free entry to and employment in Australia and there are tens of thousands of them in Australia—and are nearly as responsible for the rise in crime as the Vietnamese. Well, almost.

The Australians further resent the Kiwis' often revealed sense of superiority (they do not share the Australians' convict ancestry) and 'English ways'. There is really little love lost between them. Cruel jokes about New Zealanders' alleged sexual affinity for their sheep, and mimicking of their Scots-based accent (rendering 'fush' for 'fish') abound in Australian public life.

The Tasmanians

Now, this is an awkward one. Tasmanians (often jocularly referred to as Taswegians) are Australians. But you wouldn't think so from the way most mainlander Australians talk about them.

Tasmania (affectionately known as Tassie, pronounced 'Tazzie') is Australia's smallest state and an island, 240 km (150 miles) off the south-eastern corner of the mainland, with a population of less than half a million spread over more than 67,000 sq km (almost 26,000 sq miles).

Tasmanians are a standing joke in mainland Australia. The basic premise of every Tasmanian joke is that Tasmanians are hillbillies and country bumpkins (including lonely farmers habituated to questionable sexual practices) afflicted with the mental and physical consequences of extensive inbreeding: hence the many jokes referring to them as having 'two heads', 'pointy-heads' and the like.

But Isn't Australia Racist?

I mentioned all the above as a prelude to answering the question, 'Are Australians racist?'

When I first wrote this book in the early 1990s, against a backdrop of a Labor-government Australia officially dedicated to multi-culturalism. I answered this question with 'No, they are equally rude about absolutely everybody, of whatever colour or creed.'

I also pointed out that Aboriginal Australians are the ones suffering most from any Australian racism. I asked the reader to examine his or her nation's own glass house. I pointed out that Australia's tradition of free expression opens her up to more bruising public discussions of sensitivities like race than are possible in more restricted societies.

All of this remains true, but in the context of a Liberal government under Prime Minister John Howard replacing Labor's Paul Keating since 1996, a body of opinion previously silenced unfortunately has been emboldened to speak up. Its xenophobic, sometimes racist, voice was for a while of the former independent, now largely disgraced, Member of Parliament, Queenslander Pauline Hanson. Not, of course, that John Howard has ever actively or openly espoused xenophobia or racism; but many believe he has too passively stood aside from restraining such views, and so indirectly encouraged them.

The Hanson camp have expressed strong opposition to Asian immigration, to financial aid and welfare grants to Aboriginals, and to certain forms of foreign investment. While Hanson apparently represented many white Australians-in-the-street—only partially educated, she herself ran a simple fish-and-chips shop—her words have brought far more sophisticated toads out from under their stones. Therein lies the real danger to Australian traditions of fair play and equality that such politics poses.

But Hanson's One Nation Party is now mortally sick, with no federal political presence since the 2004 federal elections. After a brief moment of glory in the June 1998 state election when about 23 per cent of Queenslanders voted for the party, giving it 11 of 89 seats in Queensland, the party has since descended into internal bickering and fragmentation, exacerbated by external pressure. Investigations into the party have led to its deregistration in Queensland and New South Wales. In 2003, Hanson faced possible personal bankruptcy and three years' jail as a result of electoral fraud charges, in part relating to A$ 500,000 of the party's funds. This was quashed on appeal but Hanson left politics in 2004.

This is not to say that One Nation will not join the undead with the potential to rise like Dracula from his coffin. Hanson and her crew never did represent Australia or even a majority of Australians. Many Australians passionately oppose her. And though things got a little rough while Hanson was roaming the streets, the incipient violence was contained.

However, Hanson's brand of politics did influence mainstream politics, highlighting general discontent in the forgotten bush and pushing the Liberals a little further to the right to cut some ground from under One Nation. She also had a strongly negative impact on Australia's relationship with Asia. But since the Asian economic crisis in 1998 and the advent of terrorism concerns post-2001, there have been far bigger fish to fry in that relationship.

It would have been tempting to say that Hanson's political demise represents the burial of old-style racism in Australia. Unfortunately, it does not. Perhaps the lingering fear of powerful and populous Asian neighbours, for example, is inevitable in an island nation with plenty of empty land and alluring mineral resources. Deep in the Australian psyche there remains the dread of the 'Australian way of life' being overwhelmed by 'them.' Indonesia looms large in this context and there has been enhanced mutual distrust since Australian troops moved into East Timor after the new nation's bloody passage to independence from Indonesia in 1999. The appalling spectacle of ignorant and emotional Australian reactions to the drug-trafficking conviction of Australian girl Schapelle Corby in an Indonesian court in 2005 uncovered yet again the virulent forms that this fear can take. The assumption for many was that (a) Corby was innocent, (b) she was victimised by the Indonesians and (c) the Indonesian courts were incompetent and corrupt. And they said so, abusively, on talk-back radio, on the streets, and most horrifically, by mailing an envelope of threatening white powder (anthrax, some feared at first, but actually harmless talcum powder) to the Indonesian embassy.

So what is it all about? Well, try to empathise. Hanson and her ilk stood for the dying throes of the old 1950s Australia. Imagine the trauma of being jolted awake from a comfortable introspective Anglo-Celtic dream and forced to make yourself a place in the world or worse, in Asia, on pain of economic death. Of suddenly not knowing or understanding your immediate neighbours, newly arrived foreigners. For disturbed people like Pauline Hanson, the rules have been changed with brutal abruptness, the golden age has evaporated, and it all seems terribly unfair—'stop the world, we want to get off!'

But rest assured, the future of Australia is not on Pauline Hanson's side. Relax, do not become hyper-sensitive, and all will be well. There is still enough courtesy, kindness and care on the streets of Australia to more than balance the occasional outpouring of public bile.

Asians

Before we talk about Australian attitudes to Asians, let us first translate the word 'Asian' into Australian: it means, almost exclusively, Chinese and Vietnamese, and perhaps sometimes Japanese too. It does not usually refer to Indians, for example. In other words, it refers to those of Mongoloid stock. Among racists, it is a euphemism for 'slant-eyes'. This is quite different of course from the meaning the word 'Asian' has acquired in, say, London or Birmingham, UK, where it is used to refer to South Asians.

Some folk in Australia are striving very hard to make the dream of integration with Asia a reality. From 1996, a special government programme had children learning Chinese, Japanese, Malay and Indonesian at school but tragically, the Howard government has drastically cut funding to this programme since 2002 and Asian language studies are declining as a result. Coupled with an on-off attitude to funding for important Australian outreach tools such as Radio Australia, broadcasting into Asia, the current climate does not look that good for improving cross-cultural understanding, though it must be said that there are also countless academic research centres and 'think tanks' specialising in strengthening Australia's links with Asia.

The White Australia Policy

The White Australia policy dated back to the 1901 Restrictive Immigration Act which kept out non-European immigrants, following an influx of cheap Chinese labour to the Australian goldfields after the 1840s.

Among other things, the policy produced silly situations like the case of the twin brothers with mixed parenthood, one looking Indian and the other

The attitudes of those times spawned a rash of consumer products like Golden Fleece Soap, which said it would 'Keep Australians White'. This policy was not abandoned till 1973. Up to that date, Australians were taught to be afraid of the 'Yellow Peril' from the north, be it Japanese or Indonesian. It takes time to shake off such grim instruction.

The attitudes of those times spawned a rash of consumer products like Golden Fleece Soap, which said it would 'Keep Australians White'. This policy was not abandoned till 1973. Up to that date, Australians were taught to be afraid of the 'Yellow Peril' from the north, be it Japanese or Indonesian. It takes time to shake off such grim instruction.

European. No prizes for guessing which one got in and which one didn't. And many a southern European was rejected for immigration in those days, on the grounds of being a touch too swarthy. The only Asians admitted as early as the 1950s or 1960s were those who could prove direct European heritage, such as the Anglo-Indians of India or the Eurasians of Singapore and Malaysia. Sometimes it seems the Australian immigration officers making such fine decisions simply looked at the applicant's skin colour to make their final judgement.

Well-treated

Yet, curiously, I must mention here that a Chinese-Australian and Sri-Lankan-Australian friend of mine, both of whom arrived in Western Australia long before 1973, have told me that they were well treated at that time, 'like guests, like a special novelty'. Even today, I can report that a Chinese friend was hosted to a welcome tea-party by his Aussie neighbours and another Chinese lady regularly exchanges cooked dishes from her kitchen for handyman fixing about her house by her Australian neighbour.

That said, quite a few Australians do believe that the Vietnamese have brought an increase in crime (proportionately, in fact, they generate less than their share of national crime), that other Asians have brought exotic diseases like tuberculosis and hepatitis B, and that migrant Asians are taking Australians' jobs. You will find similar misconceptions about immigrants in almost every country experiencing a sudden influx of them.

Cultural Burps and Misunderstandings

Considering the country's long isolation from Asia under the White Australia policy and considering the rapid social change, if not turmoil, that large-scale Asian immigration has brought about over the past decade or so, it's surprising there is not more overt racism in Australia.

However, let us now 'sensitise' ourselves by looking at some of the things that can trigger Australian hostility.

Like the Chinese man I saw spit upon the marbled pavements of the luxurious Burswood Casino Hotel in Perth, Western Australia.

Like the Vietnamese I saw haggling over a few cents at a simple Australian neighbourhood second-hand sales fair, where nothing was priced much more than A$ 5. How to explain in a few seconds to the offended Australian vendors the long tradition of bargaining in South-east Asia? How to explain to the Vietnamese that there was an unspoken gentleman's agreement that such friendly markets were fixed-price?

Like the Chinese students I saw yelling and shouting in their native Mandarin at an Australian university bus-stop, without any regard for how uncomfortable it made the Australian commuters around them feel: 'Are we in Australia or what?'

Like the Singaporean tourists in Perth hotel buffets who piled their plates high with food they couldn't finish, simply to get their money's worth, leaving behind mountains of wasted food.

Or the Asian shoppers who transferred their market customs to their local Australian supermarket, poking their fingers into fruit and vegetables, and test-eating some of them, 'not done' in Australia. The Japanese tourist who poured tomato ketchup over his breakfast cereal didn't go down too well either. Neither did the Singaporean waving her hand imperiously at a far-off waiter to get him to come over and bring her a chair which was just behind her.

The Mystery of the Vanishing Abalone

Then there is the abalone problem off Western Australian coasts. For decades or more, ordinary Australians have enjoyed their annual abalone harvest, sticking firmly to the rules, or so they claim: take no more than 20 pieces per person per day and leave the small ones alone, to generate future stocks.

But in 1991, the Western Australian state government had to cancel that year's fishing season outright. There was no abalone left and it looked likely there might not be much more in future either. Who dunnit? 'The Vietnamese,' said some Aussies. 'The Chinese' said others. 'All Asians,' said yet others. 'Not us,' chorused the Asians. It was the big boys, the Australians with the commercial interests.

Obviously, the Western Australian Fisheries Minister at that time, Gordon Hill, thought somebody not English-speaking had done it: among the measures he announced when cancelling the season was a multilingual education programme for the fishermen.

And columnist Mike Roennfeldt, writing in *The West Australian* newspaper said: 'Everyone, including the media, has been so terrified of being labelled racists that the obvious truth has been ignored. It seems to me that tippy-toeing around the fact that the whole abalone problem lies directly at the feet of Australians of Asian descent is actually being more racist than facing squarely up to the truth.'

Whatever the rights and wrongs of this case, it is a good example of why some Australians may have reservations about Asians.

A very similar thorn in Australian flesh is the Indonesian 'poaching' of Australia's valuable trochus shell. Between 1989 and 1991, Australian patrol boats arrested 150 Indonesian vessels, mostly from Sulawesi, for fishing inside Australian waters, in a multi-million campaign to stop fishing.

From the Indonesian fishermen's point of view, fishing off Australia, for fish and shellfish, for trochus and for sea-slug (known as trepang), is a centuries-old traditional right, which in many cases they had negotiated amicably with the indigenous Aboriginals. Besides, they are poor and desperate enough to just keep on coming.

To top this all off, Australians generally feel that Asian societies are reprehensible for their lack of social and political freedom, in short, for not being like Australia.

The rows with Malaysia over the 1986 hanging in Malaysia of two Australians, Kevin Barlow and Brian Chambers, for carrying drugs (Australia does not have a death penalty for any crime), echoed in the uproar over the Schapelle Corby drugs case in Bali during 2005, the ABCTV screening in 1990–1991 of a soap opera titled *Embassy* set in a fictional South-east Asian Muslim country called Ragaan, which just happened to be located between the borders of Thailand and Malaysia, and over Prime Minister Paul Keating's infamous reference to Malaysian Prime Minister Mahathir as a 'recalcitrant', are cases in point.

The *Embassy* series was insulting to Malaysia. But the Australian government does not control the country's media, a simple fact which many Asians find difficult to understand in the context of their own 'guided' media.

The Challenge of the Crescent Moon

Islam is a topic calculated to raise the hairs on the back of many an Australian neck. This reaction stems from a blend of ignorance and blind fear. Australians are not alone in this.

People in Middle Eastern dress, especially women in veils, are too visibly different on Australian streets. Terrorism as manifested in Al Qaeda's 11 September 2001 attack on New York and the Bali Bombing in 2002, widely seen as anti-Australian, has hardly helped. As in America, some of Australia's freedoms have been subtly eroded as a result of the security crackdown perceived as a necessary response to these incidents. Since 2002, the powers of the Australian Security Intelligence Organisation (ASIO) have moved from mere surveillance to detention and interrogation without charge and the banning of proscribed organisations, while the definitions of and penalties for terrorism and treason have been broadened, among other things.

Such measures have only served to widen the chasm between Islamic and non-Islamic Australia. It will take great patience and tolerance on both sides if this chasm is to be bridged.

It certainly was alarming to hear white Australian residents on the eastern side of Australia reacting to the prospect of a mosque being erected in their neighbourhood. They howled their opposition. Their reason: property values would slump (unfortunately possible), and 'the kiddies wouldn't be safe to walk home,' as one woman-in-the-street out it to the TV cameras, a revelation of shocking prejudice. One talk-back radio caller debating another issue declared flatly: "I reckon we should not have Arabs in this country. I reckon they are all mad."

Different Attitudes

Just after the conviction of Schappelle Corby in her Bali drugs case, in 2005, one of my Eurasian friends who originally came from Malaysia was casually chatting in Indonesian with an Indonesian girl at the weekend market where they run a stall together selling jewellery. An Australian white who was looking interested in their wares suddenly turned around to his wife and said, "Do you know what language that is that they are speaking? Come on, let's get out of here." Whereupon they both left in high dudgeon, pleased at the opportunity to boycott 'Indonesians'. Yet both the stall-holders were already long-time Australians.

But try telling all this to my Singapore-Malay and Muslim friend, who is married to an Australian girl of Roman Catholic Italian parentage, Cindy, and lives in Perth (which, like many other Australian cities, is well supplied with Islamic 'halal' butchers). Cindy is now a good Muslim—the couple have found a mosque in Perth to attend every Friday—and she produces fine Malaysian food every year for the Muslim feast of Ramadan, at the end of the fasting month, clad in traditional Malay dress.

Does she ever get teased or harassed about her new religion? 'No, no—not at all', she smiles gently. End of conversation.

The Japanese

Then there is the Australian unease about the Japanese, who admittedly own huge chunks of their country, most notably in Queensland, where they hold about 93 per cent of all foreign-owned hotel rooms, for example.

This unease is deepened by actual or culturally inherited memories of the Pacific War during World War II, in which Australian soldiers, like many others, suffered bitterly at the hands of the Japanese.

If nothing else, Australia's A$ 14 billion tourism industry needs Asia. Japan and China are in Australia's top five ranking of inbound tourism markets, while the top ten includes Malaysia and Singapore.

Speaking the Language

It is a serious impediment to happiness in Australia not to be able to speak English. The Japanese often suffer from this inability. Columnist Ruth Ostrow, writing in *The Weekend Australian*, reported with outrage how a Japanese tourist was made fun of in a Gold Coast hotel bar. He kept ordering Scotch without ice. Each time, it came back with ice. 'No locks, no locks!' he kept yelling. The waitress and staff erupted into giggles every time.

Entente, But Less Cordiale

Despite the recent Asian economic crisis, Australia knows she must come to terms with Asia, for economic survival if for nothing else. Europe and the Americas have their faces turned elsewhere and are trading more with one another. Corporate Australia now understands the rules of the game well, although old habits die hard and still too many Australian exporters focus on English-speaking countries. As the English weekly *The Economist* remarked in 1989, 'The trouble is that Australians have not worked out exactly what to do with all this talk about Asia, beyond having politicians flying around the region.'

The spectacle of East Timor's descent into hell in 1999, as its people struggled to affirm their independence from Indonesia, shook the Australian nation. Australians mandated Prime Minister John Howard to initiate leadership of the UN-backed Interfet peacekeeping force that duly patrolled East Timor from September 1999 to February 2000 when UN 'blue-berets' took over.

This was the largest deployment of Australian troops (about 5,000) since the Vietnam War and, more significantly, the first time Australia had acted as a power in the region without any hand-holding from the US. A surge of Anzac-style emotion among Australians proud of their troops' conduct, has led to charges of 'triumphalism' from Indonesia, Malaysia (that familiar bête noire) and others.

Suspicions have risen over Australia's real motives. And the unseemly tug of war that has ensued in more recent years between Australia and East Timor over the rights to oilfield exploitation off East Timor and the revenue-sharing, does give ground for these suspicions. So however delicately Australia treads the region henceforth, her underlying relationship with Asia, or at least Indonesia, may never be quite the same again.

Many Australians realise the impossibility of keeping their distance as the fates of the two countries grow increasingly intertwined, yet are frustrated at how to manage the relationship. This dichotomy was evident when Australians' innate generosity rose to the surface as the nation rushed to donate hundreds of millions of dollars almost overnight in response to the tsunami disaster of Boxing Day, 2004, yet only six months later these very same people bayed for Indonesian blood when Schapelle Corby was convicted of drug trafficking in Bali, and shamefully, in some cases demanded their donation money back from Indonesia's tsunami-hit province of Aceh.

On the political front, there was a sea-change virtually reversing all that Paul Keating achieved when in 1995 he engineered a security treaty with Indonesia once the Howard government came to power. With South-east Asian governments finding greater common cause with Australia in the wake of 21st century terrorism, however, the situation has mellowed somewhat, at the political level if not on the average Australian street. Australia is the host for the APEC (Asia-Pacific Economic Cooperation) group in 2007 and this is symbolic of Australia's steadily improving integration with regional Asian fora, including such groups as the Asean (Association of Southeast Asian Nations) Regional Forum and the regular Asean-Australia forum gatherings.

Land, history and race, all these define Australia. But as in any country, so does the world of work, and the nation's attitude to it.

Democracy at a Crossroads

As in the USA and UK, post '9/11', long-cherished freedoms and assumptions about the very nature of democracy are under threat in Australia even as this book goes to press. For those who chose to make Australia their home because it looked like one of the most open societies in the world, this has come as a terrible shock.

With tensions exacerbated by a series of acts of terrorism against western nations, culminating in July 2005 with the bombing of public transport systems in London, Australia is moving towards some curtailment of civil liberties. ASIO, the government's Australian Security Intelligence Organisation, by 2005 was already allowed to hold people in secret for up to seven days and to interview them for up to 48 hours without charging them; such detainees have no right to silence and can be held even if not suspected of a crime.

Police can enter and search premises without letting the owner know in advance. Organisations can be named and banned as 'terrorist groups', and it is an offence to engage in a terrorist act or provide or receive training connected with a terrorist act. It is a criminal offence for an Australian to engage in hostile activity in another country or to enter a foreign country intending to engage in such activity.

Under active discussion now are the idea of a national identity card, nothing new to migrants from many other countries, but for long anathema and an invasion of privacy in the eyes of the ordinary Australian (although the Australian photo-driving licence has long played the same role as an identity card); widespread use of surveillance cameras in public places and on transport; stricter laws to prevent the incitement of hatred or violence, and strategies to train new Australians or foreign residents (such as Islamic clerics) in Australia's cultural values.

There is a general trend towards intolerance of free expression on the terrorism issue, including the idea of limiting what can be sold in bookshops; a Monash University student writing an honours thesis on the psychology of suicide bombers was recently interrogated by police because he had borrowed library books on terrorism. It seems possible, even likely, that the ability to detain, interrogate and even imprison without charge or trial could be on the cards, at least for public discussion, if not immediate implementation.

Among the most disturbing of the proposals now on the table is the idea of stripping citizenship from naturalised Australians if they are shown to have engaged in terrorist activity (will this include merely talking or reading about it, and who defines terror/terrorism, ask some civil libertarians?) —this could act to create a second-class form of citizenship for all those who have migrated to Australia.

EARNING A CRUST

It has never been altogether clear whether or not Australians really *want* to make money.

To take one example from everyday life, I once bought some black olives at a supermarket delicatessen counter in Australia. After the woman serving had weighed and priced them, she then said, 'Would you like some of the juice-stuff they're in as well?' Why not, said I. 'Oh yes, I always ask that *after* I've weighed them,' the woman told me, 'because you'd be surprised how much the juice adds to the weight, and to the price.' So I got my 'olives-juice' free, as an extra.

> 'Why do business with a country where "She'll be right" means she'll be wrong and the delivery will be late as well? Why bother to believe a country whose national catch-cry "No worries" really translates into "We've stuffed it up again"?'
> —Journalist John Hamilton, in Western Australia's *Daily News*, 27 December 1989.

I marvelled at this. A shopkeeper almost anywhere else would have weighed the whole lot and charged for it all. After all, if you want juice, you should pay for it, right?

Then there was the barman on a Saturday night who said lackadaisically that he'd run out of half of his printed wine list the night before and he was 'just coming to terms with how much his stock had run down'. I said nothing, but thought, is this any way to do business? Why not move heaven and earth next day to restock the bar? Don't ask.

In another incident, a shopkeeper who was regularly selling out of a particularly popular fruit juice blend told his customers he doubted he would be stocking it much more. Why not? 'Oh, I don't really like it, myself,' he explained. Any self-respecting Asian businessman would have filled his store wall to wall with the stuff.

This blunted economic drive and general lack of apology for it, is part of the country's charm, but also of its economic downfall.

When I enquired about the cost of hiring a computer from a company specialising in such hire, the reply came that it would be A$ 20 a day, or A$ 600 a month, which of course amounted to the same thing. Yet normal business practice would surely be to entice the customer into a longer hire period by charging *less* per day for a longer-term contract. This would benefit both the hire-firm and the customer. This simple way of making more money apparently had not occurred to the rather literal management of this particular company.

Another endearing feature of this syndrome is the Australian shopkeeper's willingness to send you up the road to his competitors, where, he blithely tells you, they will have just what you are looking for and maybe cheaper, too. Or the waiter's whispered advice that "the fish isn't that good today, I wouldn't if I were you."

Clearly, the desire to make money, or at least, to make profit, is consciously or subconsciously considered an evil reserved for 'tall poppies', those shooting comets so successful that their only way forward is down in most Australians' opinion.

Just Dig It Up

Australia has been able to afford such complacency in the past because it is so rich in natural resources—bauxite, iron ore, zinc, uranium, oil, gas, coal, lead and gold among them. For a long time, Australia has been 'The Lucky Country'. All you had to do to stay wealthy was go dig something else up. Linkage with England provided a ready market for Australian wool, lamb, beef and wheat. And a past pattern of government protectionism further sheltered Australian business from the real world.

Among the realities are the very small size of the Australian domestic market and the high freight costs of reaching all-Australia—the 'tyranny of distance'. A report once pointed out that Heinz UK could export canned baked beans to Perth more cheaply than its Australian counterpart could get them to the Western Australian capital from its plant in the Victorian capital of Melbourne. And I have long wondered why I can get fresh eastern-states Australian cherries in Singapore for about A$ 8 a kilo while in Western Australia I would have to pay A$ 15 or more.

Western Australian gold mine.

Australian businessmen have found it hard to keep up with a fast-changing world—the increasing self-sufficiency of the European community (including Australia's traditional business partner, England), for example, the impact of synthetics, as well as increased cotton production, on wool, and competition from almost every direction, especially from low-cost Asia, notably China.

There is little doubt about the quality of Australian products. The Achilles heel of Australian business has always been marketing.

The fatal combination of almost unbridled consumerist materialism in the prosperous 1950s and 1960s (often based on credit), and complacency about primary produce and protected industries, sowed the seeds of Australia's miseries in the 1980s and beyond.

A Cautionary Tale

Take wool as a case study of how things can go wrong. It was once said that the Australian economy rode on the back of wool.

In 1990–1991, the 70,000 'woolgrowers' of the Australian wool industry, which supplied something like 70 per cent of the world's wool, learned a hard lesson: their market crashed, leaving them with debts of A$ 2.6 billion in hand, 4.5 million bales of wool stockpiled and about 20 million of their 166 million sheep shot, because suddenly they were not even worth the food they were eating.

As Jacqueline Huie of the Australian Graduate School of Management at the University of New South Wales told *The Australian* in 1991, 'If you take your eyes off what your customers want, it is at your peril. We took our eyes off our wool customers and as a result it came as a complete surprise when in two years our major customers, the USSR and China, changed and bought next to nothing. Meanwhile, nobody told the farmers. They kept on producing. Can you imagine losing the majority of your customers in two years, doubling your production and not being able to predict any part of it? Even if we didn't know about market research, what about industrial spying?' This has a lot to do with the Australian's basically trusting, naive nature; he does not expect to be deceived or let down. In business, all too often, he can be a sitting duck.

Australia has also made the classic mistake of failing to upgrade into value-added products, rather than just exporting raw primary commodities and produce, and this too has played a role in the wool disaster. In the old days, raw wool went out to England and returned to Australia as a made-up garment (now the same applies to wool sent out to China); Australian iron ore goes to Japan and returns in a made-in-Japan car. This has been bad for the balance of payments. Fundamentally, Australia is still 'digging it up', growing it or farming it, from coal and natural gas to canola oil and dairy products. But too rarely, making it.

The State of the Economy

The nation's trade balance is in deficit, to the tune of A$ 46.6 billion in 2003. Total foreign debt is around A$ 330 billion, putting Australia in almost the same debtor-nation basket as Mexico or Brazil. Most of this debt has been incurred by private-sector borrowing, not by the public sector. Unemployment is running close to 5 per cent, much better than it was at the turn of the 20th century. On the other hand, inflation is at its lowest for almost a quarter of a century, at around 2.5 per cent—wage rises were around 6 per cent in 2003.

A major issue for the Australian economy is the delicate balancing act that must be performed between making money and being 'green'. The environmentalist lobby is extremely powerful and influences some business decisions. One estimate has suggested that several billion dollars' worth of projects are at risk because of environmentalist or Aboriginal vetoes.

Wheelers and Dealers

Australia's businessmen are much more 'real' today than they were in the 1980s. A whole breed of 'smart-guys' got its comeuppance after a decade of heady euphoria during the 1980s.

Names like Alan Bond (English-born former sign-painter), Christopher Skase (Qintex group of companies), John Elliott (Elders-IXL), and others were all powers in the land, and national heroes—yesterday.

Today, most of these multimillionaires are ruined or discredited, or both, with debts in the billions of Australian dollars, former emperors with no clothes but the debts on which their empires were founded. Their main tactic had been to use the tax deductibility of the interest payable on their borrowings, which they had used to acquire companies—and to make money by selling off their appreciated assets later. It was, as *The Australian* remarked, 'a stark reminder that money needs to be earned'. In Western Australia and in Victoria, the problem was governments fancying themselves as businessmen, taking on what should have been entrepreneurial projects in partnership with

Eminent Queenslanders have appeared in court, right up to the level of the former premier, Sir Joh Bjelke-Petersen. In 1991, after an 89-day trial, the former state police commissioner, Sir Terence Lewis, was found guilty of 15 bribery counts between 1978 and 1987 in connection with a protection racket shielding gambling and prostitution rings.

businessmen, while in Queensland, it was corruption and dirty tricks generally.

The survivors of the business fallout are big fish such as media magnates Kerry Packer, Kerry Stokes and Rupert Murdoch (hiding his Australian birth under an American passport) and lone woman, Janet Holmes a Court, who ably runs her late husband Robert's multimillion dollar empire, Heytesbury Holdings.

When doing business in Australia, you need to be aware of the scars left by all this bad news.

Australian business circles now are sobered, conservative and cautious, very wary of risk or any form of debt. Their main concern is to re-establish their credentials in the international financial community, where the very mention of Australia's businessmen now conjures up visions of fly-by-night bandits, and to deal in solid things, rather than paper.

Boom-Bust

Up to the 1990s, the Australian economy, including subdivisions like the property market, characteristically displayed a strongly cyclical boom-bust pattern.

It is still not clear whether this pattern is really over, as some economists believe—certainly property has still shown great volatility and continues to power head in an almost alarming way in pockets such as Western Australia. Part of the national psychology which has contributed to this cycle is the Australian gambling instinct, which easily matches that of those other well-known punters, the Chinese. The gambling obsession stems both from Irish traditions in Australia's colonial beginnings and from the boredom of life in the remote countryside back in the old days: for a bit of excitement, the Australian would bet on anything that moved, and still does.

The government derives considerable tax revenue from this national weakness. In 2002–2003, state and local government revenue amounted to A$ 561.9 million, the majority of which was derived from state gambling taxes of A$ 472.6 million. Foreign ownership of casinos is limited by law to only 50 per cent.

Australians are legally permitted to gamble on horses, dogs, numbers games such as Lotto (you can just trot down to the newsagent's and ask for your '12-game Slikpik for Saturday Lotto' like I do, if you don't want to dream up your own permutations of numbers) and the football Pools, as well as on slot-machines or 'one-armed bandits' ('pokies') in some states. You place your gee-gee, doggie or other sporting bet through the government's local TAB (Totalisator Agency Board) office.

National gaming takings amount to about A$ 14 billion a year, with over 60 per cent of that coming from poker and other gaming machines.

Casino Culture

Residual puritanism delayed the introduction of (legal) casinos until the first was opened in 1973, in the Tasmanian capital of Hobart. Today they exist in all states, numbering 13 in all. One casino game you probably will encounter for the first time when in Australia is the old outback game of 'Two-Up'. It is based on spinning two coins and betting whether they will fall as two heads or two tails. The simple zinc Two-Up sheds still stand on the fringes of goldrush towns like Kalgoorlie, reminding us of how basic recreational facilities were in pioneer days.

The Burswood casino at Perth sees about 8,000 people a day through its doors. The big gamblers—'the high rollers'—and often the big winners too, are usually Asians, especially the Chinese of South-east Asia. (Hence you can get some very high-quality Asian meals in Australia's casinos.)

The casinos are crammed full with 'ordinary Australians'. The atmosphere is rarely as classy as at the French counterparts, for example, although there will be private gaming rooms for very special customers, of course.

Turning Things Upside Down

Australia is now going through an economic revolution every bit as turbulent as a war. Sacred cows of all kinds are being sent crashing to the ground, or at least being chipped away at—the welfare state, the power of the unions, protectionism, state enterprise …

Much of the action, ironically, began under the auspices of an increasingly right-of-centre Labor government, in power from 1983, perhaps because Labor was the party most likely to be able to persuade the average Australian worker to go along with it. As the 1980s turned into the 1990s, Australia briefly overheated, then began to enter 'the recession we had to have' to prevent Australia from becoming a 'banana republic', to use two of former Prime Minister Paul Keating's phrases. Small wonder the unpopular Keating earned for himself the sobriquet 'The Grim Reaper'. Since the election of John Howard's conservative Liberal Party government in 1996, all the expected conservative measures have been gradually put in place, including tighter control of welfare and tax reform, looser individual 'workplace agreements' instead of mandatory conditions for workers; there will be more to come, such as the removal of 'unfair dismissal' appeal protection for sacked workers. Privatisation is also a Liberal leitmotif and the proposed sale of the major, formerly national monopoly, telecoms player Telstra is a bone of much contention in Australia.

On the whole, Australia not only remains a rich country but appears to be getting richer, with a real economic buzz by 2005—so much so that the shortage of tradesmen and technicians to staff the economy has forced the Government into much greater investment in apprenticeship programmes, and an accelerated programme for skilled worker immigration.

One of the indices that Australians watch the most nervously is the home loan interest rate chart, around 6–7 per cent in 2005.

To quote a US State Department briefing in late 2004:

'Australia commenced a basic reorientation of its economy in the 1980s and has transformed itself from an inward looking, import-substitution country to an internationally competitive, export-oriented one. Key reforms included unilaterally reducing high tariffs and other protective barriers; floating the Australian dollar exchange rate; deregulating the financial services sector, including liberalising access for foreign bank branches; making efforts to restructure the highly centralised system of industrial relations and labour bargaining; better integrating the state economies into a national federal system; improving and standardising the national infrastructure; privatising many government-owned services and public utilities; and fundamentally reforming the taxation system, including introducing a broad-based Goods and Services Tax (GST).'

Australia was one of the OECD's (Organisation for Economic Cooperation and Development) fastest-growing economies throughout the 1990s. Despite a slowdown in late 2000, it has been 14 years since Australia experienced a recession and economic growth remains robust, at around 3 per cent in 2004.

Poverty Think

'Life is not meant to be easy' said the former Liberal prime minister Malcolm Fraser in 1971. Most Australians remember, and quote, this phrase ruefully nowadays. Funnily enough, despite general economic growth, the gap between the rich and the poor is widening rapidly in Australia and the old classless egalitarian model of Australian society is under severe pressure as a result. There is an army of semi-employed, part-time and contract workers that is doing it tough, on very low earnings, many of them women, quite a few single parents.

I had never heard of 'lay-bys' until I went to Australia. A sure sign of a cash-strapped people, they are extended hire-purchase arrangements, interest-free, privately contracted between shopkeeper and customer. So if you fancy a mechanical doll for your little daughter's Christmas present, you can go into the shop in September and ask for a 'lay-by'. The doll will be kept aside for you and you will go into the shop every month to pay off a fixed sum, until you have paid for it and can take it home.

Then there are the busy, informal neighbourhood swap and second-hand markets, usually at weekends, where the elderly and desperate selling their family heirlooms for a song are sprinkled among the younger traders simply out to make a buck. And the 'op shops' selling second-hand goods are popular with almost everybody, including yours truly. There is a strong tradition also of informal groups, both in the suburbs and the countryside, using barter of services and goods instead of money. At this level, the cash economy has disappeared. Instead people are saying 'You babysit for me this Friday and I'll mow your lawn on Sunday,' or 'I'm a trained secretary, so I'll type out your letters; you're a trained electrician, so after that you can fix my light switch.'

Australia is still comparatively rich, but getting poorer by the minute. It is as well to remember this when dealing with Australians—remember that they may be hiding real distress, never assume they have money.

Scientific Excellence

Australia has sworn to transform its national slogan from 'The Lucky Country' to 'The Clever Country'. It is already well set on that path. Australian achievements in science and technology are well documented, among the best known being in computer software, telecommunications, medicine and biotechnology.

Migrants tend to pack an enormous amount of electrical gadgetry when they move house to Australia, in the belief that they won't be able to get as good or as cheap electronics in Australia. They should pause to check this one out first, however, as often the Australian technology (and design) is superior, and the price either similar or only marginally higher.

Like other countries before her, however, Australia is still making the mistake of failing to link academic research properly with the private sector for implementation. Two important bodies involved in the promotion of research and development are the CSIRO or Australian Commonwealth Scientific and Industrial Research Organisation, which dates back to 1926, and the Australian Research Council. If it were not for CSIRO's work on giving wool new properties such as being shrink-proof and capable of permanent pressing, the Australian wool industry would have collapsed much earlier, in the 1950s, when synthetics first began to gain popularity. But the CSIRO has been forced in recent years to seek linkage with, and funding from, the private sector by the Federal Government's decision to slash its own funding for the organisation.

It is generally agreed that, if Australia is to reduce her dependence on primary products, her politicians and businessmen must do much more to support the country's undoubted talent for areas such as biotechnology and information technology.

THE TAX MAN COMETH...

If I really knew all the ins and outs of Australian tax, I doubt I would be writing this book. I would be sitting back and enjoying my enormous wealth. Because everybody in Australia wants to understand the Australian tax system. Few do.

Coping with Australia's Byzantine tax regulations is a national industry. The situation is very grey indeed and it is entirely possible to get totally contradictory counsel from different accountants and tax consultants, as well as from the Australian Taxation Office itself. There has been a single taxation policy operated at the Federal level since 1942.

The GST Revolution

The Liberal Party lost an election on the Goods and Services Tax issue (the equivalent of the UK Value Added Tax) in 1993 but rode to victory on this dark horse in 1996. What exactly changed the voters' minds is a mystery to most observers. Perhaps they just hated the then Premier Paul Keating's lofty manner more than the GST, who knows.

The GST levies 10 per cent on just about everything except fresh food, hospital services, education, charitable funds and farmed farmland. This does not necessarily imply price rises though the general outlook points to mild inflation. While all this is bothersome to the consumer, what has caused even more ructions is the impact on small business of the system requiring everyone (except employees) to register for an Australian Business Number (ABN) bracketed as his or her GST registration number. Not having an ABN clearly quoted on your invoice risks a blanket top tax rate of 47 per cent.

This was partly a ploy to bring in from the cold small businesses operating in the twilight zone, often transacting in cash and avoiding tax—but there is a still a 'black economy' working underground, nevertheless. Taxi drivers, for example, must have an ABN regardless of their turnover. Technically, those with a turnover below A$ 50,000 do not fall into the compulsory GST net, but voluntary registration for the system might be wise. Many big businesses prefer not to deal with contractors who are not registered for GST, since if you do not charge them for GST, they then cannot claim GST outputs to offset against their own GST collections that must be rendered to government.

Businesses must file with the Tax Office a regular Business Activity Statement charting GST collected and due to the government and claiming credits on GST paid to suppliers to reduce the tax which must be remitted to the Government. Tax is payable on a 'Pay As You Go' basis. Employees still pay tax via 'Pay As You Earn' deductions from their monthly salaries and most tax-payers look forward to an annual 'bonus' rebate cheque when the tax office calculates their actual tax liability against what has been deducted.

Here are some simplified pointers on tax matters. Get an advisor and keep every piece of documentary evidence you can obtain for each of your financial transactions, including a log for your car use.

- **Tax File Numbers**

  If you are a tax resident (and it can be interesting defining exactly when this is—as Arthur Andersen, a consultancy expert, says, 'There is no clear-cut answer as to when a person becomes or ceases to be a tax resident'), you are required by law to apply for a tax file number. The onus is on you to do so.

- **Tax Residency**

  As mentioned above, the situation is not very clear. However, a person present in Australia for more than 183 days in a tax year may be considered a tax resident. A person who usually lives in Australia, and in particular maintains a residence there, may be considered a tax resident irrespective of the time he or she actually spends there. Permanent Resident status obviously could be another factor defining the tax resident.

- **The Tax Year**

  Australia's tax year runs from 1 July to 30 June the following year, not on a calendar year basis.

- **Residents**

  If you are a tax resident, Australia taxes you on your worldwide income, regardless of whether it derives from, or is remitted to, Australia, unless it has already been taxed in the source country; there are quite a lot of tax agreements with other countries that allow offsetting against foreign tax paid.

- **Non-Residents**

  If you are a non-resident, you will be taxed only on assessable Australian-sourced income.

- **Overseas Employment**

  A tax resident who has worked in a foreign country for a continuous period of 91 days or more will be fully exempted from Australian tax, providing he has been taxed in the other country. This exemption applies only to money derived from employment, however.

- **Overseas Income**

  Income earned by Australian companies resident in low-tax countries will be attributed to their parent companies and taxed on an accrual basis, except in a list of 61 'comparable-tax countries'. But if the comparable-tax country taxes at a low, concessional rate, accrual tax will still apply.

- **Capital Gains**

  There is no capital gains tax on profits from the sale of your first/main home ('principal residence') in Australia, even if you have been overseas for some time (providing you have not used it to earn rental income during your absence). If you have been renting it out, the capital gains tax exemption applies only for a maximum period of six years' absence from the country. Even if you sell off a second home bought as an investment, providing you time that sale carefully, for instance at least 12 months from purchase, capital gains tax can be mitigated quite substantially, and you can offset many expenses against it. Generally speaking, there are no taxes on capital or wealth per se.

- **Raids**

  The tax authorities are in the habit of instituting rigorously severe audits on taxpayers' accounts at random and without much warning. Many live in fear of such audits and there are horror stories of tax raids on private homes. This is when you may really need all that substantiation documentation.

  I know of one person who somehow suspected he would be visited by the taxman in this way. He had all his possessions and assets removed from the house by lorry and greeted the taxman with a tale of woe, saying he had been clean-sweep burgled the night before. This is not something to emulate, of course, but it does indicate the drastic nature of such tax dramas.

- **Rates**

  These are local government taxes, which vary according to the property you own and the services you enjoy. When buying a house, it is well to check on the level of rates being levied by your future local Council, since some can be quite high.

CHAPTER 3

THE PEOPLE

'He is a very nice fellow, certainly nobody
would ever guess he was born in Australia.'
—British playwright and wit, George Bernard Shaw,
in his play *Major Barbara*, 1907.

THE TYPICAL AUSTRALIAN
Image, Stereotypes and Misconceptions

I can't count how many times my decision in the late 1980s to set up home in Australia, particularly Western Australia, was greeted with curling lips and an amazed 'But, why on earth would you want to live *there*?'

This told me more about the enquirer than about Australia.

Australia seems to be one of those countries that nobody feels neutral about. Everybody has strong views, for or against. Depending on where you are coming from then, geographically, psychologically and culturally speaking, you are sure to harbour in your heart one of a well-defined range of stereotypes depicting 'the typical Australian'.

So let's clear the air first by spelling out some of these stereotypes from the start. The most widespread, unfortunately, is 'The Ugly Australian' otherwise known since about the 1960s as the 'Ocker', who seems to come in approximately three models:

European Model

If you are of continental European origin, this means the Aussie is barbaric, loud-mouthed, ignorant and uncultured, hopelessly provincial.

He is physically outsized but mentally minuscule, somewhat naive, and nearly always extremely badly dressed (this gaffe weighs particularly hard on the minds of the

Parisian French—but anyway, the Aussie is usually more undressed than dressed). He cannot hold his wine, and has the temerity to claim that his own country produces this celestial ambrosia on a par with the French original. Worst of all, he cannot understand menus written in French. Basically, he is a peasant.

But actually, most Europeans are blissfully unaware of the existence of Australia or the Australians.

British Model

If you are British, you probably see your Antipodean cousin as a rather alarming, alien being bereft of the (hypocritical) courtesies of the mother country, far too frank (which other country could have produced a foreign minister who used the 'F...' word in public while on an official tour of South Africa, or a premier who dared to put his arm round Queen Elizabeth II of Great Britain (and Australia)?), frequently obscene; a naive colonial boy in shorts, an insular sheep-farmer sporting a big hat with corks hanging off it to keep the flies away. A bit of a simpleton, really.

You find the way he tends to 'get physical' rather terrifying, although you secretly admire it too. And the way he puts himself on first-name terms with you from the word go is quite beyond the pale. He's notorious as a bloke fond of a booze-up, most often culminating in a 'technicolor yawn' or 'chunder' (in low Australian patois, a vomiting session)—which latter he performs in a back-garden 'dunny' (outshed toilet).

The Australian accent, furthermore, is execrable by British standards and unfortunately slots the Australian firmly into 'the lower classes', since it best resembles working-class Cockney from East End London, or Irish-dialect English—take the still fairly frequent use by Aussies of 'youse' for both the singular and the plural 'you,' for example.

Many of these British images derive from the Barry ('Bazza') McKenzie comic strip, which ran for years (1963–1974) in the British satirical magazine *Private Eye*, lampooning the worst traits of an Aussie on the loose in Europe.

Asian Model

If you are Asian, you probably share the European and British concern at the Australian's admittedly blunt ways, since calling a spade a spade is hardly an Asian trademark. His predilection for semi-nakedness will not have endeared him to you, either.

Faux Pas

The Aussie is notoriously oblivious to the subtleties of Asian culture and even the greatest in the land are not immune—recent years have seen premier John Howard himself fail to recognise a finger bowl of rose scented water politely proffered by the Indonesians at a tree-planting ceremony and tip it on the tree rather than wash his hands in it, as well as refer to the newly installed Malaysian prime minister Dr Abdullah Ahmad Badawi as 'Dr Badawi' when even a passing knowledge of Malaysian culture would have told him that Badawi is not Dr Abdullah's name but his father's name. Aussie VIPs mispronouncing foreign names in the diplomatic environment is too common an occurrence to merit any comment.

And most likely, you have been persuaded that the typical Australian is a dyed-in-the-wool racist, besides being lazy or on the dole and totally incompetent because he can't seem to make as much money as you can—and even more irritatingly, for some reason, does not seem to *want* to make money, anyway.

He has no drive and to all intents and purposes, has parked himself in the world's KIV tray, his nation quite literally 'a basket case'.

You are also more than a little shocked and disillusioned by various 'third world' elements in the Aussie lifestyle that you did not expect in a 'developed' country like Australia: power blackouts, police corruption, bureaucratic bungling and red tape, lying and conniving politicians etc.

Although it is true that where there is smoke, there usually are at least a few glowing coals, in fact, many of these images derive from a hostile Asian press, egged on by Asian governments intent on preventing their best and brightest from emigrating to Australia. (The Aussie media have, however, more than held their own, exchanging insult for insult, and then some.)

The culture gap is at its widest between Australia and Asia, a cause of enduring sadness to all concerned, for Asia is where Australia is located and where Australians eventually must, willy-nilly, make their psychological, cultural and economic home.

The Great Suburban Bore

A kind of sub-category within 'The Ugly Australian' classification is the Australian as 'The Great Suburban Bore'.

By definition, this view of the Australian can only be held by someone who thinks he himself or she herself is the opposite, i.e., sophisticated, intellectually dazzling, exciting, glamorous, etc. Well, we know what we think of people who think this of themselves, don't we? That would certainly be the Australian reaction to such pretentiousness, at any rate. The Aussie vernacular phrase for it is 'A bit up himself, isn't he?'.

It is true that the vast majority of Australians lead simple lives, putting great store by their homes and families, and the general philosophy of *cultiver son jardin* (with the gardening bit taken quite literally). But then, what is so reprehensible about such simple values in our troubled times?

As chief Australia-watcher Professor Donald Horne, himself a native son, has said, describing Australia as the world's first 'suburban nation' in his seminal *The Lucky Country:* 'The profusion of life doesn't wither because people live in small brick houses with red tile roofs.'

Crocodile Dundee

Another, more positive, image of Australians bases itself on the 'Australian Pioneer' stereotype, one which many Australians themselves have taken to their bosom, along with sundry others, particularly the Americans. You can tell how much Aussies fancy themselves in this role by the number of them who don bush hats, cowboy hats or 'Digger'-style Aussie army hats, especially when showcasing themselves on trips abroad. The other give-away is the urban Australian's love of the tough-looking four-wheel drive (4WD) vehicle, which

Fitting into the landscape—the author on horseback in the Avon Valley, Western Australia.

he may or may not really ever take into the bush. Former labourer-turned-comic actor Paul Hogan's sell-out *Crocodile Dundee* films of the 1980s did much to fuel this myth, and in more recent times, larger-than-life zoo personality Steve Irwin has stoked that very same fire quite efficiently, with an outsized television image (risking his own baby in the croc pool and so on) that has been beamed around the world.

This stereotype has it that every Australian is fit, tanned and courageous in the face of hideous adversities daily encountered in the bush and deserts of a harsh continent. He is attuned to the secret voice of Nature, thanks to his Aboriginal mentors, consumes goanna steaks most dinners and spends an awful lot of time fighting bush-fires, that is, when he's not locked in mortal combat with either crocodiles or lethally poisonous serpents. He is the original frontiersman (alias Davy Crockett) reborn.

Americans really relate to this myth, because many of them live its American counterpart, nursing the idea that they are all cowboys at heart, still conquering the Wild West.

A subdivision within the Australian Pioneer category falls into the *Rural Idyll* box: here, most Australians make their living herding cattle or sheep, spending much of their time on horseback, bathed in pastoral peace and romantic sunsets.

These fantasies of course completely ignore the fact that the overwhelming majority of Australians—close to 90 per cent—in reality huddle together in urban centres clustered along the coastline, in mortal dread of the outback beyond, terribly disturbed by the thought of having to deal with the Aboriginals and blithely oblivious of their own burgeoning paunches. If anything, the nearest they have ever got to the desert is burying their heads in the metaphorical sand most of the time.

The Honey-Coloured Facts

As with all extreme stereotypes, the truth lies somewhere in between.

'The truth' is also changing rapidly, almost minute by minute, as Australia itself changes, under the impact of the geo-politics of the Australasian region, and of very varied immigration inflows, particularly from Asia.

How inadequate black-and-white statements are, about any country or culture! The truth in between is, in fact, not so much grey as honey-coloured when it comes to Australia: the country's distinguished first ambassador to China, Stephen Fitzgerald, has declared that this will be the national skin colour one day soon, thanks to Asian immigration and mixed marriages.

Close to a quarter of Australia's more than 20 million people today were born outside Australia. The statistic gets closer to 30 per cent if you include all those with at least one overseas-born parent. At the start of the 21st century, 6 per cent were born in Asia. And this is not to forget the more than 410,000 original 'first Australians'—the Aboriginals.

Australia is no longer a bastion of white or Anglo-Saxon culture. The Anglo-Saxon foundations were in fact undermined long ago, with the influx of southern European immigrants after World War II, notably from Italy, Greece and Eastern European countries such as Yugoslavia. The Asian influx picked up from the 1980s, and today we see more Africans and Middle Eastern nationalities such as Iraqis and Iranians, arriving, often as refugees. But as I shall explain elsewhere, the foundations cannot be ignored, even today.

SELF-IMAGE

What do Australians think of themselves? Fortunately, like their British ancestors, they are blessed with a limitless capacity for self-mockery, always a healthy trait. Home-bred

Most Australians are a secure lot with a healthy capacity for self-mockery.

intellectuals are at times far more critical than outsiders would be.

But one mocks only when the foundations are secure, and the fact is, the vast majority of Australians believe that their way of life is the best, and the right one. In fact, they mostly are blissfully unaware that there could be any other way. They see themselves as egalitarian 'battlers' against the adversities of life, and champions of the 'fair go' for all, as straight forward, not 'tricky', always poised to help their fellow men and women in any crisis.

Their biggest failing, however, is that few of them realise just how lucky they are. They take their freedoms and the welfare system for granted, among other perks of the Australian way of life. For all their detestation of the 'whinger', they themselves are capable of whingeing about the most minute infringements of their rights. They need to travel more, to bring back sobering lessons from the tightly 'guided democracies' and outright dictatorships of the developing world.

Nonetheless, call it smugness and complacency if you will, yet there is an attractive sense of security, pride and identity in the ordinary Australian's conviction that he has got it right.

The Cultural Cringe

The only chink in this armour is the famous 'Cultural Cringe'. This originates from an uncomfortable suspicion that anything British, from the original motherland, was *per se* better than home-grown Aussie stuff. In these post-British Empire days, there are now variations on this theme, focusing on Europe: I have met Australians who are obsequiously obsessed with the notion that anything French must automatically be superior, for instance. And the increasing warmth of the country's official relationship with the USA in recent years has led to extensive 'colonisation' of the Australian mind and culture by things American too. These trends are particularly evident in 'softer' fields like the arts. There is still the lurking worry that Australian-produced cinema, literature and fashions—the whole gamut of creation—may not be as good as 'the real thing', from Hollywood, Britain or France. (But no signs of an inferiority complex when it comes to dealing with Asian neighbours; while some may pay lip service to respect for Asian countries and cultures, not so deep down, the Australian rates his own as superior to theirs).

Still, 'The Cringe' has led to extensive self-flagellation in public places and is a topic of eager discussion in the Australian press, learned works and the like. It even affects the Australian economy (which is importing too many foreign goods for its own good, in preference to those made in Australia).

THE COLONIAL PAST

Such discussions will ring a clangorous bell with other 'developing' nations who share Australia's colonial past—similar debates on the worth and universality or otherwise of local literature occur from time to time in Singapore and Malaysia, for example. It's a phenomenon quite commonly seen in new young nations, although you might have thought that 100 years or so (since Australia's declared independence from Great Britain in 1900) would be long enough to get over it.

In short, he who wishes to understand the Australian mind, needs to study the country's history and to take both convicthood and the 'colonial factor' into careful account.

The Australians who called England 'home' and valued a pukka British accent are still with us today, albeit dwindling in numbers and influence (some say they are centred in Melbourne, capital of the state of Victoria). The Queen of England is still the Queen of Australia, albeit perhaps not for too much longer, judging from the gathering momentum of the Republican movement in Australia and the deepening disaffection for the British royal family and its antics.

Despite all the overlays deposited by post-World War II migration, the key to mainstream Australian culture still lies in the 19th century working-class London and Ireland from which the first, convict, Australians were unwillingly torn—to the extent that you still hear forms of the English

I would go so far as to say that a good way to understand Australia, especially for non-Europeans, might well be to spend a couple of years in London first. A tortuous route for some, perhaps, but a worthwhile soft landing, compared with going in cold.

language in Australia which are no longer currency in modern England itself.

In this context, I continually marvel at the bravery of the thousands of Asian and other non-English speaking migrants who every year struggle to bridge the enormous cultural and linguistic chasm separating them from 'the real Australia'. Without my own British background, I do not know how I could possibly have begun to understand Australia. But even a British grounding is still only a beginning.

The Battler

The typical Australian also invariably likes to see himself as that national icon, The Battler—a working-class underdog who struggles to survive, the salt of the earth. This is the model he emulates. Hence his odd celebration of a major military defeat like the Battle of Gallipoli in 1915, during World War I, every year on Anzac Day, 25 April.

The Tall Poppy

However, should the battler actually win and come out on top, achieving success, fame and money, he immediately transforms into a Tall Poppy, a most undesirable thing, begging to be cut down to size. The typical Australian tries not to shine too obviously and does not much like those who do. As a result, it's difficult if not impossible to set yourself individual excellence as a goal in Australia.

Bogans and Larrikins

'Bogans' essentially are working-class Aussies, usually male, who self-consciously celebrate a particularly earthy interpretation of Australian-ness partly in resistance to creeping Americanisation. Basically, a bogan celebrates uncouthness and is probably related to Barry McKenzie, (*see this chapter, page 85*). According to an article by Stephen Lacey in *The Weekend Australian Magazine* in 2003, many bogans will sport a 'mullet' hairstyle—sort of 'normal' and short around the scalp, then descending into lank long locks at the back.

Snapshot of Australia

Here is a snapshot of average Australia, from the work by Professor Rodney Tiffen and Ross Gitting, in How Australia Compares, (Cambridge University Press, 2004), comparing Australia with 17 other democracies—it breaks some of the stereotypes about Australia:

- **Home Owners**

  No change for 25 years, with 69 per cent of Australians owning their own homes, while the Irish score 83 per cent and the British rate has risen to 69 per cent from 49 per cent.

- **Booze Gurglers**

  In an environment of falling alcohol consumption rates, Australians are only the seventh biggest beer drinkers and eighth wine-drinkers in the 18-nation sample.

- **Agricultural & Rural**

  Australia is second only to Belgium in the sample for the highest proportion of the population living in urban areas— 91 per cent—and first in terms of the 69 per cent of Aussies living in cities of more than 750,000 people.

- **Techno-savvy**

  With 576 mobile phones per 1,000 people, Australia comes third-last in its take-up of mobiles (try Italy, 883 mobiles per 1,000).

- **A Welfare State**

  Giving US$ 54 a year per Australian, Australia has the fourth lowest level of official foreign aid, compared with an average of US$ 112 in the sample. Domestically, Australia rates the largest gap between the incomes of the abled and disabled, and pays the third lowest rate to its long-term unemployed.

- **Egalitarian**

  Australia has the fourth widest gap between the incomes of the rich and the poor, after the US, Italy and Britain.

(Continued on the next page)

(Continued from previous page)

- **Rich**
  After the US, Australia has the second highest proportion of people with incomes below the poverty line, more than 14 per cent (the poverty line is set at half the median income). In terms of elderly people living in poverty, Australia tops the list. However, the country had the third highest rate of growth in income (real GDP) per person during the 1990s, at 2.2 per cent annually.
- **Environmentally Aware**
  The highest greenhouse gas emissions per person, the second-highest generation of municipal waste per person and the third highest petrol consumption per person, that's Australia's record.
- **Laid Back-cum-Lazy**
  Australia had the highest rate of improvement in output per worker, productivity, during the second half of the 1990s; Australians now work more hours per year than anyone else in the sample countries, even though the country has the second highest proportion of part-time workers after Holland.

The bogans also tend to live in acid-washed jeans, tight tight shorts or 'trackie daks' (tracksuit bottoms), favour loudly checked shirts, woollen 'beanies' on their heads, and the sloppy Aussie original sheepskin wool-lined lounging boots that used to be called 'Ugg boots' until Americans patented the name and stole them. They drive Australian classics such as the Holden and hang around hard-rock pubs. Larrikins have all the 'boys will be boys', 'he's a bit of a lad' cheekiness and borderline lawlessness expected of the Australian male. Look for them among the workers on building sites, among other places.

Street-Friendly

It is true that Australians have 'country ways' for the most part; this is a large part of their considerable charm. They take a direct, simple approach to things and people, and can be quite child-like at times. Their most delightful characteristic is a willingness to talk to strangers in the street, on the bus, anywhere, and to spend time with you—they are rarely in a hurry. (This principle may not apply in the centre of Sydney at rush hour—capital cities will be capital cities.)

Singaporean journalist Chai Kim Wah nutshelled this quality neatly in a travel report during the 1980s: 'A trait I came across often (was) a readiness to give you the time of day, to be matey. It is not the American gushing-on-all-eight-cylinders friendliness, but a laid-back variety you can take or leave.'

So never be afraid to greet an Aussie in the street or to talk to a taxi-driver; always take the initiative if you can, because you will inevitably be rewarded with a smile and friendly conversation.

This willingness to linger awhile also gives rise to a shortcoming in terms of modern life: Aussies sometimes do things a little slower than others, so be patient while the checkout girl at the supermarket has nice little chat with the old lady in front of you about everything from the weather to her darling little grandchildren rolling around on the floor.

This presupposes, of course, that you can speak English. Most Australians are not comfortable at all with foreign languages; and good English is still the key to their hearts.

Mateship

Once your friend, the Australian is characteristically your friend for life, for better or for worse. Loyalty, 'mateship', still counts for much.

And there probably can be no better friend in a physical crisis than an Australian. The Australian somehow seems to revert to the 'Pioneer' stereotype at the sight of fires, floods or crime—he will always roll up his shirt-sleeves (or more typically, take his shirt off) and charge in to help, oblivious to his own personal safety.

Proud and independent they may be—and they expect others to be likewise—but Australians do know how to band together in times of crisis and are quick to lend a helping hand to their fellowman, a habit learned in the bad old days of bush settlement. Asians, and others too, have often wrongly labelled the Australian 'individualistic'.

Selfless Friendship

I shall never forget how my Australian neighbours demonstrated this quality when a serious fire broke out in the wooden-hut village down my road in Singapore. They were first out of the block. By the time I got to the scene, having dithered around putting on the 'right' clothes and shoes, and then dousing myself in water first, the Aussies were already running in and out of the flames, stripped down to their underwear, carrying the villagers' sticks of furniture out of harm's way.

Mateship is what makes the difference even to the most conservative Australian. The same Australian who has just made disparaging remarks about Asians to white friends over the dinner table, will the next minute deck any white who insults the Asian friend and neighbour with whom he has been enjoying a pint of beer at the pub for the past few years—'cause mates are mates, see?' He himself is unlikely to perceive the paradox.

Scout's Honour

The Australian can be naive—long may he stay that way. It is only yesterday that most, even in the cities, kept their front doors open to visitors and never locked their cars. All that has changed, but it is still all too easy to take advantage of the Australian's innocence. He takes you at your word, and expects it to be your word of honour too.

It seems inevitable, although lamentable, that the Australians will be pushed into the harsh real world. Already, it is not as easy as it was to walk into a bank and open an account in the name of Mickey Mouse without showing any identification whatsoever. But that, too, was only yesterday.

You can still phone up and open a telecom account without any paperwork or further ado, sight unseen. You leave your passport at the Immigration office but get no receipt for it to prove that they have it. Why? Because this is a matter of trust between you two, right? You wonder if anyone else who asked for it could get it over the counter. But you are not supposed to worry about this, because it is all a matter of trust. Just as you are supposed not to worry when the passport comes back to you complete with your desired visa, but by ordinary (not registered) local mail. Neither are you supposed to worry when you deposit a large amount of cash into a bank account and get no documentation to prove you have ever paid it in—no worries, the clerk is your mate, right. The two most famous Aussie catch-phrases, 'She'll be right,' and 'No worries' assume the essence of the Latin *mañana* or Oriental fatalism at such times.

Naiveté is why Australians have had some trouble doing business in Asia. They are not used to hidden meanings behind words. As far as they are concerned, words mean exactly what they say.

The Price of Naiveté

This attitude hardly fits them for the arcane shadow-play of business in countries like Indonesia or China—no wonder Broken Hill Proprietary, or BHP, Australia's huge steel corporation, irritably announced its withdrawal from most China investments in April 1989, pronouncing itself thoroughly frustrated with 'a continuing series of negotiations and attempts at building and maintaining relationships'.

Everyone Makes Mistakes

It's generally observable that a characteristic of the 21st century is that nobody need be to blame for anything. Nobody is accountable. Criminals have had bad childhoods, parents are overloaded, so are teachers, and so are politicians, so they all make mistakes. Nobody ever resigns, that's for sure. And few are sacked. Australians, however, were masters of this particular trick long before it became fashionable. Endearingly, they do not pile the proverbial manure onto a worker who has erred, instead they forgive, and move on. One has to admit that this is a very 'empowering' environment. The less endearing flip side of this mindset though, is that the Australian's excessive tolerance of mistakes has led to a climate of permitted bungling, incompetence and error in many fields of life, ranging from flagrant spelling mistakes to Australian citizens mistakenly deported as illegal aliens.

Because, in a fatalistic way, every Australian believes it will all be all right in the end—'She'll be right, no worries'. And besides, who wants to be a 'tall poppy' and get it right all of the time?

The Soft Underbelly

Lastly, I have observed that, contrary to the machismo pervading the nation's self-image, Australians are incredibly soppy sentimentalists. It's a short step from slap-on-the-back mateship to blubbering on each other's shoulders at the pub.

You have only to study the Australian creative style in film-making, whether for advertising or for the cinema, to be struck by its lingering, lyrical quality, its preference for tear-stained soft focus.

Those familiar with the famous 'Singapore Girl' advertisements patented by Singapore Airlines, which fit very much into this genre, might remember that the image-creator behind them, Ian Batey, is a British-born Australian.

The Australian's shell is rough and tough, a protection born of his violent past in a harsh land; but if handled sympathetically, he will turn turtle and show you his soft underbelly.

THE SKELETON IN THE CUPBOARD

Every Australian who has been in the country for more than two generations carries a ghost on his shoulder, or has a skeleton rattling in her cupboard. For a start, are they really Australians, do they belong in the country, do they own any of it? The first Australians, the indigenous Aboriginals with something like a 60,000-year track record on this island continent, are still around to remind later settlers ceaselessly of their original tenancy of this wide brown land. And like it or not, Aboriginal culture sits in the heads of all Australians, who have acquired from the Aboriginals a deep almost spiritual reverence for their stunning land, many words and concepts from Aboriginal language and culture, the outdoor camp-fire cooking habit a.k.a. the barbecue and a host of other little quirks that have nothing to do with their largely European ancestry.

DREAMTIME AUSTRALIA: THE ABORIGINALS

If I begin simply by saying that Aboriginal matters are a minefield for the unfortunate author, you may get part of the picture.

There is no topic more sensitive in Australia—although the Anzacs and Gallipoli come a close second—than the Aboriginals. Approach the subject with caution; better shut up and listen, than put your foot in your mouth.

For a country as dedicated to the pursuit of democracy and human rights—and as critical of South Africa's track record—as Australia is supposed to be, the 'Aboriginal problem' is a particularly painful Achilles heel. Every Australian, and every visitor, whether migrant or tourist, confronts 'the problem' sooner or later, and deals with it in his or her own way, sometimes with grace, but often with guilty resentment, or angry aggression.

On the other hand, it is also very easy indeed to live in Australia without getting to know any Aboriginals, even without seeing any, particularly if you live in the larger cities. For many Australians, they remain but shadows on the fringes of life, phantoms that flit through the newspaper headlines.

Aboriginal children in the Northern Territory outback.

For Americans and Canadians conscious of their nation's lamentable track record with their own indigenous Indians or Inuits, for white South Africans and for many others, Australia's problem is a case of *déjà vu*. Wherever we come from, we can probably conjure up other examples in the world which do not necessarily counterpoint only whites and non-whites; many a 'coloured' migrant race too has dominated another, weaker, similarly 'coloured' native race—in South-east Asia and elsewhere.

What is 'the problem' in Australia? Basically, it is the spectacle of an underclass, which happens to be black, disadvantaged in almost every way, pushed to the fringes of society, so demoralised that it also seems to be bent on committing mass suicide in a variety of ways. And this in the midst of relative, white affluence.

They Came First

The Aboriginals themselves would prefer to be called names from their own languages: Koori in the east and south (meaning 'Our People'), Nyunga or Noongar in Western Australia, Yolngu in the Northern Territory, Anangu in central Australia and Nungga in South Australia. That's just a few of them.

These names, however, have not caught on to any great extent within white Australia, even less so in the world beyond Australia. For this reason, I am using the more conventional 'Aboriginal' in this chapter, with no insinuations attached.

'The First Australians' is the phrase most favoured among Australian liberals nowadays when referring to the original, black Australians, who may have come to Australia from South-east Asia at least 60,000 years ago. Indeed, the Aboriginals' curly hair, blue-black skins, spread noses and thick lips are reminiscent of the peoples of southern India and Papua New Guinea. My Tamil southern-Indian husband is convinced they are fellow Tamils, and prehistoric geography does make this conceivable—some of their languages even sound similar. He is often approached in the street by Aboriginals as a 'brother'.

The term 'First Australians' serves to remind all Australians, whether migrant or of many generations' standing, that they are all newcomer settlers to some degree, compared with the Aboriginals. If you are a migrant 'new Australian', do not expect Aboriginal Australians to find common cause with you as a fellow minority, not even if you happen to be black.

For the Aboriginals, post-World War II migrant settlement of Australia has simply added to their woes, adding yet more human strata above them, further blurring their claim to real ownership of the country. Immigration has pinned them even more firmly at the bottom of the social pile.

Australia's most famous old-generation Aboriginal politician, lawyer and Martin Luther King-style freedom fighter, Charlie Perkins, Australia's first Aboriginal university graduate in 1965, expressed this feeling when he spoke out roundly condemning Asian immigration in the mid-1980s.

Statistical Phantoms

Aboriginals are thought to have numbered around 300,000–500,000, perhaps even more, when the Europeans arrived in Australia in 1788. The fact that their population had fallen to around 22,000 by 1860, as the European population zoomed above one million, speaks tragic volumes. But nobody really knows the true statistics, because Aboriginals were non-persons in census terms right up to 1967.

When the whites first arrived in Australia, they declared it an 'empty land', *Terra Nullius*, as if it were uninhabited. This was very convenient as it obviated the usual legal need to negotiate any kind of lease with traditional owners; the land could simply be taken.

Persona Non Grata

As writer John Pilger has put it in his *A Secret Country*, the Aboriginals were not accounted human but rather 'part of the fauna'. As late as 1963, Australia showed its contempt for Aboriginal human rights once again when it partnered with the British government to allow nuclear testing at three sites in Australia, one off the Western Australian coast and two others in South Australia, at Emu Field and Maralinga. These tests took place between 1952 and 1963, rendering the areas affected dangerous 'no-go' sites, yet during the entire process, scant regard was shown for the fact that aboriginal families were present in the area. A Royal Commission of Inquiry in 1984 revealed the shocking impact both on the land and on the indigenous people.

Now the Aboriginals are known to number in the region of 410,000—this 2001 figure has risen from about 265,000 just since 1991. This startling rise is in part due to a real improvement in their treatment, and to a higher than average birth rate, but partly also to the increasing acceptability of declaring publicly one's aboriginality, even in the case of mixed-bloods. In the bad old days, mixed-bloods—'half-castes' as they were called then—were barred by law from claiming Aboriginal ancestry.

Only in 1967 did a referendum produce a 90.8 per cent popular vote to recognise Aboriginals as people who should be counted in the national census and also for whom the Commonwealth government could make laws (a decision that unfortunately for many of them, also gave them for the first time the legal right to drink alcohol). Many Australians confuse this referendum with the decision to give the vote to Aboriginal Australians, but the history of Aboriginal suffrage is in fact much more complex than that. Effectively however, Aboriginals did not have the federal, Commonwealth vote until 1962, and Queensland was the last state to grant them a State vote, in 1965.

Trauma of a Nation

The Europeans brought with them the flu, smallpox, venereal disease and many other ailments previously unknown to the Aboriginals, against which they had no immunity. The infinitely better armed settlers also hunted down the simple hunter-gatherer Aboriginals like animals, sometimes even putting out poisoned meat for them, as if for rabid dogs. They raped Aboriginal women and children. They ignored, despised or actively destroyed Aboriginal culture. This was attempted genocide, an orgy of cruelty.

The Myall Creek Massacre

The most famous incident among a long litany of such happenings was the 'Myall Creek Massacre' of 1838, in New South Wales state. For this wanton and brutal killing of innocent and defenceless Aboriginal women children and old men, seven of the 11 whites accused were hanged. But such justice was unusual. You will get something of a flavour of the times by watching the movie *The Tracker*.

The still unexorcised shame of this terrible time haunts the national psyche—as well it should, for it is by no means over yet. Although official policies of discrimination are long gone, you will still hear dreadful things said of 'the blackfeller' in white society all over Australia; the deeper you get into the countryside, the worse the things you hear. To far too many white Australians, Aboriginals are still 'boongs' or 'abo's', the old terms of contempt now taboo in polite urban society. Even my otherwise charming Aussie friend spelled it out for me: 'They're all bludgers (the Aboriginals), that's what they are! Never worked for any land, never bought any land, just inherited it, that's all!'

Blatant cases of discrimination still surface regularly in the press. In 1989, Aboriginal university graduate and youth welfare officer, Julie Marie Tommy, successfully sued a Western Australian pub-hotel for refusing to serve her at its bar. It transpired during the case that the hotel had also set aside separate whites-only and blacks-only bars. Such scenes are repeated endlessly throughout rural Australia today.

Not so long ago, my husband mostly 'coloured' band wa politely asked not to put u promotional posters featurin their photos at the outback pu they were playing at, lest th attract Aboriginal customers the bar.

The scandal of Aboriginal deaths in police custody erupted into the public mind, with the 1991 publication of a Royal Commission enquiry into Aboriginal Deaths in Custody into at least 105 unexplained Aboriginal deaths in police and prison cells. In so many cases, what may have begun as a simple arrest for drunk and disorderly behaviour has ended with sudden death. The Council for Aboriginal Reconciliation and also the post of Aboriginal and Torres Straits Islander Social Justice Commissioner were established in response to the Royal Commission's findings. Fingers have been pointed at the police over the issue of deaths in custody, but ultimately the finger points at all Australians. There seems to have been little progress since 1991. Of all deaths in prison/custody, 20 per cent were indigenous Australians in 2002; and whereas in 1991, 14 per cent of the total prison population comprised indigenous Australians, by 2003 this figure had risen to 20 per cent—very disproportionate in terms of Aboriginals accounting for barely 3 per cent of the total population of Australia.

For Their Own Good

By the beginning of the 20th century, the best an Aboriginal could expect from life was to be relegated to an Aboriginal reserve and get some sort of a job with the white man—on a farm, a cattle station or as a domestic servant. In some states, the Aboriginal was forbidden to consume alcohol, to marry or have sex across the colour line, or to carry a firearm. The 'sex bar' didn't stop many of their white employers, however, systematically raping their female workers.

The 1930s and well beyond, into the 1960s, saw a fully articulated policy of assimilation, with or without Aboriginal consent, for mixed bloods. Out of a sort of twisted benevolence, the white authorities systematically removed

Aboriginal children, particularly those of mixed blood, from their mothers 'for their own good', in an attempt to integrate them into white society and obliterate their aboriginality forever. Often, however, they were simply put into domestic servitude, akin to slavery.

Rabbit-Proof Fence

You need to see US-based Australian Philip Noyce's movie of 2002, *Rabbit-Proof Fence* (starring David Gulpilil and also Shakespearean actor Kenneth Branagh as the frosty 'Protector of the Aborigines') to get some sort of feeling for the enormity of suffering that such policies caused. The movie, set in the 1930s, was based on Doris Pilkington's book *Follow the Rabbit-Proof Fence*.

The basic idea was to weed, and breed out Aboriginal genes, leaving the full-blood elders to die off peacefully, thus eliminating the Aboriginal race altogether. This was thought to be the 'kindest' stratagem for dealing with 'the problem'. Descendants of Australia's poor orphans, known as 'The Stolen Generation', are still searching for their families and discovering who they really are. Some experts have estimated that two thirds of all mixed blood children—thousands—were impacted by these policies, in the Northern Territory region alone, between 1912 and the 1960s.

The Aboriginal Experience

A part of these dispossessed children's story is told movingly by a mixed-blood Aboriginal psychologist-writer-artist, Sally Morgan, in her book *My Place*.

A similar understanding of the Aboriginal experience is presented in *Dingo, The Story of our Mob* by Sally Dingo, a white Australian married to entertainer Ernie Dingo, a role model for young Aboriginals. The full story is told in agonising detail through the official report *Bringing Them Home: The Stolen Children Report'* resulting from the 1995 National Inquiry into the Separation of Aboriginal and Torres Straits Islander Children From Their Families.

In 1991 a special Memorandum of Understanding was signed to allow Aboriginals from 'the stolen generation' special access to Australia's official archives and records of policies resulting in the separation of families, so that they could research their own genealogy more effectively. But most have remained 'lost'.

An Aboriginal blowing the didgeridoo.

Absorbing the Difference

Today's policy, first set by Gough Whitlam's Labor government in 1972, is to allow Aboriginals self-determination. In line with the wider goal of building a multicultural Australia, Aboriginals are offered a share in the benefits of modern white society through gradual (and voluntary) assimilation. Every effort is made at official levels to encourage the Aboriginals to preserve their culture.

Assimilation is no easy matter, for there can be no disputing that the Aboriginals are 'different'. Differences exist within their community as well, with some members originating from tribal groups and others delineated more by whether they grew up in the towns or countryside and whether they are mixed or full-blood Aboriginals, whether they were influenced or educated by Christian missionaries or not.

Among the Aboriginals' most striking differences with white Australians is their legendary penchant for 'going walkabout'—disappearing without warning for days, weeks or months—which gives them a reputation for being unreliable. This instinct for travelling the land they inherited from their nomadic ancestors. Possession and property are alien concepts in Aboriginal culture, the antithesis of Western materialism. Nomads do not carry around much luggage, and share freely. They also expect the same of others, and this can sometimes make them appear too free with others' goods. Private property is an alien concept in their culture.

Even when tribal bands of Aboriginals in their natural state wandered through one another's territory, defined only by a delicate structure of oral precepts, there was never any attempt to 'conquer' one another or 'acquire' the land. So when the whites came, it never dawned on the Aboriginals that they had lost their land, since such a concept was unimaginable. Only when the whites erected fences to keep them out and filled the land with sheep and cattle, depriving them of their hunting grounds, did they begin to react with hostility, but in vain.

Confinement within four walls induces virtually terminal claustrophobia in many Aboriginals, once upon a time used to ranging across some of the vastest open spaces known to humankind. Hence, even when offered a neat little home, they may opt instead to create a rough camp outdoors, in the garden. They may even destroy timber structures to use the wood for making fires outdoors to cook on. In the view of unsympathetic whites, this looks like a perverse insistence on creating slums and an innate lack of 'civilisation'.

Two Families, Two Different Experiences

It is right and proper to be concerned and appalled by the plight of Australia's Aboriginal people. New migrants and settlers need to be aware that by adopting Australia, they take onto their shoulders some of the burden of guilt and shame that every Australian carries about Aboriginal disadvantage. To that extent they have some responsibility to do something about it. But they also need to know that the reality can be tough to deal with if it comes to live next door.

My husband and I have had two sets of Aboriginal neighbours. The difference between the two experiences shows that no one stereotype will fit all realities. The first family have retained friendly contact with us even after moving house. Somewhat urbanised, they are church-going Christians, aspiring, striving, hard-working and full of hope for their children's potentially difficult future in a largely discriminatory environment. We got on well as neighbours. But even they have many relatives who are constantly in and out of jail.

The second family came from the far northern outback of Western Australia, spoke mainly their tribal language, and were far more problematic in terms of adjusting to suburban life. They were poor and ran out of money and food frequently—so they came round regularly and asked for both. Their phones got cut and their electricity disconnected as they failed to pay the bills; so they came round often to make a phone call or even to ask if they could tap our power. Lack of power and hot water meant that they could rarely take a bath... Their culture is such a collective, communal and sharing one that they saw no reason not to be round our place on and off all day to ask for anything and everything—when one day I said I hadn't got what they wanted, the young girl at the door said, "How come? Ain't you been shopping today, then?" That collective spirit meant also that any relative who came visiting would stay with them, until a house meant for maybe five people was housing more like 20, with all of the accompanying noise. When grandma, about 70 years old, came, she took off all her clothes—no, I am not exaggerating—waved a big stick and did a traditional dance on the front lawn in full view of passing traffic, which slowed down in fascinated disbelief. Maybe it was dementia, maybe it was cultural; we weren't sure. Aboriginals don't much like to discipline their children in the Western way,

(Continued on the next page)

(Continued from previous page)

so they run free and wild, often without proper supervision. We shuddered as we saw tiny tots climb up on the house roof, play toreadors with the traffic across the road, and climb trees to get over our fence and toddle around our deep swimming pool, without an adult in sight. The children were never at school. The family seemed to have a lot of poor health issues and called more ambulances in a year than most other people would call in a lifetime; and they didn't settle the ambulance bills that came to our address because our phone was used to call the ambulance, so we got the debt-collecting calls. Partly because they ran out of power all the time and partly because they preferred it, they scavenged bits of wood from all over and lit camp-fires in their back garden (illegal at most times in the suburbs) to cook kangaroo joints that they had bought at the most convenient and cheapest place they could find—the local pet-food shop.

The smoke, and smell, would billow over our washing on the line outside, and we lived in fear of a spark drifting over the fence to set our property alight.

They would take off back to the north, especially during Perth's winter, and disappear for months, leaving their mail to blow across the garden as it spilled out of their mailbox, turning to slush in the winter rains; we tried to collect it all up for them and left it in a plastic bag outside their front door. Meanwhile, free bread deliveries from a local church charity group continued to arrive outside their door, so we had to make sure that was disposed of too before it putrefied in the open. Finally of course, there came the inevitable climax: one of their little boys did his last daredevil dash into highway traffic and got killed, run over. Not wishing to report them to their landlord as this would surely mean eviction for an already challenged family, we called in the Aboriginal Liaison Officer attached to the local police station. Himself an Aboriginal, he proved to be an enormous help in mediating with the neighbours to persuade them to adapt their behaviour a bit better to their new suburban environment.

I am recounting all this neither to complain nor to vilify, only to let readers know what can happen.

We found that it worked to be friendly and non-confrontational but at the same time to define our boundaries firmly and say 'No' when we needed to. They were not rude, violent or threatening in any way—indeed they were quite gentle—just very very different. There was really no way we could integrate with their lifestyle unless we severely compromised our own, and our work too, since we work at home. In many ways, we learned a lot from them about the realities—and sadness—of Aboriginal life in the urban context. There is much to learn from Aboriginal culture, particularly from the Aboriginals' knowledge of the land, but in the suburbs, a 'clash of civilisations' is often inevitable. It takes understanding, good humour and patience to peg out some middle ground.

Diet of Death

The European newcomers were the harbingers of Aboriginal death in many shapes and forms. They brought flour, sugar, alcohol and tobacco, among a host of other goodies which were to destroy the Aboriginals' health. The most visible result for the casual observer is Aboriginal obesity. Mind you, the whites are hardly immune, thanks to fast food.

Research in the 1980s and 1990s has demonstrated that the Aboriginals' spartan original diet of berries, roots, insects and occasional fish or wild animals like the goanna lizard or the kangaroo, was far better for them. Hence also the trendy cuisine style among hip whites called 'Bush Tucker'—but more of that in Chapter 6: Tucker (see pages 271–273).

The lamentable state of Aboriginal health today is certainly one more reason for Australia to continue feeling ashamed. Heart disease, diabetes, tuberculosis, even trachoma and malnutrition, AIDS too; you name it, they've got it. Taking the remote 'outback' Kimberley region of Western Australia as just one example, the area holds only 2 per cent of the State's population yet generates two-thirds of the State's notifications of syphilis, a third of those of gonorrhoea and a sixth of those of chlamydia, mostly known to emanate from Aboriginal

The goanna was the diet of the Aboriginals before the white settlers came.

communities. This is more because of Aboriginals' lack of awareness of and access to screening and treatment than because they are intrinsically sexually irresponsible. Creative ideas like 'condom trees'—wilderness trees bedecked with free condom-filled containers to give wandering Aboriginals easy access to safe-sex tools—have been devised to deal with such issues, distributing about 100,000 condoms a year in the Kimberley region.

Aboriginal life expectancy in 2001 was estimated at about 56.3 years for males, 62.8 years for females, rates that recall the rates that applied to the mainstream Australian population back at the turn of the 20th century. These rates are also about the same as for females in sub-Saharan Africa (with AIDS factored out) and as for males in Myanmar or Papua New Guinea. White males and females by contrast can expect to live well into their late 70s. This ill-health itself stems from poor diet, poor living environment and often unstable family life. Alcohol abuse, petrol sniffing and domestic violence, even incest and child abuse, are rife in Aboriginal families (not that Australian whites do not have their share, but the problem is far more pronounced among Aboriginals).

As many others have put it before me, Aboriginal Australians live a 'Third World' life in the midst of a 'First World' nation. Their trashed out-of-town settlements resemble the worst sort of refugee camps, or the black townships of South Africa. You do not want to be there on pay-day night, Fridays, when the drinking and bottle-throwing starts in the streets.

The Rights See-saw

Such conditions make it extremely difficult for Aboriginals to take advantage of the many special aid and affirmative-action schemes which now exist to help them enter mainstream Australia. They still have a very steep climb ahead of them, even despite a litany of special rights assigned to them since the 1970s, often much to the chagrin of some less compassionate white Australians.

In gradual steps, different states have, at different times since the mid-1960s, legislated first to turn over Aboriginal reserve lands to the Aboriginals themselves, and then to grant traditional ownership of vacant lands to them on application. Land within towns or already owned by non-Aboriginals is not open to such claims, however. Which means that much of the best land is still withheld from them, of course.

The acknowledged turning point was the Aboriginal Land Rights (Northern Territory) Act of 1976. Of all the states, Queensland and Western Australia have been the slowest movers, with a generally poor record in race relations.

At present, something like 11–15 per cent of Australia is held by the Aboriginal community in some form or another—often, under agreements merely allowing non-exclusive access to Aboriginal traditional owners, a very limited form of 'ownership'. Land rights battles continue today, particularly when Aboriginal aspirations come into conflict with powerful mining and farming interests. Individual agreements pop up now and again, from State to State, but there seems to be no national blueprint on how to proceed.

The elaborate bureaucracy of organisations charged with promoting aboriginal interests that for a time flourished under the umbrella of the Aboriginal and Torres Strait Islander Commission (ATSIC) was destroyed, with ATSIC itself, in

2005. ATSIC was first formed in 1990 and hailed as a form of self-government for Aboriginals, charged with acting as the Aboriginal-run middle-man between government and Aboriginals, including the distribution of government funds. But in the 21st century, ATSIC became mired in controversy, particularly over its financial management, partly over the personal conduct of its senior executives.

Premier John Howard's Liberal government, among others, lost patience with the situation and legislated the organisation, with its 35 regional councils, out of existence. The delivery of services to Aboriginals would now be 'mainstreamed' into existing agencies serving the wider community, announced the government. While a new government-appointed National Indigenous Council was set up to advise the government, this was characterised by the government itself as a temporary measure pending the possible natural emergence of new bodies from within the Aboriginal community. Said John Howard at the time: "We believe very strongly that the experiment in separate representation, elected representation, for indigenous people, has been a failure. We will not replace ATSIC with an alternative body. We will appoint a group of distinguished indigenous people to advise the government on a purely advisory basis in relation to Aboriginal affairs. Programmes will be mainstreamed but arrangements will be established to ensure that there is a major policy role for the Minister of Indigenous Affairs. This will not result in less money for indigenous affairs. It will in fact result in more resources."

Critics, however, feel that the Aboriginals have lost the power to make decisions about their own lives, and they have also pointed to the government's failure to replace ATSIC with any strong structure. On the other hand, some interesting new structures are now emerging, in the form of individually negotiated direct government-to-community 'reponsibility agreements' that demand a 'two-way street' for welfare payments given to Aboriginals; some of these have made it mandatory for Aboriginals to guarantee that their children will consistently attend school or even simply get their children to shower and wash their school uniforms regularly (both not at all the norm at the moment) in return for welfare. By May 2005, about 52 such agreements had been signed with different tribal or language groups around the country, but the Aboriginal Democrats Senator Aden Ridgeway commented that "At this rate, it will take the government about a quarter of a century to deal with the rest of the 1,200 communities."

The Land Mother

Land rights are central to Aboriginality. It is hard for outsiders to comprehend the very deep and mystic way in which Aboriginals feel they are bound to the land. This is not the feeling of the white farmer who loves his land through proud possession and control of it. Rather, the Aboriginals feel *they* are owned and controlled by the land. The earth is their 'mother'.

In a far-off 'Dreamtime', believe the Aboriginals, ancestral spirits, beings and other agents of Mother Earth travelled across the land creating people, places, plants and animals. You will hear a lot in Australia about Aboriginal 'sacred sites'. Once a place is declared a sacred site, it becomes extremely problematic to develop it or tamper with it in

Ritual spirit poles on Bathurst Island, Northern Territory.

any way. A pitched battle went on for many years now over State Government development proposals for a riverside site in Perth, formerly a brewery, for exactly this reason (but it is now an upmarket apartment complex). The sacred sites were the halting points where the ancestral beings paused on their journeys across the land. There are many other such cases across the country.

Each Aboriginal's very identity, and position within the tribe or clan, is based on the place where he or she was born, and is linked to an ancestral being, expressed through a plant or an animal. The soil is the source of all life, and the home to which all life returns after death, for recycling into life again. There is no sense of separation from other life-forms. This tunes well with beliefs found in some of the great world religions—Hinduism and Buddhism among them—and native American philosophy too.

The Aboriginals lived in complete harmony and balance with the wild land. Their burning-back patterns were an essential part of the ecosystem, regenerating and benefiting many species of plants and animals in an ecology geared for natural fires. They took from the land only what they needed to survive.

Their system of justice was harsh, but effectively meted out by the elders of the tribe—you might be speared in the leg or, much worse, 'sung to death' for transgression of tribal laws. Magic plays an important role in Aboriginal culture. Even white Australians are in some awe of customs like 'pointing the bone'—a form of curse willing an enemy to die—and 'singing', an intensive group incantation, again intended to bring injury or death to the enemy. Stories of victims (black and white) falling down dead abound.

Kinship and extended family are central to Aboriginal integrity. Many South-east Asians and the more traditional or Mediterranean Europeans will recognise this group-oriented social structure as similar to their own.

Culture and wisdom were passed on through the community's rich repertoire of oral history, stories and songs—there was no writing—culminating in the formal, and often painful, initiation ceremony for children passing into adulthood. Secret knowledge of sacred things was communicated at this ceremony. Men and women have segregated secrets—'men's business' and 'women's business'. To this day, there are many such secrets still carefully kept from the uninitiated.

The Art of Being Aboriginal

One of the most striking things about Aboriginal culture before white settlement was the existence of an estimated 230 distinct Aboriginal languages, with more than 500 dialects. More than half of these languages are now extinct.

While most of these languages, like the Aboriginals themselves, evolved in complete isolation from outside influences, in some areas there was some cross-fertilisation: in the Northern Territory, as well as parts of north-western Western Australia. For example, ancient trading links with Indonesian fishermen seeking Australia's valuable sea-slugs and trochus shells, led to Indonesian vocabulary entering Aboriginal tongues. In parts of the Northern Territory, for example, the word for 'foreigner' is *balanda*, the Indonesian word for a Dutchman or 'Hollander'.

Aboriginal languages have left their mark on white Australia, in place-names and in everyday words, from 'billabong' to 'kangaroo'. But we can only guess at what opportunities for acquiring extraordinary knowledge have been squandered over the years of white contempt for Aboriginal culture. No research body was set up to study this fascinating kaleidoscope of cultures before the establishment in 1961 of the Australian Institute of Aboriginal Studies at Canberra.

Aboriginal culture has since been revealed as vastly more sophisticated than previously understood. On the artistic front in particular, the Aboriginals have contributed to the very definition of 'Australian-ness'.

Aboriginal Australian art, traditionally executed chiefly on the Aboriginals' own bodies, on cave and rock walls, and on strips of bark, has achieved international recognition in recent decades, as Aboriginal artists have learned to transfer it to canvas and transmit it through modern media such as

Aboriginal rock painting at Nourlangie, Northern Territory.

watercolours, oils and acrylic. Especially well known are the dot-mosaic and 'X-ray' styles of painting (depicting animals complete with their skeletal structure and internal organs). The best examples are now, quite rightly, very expensive, and grace the walls of some of the world's premier galleries.

Albert Namatjira was a pioneer Aboriginal artist who scored most of his considerable success before World War II—he died in 1959. But he did it with Western-style watercolour paintings. True Aboriginal art was not to win

This reconciliation mural entitled 'The Wargul' was painted by Melanie Evans in 1999. She is from the Mudburra Poeple in the Northern Territory and lives in Fremantle, Western Australia. For her, 'the Wargul (Rainbow Serpent) represents the strength, beauty and creation of the natural features of this country'.

white acclaim until long after the war. Today, there are many Aboriginal artists of note in Australia keeping tribal traditions alive.

Just as creative as the fusion with Western art media has been the recent grafting of Asian techniques like batik—wax-resist textile printing—with Aboriginal motifs, to stunning effect in some areas of the Northern Territory.

The success of Aboriginal art has already helped restore the Aboriginals' pride in themselves and their culture, quite apart from bringing them income. But a contentious issue of today raises the question of 'intellectual copyright': whether or not white-community 'borrowing' and commercialisation of Aboriginal styles and themes constitute both - and exploitation. Aboriginal art promoters today have to take a lot more care with how they market the product and how much of the resulting income they remit to the originators, the Aboriginals themselves.

A Brand New Day on Its Way?

Less well known to the outside world are Aboriginal music and dance, central elements in traditional Aboriginal culture. Here again, Western influences have produced interesting hybrids. Many Aboriginal musicians have shown a talent for pop or country-and-western styles.

Contact between Aboriginal and white Australian musicians has also spawned outstanding fusion bands such as the former *Gondwanaland* (now just *Gondwana*, named after the super-continent of some 150 million years ago which, according to Continental Drift Theory, gave birth to Australia about 45 million years ago).

Fusion Music

Equally powerful is the fusion music of the all-Aboriginal group Yothu Yindi, led by former teacher Mandawuy Yunupingu of the Yolngu people, who in 1988 was the first tertiary graduate from the Aboriginal reserve area of Arnhem Land. To learn more, go to:

http://www.yothuyindi.com

Fusion bands like these have evolved a quintessentially Australian sound with original compositions featuring instruments as diverse as electronic synthesisers, drums and the Aboriginal didgeridoo, a very long, tube-like wind instrument carved from raw logs. The insistent, throbbing drone of the didgeridoo is the sound of Australia itself, an awe-inspiring voice from the desert speaking to the deepest, most mysterious levels of the human soul. Yothu Yindi often also features thrilling Aboriginal-style dancers and other tribal trimmings such as body- and face-paint.

An increasing number of professional Aboriginal dance troupes are now touring little-known Aboriginal dance, until only recently dismissed as primitive, akin to old Red-Indians-whooping-round-campfire stuff. Probably the best known and most sophisticated is *Bangarra Dance Theatre,* well worth making a detour for, any time you find yourself near one of their gigs. They are fine exponents of contemporary dance with an Aboriginal tone and Aboriginal themes. Visit their website at http://www.bangarra.com au.

Among Australia's best-known Aboriginal actors and dancers is David Gulpilil. If you saw the first *Crocodile Dundee* film, you will remember Gulpilil as Dundee's Aboriginal friend, but he was also outstanding in Rolf de Heer's more substantial movie of 2002, *The Tracker,* already mentioned—a subtle tale of Aboriginal wisdom set against white brutality and crudeness.

Theatre is another arena now beginning to showcase Aboriginal talents. Actor Ernie Dingo is a well-established example and Western Australian playwright Jack Davis another. Davis, in particular, has conjured up the bleakness of Aboriginal life in the old days on settlements controlled by whites. His works are now considered Australian classics and are used as secondary school study texts.

Bran Nu Dae

'There's nothing I would rather be
than to be an Aborigine
and dream of just what
Heaven
must be like
where moth and rust do
not corrupt
when I die I know I'll be
going up
'cos you know that I've
had my hell on earth—
Here I live in
this tin shack
Nothing here worth
coming back to
drunken fights and
awful sights
People drunk most
every night.
On the way to
a Bran Nu Dae
Everybody every body
say ...'

—from *Bran Nu Dae*, an Aboriginal musical,
written by Jimmy Chi of Broome, Western Australia

I was privileged to attend the 1990 premiere of Australia's first Aboriginal musical, *Bran Nu Dae* ('A Brand New Day'). The name of its creator was Jimmy Chi, the product of a Chinese father and an Aboriginal mother in the old pearling port of Broome, up in the north-west of Western Australia. The descendants of Afghan camel drivers' unions with Aboriginal women are another example of the many such exotic mixes to be found in the melting pot of Australia.
(Continued on next page)

(Continued from previous page)

Bran Nu Dae is a vibrant example of the kind of innovation we can expect from Aboriginal performers in future. Wonderfully raucous, rumbustious and ribald, the play depicts an Aboriginal boy's flight from the city of Perth back to his outback homeland. White society, from the local Roman Catholic archbishop to well-meaning hippies, is satirised mercilessly but in a good-natured sort of way.

The black protest movements of the 1950s and 1960s in the West had their impact on Aboriginal Australia and a new school of writing is now apparent as a result. One of the first and best-known Aboriginal protest writers was Oodgeroo Noonuccal, also known as Kath Walker, a formidable poetess, whose first volume of poetry, *We Are Going*, was published in 1964. Another early success was Aboriginal artist and writer Dick Roughsey, who wrote chiefly for children—works such as *The Giant Devil-Dingo* in 1973 and *The Rainbow Serpent* in 1975.

Sporting Laurels

Aboriginals have also shown exceptional talent in sports. Curiously, the very first Australian cricket team to visit England was a privately-organised all-Aboriginal team, which toured the country in 1868. (However, several of them found England's climate so inhospitable that they had to go home before time; one of them actually died.)

Most sports fans have also heard of Aboriginal tennis player Evonne Goolagong, the 1971 and 1981 Wimbledon women's singles champion. Aboriginal sportsmen have also excelled in football and boxing. Famous Aboriginal boxers include Dave Sands (1940s), bantam-weight Lionel Rose, world champion in his class at the Mexico Olympics of 1968, and Tony Mundine in the 1970s and his son today, Anthony Mundine. And who in the world did not thrill to Australian Aboriginal athlete Cathy Freeman's triumphant raising of the torch carrying the Olympic flame at the Sydney Olympics opening ceremony in 2000, followed by her epic Gold Medal win in the 400-metre race final?

Black Politics

Education is the key to Aboriginal advancement, as it is for so many other disadvantaged peoples. At the moment, Aboriginal employment rates for adults are about half those for the rest of the population. The community does already have models to follow: for example, Sir Doug Nicholls, who died in 1988, a pastor, the first Aboriginal to be knighted by the Queen and also the nation's first Aboriginal Governor, of South Australia, 1976–1977.

The year 1971 also saw the first Aboriginal Member of Federal Parliament, Neville Bonner, while 1978 saw Pat O'Shane become Australia's first Aboriginal law graduate and barrister. The first two Aboriginals to be employed by the diplomatic service in the Ministry of Foreign Affairs were hired in 1982. Aden Ridgeway of the Democrats became the second Aboriginal Member of Federal Parliament, but lost his seat in 2004. The first indigenous woman ever to sit in any Australian Parliament, Carol Martin, took her seat in the Western Australian Parliament in 2001 and retained it in the State election of 2005.

Carol Martin Speaks

The following is Carol Martin's maiden speech in the Western Australian Parliament on 2 May 2001 after her election as the first indigenous woman to sit in any Australian Parliament:

'Even as I address the House with emotions swelling inside me, I cannot help but feel a slight touch of disbelief that it has taken so long for a person like me to get here. I have been humbled by my victory and entry into Parliament. I recognise the efforts of the many people who have fought for the rights of Aboriginal people. I stand here because they never gave up their struggle. Just as I have benefited from their fight, our young people will benefit from knowing that if they believe in themselves, their law and their culture, nothing is beyond them. I hope that my election acts as an example to and provides a role model for our young people. I say to them that regardless of their situation, it is within them to take control of their lives and to achieve their hearts' desire. They are not alone; we are clearing a path for them. I am given confidence by the fact that through dedication, perseverance and hard work, all Australians, regardless of creed or colour, can move forward together. By acknowledging both the great

(Continued on the next page)

(Continued from previous page)

achievements and great mistakes of the past, we can work together to develop a new, shared future for this great nation.

Reconciliation is the beginning of that process. It is a process that allows us to view the events of today with the benefit of hindsight. It is not a 'black armband view of history', as espoused by those mean-spirited spoilers who cynically aim to divide the community. It is the opposite of that; it is a celebration. To me, reconciliation celebrates the spirit of indigenous Australia, a spirit that, after 200 years of systematic hardship and dispossession, allows us to not only survive, but also be strong and proud.'

Burnum Burnum, like Charlie Perkins, an Aboriginal lawyer and freedom fighter, is another politically significant figure. His most flamboyant gesture has been to plant the Aboriginal flag on England's white cliffs of Dover, on Australia Day 1988, to claim England for the Aboriginal 'nation'.

Burnum Burnum also masterminded the recovery of the bones of Truganini, the last full-blood Tasmanian Aboriginal, who had died in 1876. Tasmania's Hobart Museum had put them on display up to 1947 against Truganini's express wish that her body be left undisturbed. Her ashes were at last scattered on waters close to her homeland. Many other attempts to retrieve Aboriginal bones stored as curiosities in foreign museums are still underway.

Among other activist names you will undoubtedly encounter are Gary Foley, Dr Lois O' Donoghue, Peter Yu (half-Chinese) and Pat Dodson.

THE MABO/WIK MESS

Aboriginal history reached a historic crossroads with the landmark 'Mabo' judgement made by the Australian High Court in June 1992—a judgement named after deceased Aboriginal land-rights negotiator Eddy Mabo. The High Court ruled that the original colonial designation of Australia as *Terra Nullius* or 'empty land', was erroneous: the Aboriginals did have valid 'native title' to much of the Australian land.

This has generated hysteria, and more importantly, uncertainty for farmers and would-be minerals exploiters. Is the average suburban backyard secure from Aboriginal land claims? Yes, the Mabo decision stated clearly that no privately-owned land is threatened.

States like resource-rich Western Australia however had concerns because vacant State land certainly was vulnerable to native-title claims and Western Australia, for one, has plenty of that; Premier Richard Court's conservative Liberal state government therefore passed its own legislation to override the High Court judgement. But even if native-title claims do not stand on occupied land, there may now be a case for financial compensation to the original 'traditional owners', the Aboriginals.

A Native Title Tribunal set up after Mabo has been hearing claims. In many cases, all the Aboriginals want to establish is their right of access to properties in connection with visiting 'sacred sites', hunting and fishing, and their right to be consulted on the future disposal of the land. To a large extent, they want not simply access to the wealth that is land, but more the 'face' of recognition and consultation, to salve the humiliating wounds of their lamentable history—Asians culturally attuned to concepts of 'face' will perhaps be the first to sympathise with that desire.

But Australians have an additional ruling to wrestle with: 'The Wik Decision' handed out to the Wik People of Cape York Peninsula, Queensland, in 1996. The High Court in this case ruled that native title can coexist with pastoral (farming) leases and can only be extinguished permanently by a special law, which has not occurred. In other words, the farmers did not have exclusive hold on the land, although it seems their rights have priority when there is a conflict. Any new decision to mine or log such land, however, must go through a negotiation process with native-title holders first.

To muddy the waters further, the Federal Court of Australia later ruled that native title could exist over coastal waters and that in some cases 'the tide of history had washed away' that title. Nobody wants to face up to the real meaning of reconciliation with the Aboriginals, for at its heart lie the issues of land ownership and land use. Land, in turn, lies at the heart of Australia's wealth.

There has been a palpable deterioration in the tone of the relationship between black and white Australia under John Howard's Liberal government since 1996. The biggest bone of contention is that powerful little word 'sorry'. Howard refuses to apologise on behalf of white Australia for past injustices to black Australia, arguing that this generation cannot be held responsible for the sins of its ancestors, and expressing his contempt for what he has called a 'black armband view of history'. "The 'black armband' view of our past reflects a belief that most Australian history since 1788 has been little more than a disgraceful story of imperialism, exploitation, racism, sexism and other forms of discrimination," he complained in 1996 when delivering Australia's Sir Robert Menzies Lecture.

Howard's 'personal sorrow' and official 'deep and sincere regret' were expressed publicly in Parliament in 1999, but the government's position remains 'no apology'. Some say in its defence that there are serious legal liability implications to saying 'sorry'. Yet the 15,000 or so non-Aboriginal Australians who have signed an apology document (it is accessible on the Internet) and the 250,000 (overwhelmingly non-Aboriginal) who turned out for a National Reconciliation march across Sydney Harbour Bridge in May 2000 recognise a simple truth—that in their dogged pursuit of the unspoken 'sorry', Aboriginals seek, more than any concrete advantage, that form of respect known as 'face'.

This refusal to apologise is uncharacteristic of usual Australian good-heartedness. It indicates how intractable the 'Aboriginal issue' still is, despite the efforts of the National Council for Aboriginal Reconciliation established in 1991. Many decent Australians find it too hard and relapse into a conspiracy of silence, avoiding the issue wherever possible. In fact the 'S' word is so problematic for most whites that the declared annual 'National Sorry Day' reconciliation event on 26 May had to be renamed 'National Day of Healing' in 2005, in a bid to increase non-Aboriginal support.

But there are signs that the tide of history has turned and both reconciliation and an actual Treaty of Reconciliation document are possible in the near future. The Treaty would have been a fine way to greet the centenary of federation at the dawn of the third millennium, but better late than never, eh? as and Aussie might say. As journalist John Pilger concludes in *A Secret Country*, 'Until we white Australians give back to black Australians their nationhood, we can never claim our own.'

HOW AUSTRALIAN SOCIETY WORKS

'Democracy does not mean representative government or manhood suffrage, or any other piece of machinery. Democracy is a mental atitude. Democracy means a belief in equality. It is based on the coviction that we are all blokes.
—Sir Walter Murdoch, prominent Scots-born Western Australian Academic, in his *Speaking Personally*, 1930.

STRUCTURE AND FORM

To 'fit in' with Australian society, you first need to know how it is structured and how it works. It's important to understand that Australia's is a federal system, with a great deal of latitude for regional and state-based differences.

This huge continent is divided into six states and two territories: from west to east, Western Australia (capital, Perth); the Northern Territory (self-governing with an elected Legislative Assembly since 1978, capital, Darwin); South Australia (capital, Adelaide); Queensland (capital, Brisbane); New South Wales (capital, Sydney); Australian Capital Territory (home of the federal Parliament in the capital, Canberra); Victoria (capital, Melbourne); and Tasmania (an island state to the far south, capital, Hobart).

The Hutt River Province

Not everyone has accepted the federation of Australia in 1901. In 1970, Western Australian farmer Leonard Casley announced his secession from the state of Western Australia over a matter of grain quotas. His farm thus became the independent nation Hutt River Province, with himself as Prince Leonard and his wife Princess Shirley. This spot on the map has ever since issued its own passports and welcomed thousands of tourists every year. Prince Leonard is one of some 20 independent thinkers in Australia who have acted similarly. As reported by the *London Telegraph*, there's also His Imperial Majesty George II, once George Cruikshank, a Sydney sales manager, now

(Continued on the next page)

(Continued from previous page)

Emperor of Atlantium, actually a one-bedroom apartment on the Sydney waterfront. Nearby, Prince Paul of Wy too seceded from his local council in November 2004, apparently after 11 years of argument over permission to build a driveway to his home. And this is not to mention the Gay and Lesbian Kingdom of the Coral Sea, comprising some (uninhabited) islands off Queensland and touted as a final haven for gays and lesbians. It declared war on Australia in September 2004 following the government's refusal to recognise same-sex marriage

This is all in line with the English tradition of eccentricity of course.

But what it means is, there is room for all types in Australia and even if you are slightly nuts, you will fit in just fine.

DISSECTING DEMOCRACY
How Does It All Work?

The governmental system is that of a classic parliamentary democracy with full separation of executive and legislative powers, mixed with some elements from the USA. Australia was seen, and saw itself, in the 19th century very much as a repeat of the American experience.

A modification of this basically 'Westminster' system is the existence in Australia of a written Constitution dating from federation in 1901, a rigid instrument which the 'mother country', the UK, of course does not have.

Australia's Commonwealth Constitution, however, does not cover the area of civil and human rights in the way that the American one does. Chiefly, it outlines only broadly the system of national government and the relationship between the federal Commonwealth and the states. It does not even refer to the right to vote, nor to the exact structure of government and the cabinet. The Constitution is, however, supplemented by conventions which do spell out details and also control the theoretically extensive powers of the Governor-General.

Election Fever

For more on the history of democracy, see the story of the Eureka Stockade incident in 1854, *(see* Chapter 2: The Basics, *page 43)*. Adult white males were given the vote for the first time in 1856, in South Australia. Elections take place every three years. Many observers have pointed out that any Australian government's capacity to implement policy effectively is severely hampered by its need constantly to keep an eye on the popular vote. The vote is not conducted on the first-past-the-post but rather on the preferential voting principle. This gives minority parties a better chance of making an impact on politics. Proportional representation is also adopted in the Senate elections, and in some states

Government, Government and More Government

The seat of the Federal Government is at Canberra, in Australian Capital Territory (ACT), which was created in 1911 solely for the purpose of housing government and Parliament. Some have called Australia 'over-governed'. The total number of Federal, State and local public servants in 2005 stood at about 1.6 million, for a population of 20 million.

The System

Australians in the main are pretty happy with their system of government. When debates about whether or not to become a Republic raise their heads from time to time, a recurring theme is 'If it ain't broke, don't fix it!' So the Head of State still is Queen Elizabeth II of Great Britain, with Australia a valued member of the British Commonwealth, virtually Britain's reconstituted former Empire. The Queen's representative in the Australian Parliament is the Governor-General, appointed by the Queen in consultation with Australia's Prime Minister, and in theory he (there has not yet been a female Governor-General) can veto parliamentary legislation by not assenting to it. Famously, he once dismissed the Prime Minister and his Labor government (Gough Whitlam, in 1975). He can summon and dissolve Parliament, dismiss ministers, is commander-in-chief of the armed forces and may appoint judges. An Executive Council advises the Governor-General of major decisions made at Cabinet level. The federal Constitution agreed upon in 1901 can only be changed via a national referendum.

(Continued on the next page)

(Continued from previous page)

The Australian government structure is a blend of Britain's Westminster model with some elements of American forms. As in Britain, there are two houses of Parliament: the lower, the House of Representatives, and the upper, the Senate. The House of Representatives is elected at general elections every three years; the Senate acts as a house of review or checks and balances on the lower house (rather like Britain's House of Lords), with the power to reject or amend proposed legislation, and the majority of senators from the various states are elected for six-year terms. Each State Government replicates federal structure to a great extent, including each having their own Governor to represent the Queen. Local governments operate at Shire or City Council level.

Voting in Australia is compulsory, for those over 18, except for Aboriginals who may opt not to register on the electoral roll if they wish (but once they register, they must vote). One difference from the Westminster system is that voters must rank every candidate for a seat in their order of preference and if no candidate gets a majority vote, then the preference votes are distributed to reach a final 'verdict'. Australia was one of the world's first countries to grant suffrage to women, starting with South Australia in 1894, and extending to the whole nation in 1902.

THE FOURTH ESTATE

In any democracy, the media are important players, sometimes wild cards. The Australian press certainly ranks as wild, being one of the most aggressive in the world. And Australians are avid newspaper readers, as well as television watchers.

Unfortunately, their choice is somewhat restricted; there is not much light and shade, or depth, to the range of media available in Australia, partly because ownership is concentrated in a few hands—the principal owner is Richard Murdoch's The News Corporation (News Limited), and the other power in the land is the John Fairfax Holdings group, with Kerry Packer's Publishing and Broadcasting Limited (PBL) (owner of the Nine TV channel and the Australian Consolidated Press) certainly a player to be reckoned with. The country press is dominated by Rural Press Limited. The concentration of media ownership certainly runs counter to what should be found in a healthy democracy, although there are laws controlling cross-media ownership, in both television and in print media, for example. Unlimited foreign ownership has been allowed only since 1991, providing no more than 20 per cent of that foreign ownership brings with it voting rights on the board.

A rough count gives 12 national or state dailies, with a total circulation of 2.3 million, 35 regional dailies, 470 regional and suburban papers, and 1,500 magazines, 30 of them with circulations of over 80,000. The only true national paper is *The Australian* with its *Weekend Australian*, although the *Australian Financial Review* comes close.

The Bulletin, founded in 1880, is the national news weekly. Somewhat parochial at times, although it does incorporate the US magazine Newsweek, it is nonetheless a good barometer of Australian happenings and viewpoints.

Interestingly, according to the independent international media monitoring group 'Reporters Without Borders', in 2004 Australia ranked only 41st in their list of countries ranked according to press freedom, behind New Zealand (9th) and the United Kingdom (28th). This was largely because of the concentration of media ownership and also because Prime Minister John Howard had criticised reporters who questioned Australia's participation in the 2003 American invasion of Iraq.

The Small Screen and 'Wireless'

New laws now limit the extent to which media moguls can corner the broadcasting market; television owners, for example, may not have more than a 5 per cent interest in a daily English-language paper in the same capital city as their television station. Foreign ownership of broadcasting is prohibited. The Australian Broadcasting Authority (ABA) is the broadcasting regulator for radio and television in Australia.

There are 53 licensed commercial television services operating in Australia, including three national commercial television network, channels Seven, Nine and Ten. Indigenous commercial broadcaster Imparja broadcasts out of Alice Springs in the Northern Territory. There are also two public broadcasters—the publicly owned ad-free ABC (Australian Broadcasting Corporation) and SBS (Special Broadcasting Service, which takes advertising in a controlled manner, at the beginning and end of programmes for example), slated as a multicultural and multilingual broadcaster but with a much more attractive menu than this description might imply (among other oddities, its multiculturalism seems to have given rise to a regular diet of 'naughty' foreign movies). SBS does, however, broadcast in over 60 languages.

Satellite and cable pay television and digital television broadcasting are also available in Australia.

There are 272 commercial radio stations. A rough-diamond style of democracy flourishes on radio, with a proliferation of phone-in, 'talk-back' shows. But the most international mindset and highest intellectual quality is probably to be found in a combination of ABC and ABC Radio National, while SBS Radio broadcasts weekly in 68 language, more than any other radio network in the world.

In an unusual instance of media control, for Australia, the Australian Broadcasting Tribunal has since the 1970s stipulated a quota of home-made drama to be screened on commercial-licensee television. Hence the growth of Australian soap operas like the now world-famous *Neighbours*, saga of the suburbs. These local content restrictions have survived even the potentially threatening Free Trade Agreement with the USA concluded in 2004.

MIND MY SPACE

It is a delicate task to balance freedom against the risk of that very freedom's invading other people's personal space.

Freedom entails freedom of speech whether you like what the other fellow is saying or not. And democracy is supposed to mean you would die for his right to say it.

Democracy can be inconvenient. It means pressure groups, each lobbying the political process for their own self-interest—the wheat lobby, the wool lobby, the mining lobby, the environmentalist lobby, the feminist lobby, and so on. This tends to slow things down. Decisions take longer to implement. But it cuts both ways: it also means you get to have your say.

Freedom of the Personal Kind

Freedom may also mean that there is a bit more nudity and sex (both straight and gay) on television than you care for (try the notorious *Big Brother Uncut* on channel Ten, with amateur wannabes flaunting their all to the spy cameras in their 'reality TV' home), that someone has the right to open up a sex shop in your neighbourhood shopping centre, that the local pub has a lunchtime 'lingerie' strip show, and that scantily clad young people may be seen on the street kissing and holding hands.

The open display of the human body and relative sexual freedom of Western-style societies like Australia is a particular problem for visitors from Asia and other traditional societies or religions.

A quick scan of the 'Personal' classified advertisement columns in several Australian newspapers will soon reveal the scope of the services available. You can pay to do it in bubble baths, with girls in suspenders, in groups big or small, with or without rubber and leather, to suffer 'discipline', just to watch, or even just to talk about it on the phone. In such a society, the old excuse for not being able to come over—'I'm sorry, I'm tied up right now'—might be only too literally true.

And so onward through the classifieds: Under 'F', a 'French Maid, Ooh La La.' Under 'H,' a 'Hot Housewife' or a 'Hispanic'. Under 'G,' things become decidedly 'Gay'. 'Guy seeks Guy, Chinese or any nationality,' reads one ad. There's 'Lesbian Lucy' too, while one 'Lola' offers to 'dress and make up inquisitive males.' There is some elegant G-for-Gigolo begging under 'G' too: 'Gent, 23. Is there a lady out there who can financially assist one honest young man in dire straits? Genuine ad.'

By no means are all these ads placed by professionals; there are quite a few amateurs, part-timers, one-off thrill-seekers, and those just looking for love and marriage, truly.

Look the Other Way

If such things disturb you, it is important to maintain your sense of balance by understanding that most Australians go about their daily lives without a second look at this underworld. They ignore such things, treating them like the wallpaper of life, quite unshocked and often uninterested too. So just take no notice of it—walk on!

Australian attitudes to sex, violence and censorship are in any case ambivalent, reflecting the ongoing tug-of-war between the puritanism of the recent past and a more permissive present.

In general, the social premise is that non-violent erotica are a useful safety valve for normal human sexual emotions and fantasies. There is an elaborate system of film classification, to indicate films' content to the public: M or M(A) for Mature (15 and above), R for Restricted and PG for Parental Guidance, besides G for General and X for Adults-only. X-rated videos, for example, have been banned in most of Australia since 1984, except for the Australian Capital Territory (ACT), i.e. Canberra, and the Northern Territory. Western Australia too is beginning to relax on this one. As a result, the ACT, that sober seat of government, has long been Australia's chief supplier of blue movies through a multi-million dollar mail-order business, Canberra's fifth largest industry.

HOW THEY THINK OF THEMSELVES

There are internal stereotypes about what is 'typical' of a 'Sydneysider', a 'Melburnian', 'a Taswegian' (Tasmanian), or a 'Sandgroper' (Western Australian), for example. The stereotypes are:

- Sydney: go-for-it dynamic, smart and young, pushy, fast
- Melbourne: stuffy, business-minded and worldly-wise, cultured and a bit pompous in the English style
- Tasmania: slow backwoodsman, introverted and inbred

- Canberra/Australian Capital Territory: boring monochrome melange of civil service, journalists and politicians with access to some beautiful landscapes
- Brisbane/Queensland: even brasher than Sydney, bordering on vulgar, redneck and somewhat uncivilised but fun- and sun-loving
- Adelaide/South Australia: slow and quiet, rather English reserved, quite cultured
- Perth/Western Australia: isolated and behind the times, small town, conservative, laid-back and complacent, grown fat on mineral wealth
- Northern Territory: pioneering frontier 'outback' society, a bit rough and tough but interestingly offbeat.

As ever with all stereotypes, where there is smoke, there is a at least a little fire.

But overall, Australians do unite in a self-image that says Aussies are brave and tough, honest and without guile, anti-authoritarian and therefore democratic, egalitarian, loyal to their mates and willing to help others in crisis, keen on a 'fair go' or natural justice for all.

Your best bet when attempting to 'camouflage' yourself in Australia? Just be yourself—Australians hate play-acting, posing and insincerity.

JOINING THE CROWD

How difficult, or easy, do Australians make it for you to fit in with them? By and large, Australians on a face-to-face level are very accepting and will take you in as their 'mate' regardless of your ethnic origins, provided you can match a few of their most basic 'mateship' criteria. Among these criteria, paramount is your ability to speak English, even if you cannot actually produce 'Strine, the local patois. They may well prefer you if you enjoy an alcoholic beverage or two. They may prefer to avoid over-intellectual conversations and keep things light. Even better if you can discuss either cricket or 'footy' with some aplomb, but this is not essential.

Inviting them back to your home is appreciated. They will not be impressed with over-dressing, or showing off in any form at all, including spending lots of money, talking loudly and dominating the conversation. Criticisms of Australia, or negative comparisons with other nations, are completely taboo until you have been around a long, long time and hold an Aussie passport—but even then, think twice...

Differentiation may well appear not so much on the basis of ethnicity as on gender. You may have to sort out how you fit in Australian society in terms of your sex, and sexual orientation too. Australians still have quite a lot to sort out on this front. Family life, for instance, is very much in flux. Close to 10 per cent of Australian families, and rising, are headed by single parents. The number of divorces granted in 2003 was 22 per cent up on those granted 20 years earlier. Broken or single-parent families are no longer an 'alternative lifestyle'; they are becoming the norm. The agonies inflicted upon separating couples with children via the Family Court and the harsh impact of the controversial Child Support Agency structure on separated but still supporting fathers are a constant subject of national debate. Watching these traumatic personal dramas play out (everybody has a friend involved in one story or another) makes it easy to understand why many young Australians choose not to marry; but even unmarried de facto partners under the same roof for more than a year may be subjected to legal considerations close to those applied to full marriages. Working men with working or non-working wives or partners in particular need to understand that divorce or separation could lead to a 50:50 division of all their property, including their pension funds ('Super') and the family house, with ongoing close supervision and monitoring in terms of child support funding and child access or custody arrangements.

Men and Men, and Men and Women

If all you did was watch television in Australia, you might well come to the conclusion that the country was way ahead of the rest of the world in terms of men deferring to women, equality of rights, pay and opportunity for women, and the whole feminist caboodle. (On the other hand, you might watch *Big Brother*, the 'reality TV' show that beams the private doings of a bunch of artificially hot-housed 'house mates' right into your living room, and be appalled at the level of crudity and sexual harrassment that goes on among even modern young men and women).

Still, every other documentary on 'quality' free-to-air TV seems to be about something dreadful done to women and children by men—whether it be wife-battering, rape or incest. The concern demonstrated is so great, surely it must be practised in real daily life too?

Not necessarily. What you are really witnessing in the media is a sort of national self-flagellation in penance for the very real sins of the past and, it must be said, of the ongoing present. It is because things have been so bad that all the documentaries are necessary. In any case, it is by no means certain that the deep concern shown really extends very far outside of the sophisticated circle of television documentary producers and script-writers. Still, you should have heard the public outcry in 1994 when the somewhat bumbling now Foreign Minister Alexander Downer, then leader of the Liberal Party opposition, thought he would have some fun with a pun on the Liberal Party slogan 'Things That Matter' in an after-dinner speech, referring jocularly to wife-bashing husbands as 'Things That Batter.' Unsurprisingly, Downer lasted only nine months as Liberal leader.

But before we can understand how men relate with women in Australia, we must first understand how they relate with men.

Mateship and Machismo

So much has been written about this uniquely Australian phenomenon that it is difficult for me to know where to begin.

> 'My mate is always a man. A female may be my sheila, my bird, my charley, my good sort, my hot-drop, my judy or my wife, but she is never 'my mate'.'
> —Donald McLean,
> in *The Roaring Days*, 1960.

One of the first things the newcomer to Australia notices is that familiar, friendly form of address, for strangers and friends alike, 'Mate'. 'How are yer, mate?' or 'What can I do for yer, mate?'—these are all common currency. (Note that 'mate' is almost never used between men and women, or among women.)

This, however, is a mere casual greeting, albeit of symbolic significance. True mateship is an abstraction of almost mystical proportions. The term was first used by Australia's pioneer chronicler of the bush, Henry Lawson, who wrote his best material during the 1890s.

Mateship refers to that subtle brotherhood felt by men together, especially when they have had to work or fight together in harsh conditions or against great adversity. Rightly or wrongly, implicit in the concept is the idea that women can never share in this emotion (even if feminists would say that 'sisterhood' was the same thing for them). Indeed, traditionally, Australian discussions of manhood, manliness and mateship have made no reference at all to masculinity in relation to women. Women simply did not come into the picture.

The only problem with this concept in post-pioneer Australia is determining exactly what adversity it is that brings men together in mateship nowadays. One has a sneaking suspicion that 'the enemy' may in fact be women—especially wives—and the suburban stresses of home and family that they are seen to represent.

Mateship Uber Alles

Mateship in Australia—the friendship of men with men—can override all other moralities. For example, the man who would 'dob in' (inform on) his drug-dealer mate to the police, would probably be considered to have committed a greater offence than the drug-dealer himself. Like the 'old-boy' networks believed to dominate business life in England, mateship is a system that works quietly behind the scenes of both business and politics in Australia. At its worst, it can breed simple corruption—'helping out a mate'.

Mateship has its highs and its lows. At its lowest, it can descend to brute displays of masculinity akin to gorillas beating their chests. As social commentator Donald Horne has put it, in such cases, 'Men stand around bars asserting their masculinity with such intensity that you half expect them to unzip their flies.'

On the other hand, Horne also characterises mateship as a noble 'ideology of fraternalism' permeating the nation. It means that Australians believe most other people are good fellows like themselves, 'mates'. Optimists all, they believe in the essential humanity of mankind—*man*kind unfortunately being the operative word.

Last word to a woman, though: respected politician Dr Carmen Lawrence of Western Australia views mateship with benign contempt. She told journalists in 1990, "They're often extremely competitive and vicious, the so-called 'circles of mateship'. My observation is that many of the people who take part in these circles of mateship may in fact be grasping for comfort, in what would otherwise be a very hostile world. So I think we shouldn't take that away from them."

Men's Men

Hand in hand with mateship goes an almost unreasoning horror of homosexuals, tarred 'poofters' or 'queers' by macho Australia. There is a strong gay counter-culture, true, particularly in the great cities of the east, but mainstream 'matedom' vigorously avoids contact with it or, if forced into contact, bashes it, often literally. The suggestion that 'gays' of both sexes would address sex education classes in Western Australian schools in 2005 caused quite an uproar among parents.

A reading of Robert Hughes' account of the early Australian colony, The Fatal Shore, yields convincing evidence that it is precisely because homosexuality was violently and sordidly practised in convict society that Australian men have ever since expended great energy in erasing the memory of those terrifying times.

As a result, Aussie males fear seeming too emotional—too female. Among the many Australian men who have, however, bravely resisted this neurosis has been former Prime Minister Bob Hawke himself, who won a reputation for crying in public. While it is uncertain what this did to his male vote, it must certainly have endeared him to his female voters. Generally speaking, this phobia is breaking down more as young Australia becomes more accepting of the 'New Age Man' phenomenon. An American-style taste for public *schmaltz* is rapidly taking hold in Australia.

On the other hand, Hawke's public admission of marital infidelity must have redressed the balance since it would have endeared him to Australian men ('He's human, just like us'), who probably secretly admired him for it, while it may not have pleased too many women.

The Other Side of Sydney

Try, if you will, to square this softer side with the image of a macho hairy-hunky Australia: Sydney is one of the world's great gay capitals and the annual Sydney Gay and Lesbian Mardi Gras extravaganza, 27 years old in 2005, has become Australia's highest-earning festival and tourist attraction, spawning many other mini-Mardi Gras in other cities such as Perth. The 2005 parade in Sydney saw about thousands of participants and volunteer helpers, with about 450,000 spectators, on the streets with leather-clad 'Dykes on Bikes,' outrageous spangled queens, lesbian nuns and, well anything goes... The event has had some financial reverses of late but generated almost A$ 580-million after-tax profit in 2004 all the same.

On cooking, normally considered a woman's task in Australia, it is interesting to note how Australian men will take it on quite naturally when it comes to the great Australian barbecue party. There seems to be an unwritten law that it should be the husband who tends the sizzling meat—a kind of hunter-gatherer nostalgia referring to the caveman past?—while the wife may perhaps be pottering around with salads and the like.

Role-Swapping

A climate of economic decline coupled with unemployment has in a way benefited the man-woman relationship in Australia, with part-time work and even job-sharing an ever more possible option for couples. Hence, many more men are now staying at home to be 'house husbands'. Not all of them accept this situation with good grace, however; there is still some stigma attached.

Sheilas

The scenes you have probably heard tell of, the parties where the men congregate on one side of the room or garden to discuss 'footy', the women on the other to discuss cooking, babies, or just possibly nowadays, feminist issues—they do still happen.

There is not much you can do about this, as a woman. You might very well find the women's conversations more interesting anyway. If you do decide to ignore the invisible line dividing the sexes and stick with the men, better be sure you can talk about what they want to talk about, and that might mean 'footy', cricket, politics or sex. Australian men still are not entirely comfortable with women.

The Subservient Asian Female?

It seems best as a woman in Australia wanting to get on with the men to play oneself down a bit. Take note of the thriving Filipina 'mail-order bride' industry in Australia; there must be some reason the Australian male feels safer with what he believes (often wrongly) to be the more subservient, sweeter Asian female.

If you are a man trying to be a hit with Australian females, things look a lot easier for you. You need only display some of the common 'European' courtesies—offering to help carry shopping bags, opening doors, presenting flowers, etc.—and you will be viewed as totally adorable.

Convict Chattels

Another observer of the Australian female condition, Anne Summers, argued in her outstanding account of Australian myths about women, *Damned Whores and God's Police*, that the colonial experience had produced two Australian stereotypes of women—either as whores imported to service men's sexual needs, or as defenders of public morality, 'God's police'.

It seems certain that whether they were whores or not in their original state, many of the 24,000 women transported to Australia as convicts between 1788 and 1852 were indeed forced to resort to the profession, and if they did not, were raped repeatedly by male convicts anyway. Theirs, together with that of Aboriginal women, was a particularly brutalising experience.

Women convicts were exploited, beaten, enslaved and passed around or sold as mere chattels or objects of convenience. Yet for the most part, their crimes 'back home' had been little more than the pettiest of theft. Thus began the relationship of the sexes in Australia. Some say that this beginning has coloured the quality of the relationship ever since. Suffice it to say that close to a quarter of Australian women currently or previously married or in a de facto relationship have experienced physical and/or sexual violence by their partner

Puritanism vs Paganism

Curiously, as with the homosexual past for men, this early trauma for a while produced a diametrically opposite reaction: a strong tradition of puritanism took root in Australia.

For long, the place of women was at home with the children, sex was a taboo subject and censorship of the arts was the norm in almost every state—such attitudes linger outside the main cities and in some states more than others, Western Australia, for example. Sex education did not reach state schools until the 1970s and still has not reached all schools.

The superficially permissive and sometimes outright pagan society that Australia seems to present to the visiting outsider is, in fact, constantly at loggerheads with this older tradition of puritanism, just as it is in a similarly pioneer society, that of the USA.

The austere moral values of the Roman Catholic Church which held sway over the descendants of the many original Irish-born convicts, as well as other Christian groups, have for long held sway in 'middle-Australia'. In fact, until very recently, as Donald Horne has pointed out, the average Australian lifestyle was downright killjoy: bars closed at six, liquor was not served with meals, Sundays were dead, betting was illegal, books were banned, and so on.

Fair Go for Women

There are exceptions to the generally strained atmosphere between Australian men and women, particularly in the larger cities. And there is slow and steady change. Certainly, in all the official and legalistic things that matter, Australia's treatment of women now is more than proper.

The Sex Discrimination Act of 1984 makes sex discrimination against the law, giving effect to Australia's obligations under the Convention on the Elimination of All Forms of Discrimination Against Women, and parts of International Labour Organisation Convention 156. And absolutely everybody is very 'full on' with their endorsements of the need to 'empower' women (which, in a way, is a bit of a put-down since it implies that they are not already empowered).

This must be one of the very few countries in the world to have a federal post titled 'Sex Discrimination Commissioner'—currently held by a woman, as it so happens, but presumably it would be discriminatory to reserve the job for women.

Australian women have had the right to vote since the turn of the 19th century, earlier than in England, and the first female politician, Edith Cowan (after whom a new Western

Australian university has recently been named), was elected in Western Australia in 1921.

Equal Pay for Work of Equal Value
Ironically, it was male trade unionists' fear of cheap female labour that triggered agitation for equal pay during World War II. The equal-pay principle, 'for work of equal value', was confirmed in 1972 but still has not covered the entire female workforce—in fact, on average, women only earn about two-thirds of a male salary for their full-time work.

The 1970s saw many other reforms, such as the introduction of equal-opportunity legislation—classified ads in the media today often carry the banner 'We are an equal-opportunity employer' to underline the point—and a women's minimum wage, in 1974. It was in the decade of the 1970s, of course, that Australian feminism swept the world via Australian author Germaine Greer's controversial book *The Female Eunuch*, published in 1971.

Since the 1980s, there has been a boom in feminist discussions, fuelled by the mushrooming of women's studies courses in universities, colleges and even schools, as well as every conceivable feminist art form from women's cinema to women's theatre. Australia is certainly making up for lost time.

Obstacles, Real and Imagined
But many of the protection measures benevolently put in place by the early unionists now precisely stand in women's way: restrictions on what weights women may carry, for example, excluding them from many traditionally male occupations.

Increasingly, of course, automation is making such restrictions redundant anyway. But there are still many spheres of professional work also unbreached by women; the first woman judge was not appointed until the mid-1960s, for example.

Marriage and child-rearing have, until very recently, routinely meant the end of working life for most Australian women. As late as 1970, women were forced to resign from university service on marriage, and the public service limited the range of jobs they could hold. Things are still made difficult for married women teachers. Married women workers often turn out to be immigrants: about a quarter of the female workforce consists of migrant women, who feel a greater need to get ahead and make money.

As with the Aboriginals, it is not the legal structures that cause problems for female emancipation. Quite the contrary. It is the underlying social climate.

There are still many effectively Men-Only pubs or bars. There may not be any signs saying 'Women, Keep Out'. They wouldn't be necessary anyway. You have only to step inside as a woman to 'feel' the invisible signs. Few women are interested in even trying to stick around.

Australian women apparently are often willing participants in this atmosphere. A cursory perusal of publications like the one most read in Australia (one million copies), the almost 60-year-old *Australian Women's Weekly* magazine (which is a monthly), reveals a predictable diet of English royals, how-to-handle-your-husband/de facto/boyfriend, and pudding recipes, etc, although nowadays these are likely to be spliced with slightly more thoughtful topics such as 'How I Survived the Tsunami in Phuket' or 'Drugs and Your Child'. The trivial, sexsationalist, celebophiliac and British Royal Family-adoring tone of some national women's magazines is not unique in the Western world, however; besides the *Women's Weekly* (circulation over one million) and *Women's Day* (also over one million), take a look at *New Idea* (700,000) to see what I mean.

For a really blistering look at Aussie women in middle-class suburbia, follow the fortunes of *Kath and Kim*, an ABC TV 'soap' cum social commentary that mercilessly satirises the banal foibles of a materialistic, hedonistic, querulous mother-daughter duo, with wonderful comic side-dishes in the form of their husbands and best friends. It doesn't grab you straight away, has the same sort of subtlety of the British series *The Office*, so keep watching and let it grow on you; it's even worth buying the video set to catch up on past episodes. And the occasional portrayal of two snooty upmarket department store assistants, who are widely agreed to resemble a breed of woman working in the iconic Myers store, is pure genius.

Hair Talk

An interesting variation on this theme is the Great Australian Coiffure. For example, the average Australian woman-in-the-street has a predictably non-tall poppy hairstyle; usually middle-length and very tousled, the never-been-combed sheepdog look.

What this fairly typical Australian woman seems to be saying is, 'I'm feminine' (My hair's longish and kind of curly-cute, isn't it?), but 'I'm not hard or cold' (Well, look how disorganised my hair is!) and 'I'm not a threat to you' (I can't be too much of a sex-siren or my hair would be longer, wouldn't it?). So, if you are a woman set on touching an Australian man's heart, it might be wise to look a little daffy and tousled. Excessive chic seems to be a turn-off, or at least may never get you beyond the professional colleague stage.

As a man, be warned that although the base of Australian society appears to be sexist in nature, any overt expression of sexism, particularly in conversation, is now a no-no in polite society, if women are present. If they are not, probably anything goes. Neutral words like 'fore-person' (for 'foreman') are commonplace. And interestingly, note that in some circumstances, opening doors for and offering seats to women appears to have been classified by some feminists as itself a form of sexism.

Role Models

The unease Australian women sense when struggling to achieve their place in the sun is strange when you consider the number of strong female models already enshrined in Australian history, besides many new ones making their mark right now. The single most powerful model of course was the pioneer woman, who shared with her man the unthinkable deprivations of life in the bush during the 19th century and early 20th century. Only recently have several studies concentrated on her story.

Women shine in many areas of Australian life, perhaps none more than in the arts and culture. But they are noticeably thin on the ground at the higher levels of corporate business, and in politics they seem to have an unhappy bent for self-destructing. There was for instance, the former state premier of Western Australia and former Federal Minister of Health, Labor politician Dr Carmen Lawrence, who got involved in a nasty political honesty issue in WA from which she never really recovered, otherwise she had been touted as a possible Prime Minister; and then there was Cheryl Kernot, former leader of the Democrats party, who changed sides in 1997 to join the Australian Labor Party, with the possibility of the deputy premiership one day, but lost her seat in the 2001 election after a poor performance and a general demonstrable lack of fibre; and there was Senator Natasha Stott Despoja (pronounced 'Despoya'), also leader of the Democrats for just over a year 2001–2002, in 1995 the youngest woman ever elected to the Australian parliament (at 26 years old), who could not bring her party behind her own relatively left-wing policies. More robust perhaps have been characters like the former premier of Victoria, Joan Kirner (now retired from Parliamentary politics) the first woman to hold this premiership, in 1990, and the redoubtable (physically and intellectually) Amanda Vanstone, Minister for Immigration, Multicultural and Indigenous Affairs (a very 'hot' seat) from 2003.

Women have also excelled in the spheres of life most dear to Australian men: sport and the outdoors. They include Kay

A Pioneer in Her Time

Australian women have had more than their pioneer forebears for role models. There have been extraordinary women like Dame Roma Mitchell (1913–2000), for example, the former Governor of South Australia. She was thus the first woman to represent the Queen of England/Australia in this post, in Australia's 203 years of European settlement. Her 'firsts' were legion: in 1962, she was made Australia's first woman Queen's Counsel. Three years later, she became Australia's first woman Supreme Court judge, after which she was appointed the first female Acting Chief Justice.

Cottee who in 1987 sailed solo round the world in 189 days, the first woman to do so and of course the Aboriginal gold-medallist runner at the Sydney Olympics in 2000, Kathy Freeman.

Another remarkable tale is told by Robyn Davidson in her book *Tracks* (1995), recounting her harrowing solo camel journey across 2,700 km (1,700 miles) of desert and scrub between Alice Springs and the Indian Ocean. Treks like Robyn Davidson's are probably just what it takes for women really to touch Australian men. Such experiences almost confer on them the status of honorary mates.

FREEDOM AND DEMOCRACY

You won't fit in well unless you have a strong belief in democracy and a healthy cynicism about authority and government.

Australia's hunger for freedom is hardly surprising in a nation that began its life in chains.

I am referring to white Australia here. Aboriginal Australians have their own special need for, and definition of, freedom. Their definition is perhaps a more wide-ranging one too, since traditionally, even four walls and material possessions are a sort of prison for them. But the whites owe more of their psyche to Aboriginal beliefs than they realise. In a kind of osmosis between the races, the white Australian has imbibed some of the Aboriginal lust for freedom in the open under the stars.

Between 1788 and 1868, more than 160,000 white men, women and children declared criminals were transported as convicts from England to Australia, then a destination as remote, alien and terrifying as the moon today. No other nation in the world has ever been founded on such an experience.

These were the first white Australians. The bestiality of their lives in their new home is hard to describe and even harder to contemplate. I recommend a careful reading of Robert Hughes' epic account, *The Fatal Shore*. Still, it can be said that the convicts' ejection was in many ways preferable to a term rotting in an English jail. Again, Hughes' book gives a graphic account of exactly how horrible this would have been.

Despite the hardships of their initial landfall, many of the first Australians won their freedom within a short time and set out to make new lives in a new land. The Commander of the First Fleet in 1788, Captain Arthur Phillip, wanted Australia to be a free settlement and tried hard to release convicts onto the land, striving in many ways to relieve the convicts' misery.

But ever since 1788, Australians have consciously or subconsciously been concerned to remove from their lives what Hughes has called 'The Stain' of their convict past, studiously donning a camouflage of almost stultifying respectability for a while. Even in the 19th century, it was ill-mannered to use the term 'convict' in Australia; the euphemism 'government man' was preferred. This has changed in recent years to a sort of inverse snobbery where it is considered a proud pedigree to be able to trace one's genealogy to a convict ancestor.

It is in this convict context, however, that one can begin to understand why any imposition of authority, any infringement of personal liberty, no matter how seemingly petty, will arouse Australian passions to a fever pitch.

Don't Classify Me

Thus, it is almost impossible to determine with any certitude any Australian's true identity, so opposed is he to being a digit imprisoned in a computer data-bank, to being categorised in any way.

Until very recently, Australia was one of the very few countries in the world where you could stride into a bank and open up an account in the name of Mickey Mouse or Tom Jones without raising an eyebrow. Nobody checked. However, in the security-conscious 21st century, even Australian banks are getting a little more street-wise and beginning to ask for proof of identity. Nonetheless, this tendency to take you at your word, bordering on naivety at times, does linger on in the everyday social and business life of Australia. It is a direct consequence of every man's respect for the privacy of every other man.

The government strove in vain during the 1980s to introduce the 'Australia Card', an identity card for every Australian, in the hope of controlling social welfare and tax abuses. But the average Australian saw this as the thinly disguised return of the convict's number tag, a sinister infringement of his freedom. No freedom is more treasured in Australia than the right to anonymity. The outcry against the Australia Card was so loud that the government had to abandon its plan (but sneaked it in again by the back door with a compulsory Tax File Number system for all income-earners). Nowadays, the driving licence with a photo of the owner just about doubles for the dreaded identity card that Australians still fondly imagine they have escaped.

Another form of intrusion on privacy and freedom is the act of asking too many questions. In your efforts to get to know Australians, do not come on too inquisitive—What do you do? Are you married? How many children do you have? Where do you live? etc. are all considered normal questions in many other societies, but not in Australia. Excessive curiosity—'sticky-beaking'—especially at your first meeting, can make the Australian uncomfortable, and may cause him to retreat into a gruffly suspicious shell. Cool it.

Doing Your Own Thing

Freedom can be a lonely privilege. People who are used to more regimented, sheltered lifestyles, where relatives, governments, civic groups, neighbourhood groups, religious groups or whatever all combine to tell you what to do, when and how, often find that they miss this framework in urban Australia. (In the countryside, however, communities are still more intimately meshed.) Such newcomers find the sudden anonymity disorienting. Asians used to paternalistic governments and warmly interactive extended families particularly suffer from this syndrome.

In Australia, people largely leave you alone to get on with your own life, in whatever way you want to lead it. They do not interfere with you, which is pleasant; by the same token, this means you are on your own, mate. All too easily, by extension, it may seem they don't care about you. Yet on the other hand, any direct plea for help, or a greeting in the street, will always be met with a warm response.

Clearly, there are pros and cons to both ways of living. In any case, you can find support groups aplenty in Australia if you need them. Only in Australia, you have to make the effort to get in contact with them, not wait for them to arrive on your doorstep. Frequently in Australia, if you don't ask, you don't get. You are expected to stand on your own feet and fight for your rights, which fortunately, do exist.

Benign Neglect?

The area where the 'leave things alone' philosophy shows up clearest is in family life and child-rearing. Young Australians are noticeably freer and less disciplined than many other youngsters, offensively so in the eyes of Europeans and Asians particularly.

Here again, the Australian dislike for authority surfaces: parents stand for authority. Former Labor Prime Minister Bob Hawke's biographer, Blanche d'Alpuget, records that Hawke's own family was raised very much in this mould: 'Adult visitors were often shocked by the liberties in speech allowed to the children,' she says. 'Hawke was the obverse of an authoritarian father.'

Liberal parenting, and teaching styles at school too, do produce lively, creative and independent-minded—and opinionated—young people. An Asian migrant friend of mine used to a more dictatorial style of education said that for the first time he could remember, his children considered it a punishment if they were kept away from school, they enjoyed it so much in Australia.

But there are also scary incidents of major vandalism by schoolchildren, displaying that opposition to authority so typical of Australia. In one case in Western Australia, some teenage students simply went to their school at night and set fire to it. There are many other such stories. Dislocation of the family in post-industrial society is hardly a problem unique to Australia. In addition, economic hard times and the growth in single-parent families have made it genuinely difficult for Australian parents to supervise children properly.

Unemployment has exacerbated the potential for the animal energies of young people to spill over into violence. All too often, children are on the streets with nothing to do. Theirs is not a desirable freedom.

At the worst end of this scenario are children actually living in poverty, although obviously definitions of 'poverty' can be both subjective and relative. A United Nations report found in 2005 that one in seven (almost 15 per cent) Australian children lives in poverty, equated as living in a family that earns less than A$ 26,000 a year. This made Australia the ninth worst nation for this statistic, although Australia is also among only four countries (USA, Britain and Norway are the others) to have seen a reduction in child poverty between 1990 and 2005 (1.7 per cent). In 1990, the then Prime Minister Bob Hawke, Labor, famously declared that by 1990 no Australian child would be living in poverty. The Australian Human Rights and Equal Opportunity Commission says that about 25,000 Australian children are also homeless today.

An equally worrying feature of youth culture in Australia that may possibly just be a reflection of trends throughout the Western world in the 21st century is an observable lack of sense of purpose or ambition. In an easy-come easy-go atmosphere where you can always take up university studies as a mature student (although that is psychologically harder to achieve than many realise), or just go to 'Tafe' (Technical and Further Education College, tailored both for vocational training and adult education, sometimes a stepping stone to university), in an environment where nobody seems to respect or put much premium on academic excellence anyway, and anyway, it's so hard to get a job, and besides, you'd rather work and get some money than waste time on studies, an alarming number of young people get into university but then proceed to drift, somewhere around the end of their first year. Often, they will take the next year off to work in some quite ordinary waged job, with the declared intention of returning to 'uni' but in reality, many never return, thus wasting their own, and their parents' time and money. Alternatively, they start to wander through an emporium of courses, picking and choosing, chopping and changing both major and minor subjects ('No, don't like law, too hard, think I'll try engineering instead'), desperately seeking what really suits them, but never quite settling, frequently not finishing their degrees as a result.

It's not as easy as it once was for youthful 'bludgers' to live off unemployment welfare, but it is all too easy for them to drop out into the twilight world of a substantial shifting workforce in underpaid temporary, casual, part-time or short-contract jobs.

If this happens to your children in Australia, as well it might under the general peer pressure of it looking like the norm, comfort yourself that you are not alone, and also be aware that an interesting minority of young workers is simply 'working to live' in jobs they do not like, while living their 'real' lives out of office hours—frequently, these are the artistic lives of dancers, writers and musicians. In few countries is it more true to say that a person is not defined by their work or job than in Australia.

No Leaders Please, We're Australian

Crucial to the Australian concept of freedom, of course, is democracy. In its simplest form, this is seen as meaning 'Nobody is my boss.' Egalitarianism is another important pillar of the concept. Australians perversely enjoy cutting their leaders down to size to uphold this principle. Typical of the social atmosphere was the incident in 1991 when the then Prime Minister Bob Hawke was shown on television being interviewed in the back of his limousine. Unfortunately, he had neglected to strap up his seat-belt during the interview.

This point was certainly not lost on, nor tolerated by, the viewers, who promptly jammed the television channel switchboard with more than 1,000 complaints—why should

Hawke consider himself above the common man when it came to the seat-belt law? (Australia was the first country in the world to make car seat-belts compulsory, in 1971.) Hawke's reaction was wise, and the only one possible in a robust democracy like Australia's: he said he was very sorry and asked the police to treat him like any other citizen. He was duly fined A$ 100 for his lapse.

In some societies, such public criticism would be unthinkable. But Australians were quite happy to put the matter out of their minds once justice had been done, the leader levelled. Besides, they prefer their leaders to be that way: ordinary men, capable of peccadillos. As Donald Horne has said, 'Australians do not crave great men.' Great men are 'tall poppy' material, asking to be scythed down.

Contempt for politicians and political processes is a reflex emotion for most Australians. In the average Australian's mind that politicians are just ordinary blokes like himself who have been 'put up there' with the sole purpose of 'delivering the goods' and serving the people. If at any time they should cease to deliver, begin to behave like masters or, heaven forbid, leaders, they should be summarily removed by the people who put them there. The scandals of corruption in Queensland and of economic mismanagement and influence-peddling in Western Australia in recent times have served only to sharpen such attitudes.

The level of rudeness about, and to, politicians on television and in the media, for example, shocks most non-Australians, even the English and the Americans. 'It's a bit like watching soft porn,' said one migrant fresh from respectful Asia.

Fundamentally, it is a healthy attitude. Taken to extremes, it can make government close to impossible at times.

Teamwork is Australian

Here, pause a while to consider a paradox: the Australian soldier has long been saluted as an excellent fighting man. But isn't good soldiering founded on rigid discipline, hard training, hierarchy and unquestioning submission to officers' instructions? How then does the Australian soldier do it if the Australian character is inherently so rebellious?

The answer is of course that an Australian may be difficult to govern, but he responds better than most to those whom he admires and loves, and who stand beside him, rather than lead from the front. He is a team-worker. 'Mateship' reinforces this.

This principle could be extended to other spheres of life, in work and play. So do not too hastily write off Australian rebelliousness as being destructive to getting things done, nor as anathema to the collective good.

Another Way of Getting Things Done

The Australian way of doing things is eccentric and lateral rather than direct, apparently indisciplined, yet both creative and effective. And most important, humane. It is a way that works especially well for artistic endeavours and in the more arcane reaches of science—such as quantum or chaos theory and computer software-generation—which today are by definition anarchistic, as many Aussies are.

Get in Line

Another example of the general philosophy, 'I'm as good as the next man', is the Australian taxi-driver's preference for his passenger to sit in the front seat beside him: he is nobody's chauffeur. This is good behaviour to adopt when in Australia, particularly if you are male. It is not so expected of women passengers.

You should always take your place in the queue, real or metaphorical, no matter who you are. Beggar or king, you wait your turn in Australia. There should be no privilege, no string-pulling to get ahead of your neighbour.

Well, that is the official Australian ethos, anyway. When practised, it is admirable. But it should be noted that in reality, there is quite a bit of influence-peddling going on behind the scenes, harmless 'mateship' though it may seem to its practitioners.

Yet another facet of this stance is the Australian's almost automatic sympathy for the underdog, 'the battler'. Similarly, we have already discussed in other chapters his ability to elevate failure into victory. These attitudes are the natural corollary of the anti-tall poppy syndrome.

You Pays Your Money and You Takes Your Choice

Freedom is a highly valued and generally very available commodity in Australia. The individual is expected to use maturity and judgement when shopping in this supermarket of choice. It's all up to you.

SOCIAL DO'S AND DON'TS

Fitting in includes understanding all those subtle social signals that remain secret and hidden within every culture until someone alerts you to them.

You will find the usual social rituals a bit more diverse in a multicultural society like Australia's than maybe they were at home. A wedding for example, could be the traditional white affair in church, but equally might be a much more free-form affair, say, in a park or on a boat, with a registered civil 'celebrant' not a priest to solemnise the marriage, maybe fancy dress and a wild rock band or whatever. It might even be a gay 'commitment ceremony' in the absence of legal marriage for same-sex couples. Try never to look surprised.

As I have said elsewhere, keep the conversation light and human at first, until you know people really well. Try not to ask them what they do for a job, certainly not what they earn, or what car they drive, or how much their house cost. Ask rather what they thought of the cricket score the other day, or even talk about the weather, a time-honoured stratagem borrowed from 'the Poms'.

Avoid temperature-raising topics like immigration, Iraq, September 11 or the Aboriginals. Do comment on their handsome home renovations and ask them how they did it. And their children, how are their schooling/uni studies/first job going?—that's a safe topic the world over.

Deciding what to wear can be a bit of a challenge. Most Australians are religiously casual about their clothes for most events, avoiding anything more formal than a pair of shorts, but for a big dinner in a hotel, or a special dance, they will suddenly turn out in full 'tux' and ball gowns and stun you with their style. If in doubt, better ask in advance. For weddings and funerals, you can be sure there will be lots of hats and formal suits.

Don't be surprised by the many different ways that Australians may live their lives. Most Aussies don't even use the term 'alternative lifestyles' any more (very 1960s!) because these lifestyles have become so integrated with, and accepted by, a largely tolerant mainstream. So gay couples, single parents, lesbian parents (two 'mums'), organic farming communes... all these cause not even a lift of the eyebrow in Australia. Be ready for your sons and daughters to join in.

Tip and Taboos

Don't

- arrive late for dinner—while in some cultures (e.g. Mediterranean, Asian), it is more polite not to be too punctual, in western societies like Australia, it is not.
- overstay your welcome at a party, by hanging around too late (after midnight), especially not if it's a weekday night.
- bring someone extra along for a sit-down dinner without consulting the hostess in advance—numbers and seating matter at western-style dinners, although for summer-weather barbecues and pool parties in the garden, there may not be such a problem.
- bring your children with you for a sit-down dinner, at least not without consulting the hostess in advance; the western style is not to have children around at formal dinners, or at best, to ensure they are 'seen and not heard'.
- smoke in someone's home—go outside in the backyard to indulge this sin; you'll find everyone else there, doing the same thing.

Some may grumble and mumble about the 'irresponsibility' of such experimental family set-ups, but in essence, they will back off eventually, because everyone in Australia subscribes to a fundamental understanding that tolerance and non-discrimination are important if not crucial social virtues, besides being supported by a strong legal framework. It's very common to find that the organised secretary in your office is also a devotee of strange sequinned costumes and member of a drum-bashing samba group by night, while the clever young civil servant over there enjoys a nocturnal life as a febrile African-style dancer (both true-life examples, believe me). Never ever judge an Australian book by its cover.

- arrive empty-handed for a dinner party or barbecue—the customary thing to bring is a bottle or cask of wine (not expensive in Australia), or a six-pack of beer, but sometimes an extra dessert or other food offering will do just as well.
- bring expensive looking gifts for the host and hostess entertaining you at home; just something simple, whether it be flowers, wine or chocolates, will do—too much show may make them feel uncomfortable.

Do
- ask your hostess what she is cooking and whether you can 'bring anything'; though she may not have asked in the beginning, you will probably find she leaps at the opportunity to ask you to bring a dessert or a salad to complement her meal.
- help to clear the dirty dishes back to the kitchen at the end of a dinner party, and if there is no dish-washing machine in the house, offer to help wash up (because there will almost certainly be no maids around, barring the hostess); don't ever sit back waiting for them to be cleared—get up!

SETTLING IN

'The lazy country will be the lovely country, the white society will be the honey-coloured society, and the ugly duckling will become a honey-coloured swan.'
—Dr Stephen Fitzgerald, Australia's first ambassador to China, as head of the University of New South Wales Asia Centre, in *The West Australian*, 24 November 1990.

BEING A MIGRANT

This chapter is not a detailed guide to the labyrinth of getting permission to migrate to Australia. It just gives a snapshot of what it is like to be a migrant, and what migration has meant to Australia.

Even if I wanted to give you a detailed 'how to do it' guide, I doubt I could. For a start, the rules of the immigration game change fairly often—signposts to change usually are imminent federal elections and economic upheaval, as well as international terrorist incidents. A perception that multiculturalism may be failing in other countries (as per the terrorist bombing of London's train stations in 2005) has put the government under some pressure to restrict immigration; however, the evidence is that to a large extent, Australia has successfully absorbed its migrant influx with far less accompanying social tension than many countries in Europe and in reality, the economic push factor impels Australia to continue its migration programme—some six million people have migrated to Australia since 1945.

The DIMIA

You can keep up with the policy changes by checking regularly with the government's Department of Immigration and Multicultural and Indigenous Affairs (DIMIA) website:

http://www.immi.gov.au

> ### Booklets from the DIMIA
> There are a host of useful booklets at DIMIA that you can get by contacting them:
>
> PO Box 25, Belconnen, ACT 2616, Australia
>
> Tel: (02) 6264-1111; fax: (02) 6264-4466
>
> Email: dima.businesscentre.act@immi.gov.au

In recent recessions, it was often said that it was useless to import more people if you couldn't give them jobs. There does seem to be some sense in this argument at first glance. Another school of thought however points out that first, migrants and larger populations in themselves generate new economic activity as well as economies of scale, and second, that Australia particularly needs migrants with young children to strengthen the tax-paying workforce that must eventually support the large ageing 'baby-boomer' generation of the 1940s now entering old age and therefore possible welfare dependency.

At one point in the late 1990s, the immigration levels crashed to about 80,000 a year, compared with the peak of 172,000 newcomers in 1988, despite no end to the lengthening queues at many Australian High Commissions and embassies worldwide. Yet ironically, in 2005, a desperate shortage of skilled workers and tradesmen emerged in Australia and the government announced a drive to import an additional 20,000 of such people. In the same year, the Commissioner of Police in Western Australia also announced that he was obliged to look for new police recruits in locations like Ireland owing to shortages at home.

The truth is, Australia is in some senses under-populated relative to its physical size (though environmentalists will lecture you about real 'carrying capacity', i.e. the population that the land and its natural resources can actually tolerate) and needs more people to build its economy up. Hence, the migration programme for 2004–2005 had 120,000 places available for migrants, with a strong focus on attracting skilled people and people who agree to live in the more remote, rural or regional areas of Australia rather than the usual big cities like Sydney, Melbourne, Brisbane and Perth. Of this 120,000 total, about 70 per cent is now within the 'skilled' category, with the majority of these skilled migrants currently sourcing from Britain (21 per cent), India (13 per cent), China (12 per cent), South Africa (8 per cent) and Malaysia (5 per cent). The new skills now sought in addition to the traditional need for medical specialists, metal workers, mechanics, welders, fitters and toolmakers, include bricklayers, plumbers, carpenters, civil engineers, dentists, podiatrists, speech pathologists and electricians.

Add to this mainstream migration programme the 2004–2005 humanitarian programme offering 13,000 places to refugees, both of the legal humanitarian sort and the illegal-entry 'boat-person' sort (the latter usually being on a 'Temporary Protection Visa').

In summary, you can enter Australia on a business visa of some sort (there are several sub-categories), as a skilled person, as a sponsored family member, as someone's spouse, de facto partner or fiance, or as a refugee.

The grey category of another 150,000 'temporary business visas' (see discussions below) hides a large additional migration cohort, since a proportion of these visas does convert to permanent residence visas eventually.

And of course, there is the Overseas Student Programme for those visiting Australia only as students—currently hosting a total of about 250,000 students from 195 countries. For more information on this, go to:

www.studyinaustralia.gov.au

The Shifting Sands of Immigration Policy

As an example of the rapid shifts in policy, when I was applying to migrate, in the mid-1980s, it was possible to become a Business Migrant and virtually buy your way into Australia providing you could prove you had A$ 500,000 capital to invest, a business to run and enough funds to keep yourself and your family for a set period of time. (I hasten to add that this did not apply to me.) Some 9,000 business migrants were admitted to Australia on this basis between 1983 and 1991, bringing in A$ 1.5 billion.

It was also possible to bring in your aged parents once you yourself had settled in Australia for a while, on the grounds of 'family reunion'.

By 1991, these programmes in essence had disappeared, or severely mutated, largely because of migrants' abuse of the system. The Business Migrant programme was revamped because cunning would-be migrants, many of them Asian, were simply recycling lumps of money from one applicant to the next, and then failing to run a business in Australia. Now business skills and capital are checked carefully. In 1996 alone, business migrants brought in about A$ 850 million.

Many hopefuls come in on what has previously been known as a temporary residence visa ('TR') granted to those who can invest a certain amount of capital in a business and then demonstrate, over about three to four years, their ability to maintain a certain turnover and to employ a certain number of Australians. This programme has been renamed the Business Skills (Provisional) visa since 2003, offering a four-year temporary visa, during which holders can convert to a Business Skills (Residence) or permanent residence visa if and when they demonstrate the success of their business. They are then eligible within two years to convert this to full citizenship if they wish.

But beware of taking the provision visa option on when you do not have real past business experience, or without doing your homework about the very different business climate in Australia. Failures under this system are commonplace and if you are not careful you may find yourself summarily shipped back home hundreds of thousands of dollars later. This is even more tragic if you have burned your boats back home, for instance by giving up a good job and selling your home, and by transferring your whole family, especially schooling children, into the Australian environment. The 'TR' or provisional visa option requires enormous dedication and hard work to turn it into a success.

At the time of writing, the rule on importing aged parents is that the parent in question must be single, divorced or widowed, over 65 years old (for women there is some margin at the moment for this to be 62 years old) and be proven completely dependent on you, with no other source of support anywhere. The same goes for other forms of family reunion: the relative coming in must be a brother/sister or child and proven to be left completely alone overseas if not allowed to migrate to be with you.

As for the old migration-for-marriage scheme, naturally that led to so many marriage-of-convenience scams, with Australian girls often being paid handsomely to go through mock marriages with foreigners, that it had to be curbed. While the programme still exists, the sad result of past abuse is that genuine lovers now have to go through a lot more hoops to prove that their marriage to an Australian is bona fide before they can get residence in Australia. It can take a year or more to bring a fiance or de facto in; the system applies to gay de factos too, by the way. And couples will often be monitored quite closely once they are together in Australia, to check that they are indeed a couple.

How Much a New Country Costs

Don't forget that the migration process costs money, quite a lot in fact. Just taking a typical general skilled migrant's case, he/she will need to fork out, at least (Australian dollars):

- Almost A$ 2,000 for the application process
- If judged necessary, A$ 150–400 for an English language test
- A further approximately A$ 2,600 if it is judged he/she needs further English tuition
- About A$ 300 per head in the family for a pre-migration medical test
- The charge for a local police clearance certificate (proving you don't have a criminal record) or just A$ 36 if the applicant is already inside Australia
- Legal costs for legal certification of documents
- Translation costs for any non-English-language documents needed
- Actual moving costs such as airfares, freighting of possessions etc.

Taking the Passport

There is less flexibility in the migration system these days—once upon a time, a smile and a nod could well win the day. But these days, mostly, the rules are the rules.

At the time of writing, that if you want to apply for Australian citizenship, you must spend 24 months in Australia as a permanent resident, not necessarily consecutively, within the the past five years. This time must include a total of 12 months (but not necessarily continuous) in the two years immediately before you make your citizenship application.

You don't automatically lose your original citizenship and passport, so far as the Australians are concerned, when you take up Australian nationality; that will depend on the policies of your original country, not on Australia. You should note however that the Australian government's track record for protection of citizens with dual nationality who get into trouble when overseas in their country of origin, is mixed at best.

Naturalisation as an Australian citizenship has enjoyed cast-iron security until quite recently, being something that could never be taken away from you. However, the new environment caused by terrorism has for the first time stimulated open discussion in Australia of the possibility that citizenship could be stripped from naturalised citizens under certain circumstances, such as having gotten involved with terrorism. It is those 'certain circumstances' and the definitions of things like 'involvement in terrorism' that have yet to be defined. That process of definition, many thinking Australians feel, must be closely watched by those who care about human rights, lest we all lose the very freedoms that have made Australia great and a haven for the oppressed.

Familiarisation Techniques

Would-be migrants would be well advised to read the Australian press for at least a year before they make their move. I myself subscribed to *The Weekend Australian* for a year before I migrated, and picked up the odd copy of my local *The West Australian* daily whenever I could find one. *The*

Age of Melbourne and the *Australian Financial Review,* besides the weekly *The Bulletin,* are also good backgrounders.

Get a Feel for the Country First

It's a good idea too to have visited Australia before you decide to migrate there. This may sound like unnecessary advice, but not if my husband is anything to go by: a Singaporean-Indian, he was determined to migrate there without ever having set foot in the country.

Because he is black, I was just a wee bit nervous and insisted he travel across the country both with and without me first. This he did—and came back singing its praises even more loudly. So we filled in the forms, got all our official documents legally certified in multiplicate (a tedious and expensive business) and settled down to something like an 18-month wait before we got the good news. That was back in 1989. It can take longer.

The Questions Some Migrants Ask

Unquestionably the funniest experience we had in the migration process was the group counselling session at the Australian High Commission in Singapore. Once upon a time, it had been possible to offer individual counselling interviews to accepted migrants, but as numbers rose, this was abandoned in favour of group meetings.

The questions we heard asked by the predominantly Asian-Singaporean migrants at our session boggled the imagination. I take my hat off to the extremely patient immigration officer who had to handle them. She did so in typically Australian dry, wry style.

The session kicked off with 'When I come to Australia, can I bring my servant with me?' No, was the answer, ours is a do-it-yourself society. A shy couple was worried: considering the strict quarantine laws, could they bring into Australia the kangaroo skin which they had bought in Australia on a holiday? 'No worries' was the not unexpected answer to that one.

A strapping young man with no apparent health problems was extremely interested in how soon after landing he could qualify for Medicare (the subsidised medical service), the dole (social welfare payments for the unemployed) and a state pension. One could somehow guess what direction he was going in and I am sure the beleaguered immigration officer privately labelled him a potential 'bludger' on the spot (see the Glossary on page 383).

Agitated beyond belief was a Chinese man who asked whether or not he could regularly import Chinese dried mushrooms to Australia after setting up home there. Life, it seemed, would be meaningless without them. Food-import controls were strict, said the officer, and anyway, Australia grew perfectly good mushrooms of her own. No, no, insisted the Chinese, I mean our black mushrooms, our *Chinese* ones, you know? The implication seemed to be that no Australian mushroom could ever be a match for a Chinese one. (Anyway, nowadays you can get Chinese mushrooms and a host of other international mushrooms, at Australia's countless multicultural grocers' stores).

Of course, yours truly, being English, was concerned only whether or not she could import her pet dog. This used to be a very long, expensive and potentially traumatic process, but it's improved immensely. The length of quarantine required for imported pet dogs and cats in Australia varies according to the source country, but generally, you can expect about 30 days for pets from most countries (including Singapore, Japan, the United Kingdom and the United States of America, for example).

You Can Take It With You

What *can* you take into Australia when you go? Probably everything you own, although as much as possible should be over 12 months old, and you should have the documentation to prove this.

The rest of the documentation should be handled by your freight-forwarding agent, who will let you know whether or not you are required to be present

When my husband and I first landed, we had a typed checklist of the property we were carrying with us (including a large fax machine I had refused to ship, because I needed it immediately for work in those pre-Internet days), complete with every item's value, age and serial number. This was much appreciated by Customs, and speeded clearance considerably.

for a meeting with Customs when your cargo arrives. In our case, we were not.

Some items can be a particular problem: for example wooden objects or cane/bamboo/rattan may be treated as a hazard to Australian agriculture because of the bugs they may hide, and this will mean careful fumigation at the very least. Once again, with such problems, you should check carefully on the latest rules with your nearest Australian government representative office.

But remember, once you have taken up residence in Australia, you will be travelling as an Australian; when you re-enter Australia, your allowance for purchases (such as radios from Singapore and the like) will be restricted to a value of A$ 900 per head (A$ 450 if under 18). Anything above that must be declared, with a supporting document proving its sale value.

If you are travelling regularly in and out of Australia with an expensive item of equipment that is still fairly new, and obviously so—a lap-top computer, say—we have found it useful to ask Customs to note down the serial number on a Customs form before leaving Australia, so that you can later prove you did not buy it on your trip abroad and are therefore not liable for duty. Customs will often tell you there is no need to worry when you first approach them with this one, but we suggest you insist in case the next Customs officer is less understanding.

Australian Quarantine and Inspection Service Statement

NATURE MADE AUSTRALIA UNIQUE—

QUARANTINE KEEPS IT THAT WAY

Australia's remoteness created an environment unlike any other on Earth. Quarantine helps protect it. Food, plant material and animal products from overseas—including many common souvenirs—could introduce some of the world's most serious pests and diseases into Australia, devastating our valuable agriculture and tourism industries and unique environment.

DECLARE OR BEWARE

In general, when returning to Australia, we have found that honest declaration when in doubt really pays. On the few occasions when we have had to pay

What to Bring, What Not

Basically, as a migrant, your personal effects are brought in pretty much duty-free on the understanding that you have owned and used them for more than the past 12 months. You will find the Australian Customs generally lenient when it comes new migrants's container-loads of possessions, but do not try to push your luck too far by importing masses of newly bought stuff. Your property will only be considered part of your migration within the first 12 months of your visa.

- **Electricals and Electronics**
  Bring what you have with you—the prices aren't hugely different in Australia, but often the latest models and technology takes longer to get to Australia.
- **Mobile Phone**
  If you are from the USA, don't bring it! It won't work in Australia. Otherwise, you can get good phones on contract packages in Australia, but you can always just bring yours and change the SIM card.
- **Car**
  Don't bother, the process might cost you quite a bit, and cars are so cheap in Australia, including high-quality second-hand ones.
- **Fridge, Washing Machine, Television, VCR**
  Probably not worth it – and do check their compatibility with Australian systems first, as they may not work as well in Australia; it's probably more worthwhile to buy new when you arrive.
- **Furniture & Bedding**
  Yes, bring it, quality stuff is quite expensive in Australia.

duty, we have always found it very reasonable, being usually around 20 per cent of the sale value, above your A$ 900 allowance.

- **Food**
  Never, never never! It cannot be stressed too much how seriously Australia regards the importation of foodstuffs, a major offence.
- **Plants and Animal Products**
  Live plants, never, dead plant material like woven reeds or wood carvings, must be clean, declared carefully and may be treated/fumigated or confiscated. Animal products are a bit of a no-no too. Corals and shells that may be in your jewellery are prohibited. If you have some nice Indian or African drums you wanted to bring, forget it—any raw hide is taboo, even in 'dog chew' snacks for your pet dog. Feathers and bones etc. must be free of any flesh or tissue. Even the sheepskin you bought on your last holiday to Australia had better be declared, just to be safe! If you had a store of unused canned pet food for your dog that you thought you'd bring along, forget that too—it cannot come in. Got some bee pollen beauty products? It's unlikely that can come in either. Whatever, make sure you declare anything remotely of animal origin.

Tip: don't forget to clean all shoes packed, and to empty the vacuum cleaner bag—the dirt these may carry could be of serious interest to the Australian Customs and Quarantine officers!

Note: Australia's electrical plugs are virtually unique—three flat-pins in a triangular formation, with the two upper pins slightly slanting—so you will have to get ready to change the plugs on just about everything you have.

Toughing It Out

But don't get too smart by arranging for under-invoicing at a fantastic bargain-basement price; Australian Customs officers know very well what are the likely selling prices for most items, whether you are coming from Singapore or from London. Like Customs officers everywhere, they react pretty brutally if they discover you have been trying to take them for a ride.

Be careful too with illicitly-copied computer software: Australia strictly enforces copyright protection laws.

Never, ever try to sneak in food or plant material (that includes cut roses and orchids, Mum's home-made jam and Auntie's fantastic curry powder in a jam jar) without declaring it. It's a very serious offence. You may get it approved if you declare it; or like my friend with the tupperware of unwrapped smelly cheese he didn't want to leave behind in his fridge at home, you might not.

For importing undeclared food, you risk being fined around A$ 200 or so on the spot, or in serious cases, being taken to court and fined over A$ 60,000, with the possibility of ten years' imprisonment.

Under Suspicion

Everyone has had at least one horror story with Australian Immigration/Customs officials. They can be toughies, although they come on initially with brighter smiles and more friendly chat than any of their counterparts worldwide. So relax. Still, I shall not easily forget one unsmiling lady at Perth airport who had our entire luggage searched, apparently for drugs, just because we had travelled in and out of Malaysia once too often for her liking. Nor how she thrust her hands triumphantly into the tatty, torn silk lining of my suitcase—at last, a false bottom—flipped suspiciously through the pages of my notebooks, and even had my Indonesian wooden puppets' heads X-rayed for secret compartments.

The customs officers can even be laid-back, but may then become fallible. Although emotionally scarred, we survived one of our migrant residence visas being accidentally cancelled at the airport (inspect your passport carefully to see what has been done before you leave the airport)—a frightening discovery made only just before our next flight.

On balance, though, a cool temper combined with a modest and pleasant demeanour will see you through. No showing off, please. One well-heeled Chinese visitor learned his lesson. Asked what he had come to Australia for, he facetiously replied, 'To spend money.' This was not a sensitive remark in the context of the Australian dislike for 'tall poppies', nor the average Customs officer's salary. Needless to say, they took him apart.

WHAT USE ARE MIGRANTS?

Why then, does Australia want migrants? Well, some segments of Australian society in fact do not want them at all. Others, possibly as much as half the population, would prefer them to come from white Europe. But all major political parties currently accept migration as necessary. Disagreements tend to focus on how many should be admitted, and what type—European or Asian, skilled or unskilled, English-speaking or not, and so on. In the old days, it was believed that the only way to resist the 'Yellow Peril' from the north was to breed and multiply—'Populate or Perish', the slogan went. Nowadays, part of the official credo is that, to integrate with the booming economies of Asia, Australia needs Asian immigration.

Immigration doesn't just make money by stimulating the economy; it makes money per se. Migrants brought A$ 4.3 billion into Australia in 1989 alone, making immigration the nation's third biggest earner after tourism and wool at the time. Just the additional 20,000 skilled migrants expected in the four years from 2005 are likely to bring in over A$ 1.5 billion extra in tax revenue.

The same things are said about unwanted immigrants all over the world, no matter which cultures are involved: they contribute to social disorder, they cause rises in crime, they import new diseases, they pinch local jobs... In Australia, they said it about the Greeks and Italians, even the British, when they first arrived; they said it now about the Vietnamese, Chinese and Japanese in the 1980s and

1990s, and now it is the African and Middle Eastern refugees' turn—and some of the people saying it today are in fact Italian-Australians, British-Australians and the like, former migrants themselves.

Each generation of immigrants must undergo its own baptism of fire, emerging tempered from the crucible.

A Migrant Nation

Much is said nowadays about Asian migration to Australia. It is sometimes forgotten that between mid-1947 and the end of 1951, Australia took in 170,000 of post-World War II Europe's 12 million displaced people. There is a fascinating account of this programme, written both from the point of view of Immigration officers and migrants in a study titled *Angels and Arrogant Gods,* from the Australian Commonwealth Government Publishing Service.

At first it was 'whites only, please'. Migrant Britons were offered financially-assisted passage to Australia from 1946 to 1982, when the practice was discontinued. Many an Asian and other migrant today arrives by plane with a substantial bank balance (having sold a house back home), a container-load of possessions and university qualifications to boot.

It is humbling to reflect on the fact that those early European migrants often arrived in Australia only after a harrowing journey aboard an overcrowded ship, without a penny in their pockets and committed to a compulsory work contract (usually hard manual labour) with the Australian government in some remote corner of the country, where they were housed in makeshift huts at best.

You had to stay and work two years before the government would even give you your passport back. But then, where you had come from, you didn't even have food...

Such were the original New Australians. There was no talk about 'multiculturalism' in those days. You were supposed to become Australian, as quickly and as convincingly as possible.

It was not until Gough Whitlam's Labor Party came to power in 1972 that the racist immigration policy was finally laid to rest. In 1976, the first Senior Immigration Officer was appointed to an Asian posting. These changes came just in time to accommodate the Vietnamese boat-people refugees of the 1970s. By 1986, Australia had taken in more than 100,000 Indo-Chinese refugees. The total number of refugees from all sources taken into Australia between 1945 and 1985, however, was a massive 430,000. In the decade between 1992 and 2002, another 100,000 or so were admitted to the country.

Before mass migration programmes began, back in 1947, fewer than one in ten Australians had been born outside the country. The population then was about seven million. Now, migration accounts for more than half of Australia's population growth.

Australia today is recognised as one of the most multicultural countries in the world, with approximately a quarter of the 20-million population having been born overseas, and close to 30 per cent of those born in Australia classified as 'second-generation' migrants by virtue of having at least one parent born overseas. Australia is a country of 130 nations. Some Sydney suburbs are 42 per cent of non-English speaking origin. By 2021, the total population should be about 25 million if present migration patterns continue. By the year 2010, say some studies, the Chinese-origin population of Australia alone could exceed one million. But the traditional countries, United Kingdom, New Zealand and Italy are still the leading sources of overseas-born residents of Australia, with Vietnam and China close behind.

MULTICULTURALISM—HANDLE WITH CARE

Beyond simple migration, Australia has further espoused multiculturalism within Australia and has put its money where its mouth is, until very recently.

Multiculturalism is reckoned to cost the Federal and State Governments about A$ 514 million a year, or about A$ 30 for each Australian, revealed *The Australian* newspaper in its own 1991 investigation. These costs are incurred in a range of activities, from the Special Broadcasting Service (SBS) catering to minority culture, to ethnic language booklets on everything under the sun and English-as-a-second-language programmes.

This policy worries even some proponents of Asian migration, let alone conservatives concerned with preserving Australia's British heritage. They worry about 'ghetto-ism'. They fret slightly about the proliferation of ethnic clubs, and they froth at the mouth when migrants are discovered still promoting forced arranged marriages of under-age girls, or worse, continuing traditions of female genital mutilation inside Australia.

The upheavals of the late 1990s in Eastern Europe amply demonstrated the problem, as did the Gulf War of 1990–1991: émigré communities of Serbs, Bosnian and Croats in Australia avoided, or attacked, one another in tandem with the factions developing in what was Yugoslavia, while Rumanian-Australians denounced the Ceausescu 'moles' in their midst after the Rumanian revolutionaries had despatched their former dictator. I even know of a Eurasian group in Australia which has fractured along lines demarcated by whether one is of Dutch/English or Portuguese origin.

Many migrants and refugees have, perhaps understandably, imported their domestic political and social problems into Australia. These nations within a nation have made many uneasy.

A multicultural mix—people from different ethnic backgrounds come together for a meal.

This is an ongoing debate, as it is in some other countries too, such as Britain: should migrants be forced or persuaded into cultural integration? For instance, can Muslims be obliged to submit to Australian customs and laws?

Rubbing Shoulders with the World

As a migrant yourself, you may well find multiculturalism exciting. For the first time, you will find yourself side by side with exotic cultures you never dreamed of encountering before.

How, for instance, could my Sri Lankan engineer friend ever have guessed he would end up marrying a Colombian girl in Australia? Listening to the interplay of this family's three different accents when conversing together in English at their Australian dinner-table was something of a treat: his voice still heavily Indian-inflected, hers distinctly Spanish, and their little girl's, why Australian, of course.

You may have to be more careful than you were before. 'Irish jokes' may prove problematic in the wrong company. There are other potential social gaffes to avoid: you may find it next to impossible to mix your Serb and Croat friends from Yugoslavia, for example, and it would be most ill-advised to invite an Armenian and a Turk, or a Tamil and a Sinhalese, together for tea.

Yet multiculturalism is a furnace in which hitherto unheard-of new alliances may be forged: I think, for instance, of the Portugal Day hosted by the Portuguese Consul in Perth, which saw peoples of all the former Portuguese colonies come together in song, dance and festivity: from Indonesian Timor, from African Mozambique, from Latin American Brazil, from Goa in India, from Malacca in Malaysia and from Macau off China. And yet they were all Australians too.

Indeed, one's definition of an 'Australian' blurs somewhat when confronted with pedigrees like those of my friends. Former residents of Singapore, they now live in Perth. My girlfriend's mother was born in Shanghai and looks

Chinese, but doesn't speak the language. (Her parents were Czech-Japanese on one side, Irish-Chinese on the other.) My girlfriend's father, on the other hand, was a Latvian who had fled his Baltic home-state during the Russian Revolution of 1917, to Shanghai via Siberia; in Shanghai, he had been adopted by a benevolent Iraqi-Jewish opium trader.

This couple got out of China in 1954, using the wife's part-Czech descent as a pretext for exit. And so to Singapore, where my ostensibly Singaporean, now Australian, girlfriend was born to them. She married a mixed Irish-Eurasian from Singapore. Should anyone be surprised that their little girl, dinki-di Aussie, has turned out fair and freckled of skin, with stunning red hair? I challenge anyone to top this family on the multiculturalism scoreboard.

Singaporean Anthony Quahe is the Honorary representative for Contact Singapore in Perth. This long time migrant to Perth—pictured here with his wife Francisca and children—now runs a sunccessful law practice in Australia.

Dr Eric Tan, the Malaysian-born Chancellor of Western Australia's Curtin University of Technology, in discussion with students at the university.

Multiculturalism and the promotion of ethnic politics has led to ethnic lobbying. Former Malaysian-Chinese Dr Eric Tan, a prominent surgeon and community leader in Perth, has a shrewd idea of future directions. Himself an 'Asian-Australian' for 30 years now, he told me, 'You can expect a trend towards the Chinese community entering Australian politics Australia-wide.'

Perhaps a Chinese-Australian Prime Minister of Australia could even be on the cards one day. In 1990, Bill O'Chee of Queensland, then 24, became the youngest person ever elected to the Australian Senate (for the National Party, straight from the rural heartlands). His grandfather was China-born but Irish-ised his name to 'O'Chee' to fob off

Mrs Cecilia Wee of Singapore is a successful hotelier in Perth, Western Australia, with some four properties to her name. Here, she is pictured at the Reception of her Red Castle Motor Hotel in Perth.

Australian racism. Bill's mother is Irish, his father Chinese. He is no longer in politics, however.

Then there is Hong Kong-born engineer-entrepreneur Michael Choi Wai-man, MP, the first and only Chinese-Australian member of a state legislature in the 2001 state elections.

Hongkong-born Labor MP for Capalaba, Queensland, Michael Choi (far left) gets some support for his election campaign from famous former Labor Prime Minister of Australia, Bob Hawke (far right).

Making Things Different

'I want to tell the world that, despite some narrow-minded, uninformed and oversimplified comments from certain high-profile politicians, Australians are not racist and in fact are very fair-minded people... Multiculturalism has brought richness to Australia... Multiculturalism is not about taking one previous culture into this country lock, stock and barrel, it is about keeping the good and discarding those things that are perhaps incompatible... There are parts of my parents' culture that I would not want my children to learn because I know that they have no place in this country. But there are other parts of the Chinese culture that I want not only my children to learn, I would dearly like my fellow Australians to embrace them also, because they are simply good for our nation-building. Multiculturalism is about being the best of the best. I do not want Australia to be Asianised, whatever that word means. I do not want Australia to be Europeanised, whatever that word means. I definitely do not want Australia to be Americanised, and I know what that word means. I want Australia to develop her own culture and be the envy of the world because she has developed her culture from the best of the best.'

—Michael Choi Wai-man,
in his maiden speech as a new Member to
the Queensland Legislative Assembly, 2001.

Singapore-born Henry Heng (far left) and Edmund Teo (far right) together with Malaysian-born civil engineer Thomas Yap (centre) are joint directors of Refresh, a distilled water and foods company in Perth, Western Australia, and do thriving business both inside and outside Australia.

Integration Without Tears

You, as a migrant, should at least be sensitive to Australian concerns about multiculturalism. It is natural, and also helpful in the initial stages of migration, to turn to support organisations comprising your former compatriots. In every Australian city, you will find the right club for yourself: Greek, Italian, Austrian, Polish, Serb, Croat, Tamil, Malayalee, Sri Lankan, Timorese, Eurasian, Anglo-Indian, Singaporean or what-have-you.

But you would do well to make an effort to meet Australians by joining some of their activities too—from your street Neighbourhood Watch (crime-watch) committee, to the local church, the local heritage/history society, or a nature-walking group. Trouble is, you find that many of the 'Australians' around you prove to be migrants too. But even this discovery serves to make you feel more at home, less of an oddity.

Remember that Australia is remarkable for the ease with which you can strike up a conversation with a stranger. Don't be shy, speak up if you want to make friends, whether on the bus or when picking up the children from school along with other parents. This dictum applies especially to naturally conservative Asians. Remember that your accent may be as unfamiliar to older Australians as theirs is to you, so take it slowly and enunciate clearly. There will be some who don't feel comfortable with you, but many will respond kindly.

Remember too that elaborate structures are already in existence to help migrants: consult your local phone directory for contact with bodies like the Ethnic Communities Council or the Multicultural and Ethnic Affairs Commission. Ask them for advice, and the contacts for other migrant assistance centres.

As for general information, if you look up your phone directory listing for Recorded Information Services, or letter 'D' for 'Dial-It', you will be astounded at the range of things you can find out over the phone. Similarly, Australia excels in the prolific production of first-class information leaflets and brochures. A browsing session at your local library, Council and other local government offices, as well as hospitals, and medical and migrant resource centres, will harvest a sheaf of such literature.

Take an active interest in Australian politics and social issues by reading the local press; sample typical Australian activities, such as the local footy (Australian Rules football) or cricket matches. Watch television and listen to the radio; make a point of seeing the latest Australian movies and plays, art exhibitions and so on. This will help you converse with Australians on their own ground.

If, by any chance, your English is less than perfect (and not all migrants find it easy to recognise this simple fact—many Singaporeans, for example), work on it. The language is absolutely crucial to your integration.

Mum's the Word about Home

In the same box comes the problem of the 'Back home, we do it this way…' syndrome. Or the equally common

'I can't understand why Australia doesn't… what's the matter with them?' Avoid at all costs making public comparisons, particularly invidious ones, between your motherland and your newly adopted home, Australia. This goes down very badly with Australians. Put yourself in their place and this becomes very easy to understand. Also taboo—and many Asian migrants need to learn this—is talking about money and the cost of things (property, cars) all the time. Listen, Look and Learn—But Keep Quiet. Until you know people better, look for the common conversational ground found in children, sport, food, and as a last resort, the weather.

The Migrant Blues

No matter how gungho you have been initially about making a new life in Australia, there will come those moments when you feel depressed, alienated… You wonder if you have made a mistake. This applies to all—and I include those of Anglo-Saxon background, who may be all the more shocked to discover how 'foreign' Australia can be. How much more, non-European migrants.

In many ways, the respectable, older middle-class migrant may suffer more, and more silently, from culture shock than a refugee. For refugees, there are all sorts of support and aid groups. For simple migrants—once you land, you're on your own, mate. The older you are, the harder it is. You will find that your young children, in contrast, take to it like a duck to water. I have noticed too that women often fare better than men. However, women's ability to adapt also depends on how much 'permission' they get from their men to go out and get things done (not always automatic in very traditional cultures, for example from Asia and the Middle East). You must accept that it usually takes something like two or three years before you feel comfortable, begin to 'fit'. Whatever you do, don't give up before you have given it a go for a couple of years. Believe that it will get better. Statistics show that migrants usually quit within the first three years, but rarely later than that.

Often, it is necessary to arrive with a passionate commitment, knowing that above all, you want to live in Australia. That must be the first premise. Then you adapt. Refugees have no problem with this; most of them recognise their luck when they come to a country like Australia and eagerly accept the rough with the smooth.

If you arrive believing that everything will be the same as back home—you will do the same work, have the same status and income and the same sorts of friends, and your children will continue to behave exactly the way they would have in your own culture—but just in a different physical setting, then you will fail as a migrant. I have seen many new arrivals pull out within a year because they couldn't make a big enough buck fast enough, or because they were puzzled by Australian bureaucracy and democratic rules that say you cannot just willy-nilly put a second storey on your house without your neighbours' consent, or you cannot develop a site because of heritage listing, or because of Aboriginal sacred-site rights, or just because their children were beginning to be a bit ruder and talk with a broad Aussie accent.

You must be prepared for big changes in your life. Very few migrants end up doing the same work in Australia as they did back home; teachers may drive a taxi, scientists open a restaurant. Many find that they 'lose status' in the terms set by their own culture and friends back home; but they need only to relax and realise that the status thing hardly figures in the Australian mind, to be happy. Yes, it's probably a waste of talent and skills, but that's how it has always been for migrants throughout the ages. If you have children, you can just look ahead and enjoy the new opportunities that they are certainly going to get in Australia.

But admittedly, it's the little things that get you down.

For those used to lively, noisy city streets and housing estates at night, it can be the lack of people, the silence of the dimly lit streets of suburbia. Many residential areas resemble menacing black holes at night: Australians seem to live mostly at the back of the house, turning off all the lights at the front as an economy measure, leaving a faceless and unwelcoming streetscape.

Can't Stand the Quiet

A Singaporean Malay friend in Perth recently bought a plot of land and decided to build his own house on it. When I looked at his plans, I exclaimed, 'But why have you chosen to live so close to a highway?'

'It's the silence,' said he. 'I just can't stand it. I just have to have more noise, else I get lonely.' Some call it peaceful, others lonely.

No more food-stalls or cafés in the street, unlike Singapore, Kuala Lumpur, Athens or Paris, except in the very heart of the city centre. Faced with steep restaurant prices and early closing times, you do more home entertaining than ever before. Not a soul on the streets; and it's not all that safe to walk the streets alone at night, either. And in the winter, well, you wouldn't want to.

Beaten, you retreat behind the four walls of your home like the rest of Australia. Having read the over-active local press for the latest, often horrific, crime stories, you fearfully lock up the house and barricade your bedroom door with chairs for good measure.

Unfortunately, the fear of crime is to some extent justified. It was only yesterday that Perth-dwellers still left their doors and windows open all the time, and never locked their cars, but alas, no more. I myself was greeted by a friendly brick through my window before I even moved into my new house. Just a minor burglary attempt, but still… Allegedly sleepy Perth surprisingly has been tagged 'the burglary capital of Australia.'

I got a burglar alarm and paid a monthly fee to connect it to a monitoring station that would call the police if it went off. I would recommend a dog too if you have the time to maintain one, as well as metal grille-reinforcements to windows and doors.

But you soon learn which places to avoid at which times, how to protect yourself, and the fear eventually recedes into the background as you become more street-wise.

TRANSPORTATION

If you have never driven before, which was the case with me, thanks to tiny Singapore's excellent public transportation and punitive car costs, those four walls of home quickly become a cosy cage. One crucial element in entering Australian society can often be whether or not you can drive a car. If you can't, the result may be extreme isolation. Mum, your favourite nanny, is no longer just around the corner; your best friend no longer just a phone call away.

You need to tackle this issue very early on. I know this, because it was my problem too when I first arrived in Australia. One of the keys to happiness in Australia is having a driving licence: don't leave without it. (If you hold one already, you'll probably only need to pass a simple oral or Highway Code test within a few months of arrival in Australia in order to convert it to an Australian licence—but check this with your local police station). In Australia, anyone over 18 can drive a car. As a visitor, you can drive on your own driving licence for up to six months, after which you need either to convert to an international driving licence, or else obtain an Australian licence. When you pass your test, you get a 'P' plate announcing you as a probationer, a badge you have to wear for two years. Penalties for driving offences, particularly in the case of young drivers, are often higher for drivers still on 'P' plates, so you need to mind your Ps and Qs for a couple of years.

Buying a car in Australia is pretty much a breeze: there are plenty of choices, including a lively second-hand market featuring quality cars at bargain prices. Maintaining the car is also affordable, although you need to shop around a bit when choosing a garage to service your car—car yards are notoriously predatory and often down right tricky. And remember, Australians don't really care whether you run a smart car or not; on the whole, they don't measure your worth that way.

While driving is the key to freedom in Australia, on the other hand, you need to understand that driving a car in Australia is very different from driving back home, especially if your experience is limited to a very urban context. Americans and Europeans have to deal with driving on the left in Australia. In the cities, be aware first that drink-driving laws are strictly enforced, so don't do it—in Western Australia,

Driving on the streets of Sydney can be a different experience especially if you come from a more urbanised city or if you are used to driving on the right.

for instance, the limit for alcohol in the blood is 0.05 g per 100 ml, and while a first offence at this level will attract a fine of A$ 500, a first offence at 0.08 g per 100 ml will bring you a fine of A$ 800 and removal of your driving licence for at least three months. Most groups of people going out for the night either negotiate for one of them to remain sober and be the driver for the night, or else arrange taxis if they are going to drink.

Seat belts are compulsory and driving while using a mobile phone is illegal.

If you are used to a free-wheeling situation (as in many Asian cities) where you can zig zag among lanes almost at will, please re-train yourself to the safer and more courteous procedure of signalling your intentions before you change lanes, as most Australian drivers do. Learn to be patient

The Cost of Four Wheels

Running a car is affordable in Australia; in 2005, petrol costs were around A$ 1 or more per litre, with diesel higher, and prices generally moving up as you drive deeper into the countryside, but that was a consequence of global petrol supply and demand patterns. Hence, watch out for fuel-guzzler car models if you are going to drive outback a lot.

- **The Car**
  Anything from as little as A$ 8,000 for a five-year-old second-hand Japanese or Korean car, to around A$ 15,000–20,000 for a brand-new one, or moving to between A$ 30,000–50,000 for luxury cars, specialised trucks, sports and 4WD (four wheel-drive) cars.
- **Your Licence**
  About A$ 100 for a five-year licence.
- **Registration and Third Party Insurance** (government/police—known in Strine as 'reggo'):
  About A$ 470 for a 12-month standard vehicle that can be used for both business and family purposes.

while polite Australian drivers slow down in front of you to allow an elderly person, or indeed any pedestrian, to cross the road, even when not at a pedestrian or zebra crossing. Generally, learn to exercise plenty of patience and consideration.

In town, in most built-up areas, a speed limit of 60 kmph is the norm, sometimes dropping to 50 kmph in suburban streets, or 40 kmph in zones around schools. Outside of the cities, and indeed on many freeways inside cities, speed limits can be as high as 110 kmph. Handling speeds like this on winding country roads—sometimes only partially surfaced—and even more so, at night on only partially lit roads (you will find road lighting generally dimmer than what you are used to), can take some skill. Quite a number of visiting Asian drivers have come to a bad end on Western

- **Royal Automobile Club membership** (optional, but you'll regret not having it when you next leave your lights on and burn the battery, or lock yourself out of the car in some lonely spot and have nobody to call for help):
  A$ 64 for the year.
- **Royal Automobile Club general car insurance** (there are other options for insurance but this is just offered as an example):
  About A$ 300 a year.
- **Annual service in a garage:**
  You need different levels of service according to how many kilometres your car has done. A simple 'A' class service with just a change of oil and simple check-up might be only about A$ 100, whereas a full 'C class ' service with 'all the bells and whistles', for an ordinary car that has done about 100,000 km, might be more like A$ 400.

Australian country roads, for example, and it has often seemed that unfamiliar speeds might have been a factor in many of these accidents.

Australians are used to distance in their daily lives, so may think nothing of driving a couple of hundred miles to visit a friend. Be ready for this, and if you are not used to this idea, take care with the risk of fatigue on long journeys on roads that seem to stretch for ever into the horizon.

Another, more unfamiliar, hazard, in the countryside, is large wild animals, such as kangaroos or buffaloes. As a rookie, it is best simply not to try to drive at night at all, since kangaroos start to move around from twilight into the early morning; believe me, a collision with an angry adult kangaroo about 1.8 m (6 ft) tall, can cause an accident that will kill you, especially if the animal crashes through your windscreen into the car. It seems that 'roos' are in some way attracted to car lights, or dazzled and confused by them, so this event is a distinct possibility.

Often, the roads go for set distances without any provision for overtaking lanes, which appear only sporadically, signed in advance. When stuck behind a big vehicle, you should take advantage of these opportunities.

By day or by night, outside of the city, you may also be confronted with enormous 'road trains'—lorries towing joined, articulated containers or trailers stretching quite some length behind them, sometimes 50 m (165 ft)—steaming along the main freight roads, across the vastness that is Australia. You have to learn to pull off on the shoulder and let them pass, or when and how to overtake them safely (they will often help you by flashing their right indicators to say that you can go), or they may make your life a misery; absolutely no point, dangerous too, in 'having an argument' with a road train. Apart from these juggernauts, you can also drive for hours in Australia without seeing a soul, so huge is the land and so small the population. This combined with a general inadequacy of mobile phone signals in the countryside means that you must be very self sufficient—have your own spare tyres and wheel jack (and know how to change a wheel) for instance, carry water, oil, maybe even a safe container of some extra petrol, ropes, spades, refrigerated boxes with food and water, and never move without good maps. Petrol stations may be few and far between once you 'go bush.' If long-distance driving is going to be your thing in Australia, having a GPS (Global Positioning System) facility built into your car is never a bad idea, likewise some kind of radio-phone system.

With outback driving, you need to be careful. Every year there are stories about unwary visitors who have become stranded in remote areas for lack of a spare part in a breakdown, even because they run out of fuel, or get bogged in sand or floods, and who quite simply die as a result , either because they are not found in time and have insufficient food and water, or because they try to walk for help, get lost and find themselves in some of the world's most inhospitable country. Never leave your vehicle in such a case—air search crews will find you so much more easily if there is a vehicle to spot, and the vehicle may offer some shelter from extreme weather. Always inform national park rangers or policemen when you are driving into the interior about your planned route and return date. Listen to the locals and acquire their know-how. Don't do silly things like camp close to pretty creeks —there are very large crocodiles around who are smart enough to stalk you and observe your habits for several days before they strike—and don't swim in un-patrolled ocean bays where you know nothing about the tides and currents, let alone the resident jellyfish and sharks.

Saved by EPIRB

One British tourist recently stranded for three days in the remote Kimberley region of the north-west after getting bogged in a marshy area near the coast, was saved just as he was running out of food and water, because he had an Emergency Position Indicating Radio Beacon (EPIRB), which he set off. The beacon's digitally coded international distress signal alerted the Australian Search and Rescue Services far away in Canberra, who asked the Coastwatch unit to get a rescue helicopter out to him. You can buy an EPIRB for around A$ 300–500.

Other Transport

There are transport systems other than the car in the city centres of Australia and some of them very good ones—there are trains, trams in Melbourne, and often networks of free buses within the city, such as the 'CAT' bus system in Perth and Fremantle, Western Australia. If you are travelling a regular route every day to work, you can often buy a cut-price season pass or 'multi-rider' ticket which just deducts cash once inserted into a special reader machine on the buses; a convenient, cheap and fast way of moving around that is often valid for both buses and trains. In Sydney, Perth and other places, there are also ferries crossing rivers and harbours.

MORE BUMMERS

For those accustomed to 24-hour shopping—as many Asians are—it takes some getting used to that the shops often operate within quite restricted hours—they close by 5:30 pm on a weekday, except for Thursday or Friday late shopping nights, in Perth, one of the most backward locations in Australia in this respect. Things are marginally better in the big cities of the eastern states. In Perth, just forget Sundays (except for that nice Thai lady's delicatessen shop, the Asian food centre and the Italian family-run fresh market). But again, you learn to adapt if you keep looking at that brilliant blue sky, reflect on your freedoms and savour the pleasures of life in the backyard with your friends and family.

Some migrants, especially Asians, are uncomfortable with the degree of freedom and free speech they find in Australia. They feel bombarded by brutal frankness, harassed by the sight of nudity and sex on television and in the cinema. In a way, they miss the firm framework of stricter rules and the soothing absence of moral choice. They are used to governments making decisions for them, like proxy parents. But suddenly, nobody cares what they do. So they feel uncared for—freedom too can create culture shock.

Another 'bummer', to use an Australian phrase, is the Australian pace of work, much slower than say, a Singaporean, a Hongkonger or an American might be used to. One former executive with a multinational corporation, whom I know resigned in frustration from a civil service job, told me, 'I was going crazy, just twiddling my thumbs doing nothing all day. I had finished my work!' Needless to say, she wasn't very popular with her laid-back Aussie colleagues. Another rule—don't show off by working too hard if you want to be loved. Or work hard, but disguise it somehow.

More serious is the discovery on arrival, too late, that your professional qualifications are not valid in Australia. This is a very common problem, so do check carefully what you need to do to re-qualify for work in Australia, well before you arrive. Otherwise you will join the growing band of doctors, teachers and engineers running takeaway food shops or struggling on student study grants.

MONEY MATTERS

The Australian dollar has been quite strong for some time now, running between A$ 0.76–0.79 to the US dollar for a few years now. The Australian currency is decimal, featuring some attractive plasticised notes (yes, you can wash them by mistake in the laundry and they come out just fine!) and some of the world's clunkiest silver coins (my husband piggy-banks them all and then takes them to the bank to change into notes, so fed up is he with carrying them around), such as the enormous wavy-edge 50-cent coin. Inexplicably, of the two gold coins available, the A$ 2 coin is smaller than the A$ 1 dollar coin. Entrance to charity events and the like is often by 'gold-coin donation' meaning you can give either A$ 1 or A$ 2.

The banking system has been under fire in recent times because of an array of transaction charges, duties and taxes generally considered rather unfair. They can certainly add up.

The big names are the Commonwealth Bank of Australia, the Australia and New Zealand Banking Group (ANZ), Westpac Banking Corporation and the National Australia Bank (NAB).

Opening an account is usually fairly easy. The only identity you will need to present is either your driving licence or your passport. Do check on the necessary arrangements for using Internet banking and linking all your accounts so that you have full freedom to bank online. If you are in the habit of moving large sums of money around among bank accounts, particularly from overseas accounts into Australia, be aware that transactions of A$ 10,000 or more have to be reported specially by your bank, and so could attract government interest; by the same token, you are obliged to declare cash in any currency amounting to A$ 10,000 or more if you are carrying it *in or out* of Australia.

Take advantage of credit cards supplied by the banks that offer you frequent flyer points on airlines; compare carefully the relative interest charges for credit cards, personal loans, overdrafts, home loans and car loans before you decide which way to go.

Banks are open from about 9:30 am till 4:00 pm and on Saturday mornings too, an improvement made only in recent times.

KEEPING IN TOUCH

Telecommunications in Australia is in a bit of a mess at the moment, to be frank, with the original core supplier, the once government-owned, now corporatised and semi-privatised, Telstra (still 51.8 per cent government-owned). Telstra is now on the threshold of being split into retail and wholesale units, all to be sold off to private bidders some time in 2006. The wholesaling at present involves Telstra selling capacity to its rivals, such as Optus; thus it is Telstra's charges that may determine how much your own phone service company is obliged to charge you for services. Telstra's profit in 2004-2005 was A$ 4.44 billion— 'nuff said.

The biggest row, still ongoing, is whether and how, and at what cost, services to 'the bush' can be improved

Rural Australia's main defender, the National Party, in coalition government with the Liberal Party, only acceded to the idea of privatisation of Telstra after a A$ 3.2 billion plan was agreed to support 'the bush' in telephone and Internet service development.

While other nations, including small Asian nations like Singapore, were already speeding along the Internet highway and getting their entire populations totally wired, in 2004, Australia ranked third last in broadband penetration rates among other members of the Organisation for Economic Cooperation and Development (OECD). The figures show Australia lagging behind at the bottom of the pile for the developed world, behind South Korea at the top (25 subscribers per 100 inhabitants), Japan (15 per 100), the USA (about 13 per 100) and Italy (about 8 per 100). There are still plenty of irritating 'black spots' right in the heart of major cities, where broadband somehow cannot be connected. You need to check on this before deciding where to live, if Internet matters to you.

You can opt to place your tele-custom with a multiplicity of operators—Optus (actually largely Singapore-owned), Telstra, Vodafone, AAPT, to name only a few—but for the moment at least, the fellow charging for line installation and rental will still be the giant Telstra. A typical monthly line rental charge is around A$ 27. Trends reveal that Telstra's fixed-line business is however collapsing, as many younger communicators opt for their mobiles as their only phone instrument. There is full portability for mobile numbers, so you can switch operators as often as you like.

The telecoms environment is highly competitive so you can shop around quite a bit. There are many Internet/email providers but among the best known are iinet (sic, no caps, double 'i'), Telstra's BigPond, iPrimus and OzEmail.

HEALTH

For your first two years as a Permanent Resident of Australia, you will not be able to access the national Medicare health and welfare net. But eventually, you will find that you are well protected, though the majority of Australians now also opt to pay for extra private health insurance as well (big names, Medibank, HBF). Note that there is an actual tax penalty on high income-earners who do not take private health insurance. Mercifully, the old are helped with private health insurance costs: as an incentive, the Federal Government offers a 30 per cent rebate on private health insurance premiums for all those aged under 65. Those aged 65–69 are eligible for a 35 per cent rebate and those aged 70-plus for a 40 per cent rebate.

You can sign up for different plans or levels of private health insurance: some levels cover everything including dental, optical and even chiropody or podiatry treatment, while others may be more restricted. Often, you can claim for some rebate on the cost of consultancies with alternative or holistic practitioners such as homeopaths or acupuncturists, but not the cost of their actual treatments or medicines.

You need also to be aware of the Pharmaceutical Benefits Scheme under which government subsidises the costs of prescriptions for most ordinary consumers.

There are both private and public hospitals, all offering high-quality services, although treatment in the city centres may well be preferable to treatment in remote rural hospitals—the figures for cancer survival in country areas, for example, have given cause for alarm and suggest that services are not adequate in the bush. If you have private health insurance, you are more likely to be able to choose exactly where you are treated. It's a good idea to consult your general practitioner, family doctor, first before deciding on a specialist, as his or her referral to a specialist may make the difference in how much money you can save on the process.

SHOPPING AROUND

Shops open from about 9:00 am and as discussed elsewhere in this book, do not often open till late at night and sometimes not on Sundays either. Do not look for alcohol in supermarkets; you need a separate 'bottle shop' (which also may not be open on Sundays). For Sunday trading, look for very small family-run 'delis' (from delicatessen, but many of these are not really delicatessens), and corner shops.

There's plenty of choice for shopping around in Australia, from fancy department stores to shops specialising in second-hand 'pre-loved' gear, often channelling their proceeds to charities, and both covered and open markets, including non-commercial neighbourhood 'swap markets' —even some of the suburban and rural church fêtes and agricultural fairs can

One of the glories of clothes shopping in Australia for we 'mature ladies' is that there are quite enormous sizes available, up to size 22 or 24 (when the average is more like a 12 or 14), so if you are a European living in Asia and sick of schoolgirl sizes, Australia is the place to shop.

be an excellent place to shop, especially for items like crafts and home-made jams or other local produce. For fresh food and value for money, seek out your local 'grower's market'; many such markets are run by Italian or Asian immigrants and offer a wide range of foods as a result. Every Australian city however has its own network of 'Oriental' stores, and the beauty is, they stock everything from Sri Lankan to Korean ingredients, all in one place. Generally, it's a good idea to seek out speciality stores rather than visiting only the big chain stores (David Jones, Myers, Aherns, Target, K-Mart, Woolworths and so on), if you want real choice and quality. Fixed weekend markets—of the type seen in Fremantle and Subiaco in Western Australia—are good fun, offering plenty of life and colour, as well as good buys across a wide range of goods, from bakery to furry koala toys and sheepskin-lined boots. The community markets where you, too, can turn up with your car and sell things out of the boot, can offer surprising bargains.

You will find clothing stock sharply seasonal; it is very difficult to buy summer clothes in winter and vice versa, which is a bit of a pain if you are going overseas to another climate. On the other hand, if you can get into the end-of-season sales, you can pick up whatever you want at rock bottom prices.

If you are looking for 'Australiana' as gifts, try to look for it in reputable large stores, rather than tacky little souvenir stalls festooned with koalas and rude teeshirts. There are tasteful things you can choose, from macadamia chocolates and good wine, to unusual items like the version of Italian panforte cake made by the only Benedictine monastic community in Australia, at New Norcia in Western Australia (available in some mainstream stores, such as David Jones), or the fun novelties and environmentally-aware items stocked in millionaire Dick Smith's chain of Australian Geographic shops.

Remember the GST

Whatever you are buying, remember to check whether the 10 per cent GST (Goods and Service Tax) has been included, because it will be, in the end.

Generally speaking, bargaining is not appreciated in Australia, except perhaps in simple open markets; however, you will frequently come across kind souls who will round prices down for you if you have struck up a friendly relationship with them.

AWFUL THINGS THAT COULD HAPPEN

You learn the hard way about certain basics of Australian life: if you forget to leave the rubbish bin out on the kerb for emptying on the appointed day (usually once a week only), too bad. After the third visit in a week from a door-to-door canvasser for charity, you learn to say 'No,' or ask them to send a letter instead. You might even learn to abuse the army of telemarketers that specialise in phoning you to promote home security systems or insurance just as you are making the evening meal.

You thought that swimming pool in the back garden a great idea, but now you find it costs a bomb to maintain in tip-top condition, the local Council has passed a rule on regular pool inspections (charging you an inspection fee for good measure) and any pools considered too accessible to children (your own or other people's) must be surrounded by an ugly isolation fence that will cost the earth to install.

You are terrified of your first winter after many years of living in the tropics, so you decide to order three tonnes of firewood in advance. Trouble is, there was no arrangement for when exactly it would be delivered. The wood arrives while you are out. It has been dumped in the back lane outside your garden fence, a good distance from your woodshed. You spend the next three days trudging back and forth with wheelbarrows and baskets to transport it all into the woodshed.

When you get more localised, the same happens with a huge Everest of wood-chip mulch that you have decided to spread over your garden to protect native plants against soil and water loss.

Yes, all this has happened to me.

CHILDREN CHANGE

Luckily, however, I am not a parent. Migrant parents get upset when their children show signs of assimilating too well.

Cutting the Apron Strings

Singaporean friends of mine were typically protective Asian parents: they were driving their young son to and from school every day. But the boy soon asserted his new identity, demanding the same independence as his Australian schoolmates, who were all left to cycle to school by themselves. He didn't want to be seen as a sissy by his peers; he was going to be an Australian. The parents agonised for some time over road safety before giving way.

More serious identity problems may surface later. All that a migrant parent can do is be ready for these when they come, and perhaps just try to live with them.

Although such parents invariably will assure you that they migrated 'for the sake of the children', paradoxically they are filled with dread at the thought that their offspring may become loud, boorish and rebellious, or generally fall victim to sex, drugs and rock 'n' roll, as it were. Some kids do indeed react against their own background. That is a natural part of their adjustment process and must be accepted as such. The first symptom of mutation is the child's changing accent.

I witnessed an extreme teenage reaction to Malaysian roots. Gathering together for a home-cooked curry, the adults sat down with gusto to whack the goodies in time-honoured Malaysian fashion: with their fingers. When the family's daughter arrived home with her Australian friends, loud expressions of disgust were heard from her. The adults understandably told her to get lost. From the girl's point of view, she had been shamed before Aussie mates by her parents' primitive table manners, quite unacceptable to an Australian.

Yet I have also seen the Australian children of first-generation migrants cheering for their motherland's soccer team in matches against Australian teams. So you never can tell ...

Australian education in democracy and rights can make a parent's life perilous indeed. My Eurasian lawyer friend from Singapore got his comeuppance when he discovered that his Australian-born teenage daughter had reported him to the local Human Rights and Equal Opportunity Commission for giving her a typical Asian 'tight slap' over some minor cheek the day before. She should have reported him to the local welfare authorities; but the incident did give him some pause for thought about brats' rights as he prepared his defence ...

Admirable environmental education in Australian schools can also produce annoying little home preachers, demanding you buy only dolphin-friendly, ozone-friendly and recycled-paper products.

Going to School

Surprisingly, school in Australia is not compulsory after the age of 15 (although there are moves to raise this age), but it is free. There are four terms and their exact timing varies state by state, but roughly speaking they are:

- Term 1   February–April
- Term 2   May–June
- Term 3   August–September
- Term 4   October–mid-December.

As with the world of work too, everything comes to a grinding halt over the December–January summer holiday period, although Australian families are showing increasing interest in private tuition and extra coaching during holidays, and outside of school hours.

Children in very remote outback areas study at the 'School of the Air', with homework arriving by mail, and instruction via two-way radios, as well as the Internet.

Public Schools

For the British especially to note, 'public schools' in Australia are not elite institutions—they are the government schools open to all, and unfortunately, often very far from elite. The other system comprises high-fee private schools, including independent and community or religion-based schools (the Jewish school, Roman Catholic schools etc).

Many parents are beguiled by Australia's charming attitude to early education, which is unpressurised and emphasises creativity, individual expression and so on, giving the child a lot of freedom, well, to be a child. This contrasts favourably with pressure-cooker environments in Asia, for example, where even streaming of children may be common at primary-leaving age. However, things suddenly toughen up towards the tertiary entrance examination level, reached in Year 12, usually at the age of 17 (a bit too young to be a school-leaver, in many observers' opinions). The pace starts to heat up some time after Year 10, through Year 11.

The tertiary entrance exam (TEE) goes by several different names across the states but a rose by any other name would be just as thorny—it's a demanding test and if your child is not academic by nature, it's better not to push him or her through it. It is possible also to stretch the TEE preparation year into two years, on request. For non-academic children, and for the many who—at any age—decide to repeat or sit their tertiary entrance exam outside school, there is always the excellent Technical and Further Education (TAFE) college network, which also offers good vocational training courses. TAFE courses can also be a stepping stone to university courses.

Tertiary Entrance, Its Many Names

As of 2005, the tertary entraince exam is known in the different states by the following names:

▪ Australian Capital Territory	University Admissions Index (UAI) statement
▪ New South Wales	UAI statement
▪ Western Australia	Tertiary Entrance Examinations (TEE) with a statement of the Tertiary Entrance Score (TES) from which the decisive Tertiary Entrance Rank (TER) is derived, determining university entrance
▪ South Australia	Tertiary Admissions Rank (TER)
▪ Tasmania	Tertiary Entrance Score (TES) and Tertiary Admissions Rank (TER)
▪ Northern Territory	Tertiary Admissions Rank (TER)
▪ Victoria	Equivalent National Tertiary Entrance Rank (ENTER)
▪ Queensland	Tertiary Entrance Statement (TES)

The tertiary entrance exam is one good reason you should not wait until your children are already in their mid-teens to migrate; many children switching from a different system too late really flounder at tertiary entrance level in Australia. Often their chief difficulty is a change of mindset: if they have come from a system where learning the facts off by heart is enough, they will have a hard time learning that the Australian exam system values opinion, judgement, intellectualising and analysis more than knowledge of the facts. They will find. for instance. that English Literature is analysed more in terms of gender, race, politics and prejudice, than in terms of the elegance of the language, or the nature of structure, character and plot. Children who have migrated before their teens grow with the system and by the time they get to tertiary entrance, are well accustomed to these ways of thinking.

During the tertiary entrance exam year, Year 12, the student will be assessed during the entire year, with project scores during the year contributing to his or her final results— hence the pressure is on for the whole year, not just on the examination day. Another thing to remember is that marks in a class or year tend to be averaged out, so that if your child has the highest mark in the class but everybody else is closer to another, lower, level, then his or her marks will likely be brought down to match the average more closely. True!

Unfortunately for you, the education system in some states, notably Western Australia, is currently in virtual uproar, being in transition between two vastly different systems. The new system, known as Outcomes Based Education (OBE), already known to the USA and UK, has only begun to take hold in Australia in the late 1990s. OBE has upset some teachers so much that they are in virtual revolt, insisting they cannot implement the system as quickly as required. At the time of writing, there is nothing better than a tense stand-off between government and the teachers in Western Australia for example, and the future is very unclear. Once OBE takes hold, the tertiary entrance exam is defunct. OBE is too complex to describe here but in essence, it requires a far more subtle and somewhat nebulous curriculum and an extremely flexible style of assessment. Instead of rigid marking systems, teachers are now supposed to assess students for their ability to exercise certain skills and even attitudes, within very broad categories rather than marked grades. The mixing of subjects is also very fluid, so that scientific knowledge can for instance be expressed via the medium of a drama which also tests English language ability as well as a capacity for confident self-expression onstage. In a nutshell, OBE requires a student to demonstrate more deeply what they know and how they can apply it, rather than rewarding them for picking 'the right answer' out of a few choices in an exam paper. Creative and analytical skills are highly valued in this system. But it's much harder for parents to understand how well their children are doing.

'Uni'

Going to 'uni' or university frankly is not respected as the privilege it is by the current generation of Australian students, but perhaps that is also a worldwide phenomenon. Many Australian kids do not even bother to try to go there. A worryingly large number drop out, or else 'shop around' their university, changing courses every so often and never really achieving anything. The number of students who quit in the second year, ostensibly to go to work and earn some money 'for a while', but who for one reason or another never go back, is striking, and depressing. You will need to keep a careful watch on your child if you want him or her to resist the peer pressure of seeing plenty of examples like this around on campus. I think the problem is partly attributable to the inherent immaturity of 17 year-olds fresh out of Year 12. In other words, they are too young to settle down to a university routine as yet—partly due to the low status, and pay, accorded to degree-holders in Australia, and partly due to the spectacle of so many people regularly losing their jobs, or else surviving on makeshift part-time and temporary work contracts. Employment does not look like the secure rock it was for the 'baby-boomer' generation, or indeed for 'Generation X.'

I myself think it is a good plan to pre-empt this desire to quit university mid-stream by encouraging your 17-year-old youngster to go see the world, or even just Australia, for a year, do some voluntary service overseas, or within Australia, to get it all out of their system before they enter university. That way, there is some hope they will by then appreciate all the opportunities they have in Australia compared with other countries, and will want to use their chance to its fullest. (However, I should declare my inexpertise here— I am not a parent).

Shy Asians and others need to understand that in Australia debate is considered desirable, so expressing yourself publicly is no shame and expressing views that are different from your teacher's is not a problem, rather it is expected of you, especially at university.

If you are Australian or an Australian permanent resident, as a full-time student you can benefit from the Austudy financial assistance scheme to support you in your studies, subject to some income and asset tests. But most Australian students have to repay to the government the 'HECS' points (Higher Education Contribution Scheme) that they have accumulated during their student years, representing the value of their education; they do this in the form of deductions from their salary incorporated into their income tax payments when they get their first job after graduation. So to that extent, university education is not free in Australia.

ON THE POSITIVE SIDE

It would be negligent not to warn you of the migrant blues. But there is a brighter side, some of which I hope will emerge in other sections of this book. Among the plus points are the exhilarating experience of freedom, space, and that special bright light that the Australian climate and geography produce. Enlightened attitudes to medicine, to education and to the environment abound. There is an easy friendliness on the streets and the peacefulness of daily life—and real, wild democracy. There is the excitement of a vast, largely wild land.

You may decide you like it all so much that you want to become an Australian citizen. Check on your own country's rules about dual citizenship (allowing it or not allowing it) before you take the plunge.

Having spent 24 non-consecutive months within your first five years in Australia, you are eligible to apply, and the letter confirming your citizenship can come as quickly as a surprising two weeks after you apply. The ceremony at which you receive your Certificate of Australian Citizenship, necessary before you can get an Australian passport (without which you cannot safely leave and re-enter Australia once you are an Australian national), could be a few more weeks.

Here is one new citizen's account of the modest ceremony at which he received his citizenship, in Perth, Western Australia:

'We all trooped off to the Mayor's office, me and my two witnesses (you are not allowed more than two). On the seats in this room upstairs was a small package with our name tags on and a leaflet explaining our rights and duties as citizens. Altogether, our group of new citizens numbered 30.

'The Mayor's deputy made a speech and then they called us up in groups of about four or five to recite the oath of allegiance to Queen Elizabeth II (that probably won't go on much longer) and the country. ... The Mayor shook our hands and gave us our certs, and also a little badge with the Aussie flag on it for us to wear. Then we posed with the Mayor for a photo if we wished, holding up our certs.

The Citizen's Pledge

This is the pledge recited at the citizenship ceremony for newly naturalised citizens:

'From this time forward, under God*,
I pledge my loyalty to Australia and its people,
whose Democratic beliefs I share,
whose rights and liberties I respect,
and whose laws I will uphold and obey.'

The irony is, Australian-born citizens never have to pledge anything to anyone!

those who wish may affirm their loyalty without a reference to God.

'Our local councillor made a speech: he said wasn't it wonderful how the Aussie World Cup soccer team was almost all migrant and how migrants introduced soccer and in such a short time took Australia to world standard, etc. Then we had some beers or sherry and what the Aussies call 'finger food' (otherwise known as 'bites', 'dim sum' in Cantonese or 'makan kecil' in Malay), and we all sang 'Advance Australia Fair', and then went home.'

The National Anthem

Composed by Peter Dodds McCormick, a Scot, 'Advance Australia Fair' was first performed in 1878. A revised version of the song was officially adopted as the Australian national anthem in 1974, by the Labor government led by Prime Minister Gough Whitlam, but tensions between the British 'God Save the Queen' brought a reversal to this royal anthem under subsequent governments. Finally, after extensive surveys of public opinion, 'Advance Australia Fair' was firmly adopted as Australia's national anthem in 1984, with 'God Save the Queen' reserved only for occasions when members of the British royal family are present; on such occasions, both anthems are played.

Advance Australia Fair

Australians all let us rejoice,
For we are young and free;
We've golden soil and wealth for toil;
Our home is girt by sea;
Our land abounds in nature's gifts
Of beauty rich and rare;
In history's page, let every stage
Advance Australia Fair.
In joyful strains then let us sing,
Advance Australia Fair.

Beneath our radiant Southern Cross
We'll toil with hearts and hands;
To make this Commonwealth of ours
Renowned of all the lands;
For those who've come across the seas
We've boundless plains to share;
With courage let us all combine
To Advance Australia Fair.
In joyful strains then let us sing,
Advance Australia Fair.

My own citizenship ceremony was rather rushed, because I asked for an individual date owing to a need to travel on business. But I enjoyed the fun it all provided to

Author Ilsa Sharp (back, second left, holding the citizenship certificate) on the proud day she received her Australian citizenship, in 2002, from the City of Canning offices in Western Australia (Canning official on far left), with her Singapore-born husband Siva Choy (far right) and her favourite Aboriginal neighbour, Stephanie Eade, with two of her three children, Wayne (centre front) and Courtney (front right) as her witnesses.

my neighbours, an Aboriginal family, whom I invited along as witnesses.

HOMES AND GARDENS

A detached house set on at least a quarter-acre garden, with about six rooms, is central to the Australian definition of happiness. 'The first suburban nation', Donald Horne has called his own country, in his seminal psycho-analysis of Australia, *The Lucky Country*, of 1964, a classic to which all subsequent studies owe a debt, including this one.

Certainly, an Australian's home is his castle. A home of your own is the Great Australian Dream.

Impossible Dream?

Unfortunately, that dream has been punctured over recent decades, as house purchase prices and bank-loan interest rates have soared in tandem, with the latter heading towards 20 per cent or more at their worst in the late 1980s— at the time of writing, the rates are a lot more reasonable, around 7 per cent.

Rising prices and the preponderance of part-time work have left many young couples unable to contemplate buying their first home. To Australians, this upset has seemed akin to an infringement of their human rights. This is a key election issue every three years. All across the nation, resentment hangs in the air like smoke over a barbie; the government struggles constantly to meet its people's expectations of affordable homeownership. If you have been able comfortably to buy your Australian house outright, do not flaunt the fact.

Still, something like 70 per cent of Australians are homeowners (close to 40 per cent) or mortgagees, a pretty high rate in world terms. Public housing has become the mark of virtual welfare cases—broken families or families otherwise in crisis, single mothers, the unemployed, refugees and so on—and the housing provided, albeit low-cost, is often only minimally maintained.

Land Hunger

The quarter-acre fixation is also being re-examined, by thoughtful town-planners in particular. How much longer can Australian cities spread outwards in massive suburban sprawls, as can already be seen in Melbourne and Sydney and as is happening apace in Perth?

Not only does the Australian homeowner expect to own a fair amount of land, but he also expects literally to sit on it. Apartment living, even medium-rise, is only just beginning to occur as an option to most Australians, and the vast majority abhor high-rise homes. One of the most striking characteristics of the Australian city is its low skyline, except perhaps in the very heart of the central business district, where skyscrapers are considered reasonably appropriate for work—but not for home.

I personally find this a much more human way of living. With the population so small in such a huge land, one can sympathise with the Australian's instinctive insouciance about using up land. However, it must be admitted that a widely spread population makes the planning, administration and servicing of cities very difficult indeed. The provision of

Homes of the wealthy overlook Sydney Harbour's north side.

sewerage, roads, transport and a host of other infrastructure and services becomes a costly problem. Suburban sprawl is not acceptable either to environmentalists eager to protect wild Australia.

It seems most likely then that residential areas within a certain radius of Australian city centres will no longer be able to corner quarter-acre blocks for each housing unit in the future. Noises in this direction have already been made by various city authorities; 'high-density housing', a phrase which would have caused an uproar only a couple of decades ago, is now an Australian planner's buzz-word. An influx of Asian and American investors, more used to apartment-block living, has also fuelled the building of high-rise residential blocks (not that 'high-rise' is necessarily synonymous with 'high-density', however).

The Great Australian Dream is steadily receding to the outer suburbs and the outback countryside itself. But you can rely on the Australian homeowner to fight this 'reform' all the way. He feels as strongly about holding land as some Americans do about the right to own a gun, or the English about the importance of pet dogs.

Australian Style

The vast majority of Australian homes are single-storey, what are known as 'bungalows' in some parts of Asia, and each home is gloriously individual. It is still extremely unusual in Australia, I am glad to say, to be confronted with serried ranks of exactly identical estate homes looking as though they came out of the same plaster mould, off a factory conveyor belt, of the sort now common in many other parts of the world.

Very much in vogue, at a price, are historic, or even imitation, 'Federation' homes, harking back to a colonial architectural style popular at the turn of the century: these charming buildings usually feature porches and verandahs supported by pillars and elaborately lacy wrought-iron work, among other things. Other recognisably Australian housing styles are the neo-classical and Spanish designs of Mediterranean origin, 'weatherboard' wooden cottages, and the 'Queenslander', a largely timbered tropical exotic set high above ground level, usually with open verandahs.

The 'Greenie' movement is taking some designs closer to Nature, so timber and stone, or mixtures of the two, can also be seen. A most attractive, but not cheap, 'back to Nature' option is rammed earth, very popular in southern Western Australia, which produces a marvellously smooth caramel-brown surface. It's a strong material and naturally well insulated. Cheaper are baked mud-bricks, but it's an exhausting labour of love to construct a home of these.

In the older homes, all kinds of antique fixtures may be found. Like the wood-fired cooker I found in my 1950s home, on the edge of metropolitan Perth, when I moved in, in 1989. It was perfect for baking bread, and ingeniously linked up to the water piping to provide hot water, and a constant source of warmth, but eventually I tired of it and passed it on to a couple living in more rural parts, where such cookers are still found.

On the Ground

One of Australia's greatest attractions is surely the fact that it is still possible to acquire large chunks of wild land, and also to own a home on the ground for a reasonable price. Many a homeowner buys his land and then designs and builds his own house. A whole industry is geared to helping him do this, once planning permissions have been cleared with the authorities. There are catalogues of ready-made doors, windows, roofing, tiling, you name it.

Usually, you call in a professional to lay the foundations at least. After that, you could build it stick by stick yourself if you really wish. But most people use professional builders under their personal supervision. Be aware though that Australians dine out regularly on their horror stories of negative encounters with irresponsible or outright crooked builders. You must monitor your building project closely and do your own homework so that you understand what is going on.

When buying land, you need to have good advice and to be aware of all sorts of pitfalls. You may well find that you are not allowed to keep your land vacant of a building for more than a set period of time, say, about two years. There may also be requirements that you fence the land, which could be expensive, and there will certainly be strict rules about maintaining fire-breaks and burning back the land every so often.

You could also find that although you own the land, you do not own the soil beneath it, as the government may have reserved mining rights. This could put you in a sticky position if gold or iron ore is found beneath your house. In the countryside, be sure of your water sources, and understand thoroughly the local fire risks.

As in any other country, you need to study planning programmes for the area where you are buying: will your beautiful wilderness be a new town in a few years' time?

These are but a handful of the most common problems with land ownership. Tread carefully. For all these and other important considerations, such as taxation, please do refer to a professional consultant.

Shop Around

Any day, the newspapers are chock-a-block with house-sale ads. In Perth, I found that it was an accepted Sunday leisure activity to tour the various homes up for sale and open for viewing, sometimes just for fun, sometimes to update one's

Residential housing in Cannington, Western Australia, complete with swimming pool.

understanding of the market. These are not display homes, but real people's homes up for sale—the owners just have to go out for the day while a pack of strangers tramp through their home.

Most Australian home sales are done through a real estate agent, followed by a 'settlement agent' or lawyer who actually sees all the various, final payments through. The real estate agent will be sitting around in the house open for viewing (complete with all the occupants' furnishings). While Australian agents are no more honest than any others, I have found them pleasantly un-pushy, in that they rarely speak unless spoken to.

Here's the drum, as the Australians say, the latest on property, at the time of writing...

Taking Perth in Western Australia as an example (but don't ever forget, there are enormous differences, state by state, among Australia's property markets; generally speaking, the east, especially Sydney, is always the most expensive area), residential properties saw a 30–40 per cent decline in value after peaking at the highest ever level in May 1989, but in the early 20th century, prices started to soar again.

As William F Shire, Director of Australian Business & Property Services in Perth, says, "Prior to this boom period [in 1989], an average four-bedroom, two-bathroom brick-and-tile house could be bought for approximately A$ 72,000." As this kind of property now proceeds to more than double, the same kind of gains are now materialising for the buyers of 1989 who may have paid perhaps A$ 120,000 .

Another Australian, Peter M Brown, Associate Professor at the National University of Singapore's School of Building and Estate Management, who is hung about with qualifications much like a Christmas tree with lights (including being a Fellow of the Australian and New Zealand Institutes of Valuers), apparently has got the Australian real estate cycle all figured out. It follows an eight-year boom-bust pattern, he says. There have been property price peaks in 1973, 1981 and 1989, and then again at the turn of the 20th century, so this looks about right—say a ten-year cycle then, all other factors being equal.

Buy Now

When to buy? Well, you could wait for a peak to decline. But quite honestly, if you are not speculating and are prepared to sit on your property a while, you probably cannot lose, whatever time you buy. But it's always worthwhile keeping an ear out for what might happen in the next federal, and state, Budget. And in general, it's a good plan to buy in winter when the market is much quieter. Australian property owners who want to sell always try to capitalise on the euphoria that spring or summer sunshine stimulates in buyers confronted with nice fresh winter-watered gardens crammed with flowers.

How and What to Buy

First, do be aware that buying an Australian property does not in any way enhance your chances of securing permanent residence or citizenship. And if you enter on a temporary residence/business visa that later fails, you will have to sell whatever property you have bought in the interim.

The FIRB

Visitors and non-residents can only buy brand new properties, or buy an old property and demolish it to build a new house or a building that is at least a 50 per cent renewal of the old building—but to buy an old property, you need Foreign Investment Review Board (FIRB) approval, which is usually available within about 28 days. Or you can buy land for building but must build on it within 12 months of buying it.

For commercial properties, the FIRB is likely to approve any non-resident if the purchase involves a shop or hotel.

For your first information on what's available, the local newspaper's real estate section and local real estate magazines are a good start. About a year before you move, get friends in Australia to send you pages of the newspaper, cruise around Internet sites, and generally do your homework. Make up your mind what exactly it is that you want—how many bedrooms, bathrooms, a big yard or a small one, a swimming pool or not—and what will be the best location for you in terms of proximity to schools, work and so on. Take the occasional flight into Australia and look around a bit just to familiarise yourself. Buying sight unseen does happen—especially with cashed-up investors, as has been the case in Singapore at certain travelling real estate exhibitions—but it can be a foolish and unnecessary risk. One real estate agent friend of mine has told me that the average agent's commission for property sales at such exhibitions is easily A$ 5,000, so exhibitions and their costs can easily become part of the buyer's cost.

The vast majority of property available in Australia will be freehold, a concept of complete ownership that is commonly referred to as 'fee simple'. 'Green title', you should note, means your title is complete, you can do anything with the property. That will not be the case with a shared 'strata title' however—there will be other owners to consult.

If you want to develop the site as, say, a 'duplex', i.e. with two smaller homes on it, be aware that there will be rules on what size the block must be to do this, particularly about the width of the frontage and the amount of spare land available for creating full access at the sides (for cars, emergency vehicles like fire trucks etc).

In some areas, there may be restrictions like 'R' (Residential only) coding that will dictate what you can do with the property; be sure to consult the local Council about such rules, as well as special issues like heritage areas. Your real estate agent, however, is legally required to divulge such issues to you in advance. Other issues may be Council plans to take land for the widening of roads ('road resumption'), in effect compulsory acquisition but usually compensated with the market value plus 10 per cent.

What kind of Australian house is a good buy then, in capital gains terms when you sell? (There is no capital gains tax for the sale of a 'first home' or principal home).

When you buy an established property, you buy it as is—it must be in the same condition in three months' time as on the day you agreed to buy it. So it's the vendor's responsibility to ensure that the condition remains the same. But if the water heater is not working when you buy it and you didn't check it then, then you cannot complain if it is not working when you move in. On the other hand, if the reverse is true, you can complain when you move in.

Here, the experts recommend purchases of brick-and-tile (brick walls, tiled roofs) homes in the A$ 200,000–300,000 bracket, and careful attention to location—not more than 15 km (9.3 miles) from the city centre, with easy access to the nearest freeway, to schools, shops, parks and bus routes, and so on. Get to know the local geography and understand details like, in Western Australia, the fact that nobody actually lives in 'Perth', since Perth is only the city centre; people live in a suburb with its own name, like Bentley, Victoria Park, Mirrabooka or Mount Lawley. Be careful when ads say '5 mins from the city'—which city? It could be the city centre of a satellite city like Rockingham, well outside Perth, not Perth city itself.

'Brick-and-tile' as opposed to what, you may ask?

Many older Australian homes are built of 'weatherboard'—

overlapping timber planks—or of 'fibro', compressed-wood fibreboard, or even metals like zinc or anodised aluminium. In the case of metals, particularly, there will probably be an asbestos insulation layer under the metal cladding. In many old buildings, roofs are either of zinc or other metals, or also of asbestos. The weatherboard styles often have a pretty, old-fashioned and traditionally Australian look about them, but brick-and-tile immediately confers greater prestige, something you have to consider in terms of resale value.

There is also a psychological problem with asbestos owing to a prolonged health scare about asbestosis in Australia. Loose asbestos fibres certainly are not great for your health and intensive exposure to asbestos, in the industrial, manufacturing context, has been proven dangerous, even fatal. But there really is not much hard evidence about how dangerous it is just to live in a house with asbestos insulation. However, in view of fairly hysterical public perceptions in Australia at the moment, asbestos is probably something a home buyer should worry about, again in terms of resale value if nothing else.

Also prestigious are fenced or walled gardens, although a pleasantly free and open, trusting feeling is visible in the suburban Australian landscape, thanks to the many unfenced gardens. The wealthier the area, however, the more money will have been spent to purchase privacy behind creeper-laden walls. But these are sure insignia of the tall poppy.

Older Australian properties will not necessarily have more than one bathroom and may have the toilet separate, even distant, from the main bathroom, nor will they have ensuite bathrooms, so if these are important for you, you need to check carefully on this.

Most properties will be sold fittings included—fittings such as carpets, window and light fittings, perhaps even with cooker, washing machine, air conditioners and fans. Be clear about this before you buy, and check that what has been promised is indeed in place before you take possession.

GETTING STARTED

You'll probably start your property hunt with a real estate agent. Make sure he/she is a member of a proper professional association with certification—in WA, this would be REIWA, the Real Estate Institute of Western Australia.

Beware of loans taken outside Australia, as they may attract a 10 per cent Australian withholding tax. In Australia, you can go to a bank or a finance broker and mostly, a 10 per cent deposit is expected when your offer is accepted, although this is sometimes negotiable. The deposit is fully refundable if the finance is not approved or if the sale does not go through for any reason that is not the buyer's fault. If you, the buyer, just change your mind, the owner can re-offer the propery on the market and sue you for the difference he has lost, with costs.

You can have the property you fancy valued, for a fee of about A$ 600, using a 'Sworn Valuer'. A real estate agent can only give you an appraisal, which is little more than an educated opinion. A sworn valuer on the other hand must be ready to substantiate his valuation, in court if necessary. These valuers take a four-year course and valuing is their sole profession. But in truth, many valuers do call up real estate agents for extra information and help! Check out the current median price in the city of your choice, and then check out what price houses are routinely changing hands at in the area you have picked. Pay the local price, not a foreign sucker's price!

Help for First-home Owners

If you are buying your first home in Australia, you can get the 'First Home-owner Grant' introduced for the federal election of 2001. It was a generous A$ 14,000 then, but has now been reduced to A$ 7,000. It's not means tested and permanent residents can access it. You must move into the property within the first 12 months of ownership, you must live in it and you cannot rent it out. The purchase is free of stamp duty up to a property value of A$ 220,000, after which it is charged pro rata.

What to Check Before Making an Offer

Having identified your property, follow a few more steps to check things out before you make an offer:

- Check on add-on structures in the back garden—sheds, studios and 'sleep-overs' or 'granny cottages' and double-check whether they have all had Council building permission or not;
- Be sure to check on whether the fencing on the property reflects the actual boundaries of the block of land that you are buying, and whether any neighbours have intruded beyond their boundaries into your site.
- Check on how much the local property rates are—an average locality might be around A$ 600.
- Check there is sewerage already laid and connected, make sure old leach drains (covered drains) and septic tanks have been decommissioned, otherwise this may have to be done later—and septic tanks will need emptying every five years.
- Check that gas connections have already been laid; if not, this is something you may wish to do later, and will have to pay for. I didn't have gas on tap in my house when I moved in, in 1989.
- If there is a swimming pool, check whether there is an automatic pool-cleaner machine already in place that you can inherit, how old the pump is and whether it is a self-chlorinating salt-water pool (a good idea).
- If there is a well-planted garden, consider whether you really want to maintain a full garden, or how much it would cost you to pay someone else to do it; take note that beautiful green-turf lawns guzzle expensive water in the summer, and check on the local Council's probable water restrictions in summer to see whether you can really maintain that lawn; native plant gardens are easier on water consumption, but still need some, and also need regular re-mulching every couple of years.
- Check on whether there is a built-in burglar alarm system, monitored or otherwise, and check the quality of all security locks on doors and windows.

(Continued on the next page)

What to Check Before Making an Offer

(Continued from previous page)

- Check that the house is insulated.
- Check whether there is a cooling system in place for the summer—evaporative air conditioning (water circulating over wood chips) is both economic and environmentally friendly, and quite efficient, with the plus over traditional air conditioning that you need to keep the windows open not shut when operating it.
- Check whether there is a heating system for the water, such as a solar heater unit on the roof—these are very efficient and economical considering the amount of sunshine Australia enjoys.
- Be sure you know how old the house is. You might like to check when it was last roofed. If it's raised on stumps, you will want to check when it was last 're-stumped', i.e. physically lifted and re-stabilised on a new footing. Both these issues have confronted us in our house in Perth—the roof had to be replaced within five years of moving in. But if you are buying more for the land value than the building value and intend either to sell or develop soon, these issues may not bother you so much.
- You can expect—and demand—that full treatment of the house for preventing termite damage has recently been done, if there are any timber structures at all.
- Check out the neighbours and the neighbourhood, ask Australians about your chosen suburb's reputation. If there is public housing next door, or a high crime rate in the area, you may wish to reconsider.
- Visit the area and the house if possible without your real estate agent, and at different times of the day and night, to get a real feel for it.
- If high-speed broadband and the Internet matter to you, check whether they are available in the area you have chosen; you would be surprised at how commonly 'black holes' in broadband supply manifest themselves even in apparently metropolitan areas.

Making an Offer

If you like the house and the market is currently busy, then don't fall into a tedious bargaining process, just offer the stated price, or you may lose the place during the delay. But in some circumstances, you may wish to make a lower offer. Always remember that the real estate agent selling the property is acting for the seller-owner, not for you the buyer. If you have cash in hand, you are in a very good position to knock the price down, but if there are long-winded procedures to endure, moving money around banks etc, then you can expect the vendor to exact the full price as originally stated. Even when you make an offer, you can still hedge it around with conditions, such as 'subject to checking for termites', or 'subject to the structure being checked for wiring and plumbing', or even 'subject to property being cleared of all rubbish.' If you have certain considerations before you can raise the money, you can say things like ' subject to me selling my boat' or 'subject to me getting my accident insurance settlement.' You can also state in your offer that you would like to take over some of the furniture that you have seen in the house, or the pot plants or whatever. Make a point of stating in your offer that all plumbing, electricity and water must be working at settlement time—this will force the vendor to ensure any repairs needed are done before you pay up. You can also make your offer subject to structural inspection—this must then be done within about seven days, at your own cost, probably about A$ 500. Once you have made an offer on the place, this is a sort of legal contract, but only truly binding once your offer has been formally accepted by the owner. He or she has the option of accepting or rejecting your offer, or making a counter-offer to you, in terms of price, terms, conditions or settlement dates.

You can refuse to settle until all the items you want fixed are indeed fixed, although you cannot actually withdraw from the promise to purchase. Or else, you can deduct the cost of fixing the items needing repair from your final purchase price. Your offer will state the final settlement date and finance terms.

Settlement

The 'settlement' system is unique to Western Australia—in Sydney or Melbourne, you can use lawyers to handle your property purchase (as with conveyancing lawyers in Singapore, for example), but the upside is, WA's settlement system is cheaper than using lawyers. You can't progress a property purchase or sale in WA without a settlement agent. Make sure you choose one that is registered with the Settlement Agents Supervisory Board. The settlement agent then does all the legal paperwork for you, liaises with your bank and organises the stamp duty—which can be substantial, at about A$ 11,000 on a A$ 300,000 home, due about one week before settlement. You'll need to budget for the settlement agent's fees, say about A$ 10,000 on a A$ 300,000 property. Amongst the paperwork the agent will handle for you will be items like the settlement of your share of rates and taxes or utility bills outstanding on a property you are selling.

What if you have a complaint against your real estate agent? The Real Estate Practices Act has set up the Real Estate and Business Agents Supervisory Board to take care of such incidents. You can complain to the Board, or to your nearest Consumer Affairs unit, under the Trade Practices Act.

And what about cutting agents out of the process altogether? You may see private sales advertised, with no agent involved. This is not necessarily cheaper from the buyer's point of view; it is the seller who is saving money, not you. The property could still be over-priced or agents may not have wanted to handle it for some reason—an ominous sign for you too.

Even if the price is good in a private sale, there is now little or no protection for you as the buyer. Since the owner is not a member of any formal real estate agents' professional association and your only recourse with any complaint will be in the civil courts. In contrast, when the agent belongs to a professional association, a complaint to that association threatens him or her with loss of his licence. And from your point of view, any agent belonging to a formal association will have professional indemnity insurance and professional liability insurance to cover against complaints such as yours, so there is the possibility of quite speedy compensation for you. So private sales are not as attractive as they might seem at first glance.

Some Real Estate Jargon

When you scan the Australian classified ads for house-sales, there may well be some abbreviations which are a mystery to you. Following are a few examples—for the rest, consult an Australian friend or real estate agent.

- **Backyard**

  A general term for the patio plus garden, poolside area, and everything else at the back of the house that is related to the outdoor life that is so central to the Australian lifestyle.

- **Bgp**

  Below-ground pool. A much better sort of swimming pool than the above-ground sort, this is a properly sunken pool.

- **Blt in robes**

  Built-in wardrobes.

- **Bore**

  A deep well driven into the ground to tap deep aquifers or ground water, and equipped with a pump to bring it up. This is an important plus for homes with gardens and reticulated watering systems, not least because it saves on the cost of what is sometimes called 'scheme water', or the the more expensive treated drinking water supplied by local authorities for delivery to your household taps.

- **Brick veneer**

  Simulated brick facing for houses, used as a disguise over inner walls of other materials such as asbestos or aluminium.

- **Dbt**

  Double brick-and-tile, a better quality, better insulated version of simple brick-and-tile.

(Continued on the next page)

(Continued from previous page)

- **Games room or Family room**
  A large living room where the family congregates, usually separate from the dining room, and often also separate from a front lounge room or what sometimes may still, in old fashioned parlance, be called 'the front parlour,' a kind of guest reception room away from the more private family areas.
- **Harbour glimpses**
  Common in Sydney, this half-promise means that if you stand on a stool, or if you are about 2 m (8 ft) tall, you can, by squinting through the bathroom window, spot a small part of the spectacular harbour view.
- **Retic**
  This refers to 'reticulation', the system of below-ground piping which pumps bore water up through automatic sprinklers to tend your garden. When buying a home, it's best to ensure this is already in place as it could be expensive to lay.
- **Weatherboard**
  These are the old wooden cottages of 1950s Australia and earlier, with overlapping planks of wood, very commonly seen in Perth, Western Australia. Today they are charming heritage properties. Though often poky inside, they characteristically sit on a 'quarter-acre' block of land and have a cottage-like look, with curlicued wooden ornamentation on pillared front verandahs.

HANDYMAN MANIA

Because the home is such an important possession, Australians spend an awful lot of time 'doing things around the house' (when not tinkering with the car). In fact, they are forever renovating, rebuilding or extending.

If you want to be a real Australian, you should always have at least one room of your house in total chaos when visitors call on you: 'Oh, we're just renovating the lounge/bathroom/kitchen.' The wreckage of broken timber, drilling dust and stripped wallpaper should be strewn over the floor. The man of the house (yes, they're still traditional that way in Australia)

A dinkum Aussie lifestyle—constantly renovating your home.

should be glimpsed, paint-roller, electric saw or wallpaper-steamer in hand, slaving away in his filthy dungarees, or, more likely, shorts.

Alternatively, the whole house, including the tea-set crockery, could be coated in a fine film of red wood dust—'We only just finished hand-polishing the wood floors.' Or there could be a curious odour—'The pest men just came to spray for termites.' All these constitute a perfectly normal state of affairs in any Australian home at any one time.

DIY is Dinky-di

If you are in any doubt about my telling the truth in this matter, just take a look at the *Yellow Pages* phone-book for any city in Australia and see how many 'DIY' (Do It Yourself) centres you can count.

I guarantee they will take up several pages.

DIY is a massive industry in Australia, partly because the cost of labour makes hiring contractors prohibitive, but also because it is the approved, macho way of 'doing things around the house'. It's part of the 'pioneer, frontier syndrome' that infects every Australian mind. A visit to any major DIY emporia reveals vast warehouses stacked with every conceivable thingamajig to do every conceivable practical thing from building your own greenhouse to mending a leaky tap. My husband says it's Heaven; others have more mixed feelings.

Most Australian homes have a workshed in the garden, crammed full of tools for this and that, paint tins and so on. And garden tools. Sometimes home brewing equipment too. Sadly, it must be said, sometimes it is difficult to appreciate what has been achieved by all this toil, when gazing at the ill-matching but all equally awful wallpaper and carpets in many Australian homes.

On the other hand, there is a certain vitality in Australian home décor. Often, in younger and more educated households, the furnishings will reflect the new multicultural society in which Australians now live, as well as a consciousness of Asian neighbours—Italian touches, Aboriginal artefacts, vases bought in Singapore, batik paintings from Indonesia and so on, stone statues from Bali and 'water features', tinkly little fountains, from somewhere in South-east Asia or Japan.

GARDEN GNOMES

The garden is the other Australian obsession, very much part of the British heritage. Older Australians (39 per cent of gardeners anyway) illustrate the origins of this heritage beautifully, as they lovingly tend look-alike English country-cottage gardens full of roses, chrysanthemums and dahlias, with verdant lawns tediously kept alive by a water-sprinkler system using bore water from beneath the soil.

Australian grass, such as it is (you will soon become familiar with the menace of everything from buffalo-grass to couch-grass, among various kinds of undesirable grass), is not meant to be green and lush, particularly in the summer.

Shopping at Xanthorrhoea, which is a native plant specialist nursery in the Perth hills.

The natural state of an Australian lawn is dry, brown and sparse—come and see mine in Perth any time!

Such English-style gardens are of course quite ridiculous in a largely arid ecology. The 'soils' in Perth, for example, consist almost entirely of sand.

Among the foreign plants which do seem to do well in Australia are those which come from a very similar setting, in South Africa. Thankfully, recent decades have seen the growth of a 'Native Gardens' movement (about 23 per cent of styles chosen) which encourages the cultivation of indigenous

Kangaroo's Paw.

Australian species. These 'natives' include the Eucalypts, the Acacias (Wattles), the flowering Grevilleas, Bottlebrush, Banksias, Kangaroo Paws and so on. They are much more sensible choices than roses since they demand less attention and waste less water: native plants are geared to manage with very little water—but not no water, as many beginners fondly imagine.

This great change signifies that at last, the white Australian is coming to terms with his real environment, the Australian ecology, and breaking away from the English motherland of the past.

Here are a few things you need to know about native gardens that are quite different from European temperate or Asian tropical gardens:

- Native plants do *not* like highly nutritious phosphorous and nitrogen-rich fertilisers and manures—they are adapted to much less rich diets; use only a designated special native-plant slow-release fertiliser and don't place it too close to the plant's roots.

- You may still have to water some native plants in the hot dry summer and also during their first year when they are still young, but it is better to water infrequently and deeply than to water frequently but too shallow—if you do the latter, the roots will spread all over the surface with only fragile grasp and eventually the plant will just fall over; you need to encourage the plant to drive its naturally

The Wollemi Pine is a 'living fossil', a prehistoric tree thought extinct until its rediscovery in the Blue Mountains in 1994. There are only a few trees, about 40, in existence, apart from the seeds and saplings now being nurtured by excited Australian botanists and foresters. This picture shows a new sapling recently grown from one of the seeds.

deep tap roots way down into the soil, seeking out water. Generally speaking, you need to water native plants only at the height of summer, and even then, not much. Many natives need water but also dislike 'wet feet', preferring good drainage, so sometimes it's a good plan to place them on a slope, mound or embankment.

- Once planted, a native plant will dislike any further moves, as its root systems hate to be disturbed.
- Many native plants need full sun if they are to produce good crops of flowers, but not all of them; study the local species well, read books, identify your local native plant specialist nurseries and visit them often, asking for advice when needed.

- Planting time is in winter, with most flowering plants achieving their full glory in spring and early summer.
- If you don't mulch, mostly your garden just won't work for you. Try a nice wood-chip mulch to give it a nice bushland look, but take care not to pile the mulch high around the stems of plants and trees, as this can encourage moisture accumulation and fungal rots; leave a circle of non-mulched area just around the base of the plant;
- In areas like coastal Western Australia, much of which has only sand for soil, water runs off or seeps through too quickly, so you may need to use a soil-wetting agent to help soils retain the water you apply, or water granules in your pots and baskets; if you see the soil surface crusting in pots and baskets so that the water just runs off and never penetrates to the plant's roots, apply a simple dilution of a little washing up liquid and water to loosen up the soil structure—it won't harm the plant.

Putting on a Front

Whatever the character of their gardens, you will see them on weekends, all the gardeners, toiling long and hard at weeding, digging, pruning, mulching (using woodchips, newspaper, lawn mowings and the like) and mowing their lawns.

Businesses providing services such as 'garden bags' delivered empty and collected full of garden rubbish at regular intervals, are thriving. So are lawn-cutting and tree-pruning services, for the lazy.

Interestingly, it is always the *front* garden above all that is so lovingly tended. Traditionally, the back garden, or 'backyard', has two areas, the smart entertaining area around the patio and pool, and a discreet bit you can hardly see, usually around the garden shed, that is a much messier, more utilitarian place, where the washing is hung out, the dogs and cats hang out, handyman activities take place, and a vegetable patch might be cultivated for cheap, fresh food.

The front garden is the image the householder wishes to present to the world; the Australian cares about what his neighbours, and passers-by, might think of him, in terms of middle-class decency.

THE FAMILY DOG

Australians have inherited the British love of pets, particularly dogs. Take a look at any public park over the weekend and see how many dogs you can spot being walked; you are bound to see an amazing number, and variety.

If you are settling into Australia and want a dog, you should take a look at typically Australian dogs, most of them stemming from sheep- or cattle-mustering breeds. Breeds include the Blue-heeler and the Kelpie. The smooth-haired Kelpie is a cattle-dog that derives from the border collie. But remember, they need a lot of space and a lot of walking; energetic dogs, they will probably chase anything around, including your neighbour's cat, and should never be left out of your garden unaccompanied.

Also typically Australian are the Australian Silky, a long-haired toy dog, and the Kangaroo Dog, a greyhound-Scottish deerhound cross once used to fight off kangaroos and dingos (wild dogs).

FRONT-ROOM FORMALITY

A strange thing about the Australian suburbs is the deathly quiet, and darkness, of the streets at night. This is partly because the seasonal weather does not always encourage people to be out on the streets, as you might expect in Mediterranean or tropical Asian settings, and partly because the level of urban crime (or at least the *perception* of the level) does not encourage it either.

But it is also because the front room is never in use and therefore never lit up. 'The front room', also known as the lounge-room, plays much the same role as the parlour did—and still does in some North-country parts—in England. It is a starched, tidy, formal room for 'serious' socialising only—a visit from the local priest perhaps, the police, the family lawyers, the doctor or prospective in-laws. It is not really meant to be lived in.

The underlying idea, of course, is that most visitors are (a) unexpected and (b) unwelcome, so they should be contained at the front of the house and got rid of from there. Australians are paradoxical in that, although they are very friendly on the surface, they in fact have a highly developed concept of privacy.

Real life takes place at the back of the house, in and around the kitchen, in the larger 'family room' and, in the summer, in the backyard, on the patio or verandah as well as the decking around the barbie (barbecue pit) and perhaps also in and around the swimming pool.

Kitchens are often open-design, allowing for maximum social interaction. A great deal of social life takes place in the kitchen. It is rare to be invited to a sit-down dinner in a separate dining room. More likely, you will find yourself milling around the kitchen talking to the lady of the house cooking at the stove, snacking from a mobile buffet, or standing in the garden around the barbie pit.

LOO LORE

Another odd thing about Australian houses from the non-Australian point of view is the bathroom and 'loo' configuration (john, WC, toilet, lavatory) disposition. Only the newer houses will have more than one loo. Older and rural homes might even have the loo in a separate shed in the yard—the 'dunny' of Aussie folklore. Writing in *The West Australian* in 1993, Pam Casellas remarked, 'We grew up with good bladders, us country kids, because we were too scared to venture out to the lav in the middle of the night.'

Very few homes have loos in the bathroom itself (the place where you shower or bath)—they are usually separate. So do not ask for the 'bathroom' nor to 'wash your hands', if what you really want is to relieve yourself, as you will probably find yourself facing only a hand-basin and a towel-rail. You will have to be more specific and ask either for the 'toilet' or the 'loo'.

I am pleased to say that the more sophisticated homes are improving on this lamentable situation by installing more than one loo, and also incorporating loos with the shower-room in some rare instances. Despite the British tradition of taking a bath in a tub, or 'long bath' as some call it, most Australians opt for showers in preference, by the way.

The 'John', 'Loo', 'Dunny'

'The night was dark and stormy
The dunny light grew dim,
I heard a crash, and then a splash,
Good God, he's fallen in!'

A childhood ditty retailed to the author by Beth Kennedy, a native of Albany in Western Australia. The outdoors toilet or 'dunny' in old Australian homes, still to be found in the countryside, is at the centre of countless jokes and tall tales, including those of fearsome spiders attacking one's rear end.

Other Rooms

Bedrooms and the master bathroom, if there is one, are designed to be out of the way of visitors and it is expected that they should be treated as strictly private areas.

THE BARBIE

Some have called this 'the high altar' in the ritual of outdoor living. The outdoors area of the home is very clearly a male domain, controlled by the man of the house. As mentioned earlier, the hunter-male cooks the 'primitive' meal of raw meat burned on charcoal. Visiting females should not attempt to interfere. Outdoors settings are the ideal environment for the naturally sociable and easy-going Australian to mingle without formality.

Cooking up a storm at an outdoor barbecue.

The barbie party is the Australian's safe route to nostalgia about life in the bush, brewing tea in a billy over a campfire. The same macho psychology pushes suburban Australians to wear cattledriver 'cowboy' hats, display huge 'roo bars' on the front of their cars (for fending off kangaroos crossing the roads) or to purchase impressive 4WD (four-wheel drive) vehicles, meant for heavy bush-driving, when in fact they hardly ever go bush (making them a complete menace on ordinary suburban roads, where drivers behind these monsters can never see past them).

Incidentally, you will hardly ever see the word 'barbecue' spelled properly. It appears everywhere, in advertisements, party invitations and so on, as 'BBQ', 'Bar BQ', and 'Bar-b-que'.

VISITING

There is certainly more visiting without a prior appointment in Australia than there would be in England. All the same, you have to be careful about your timing.

In Asia of course, and many Mediterranean countries too, the problem simply would not arise: the family would naturally invite their friend to share the evening meal with them. But this kind of familiarity does not come easily to Australians, so do not expect it; instead, leave at the unspoken but appointed time, i.e. by about 6:00 pm latest. Neither is it as automatic to Australians to offer visitors a drink on arrival as it is in some cultures, particularly Asian cultures.

A very pained Asian friend complained to me once about how he could feel the atmosphere tense up if he called on his friends shortly before 'tea' (the evening meal, or dinner, in Australia). They would sit chatting very politely, but clearly waiting for him to leave, indeed dying for him to leave as time wore on.

If you come from a society where home-help or servants are easily available, pause to remember that this is not the norm in Australia. It would therefore be a good idea to offer to help clear the table and to wash up. The offer may be refused, but it will certainly be appreciated.

TROUBLESHOOTING CHECKLIST

Here is a random and by no means exhaustive checklist of potential problem areas.

Swimming Pool

'Just what I always dreamed of, my own backyard pool!' you may sigh as you move into your new Australian home. All pool-owners quickly learn how costly it is to maintain a pool in proper condition. You will be forever measuring the chlorine level, the pH level, the alkaline-acid ratio, tipping in great sacks of salt (for salt-water chlorinators), repairing pumps and filters, and so on.

Pool maintenance is a serious matter in the scorching Australian summer—the hotter it gets, the more likely a badly maintained pool may breed bacteria, the sort that cause meningitis in children, for example. The chemicals necessary to maintain balance in your pool are costly. So budget carefully before rushing for one.

Take note too of our salutary lesson when we accidentally emptied our pool. We had turned the pump onto 'Backwash' to clean out the filter, which entails draining some water out of the pool. We then went to bed and forgot about it. Next morning, hey presto, no pool! Well, no water anyway.

We decided this was a blessing in disguise since the swimming season had just ended and winter was on its way, and thought nothing further of it until someone wiser remarked that he hoped our pool was not fibreglass. Yes it was, we told him.

In that case, said he, better get it filled straightaway, as the sides would probably buckle under the pressure of soil subsidence around the pool during heavy winter rains. Sure enough, when we anxiously inspected our pool, there was a distinct bulge on one side. That meant hosing in about 30,000 litres of water as quickly as possible—and the consequent water bill.

Trees

For those who have previously lived in city apartments, it may be quite marvellous to find you have trees in your Australian garden, perhaps fruit trees as well. But be aware that all trees, and especially fruit trees, need special care.

Some species, such as the paperbarks (Melaleucas) may have acid foliage which renders all the soil beneath their canopy bald of grass. Some may be poisonous to children. Others (like lemon trees) may detest exposure to strong winds. Some unique Australian ones, like the iconic Blackboy (aka Grass Tree, aka Balga, aka Xanthorrhoea sp.), may need to be set on fire every so often, not to mention the huge area they need for their extensive root system. Besides which, they grow at tortoise pace, so you need either to plant a fairly mature one (not always easy to transplant) or be patient and plant for posterity.

Wattles look great, with their gorgeous yellow blossom, but don't plant them close to the house or drains, as their

The Blackboy of Western Australia.

root system will one day invade and destabilise the building or the drainage system.

Bottlebrush also look wonderful with their drooping candle-like red blooms, but if you or anyone in your family are asthmatic or susceptible to hay fever, the flowers could make things worse for you. The high pollen index during most Australian spring seasons often disturbs such people badly.

Once again, you may have to make the difficult decision whether to use chemical fertilisers and insecticides—fruit flies are among the pests attacking stone fruit like nectarines and apricots, for example. Check out your local gardening societies, including the organic ones, and ask their advice—I discovered from an organic gardener that you could hang fruit tree branches with tins full of water mixed with the salty Australian yeast-and-vegetable bread-spread, Vegemite, to act as natural fly traps. But you have to change them every week...

With other plants, you have to watch out for snails and slugs—guess what, a small saucer full of beer embedded in the ground next to your plant will attract snails, who will joyfully drown in the amber fluid.

Wooden Houses

Termites, or white ants as they are more commonly called in Australia, are a problem, but so are the chemicals used to spray against them. Spraying once may be necessary, particularly if your home is weatherboard and has wooden floors, as many of the older homes do. But do not listen to the pest-control companies who want to persuade you to treat your home every year—chemicals usually have an effective life of at least three or four years, and could be toxic if they leech into your garden soil, where you might have a vegetable patch ('veggie' patch as the Aussies call it), for example.

Do some research before making this decision, sample a mixture of views, from those of your neighbours to consumer advice bureaux to 'Green' conservationist groups.

Creepy-crawlies

Spiders stand out in this category, with some 2,000 species identified in Australia. Some Australian spiders commonly found in the garden and the house are a lot more dangerous than anything you are likely to have experienced before.

In the eastern states, there is the Funnel-web, named after the silken tube it builds at its burrow entrance, one of the world's deadliest spiders—the antidote must be administered almost immediately after the bite to be effective.

In the west, there is the Red-back (related to the Black Widow), a small glossy black spider with a red patch on its abdomen, brightest in females, which are also the more dangerous—again, an antivenin is available, however. The Red-back loves to hide in places like the top of fences, inside letter boxes and on the handles of gardening tools among other places. This spider's bite has been known to kill.

Flies

Your image of elegant luncheon parties on your patio on sunny Sunday afternoons could be marred by a common Australian pest, the fly. There are about 7,000 species in the country.

In rural areas, the flies are notorious for their persistence, and their tendency to sit anywhere moist, including your nose, eyes, ears and mouth. Hence the famous 'Australian salute', the constant rhythmic flicking of the hand across the face to keep the flies away. You will find this gesture comes very naturally indeed.

Houses are suitably equipped with extra mesh-and-metal fly-screen doors besides the usual doors, as well as window fly-screens. If you want to enjoy peace in your own home, and if you want to stay popular with your Australian hosts, remember always to close the fly-screens, leaving the normal doors and windows open for good ventilation during the summer. And keep your own fly-screens in good repair, free of holes.

Burglary

House-breaking is definitely on the increase in Australia, with drug-taking and youth unemployment among the causative factors. If you are alert and careful, you should be able to protect yourself. A dog is a good idea. So is a burglar alarm.

The sort of alarm system that links up to a monitoring system connected to the nearest police station is probably best; a loud alarm bell might possibly scare a would-be burglar off, but it wouldn't necessarily get help to you quickly without such a monitoring system (and be aware too that there is a general public outcry in Australia at the moment about the slow police response to emergency phone calls). Alarms that use sensor beams to detect movement across rooms are quite effective. Make sure you have a 'panic button' activating the alarm and a working telephone near your bed for emergencies. Alarm systems that can generate their own battery power should the mains power in the house be cut off are also a good idea. Now plaster the house with the stickers provided by your security service, announcing that 'This house is protected by X Monitored Alarms' (even if it isn't).

Leave lights on and radios or televisions playing when you go out. (Cent-conscious Australians never leave lights on, though.) Sensor-lighting systems that switch on in response to movement are also a good idea, to light up the front drive when you drive your car back home, or to light up the garden suddenly, if an intruder climbs over the back fence.

Lock up properly at night and when you go out. Fix metal-grille screens on windows and make sure fly-screens are also reinforced with metal. Never answer the front door without ensuring the second, fly-screen, door is locked; as an extra precaution, use a peephole to view who is calling before opening either door.

Get a house-sitter rather than leave the house empty when you go on holidays. Note that in car-oriented Australia, a car in the driveway usually indicates someone is at home, while absence of a car means everybody is out and it may be OK to break in—one of many good reasons to own a car.

Charity Canvassers

The newcomer is at first intrigued, later astounded, and finally infuriated by the number of people who come to the front door collecting for charities. This is a great Australian nuisance.

Many of these people are professional, paid collectors and while many may need the job, it is very difficult to sort out who is genuine and who may be just operating a neat little scam. The best tactic is probably to ask them to write to you instead, so you can decide at your leisure whether you want to donate, how much and to which charities. Don't feel bad, just send them away. There are just a few groups I rarely send off without some money—'The Salvos' as the Salvation Army is often called in Australia, and sometimes the Red Cross too. They do tremendous work across the board with the poor and disadvantaged (of which there are a surprising number in Australia). They will often announce a door-knock campaign well in advance, in advertisements or newspaper announcements, so you can always know when to be ready for them.

Fire

You must always be aware of the very great danger that fires pose in Australia, especially during the summer, when everything is tinder-dry. Keep an eye on the daily television announcements for the level of Fire Hazard and obey instructions on whether or not it is safe to light fires (including barbecues), at home, in the park or camping in the countryside. Check with your local city council on rules (legally enforced) about firebreaks on your land. In many suburban areas, it is illegal all year round to burn off rubbish, leaves etc., so it would be best to check with your Council whether and when you can do this.

You may always have dreamed of a country home surrounded by tall trees, but think hard before you act on your dream—ten terrifying days of walls of fire and fireballs hurtling through the skies in January 1994 reached right into the suburbs of Sydney, let alone the country, leaping from tree to tree. Thousands of volunteer firefighters demonstrated Australia's gutsy civil spirit, but countless homes were lost. Such scenes are repeated all over the country every summer.

How to protect yourself if it happens? First, leave the area, abandon your house, *but early*, never at the last moment, that will be too late—when the flames are upon you, it's marginally better to stay put than to run. Out there in the firestorm itself, you could die of radiation or smoke inhalation. (Equally, even the swimming pool may not be a safe retreat if you have your head above water breathing the smoke, or if the water heats up.) Preventive measures include making firebreaks, removing all dead twigs and debris on your land, clearing gutters of leaves, plugging all holes, including downpipes, and sealing windows, hosing down your property and the land to drenching point, not just before the fire comes, but for days before. And of course, get rid of all inflammable items such as tins of paint or firewood and heating oil supplies.

Rubbish Disposal

We had come from tropical Asia and so were quite taken aback at first to discover that refuse collection did not take place daily. If you forget to wheel your bin out onto your front kerb on the designated night for emptying the next day, too bad—you wait for another week.

Most suburbs have two or three separate bins—one for real rubbish and wet kitchen waste etc. (if you haven't yet got wise to composting) and perhaps some light 'green waste' from the garden (not huge tree branches though); one recycling bin for paper and cardboard; and one other recycling bin for plastics and aluminium cans. (In some places there will be only one recycling bin, however.)

Recycling bins for bottles at a local supemarket.

At regular intervals, your Council will inform you of the dates for its 'Verge Junk Collection Service' and you can chuck out on your verge the equivalent of one car trailer-load of household junk ranging from old fridges to broken furniture, but not construction waste such as bricks and cement rubble. Another regular collection will be for 'Prunings'—this is the time to get your trees lopped and place all the big branches on the verge for the Council to take away.

Mail Boxes

Your 'postie' (postman) will probably cycle past at great speed on the pavement at the front of your house. The idea is that you should have a mail box out on the pavement at the front of the house so he can drop the letters in as he passes. He will not expect to get off his bike and walk up to your front door to deliver, although you might get that favour from the newspaper delivery man. If you don't want sheaves and sheaves of junk mail flapping about in your mail box, put up a sign saying 'No Junk Mail' and that will likely be respected; my husband on the other hand says that he loves the junk mail and it helps him make informed decisions on where to buy the cheapest hand-saw, cutest tool-kit for a Christmas gift etc., while I have girlfriends who instantly rush out to Target or Myers stores the minute they see a brochure saying '50 per cent off all knickers and bras.' These flyers certainly are good guides to all the 'Specials' at the supermarkets.

And some poor soul does make a living delivering the junk mail to your mail box every week, rain or shine.

Heating

If you are not used to winter, remember that the idyllic Australian summers in the garden do not go on forever and you will need to keep warm, eventually. The most economical and environmentally acceptable way of doing so is to wear good woollen clothes, especially under-vests, hats and socks, and sleep under a heavy feather 'doona' as the Australians call the duvet or continental quilt.

Take note of our backbreaking experience when wood suppliers delivered 3 tonnes of firewood outside our gate, in the public back lane, while we were out. We had to cart the whole lot into the woodshed—this took us three days!

The winters are generally not very severe—in Perth, for example, winter night temperatures only rarely fall below 5°C (41°F), daytime rarely below 15°C (59°F)—although Melbourne and Tasmania are another story in this respect.

Depending on where you are in Australia, you may feel you need heating, particularly to provide hot water. The 'sunburnt country', Australia, is the ideal country for solar heating and many homes already have it. You should certainly consider installing it if you have a new house without it, or are building your own home. It's a cheap and very efficient option.

There is enormous romance, of course, in a flickering log fire of a cold winter night. But you should consider what you are burning: Australia's native forests—such as the jarrah trees of the south-west—are precious environmental resources, which should not really be allowed to go up in smoke. Besides which such fires cause air pollution.

However, you can ask for 'mill ends'—the waste chips and blocks left over from processing at furniture and plywood factories—which are cheaper and somewhat more environmentally acceptable. 'Mallee roots' are another choice, although they too are part of the unique Australian ecology, being eucalypts.

A better path might be to use kerosene oil, a fuel resource with which Australia is richly stocked, as with liquid petroleum gas (LPG) for cooking and so on. But of course, every heating fuel comes with some environmental cost or other. Natural gas is the newest option and very much the way to go in terms of affordability, cleanness and efficiency; once you have laid down the capital investment necessary for the fires themselves, the gas supply itself is very cheap.

Cooling

The Australian summer will take some newcomers aback, reaching temperatures of 40°C (104°F) and above at its height. It is a dry heat, and the sun comes at you out of a dazzling clear blue sky.

We installed an evaporative air-cooling system in our home, much nicer than conventional air conditioning, and vastly cheaper to run. One attraction with this system is that you actually have to leave windows and doors open to make it work well, instead of being hermetically sealed into the house, as you are with air conditioning. Air passes over recycling running water which cools it.

We manage to reduce 40° temperatures to 30° or lower with this system (and 30° down to 20°), which is comfortable for us considering we came from tropical Asia. Another advantage is the fact that such systems tend to add moisture, humidifying the extraordinarily dry atmosphere during the Australian summer.

Antique Furniture

If you have brought precious antique wooden furniture to Australia, beware of the dry summers I have mentioned. Most timbers will eventually crack and split as a result. The safest policy is to give your furniture an annual oil rubdown (linseed oil is one option).

'We're happy little Vegemites, as bright as bright can be,
We all enjoy our Vegemite for breakfast, lunch and tea.
Our Mummy says we're growing stronger every single week.'
—Advertising ditty of the 1950s.

NOTHING DIVIDES OPINION QUITE LIKE FOOD—'tucker' is the Aussie word for it. Different strokes for different folks... And perhaps in no other area have Australians changed more radically or more rapidly than in the kitchen, over the past decade. Post-war migration, first the Italians and Greeks (go to Melbourne for their cuisine), followed by the Lebanese and other Middle-Easterners, then latterly of the Chinese, Indians and Vietnamese, has transformed Australian eating and cooking habits. It's probably best summed up by a recent item on the menu of one of my favourite South-east Asian restaurants (which calls itself in good Aussie fashion, 'The Tucker Room'), announced as 'Chook Masala' (i.e. Chicken Masala curry).

Overall, Australian cuisine has traditionally followed in the lamentable footsteps of its English counterpart. Despite England being my own birthplace, I really hesitate to call it a 'cuisine' at all.

Time was, 'food' in Australia meant a roast joint of beef or lamb—or cheaper meat items such as tripe, offal ('fry') or salt-meat—with potatoes and over-boiled greens (they thought them safer this way in the old days), followed by a treacly pudding with custard. Dairy foods were also important staples.

The Australian, his country being a beef and lamb-producer, consumed meat in prodigious quantities and, like the English, was often overweight. This gastronomic 'culture' still survives in Australia outside of the major cities and in suburban heartlands—French and Chinese gourmets, you have been warned—but the cosmopolitan minority is expanding its influence steadily.

The turn of the 20th century also saw the rise of what is known as 'Modern Australian' cuisine, an eclectic and innovative style drawing on multiculturalism, which is fast acquiring a unique Australian identity. You can get everything from lemongrass to couscous in Aussie markets nowadays, and chefs are going to town with some of the world's freshest, purest ingredients.

As an example of the style, cited in *The Weekend Australian* paper, 1997, from the Paramount restaurant in Sydney, try Duck Pie with Shitake Mushroom Sauce and Ginger Glaze— 'Everyone identifies with a pie—the term is Australian, the taste is Chinese, the appearance is French,' says chef Chris Manfield. Nowadays you are quite likely to encounter prawns, kangaroo and papaya in the same dish. It's an enormously exciting new scene, and, combined with the 'Bush Tucker' movement (*see later in this chapter on page 221*), it's anyone's guess where it will ultimately go.

Recommendations

To get a feel for the finer points of traditional Australian cooking, do consult Shirley Constantine's excellent Traditional Australian Cooking, which is more than just a cookbook; it's a readable social history too. There are some good basic recipes, too, in Margaret Nicholson's The Little Aussie Fact Book.

THE ASIAN INVASION

Wandering around historic Fremantle, Perth's twin port-town, not long ago, I spotted an odd item on a traditional Aussie fish-and-chips shop blackboard menu, reading, 'DIM SIM'. 'Wozzat, mite?' I enquired amiably of the proprietor in my newly acquired super-casual Aussie vernacular.

"'Ere 'tis, luv," replied he, indicating a squat little item somewhat like a half-spring roll, a pastry case stuffed with veggies and minced meat of some sort. It was priced at about US$ 0.60.

'Nao fanks, mite,' quoth I, quailing, recalling with nostalgia the infinite variety that the classic Cantonese Chinese snacks-buffet, *dim sum*, usually offers. (*Dim sum* or *dian xin* is a range of small steamed and fried snacks eaten for lunch or breakfast from mobile buffet trolleys.)

But this was just another example of Asian migrants' subtle subversion of Australian cuisine. Or, to look at it another way, it was an example of Asian cuisine absorbed and mutated within Australian cuisine. Tough to tell who is dominating whom when it comes to 'Dim Sim', Australian-style. It works both ways—it's common to see western dishes like 'wedgies and sour cream' appearing on Asian menus, in a desperate attempt to keep the children quiet while the parents slurp their noodles.

No Need to Bring Your Own

Anyone who's ever flown into Perth airport on one of those ghastly flights that get in at almost 3:00 am will be familiar with the sight of Asian visitors and returning residents arguing their way past Customs officials with bags of spices and unattractive-looking dried foods, from squid to waxed duck.

Grave Concern

There are all sorts of stories, apocryphal and otherwise, about Australian Customs' reactions to some of the foodstuffs that Asian migrants typically try either to import legally or to smuggle through when they land in Australia. A food-related story that I particularly like concerns that traditional essential in the Asian kitchen, the often massive, heavy granite, slab that Indian housewives, especially, use as a base for pounding or roller-grinding the fresh spice pastes that are the foundation of good curries. "What's this, then?" cried one Aussie Customs officer at the airport on being confronted with one such slab, a particularly large specimen (an ammi for those South Indians among you). "Oh, it's just for grinding," said the timid Indian lady lugging this heavyweight piece of hand baggage. After further suspicious exploration of the stone, almost as mysterious to them as the mystic obelisk in the cult sci-fi movie 2001 Space Odyssey, the Customs officers gave up and let it go. As the ammi's relieved though puzzled owner left their desk, one officer turned to the other and said, "These Asians, now they're even bringing in their own tombstones!"

Australia understandably has to police imported food and agricultural items sternly to protect its own agriculture against foreign pests and diseases still foreign to its own continental island environment. But I don't know why these would-be gastronomic smugglers persist in running the gauntlet of Customs when Australia is fast producing the goods for them on the spot.

Take my own Perth suburb, for example. Within 10 minutes' drive in any direction are two 'Oriental' provisions stores stocking everything from Chinese *wok* (frying pans) and chilli powder to fresh Indian *roti canai* (bread; Sundays only) and crisp Indian-style *samosa* snacks (pastry triangles stuffed with meat and vegetable), and two 'international food centres' featuring stalls offering Indian and Chinese favourites—besides the Italian, Lebanese and Greek dishes which have long been Australian standards.

At one of these centres, white faces are in a distinct minority, the southern-Chinese Hokkien dialect of Singapore and Malaysia is spoken, several characters are to be seen slopping about in thongs (flip-flop rubber sandals), shorts and singlets, and the *char kway teow* (a sort of fried fettucine) could comfortably compete with the Chinese original back home in Malaysia.

A food centre that has a variety of cuisines from different countries, attracting customers from different ethnic backgrounds.

Eating habits have changed with Asian immigration.

It's not just the food centres that have gone Asian, either. Any Australian city restaurant area will feature at least a Cantonese- and a Peking-style Chinese restaurant, a Lebanese falafels-and-kebabs café, a Malaysian *satay* (barbecued kebabs) joint, an Indonesian *nasi goreng* (fried rice) restaurant, a Thai seafood spot, besides a Vietnamese restaurant and an Indian curry house.

Unfortunately, you have to shop around quite energetically to identify the ones serving the real thing, because many Asian restaurateurs have adversely tailored their cuisine to Australian taste.

Even the fish-and-chip shops have mutated. Increasingly now, these typically Australian establishments are being taken over by Asian migrants. Few of them offer only good old fish and chips lathered in batter and salt and served in brown-paper packets (more traditionally, they should be newspaper). Nowadays they also serve *calamari*, or batter-fried squid, a borrowing from Greece, Chinese-style spring rolls, Indian *samosa*, and other alien imports. Health freaks can also get their fish grilled rather than fried.

Memories of Days Gone By

By the way, if by some chance you have never experienced the great British working-class tradition of batter-fried fish and potato chips served up in paper packets, liberally doused in salt, pepper and vinegar, you must go through with it at least once in Australia. After years in Asia, visits to the Australian fish-and-chip shops brought back my childhood and student years in northern England, scoffing the sizzling, calorific stuff from newspaper as I walked along cold wintry streets at night. Very nostalgic.

Asian DIY in the Kitchen

Some pioneers have been busying themselves for many years to make all this come about. One such is Charmaine Solomon, nee Poulier, one of Australia's best-known Asian residents, a Sri Lankan-born 'burgher' or Eurasian by origin. She has lived in Australia for more than 30 years. If you are an Asian migrant to Australia, afraid you will no longer be able to eat your traditional food, either because you will no longer have a servant to do it for you or because you fear Australia will not have the ingredients, take heart from Charmaine Solomon's work, showcased in her 16 cookbooks, almost every one of them an ambassador for Asian food to Australians. The most famous, back in 1976, was her groundbreaking *The Complete Asian Cookbook*. Her goal has always been to prove that good Asian cooking can come out of a Western-style kitchen, and she has amply succeeded. Her books have been vital to the task of preserving Asian heritage among second or third-generation Australian-Asians.

In this book, too, it is revealed, for instance, that Australians refer to snow-peas but Americans talk about sugar-peas or mange-tout, while green and red peppers may be described as capsicums, sweet peppers or bell peppers, depending on where you are from. *The Complete Asian Cookbook* also lists Australia-based suppliers of Asian ingredients and foodstuffs. Here again is a sign of the times; in 1976, Charmaine could list only one shop stocking Chinese goods in Perth, and none selling Indonesian, Malaysian, Indian or Sri Lankan goods. They are all over Perth now. What isn't in the shops is growing in people's gardens—all the Asian herbs, *lengkuas*, *pandan*, *daun kesom*, *serai*, the lot. They got past Customs somehow.

COOKBOOKS TO CONJURE WITH

You will also come across other Australian culinary luminaries (I just like the sound of that—I mean 'celebrity chefs'), such as Ian Parmenter of the former ABC TV show *Consuming Passions* and the author of books of the same name, who is famous for a quirky style seasoned by his cheerful quaffing onscreen of quantities of vino; earnestly bespectacled Australian-born Chinese Kylie Kwong (*Kylie Kwong Recipes and Stories*), another ABC TV chef ("Kylie never wanted to become a chef and hates her first name," says her website bio); veteran Stephanie Alexander ("Not a stalk of *buk choy* or *gai lan*, or a sprig of coriander in sight in those days," says Stephanie, author of the best-selling *The Cook's Companion*, recalling her heyday in the mid-1970s)—her own journey from a classic French style to something more defiantly Australian mirrors the nation's culinary odyssey; newer names are those like Sri-Lanka-born Geoff Jansz (who says Aussie cuisine is "Fabulous, playful, unpretentious, affordable."), the author of *Taking The Freshest Approach* and *Favourite Recipes*, and the hottest, youngest one of all, New Zealand-born Jason Roberts (author of *Graze*, a book about "lots of little meals fast", and written in six weeks, so he says). In the domain of the kitchen, Donna Hay is an Aussie mega star; look for her big-selling *Modern Classics* cookbook series and also *The Instant Cook*. Unfortunately for 'Sandgropers' like this author, most of the nation's star chefs seem to be centred in the east, in Sydney or occasionally Melbourne; Ian Parmenter of Western Australia being one notable exception.

CUTLERY

There is one very odd thing about Australian eating habits, especially when it comes to consuming Asian food. I can understand a general reluctance to tackle eating instruments as esoteric as chopsticks, or as alien as one's own pinkies (connoisseurs of Indian and Malay food, however, always prefer to use their hands, as the natives do).

But it does seem really benighted to try to eat fried rice with a knife and fork, as most Australians do. The less uptight Australians do at least relax with just a fork. But why, oh why, is there a hidden taboo against eating it with a spoon and fork, as sensible South-east Asians themselves do nowadays?

Apparently, for Australians, it is somehow not nice to use spoons for anything other than soups or desserts, but nobody has ever explained to me why this is so. Even long-term Asian residents in Australia have given it up as a losing battle and are to be seen stabbing away with forks instead. Logically then, the American custom of cutting food into small pieces and then picking it up with a fork should be quite acceptable in Australia.

Mine and Yours

For Asians in particular, the 'my dish' syndrome evinced by Australians will seem quite remarkable. Each diner has his own plate of food in a typical Western-style Australian meal. If a Western-style meal is served at home, care should be taken that food is available in multiples of the number of guests (six carrots for three guests, for example, i.e. two each), as the guests are likely to feel more comfortable if they can actually count how many pieces they are 'supposed' to take for themselves. It is all very precise.

This kind of thing can occur even at Asian restaurants in Australia, where some Australians will order for themselves one plate of noodles or one plate of fried rice, rather than ordering several dishes to put in the centre of the table to share, as Asians would. Call it individualism, selfishness or meanness if you like, but you will have to go with the flow.

Allied with this situation is the 'my drink' phenomenon. In Asian societies, the bottle of whisky, brandy or whatever will be plonked on the table for everyone to help themselves as they wish. In Western societies like Australia, the host will ask you whether you want a drink, serve you a carefully measured measure and wait until you seem to need another one before asking if you do, and then refilling your glass. Appalling as this may seem to some Asians, again, just learn to live with it.

QUICK FIX

Unfortunately, one of the less welcome post-war food imports has been 'fast food'. Australians eat far too many 'takeaway' meals, from fish-and-chip cafés as well as from 'Chinese takeaways'—estimated at four to five times a week—and the national expenditure on fast foods of all kinds is about A\$ 1.5 billion a year. In the mid-1990s, it was revealed that more than 8 per cent of the Australian family food budget went on snack or 'junk' foods, making Australia the world's fourth most enthusiastic consumer of such 'food'.

The Fat File

- More than half of the Australian population is overweight or obese.
- An estimated 1.5 million people aged under 18 are considered overweight or obese.
- About 20–25 per cent of Australian children are overweight or obese, with the proportion fast increasing, particularly since the mid-1980s—a trend which reflects international patterns.
- Approximately 9 million Australians over the age of 18 were estimated to be overweight or obese in 2001. This showed a rapidly increase over the previous 20 years.
- The Australian National Health and Medical Research Council (NHMRC) recommends at least two servings of fruit and five servings of vegetables per day. The 2001 National Health Survey showed that only 30 per cent of people aged 12 years or more usually ate four or more servings of vegetables per day while 53 per cent ate two or more servings of fruit.
- The financial burden associated with obesity in Australia was estimated to be A\$ 1.2 billion in 2000.
- Outside of school hours, only 62 per cent of children aged 5–14 years participated in organised sport in 2003.

—Australian government figures 2004–2005

Perhaps not surprisingly, 60 per cent of Aussie adults (over 19 years old) have been classified as obese or overweight. Some experts reckon the situation is rapidly heading towards as much as 75 per cent of the population being obese by about 2020. The situation is even more alarming when it comes to children: a quarter are now considered obese, whereas 20 years ago, the statistic was only 10 per cent. As in other countries, long hours at the TV and computer monitor are part of the reason—and, on top of that, Australia has the greatest amount of junk food ads per hour of television of any country in the world, including the US and the UK. About one third of the TV ads screened during kids' viewing times are for food or drink. Medical surveys reveal that of these, about 99 per cent are for junk food: burgers, chips, soft drinks and sweets.

However, a vocal health-food lobby, backed by an array of official government programmes, particularly in schools, is fighting back. And a 1996 survey found that Australians had a guiltier conscience about what they ate than any other nationality.

THE AUSTRALIAN SHOPPING BASKET

Within the past 15 years, the fondly remembered era of the milkman (the 'milko') and his daily doorstep delivery has disappeared from the suburbs of Australia. The phone directory reveals a host of 'Dial-a-Meal' services and there are endless pizza deliveries on call, but most Australians do the bulk of their shopping in supermarkets and at the many fresh fruit-and-veg markets, especially the wholesale growers' markets, very much in the American style: they load up their big cars with a week's supplies, wheeling their laden supermarket trolleys out to the car across the huge car park, and store many things in deep-freezers. (The trolleys, by the way, are sometimes obtainable only through a coin-slot machine which consumes, say, a 20-cent deposit, refundable when you return the trolley).

The average Australian family's diet includes essentials like eggs, milk, meat and vegetables; Polony sausage (a European infiltration); pizza; pasta; spaghetti (the latter two are listed separately) and tomato paste—the Italian influence. Anglo-Saxon favourites like custard powder and pickled onions are still there. And, oh dear, canned baked beans too.

Consumption figures from the Australian Bureau of Statistics show that Australians are upping their veggie intake but still don't eat enough of them for good health, and they certainly haven't abandoned meat. Their average annual consumption of meat and meat products is about 71.6 kg (about 158 lbs) per person, with pork consumption rising particularly noticeably in recent years.

Hurry Up, The Shops are Closing!

Australia's shopping hours are in transition as federal National Competition Policy reforms start to bite, so how late you can shop for your groceries all depends on where you are: the spectrum runs from fairly recently reformed retail trading hours in the east, New South Wales and Victoria, allowing weekday night and Sunday shopping, to the still puritan extreme of Western Australia where everything shuts down by 5:30 pm on weekdays, and nothing moves on Sundays (least of all any form of alcohol sale).

In regimes such as WA's, there is usually one night a week declared 'late shopping night'—Thursdays in the suburbs or Fridays in Perth city, for instance. Suggesting that late-night and weekend shopping might be a boon to families, tourism and employment can raise passions, and hackles, in WA where the ideology is that in a deregulated shopping hours scenario, the big chains (Woolworths, Coles etc) will dominate and kill small business, family life will be devastated either by long retail working hours or distractions in shopping centres, and anyway, what about the Sabbath? A referendum on whether or not to reform shopping hours drew a resounding 'No' from Sandgropers (about 60 per cent) in February 2005 and there the matter rests, probably for the following decade.

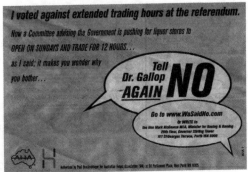

An ad in the West Australian newspaper in 2005 by the Australian Hotels Association of Western Australia, who have a vested interest in people coming to their 'hotels' (Aussie for 'pub' or 'bar'), not go home with a bottle, to drink on Sundays!

Trial by Yeast

The shopping list would not be Australian if it lacked one particular item—I refer of course to 'Vegemite'.

Vegemite is the trade name devised back in the 1920s for a bread spread that describes itself as 'concentrated yeast extract'. It is the Australian equivalent of Britain's Marmite but different. Indeed, Vegemite was created specifically to compete with Marmite. It was launched in 1923 as 'Parwill' but then changed its name to Vegemite.

Vegemite offers the same kind of test for whether you have integrated with mainstream society as that posed by warm beer in Britain for wannabe Brits or by the odiferous durian fruit in South-east Asia. This thick dark brown goo usually comes in a small glass jar with distinctive yellow and red labelling and packaging. The strongest impression left by its taste is, well—salt. With yeasty undertones, naturally.

Vegemite is considered quintessentially Australian. If you don't like it or don't eat it, your Australian-ness is open to question. But take heart, some Australians don't.

The ingredients are listed on the packaging as: yeast extract, salt, mineral salt (508), malt extract (from barley), natural colour (150d), preservative 220, vegetable extract, and the vitamins thiamine, riboflavin, niacin and folate. The numbers are the official food additive codes. The label further points out that five grammes of Vegemite gives you half your daily allowance of Vitamin B1, riboflavin and niacin. I personally can recommend the stuff as a piquant backdrop to a robustly-flavoured Australian Cheddar cheese sandwich, topped with a layer of watercress or fresh sunflower sprouts. Go for it.

The Meat Pie

Least attractive of all is the unofficial 'national dish', the Great Australian Meat Pie—meat and vegetables in a pastry shell. A particularly dreadful version of this is the 'Adelaide floater' which features the said pie, with peas, awash in a gooey gravy soup.

As columnist Buzz Kennedy has said in *The Weekend Australian*, 'Meat pies are not meant to be healthy. They are

The Great Australian Meat Pie—this photo was first used to publicise the opening of 'The Jolly Pieman' store in Mirrabooka, Western Australia.

meant to be squidgy and dribbling with gravy thickened with white flour and eaten in great chomps.'

All part of the Australian gastronomic experience, but definitely an 'acquired taste'.

Other Australiana

There are many other Australian endemics when it comes to food. Take 'puftaloons', for example, increasingly rare nowadays. ('I haven't seen a puftaloon for 40 years,' complained one reader not long ago, in a Western Australian newspaper, 'but I suppose that my body, nowadays conditioned to forever seeking low-cholesterol tucker, would not allow me anywhere near one.')

This is a fried dough-scone, which rises high and fluffy during the frying. Puftaloons have been recorded as far back as 1853—some older Americans may recognise them as 'puff-ballooners'. They were used to fill families up when times were hard and meat was short.

While most puftaloon recipes are simple, using just self-raising flour, butter and salt, mixed with milk or water, there are variations incorporating egg, a dash of tomato sauce, chopped onion and mincemeat. In the old days of pre-cholesterol-scare innocence, you would have fried the puftaloons in 'dripping'—fat dripped from cooking meats like lamb or beef, for long Australia's favourite cooking oil. As with waffles, you are supposed to smother puftaloons in treacle or honey before eating them fresh and golden brown from the frying pan.

Still household names today are Arnott's biscuits, Jaffa cakes, and Minties, the mint 'lollies' (sweets, candies) wrapped in green and white paper with red writing on it. Chewiness, say Aussie aficionados, is the factor that elevates the Mintie above the 'Pommy' Minto or Polo Mint. A traditional Australian children's party game is the 'Mintie Hunt', where a trail of clues laid outdoors leads to the treasure-trove of Minties.

Among the snacks you will find at venues such as the fish-and-chips shop, are sure to be 'Chiko Rolls'—crisp-fried semi-cylindrical pastries stuffed with corn, potato and gravy, nearly as Australian as Vegemite. Similarly Australian are Anzac Biscuits, substantial constructions of rolled oats, syrup and coconut, named after the Aussie soldier boys who gratefully received them at the Gallipoli warfront in parcels from home during World War I.

Food traditions dating back to the days of the bushman are Billy Tea—tea brewed in a metal mug or can of boiling water over a campfire—and another camp-food, Damper, a heavy unleavened wheat bread baked in hot ashes, which could 'damp' your hunger.

FRUIT

Most fruit grown in Australia today has foreign origins. A thought that would annoy the vociferous campaigners of today in the growing movement to ensure that all fresh food in Australia is labelled with its country, and preferably also its Australian state, of origin. Australian consumers increasingly want to support their local farmers. There are also a few racists and political activists who want to boycott foreign food whether for its own sake or in order to send a political message about one thing or another.

What some of you may know as a 'papaya' is a 'paw-paw' in Australia and along with bananas, pineapples, avocados and mangos, is common in the tropical regions of the north, mainly in Queensland. Citrus fruit and apples are the most abundantly produced—apples from Tasmania are particularly famous and the Granny Smith apple variety was first developed from a Tasmanian seed. The zappy, crisp 'Pink Lady' branded apple first developed during the 1970s in Western Australia, derived from the Cripps Pink apple variety, is also a legend at home and abroad, in England and beyond.

There are some spectacular stone-fruit to be had in season—nectarines, peaches and apricots among them. And there are also home-grown berries such as strawberries and raspberries. And what a luxury it is to be able to gorge on cheap Australian-grown avocadoes.

DINING OUT

The single most alien aspect of Australian dining and wining is the BYO phenomenon. The acronym stands for Bring Your Own (Booze/Grog). Few restaurants are licensed to sell liquor, but most will let you bring your own. You will have a pretty miserable time if you forget this custom, only to find yourself without wine to go with your special dinner. So the routine preliminary to dining out is nearly always to visit the bottle-shop first. This custom is in fact a blessing in disguise, since you get a wider choice of wines, no restaurateur's mark-up on prices, and no corkage charge either.

> **No Drinks Only**
>
> Note that it is often impossible to order just a drink, such as a glass of wine, as in many areas the law insists that all alcohol in restaurants must be served together with food.

Australian restaurants usually close fairly early (in traditional homes, 'tea', i.e. dinner, is eaten as early as 6:00 pm). Tipping is rarely necessary. Water is just as rarely offered unless specifically requested.

You will find Australian portions extremely generous. The nation eats heartily, mostly scorning the inadequacies of 'nouvelle cuisine' with all those fancy white spaces on the plate. Some of the best-value meals are those to be found in pubs, sometimes stand-up style at the bar counter. Counter lunches are especially good.

SHOUTS AND SPLITS

The custom of 'shouting' rounds of drink in the 'pub' (anything from a bar to a hotel is a 'pub' in Australia), taking turns, is entrenched and woe is he (less often she) who forgets it. Remember that Australians are not too well off nowadays,

The pub bar is important to social life.

Drinkers people-watching from the window of Fremantle's Sail and Anchor pub.

so pull your financial weight at the bar. On the other hand, they are proud as well, so offering to pay more than your share of shouts could also be taken amiss.

Pride really comes to the fore when the bill for a restaurant meal is delivered. The Australian is pathologically opposed to carrying a whole dinner tab, and equally opposed to letting anybody else carry it for him. If you are a man dating a woman, be warned that there is a distinct suggestion you may be angling to bed her pretty soon if you go so far as to pay for her meal. Play safe and offer to 'go Dutch', as the English saying has it—that is, unless you are trying to tell her something.

Asians, and some southern Europeans too, find this particularly difficult to cope with; they are used to immense shows of generosity, hosting whole dinner parties, on the quiet understanding of course, that the others will owe them a debt in turn when the time comes, some time later.

But it is precisely the unspoken indebtedness that the fiercely independent Aussie dislikes about this system. An Australian married to an Asian woman had encountered this embarrassment many times and he explained it to me thus: "We feel our independence has been compromised when somebody pays the whole bill. It's kind of throwing your weight around, showing your power. And when they do that, you haven't any choice in the matter; the next time around, you will have to do it, but you haven't any choice about it."

So when in doubt, always split the bill.

TRADITIONAL FARE

Conventional or traditional Australian cuisine divides into two streams: classic Continental European cum cordon bleu, and good old Australian tucker.

It is possible still to eat quality European food in Australia, however, sometimes in the most surprising places: like the exquisite French meal I enjoyed at the 1885 Inn and Restaurant in the Margaret River wine country of south-western Western Australia, for example, the best I think I have had outside of France itself.

Old Favourites

In an attempt to characterise traditional Australian food as compared with any other, one newspaper writer came up with the word 'gutsy'. We have already discussed some of the more hardcore dishes in the genre.

Setting aside the old 'meat and two vegs' formula, however, the strongest item on any truly Australian menu would have to be seafood and fish dishes. Prawns and 'yabbies', or small freshwater crayfish, are delicious. The Barramundi fish, the John Dory and the Dhu fish are among many great Australian epicurean experiences. Mud crabs are well worth the effort, oysters world-famous.

More puzzling may be the mention of 'Bugs' on the menu. These are a small seafood item, allied to crayfish, some from tropical Moreton Bay, others from the southern Balmain region.

A tolerable introduction to traditional Anglo-Saxon fare is probably the Yorkshire Pudding. At its crispy, piping-hot best, this is a delicious batter pudding consisting of egg, milk and flour baked in dripping served as an accompaniment

Sausage sizzle at the Perth garden centre.

to the main dish. Another tasty standard is Steak and Kidney Pudding.

The salad is growing in popularity and variety on Australian menus and Australia's abundant fresh vegetables and fruit make it an ideal option. Asians not used to so much raw food may find it all a bit alarming, but it is indisputably healthy. By the way, you will find it extremely difficult to avoid beetroot, that violently purple vegetable. Australians love it (I loathe it).

Outdoor barbecues are a favoured setting for most Australian food. The ultimate Aussie of his day (pre-Steve Irwin era) was Paul Hogan (he of *Crocodile Dundee* fame) who made the catchphrase 'Toss A Prawn On The Barbie' ring around the world in the bicentennial year of 1988. A favourite way of raising money for good causes, or attracting customers to a shop, is a 'Sausage Sizzle' or 'BBQ' tempting passers-by with the wafting aroma of 'snags' (sausages) and lamb chops charring on the barbie.

And Now for Afters

Australian desserts, cakes and puddings—'afters'—are quite unique. Perhaps the best known are the Pavlova dessert and the Lamington cake. Both of these are delicious.

The Pavlova, it is claimed, was created at Fremantle's Esplanade Hotel in Western Australia, for the prima ballerina Anna Pavlova, when she toured Australia in 1935. It's a mouth-melting froth of meringue, whipped cream and fresh fruit.

Lamingtons, probably a Queensland invention in the early 1900s and named after 19th century Queensland governor, Baron Lamington, are small sponge blocks layered with raspberry jam, covered with thin chocolate icing, like a skin, and then rolled in desiccated coconut.

Other more traditional English puddings personally make me cry, remembering my schoolhood in austere post-war northern England, made miserable in gastronomic terms by the effort of desperately trying to shovel down monumental stodge like Suet Pudding, Golden Syrup Dumplings, Bread and Butter Pudding, or Steamed Jam Pudding, afloat in dreaded yucky-yellow custard…

CHRISTMAS

No matter if the sun is high in a bright blue sky and the temperature well over 40°C (104°F), Australians will still have their Christmas Day lunch very much in the traditional English mode, complete with turkey, stuffing and 'Christmas pud' (more archaically known as 'Plum Duff').

There are some concessions to Australia's 'reversed' seasons. Ice-cream cake does sometimes replace or supplement the Christmas pudding, for example. (They say that in the 19th century gold-rush days, miners would put gold nuggets in the Christmas pudding instead of the traditional sixpence coins).

Suggested menus in the daily press sometimes even propose a curry as a way of getting rid of Christmas leftovers. Curry in most Australian households has always been used as more of a disguise for leftovers than considered as an art in itself.

The more sensible option is to perform the 'Christmas in July' charade, thus reserving all the heavy festive-season food for the Aussie winter.

ABOUT TEA

"They can't even make a decent cup of tea over here," a disgruntled migrant Sikh once told me. He leaned over the table with confidential mien, "I mean, it's like dishwater!" He snorted his contempt, pausing only to swill down some of his own dubious brew of sugared milk laced with coffee.

Such criticism would shock Australians if they heard it. They reckon they know about tea. After all, they take after their English forefathers when it comes to tea: they are addicts. They are the fifth largest per capita tea-drinkers in the world, brewing up about a kilo per person per year. But it has to be said that coffee is overtaking the tea tradition in Australia, with annual consumption at more than 2.5 kg (5.5 lbs) per person.

Indians like my Sikh friend, of course, are used to a stiff brew of fine tea-dust cooked up for some considerable time, with the milk and sugar, as well as some spices, already in the drink. Whereas the Australian will add the milk and sugar in the cup, whether before or after pouring the briefly-brewed tea.

Once again, do not forget that an invitation to 'tea' is in fact an invitation to the evening meal, a tradition deriving from old-fashioned north-country England.

BUSH TUCKER

When the first whites arrived in Australia, they took no notice at all of whatever it was the Aboriginals were eating, nor did they even attempt to farm the land for the first five years or so. They simply imported all their food. At times, they well nigh starved on account of this stupidity, or worse, almost killed themselves.

Once, seeing that the Aboriginals ate the roasted seeds of the *Zamia* cycad (an ancient, primitive palm-like tree), the white settlers did likewise. But because they had not observed carefully enough, they died from the potent poisons contained in the seeds. The Aboriginals had learned how to soak and prepare the seeds for consumption, removing toxins, for many weeks prior to cooking.

Over the past decade, there has been a growing realisation that the Aboriginals knew, still know in some cases, how to live off the land, and that this 'bush tucker' can be quite good for the health. It was certainly better for Aboriginal health than the whites' imported flour, sugar and alcohol. Take a food like Billygoat Plums. They have the highest concentration of Vitamin C of any food in the world, as much in a single plum as in a dozen oranges.

Needless to say, knowledge of bush tucker could be the key to survival if you were unfortunate enough to get lost in the outback.

It is estimated that there may be 30,000 types of bush tucker. Perhaps only about 30 or 40 of them have been introduced to urban Australia so far. The first moves are now being made towards mass production and processing of some of these traditional foods, which already appear on the menus of chic restaurants in the eastern states. If you visit an Australian bookshop, you will surely encounter perhaps half a dozen or more major books on bush tucker.

This back-to-nature movement got an immense kick-start from a television series in 1990 titled *Bush Tucker Man* and hosted by Les Hiddens, an army major who is an expert on edible plants from the survival-skills point of view.

Buffalo, kangaroo (raised on farms, not taken from the wild, they say), camel and crocodile hardly qualify as bush tucker any more, so commonplace have they become. Camel meat is turning up in the Australian meat pie. Crocodile, like kangaroo, is considered a particularly healthy meat, being low in fat and cholesterol, with a chicken-like texture and a flavour much like veal.

Aboriginal women have traditionally been the gatherers of tubers and roots, such as yams and ground orchids, in particular, hence the woven or wooden collecting trays, 'coolamons', and 'dillybags' they often carry around with them.

There are grass seeds and ferns which can be eaten, also many fruits and berries. The blue-black Davidson's Plum of the rainforest makes a delicious, sourish jam, for example.

Aboriginals in their natural state also eat wildlife, of course, such as the goanna, a monitor lizard, reputed to be pleasantly edible if a little gamey, and the fatty mutton bird (short-tailed shearwater) of the south-eastern coast. Goanna is another example of the healthy lean meat available in the bush.

In some areas, Aboriginals also nibble on live green ants—the green comes from chlorophyll in the plants eaten by the ants and the ants as a result have an attractively tangy taste, rather like lemon juice (Yes, I've tried it). One imagines it would take an awful lot of these to make any nutritional impact or to affect energy levels, however.

Gourmet Grubs

And then there is the witchetty grub. The Aboriginals' consumption of these fat maggot-like creatures, live and raw, has acquired a horrid fascination for outsiders, thanks to Aussie tour guides' propensity for macho demonstrations.

Witchetty grubs are in fact insect larvae, usually of wood-boring moths. You do not have to eat them raw (when they taste creamy and squashy—you bite off their heads first); they can be cooked in hot ashes, which renders them something like underdone pork crackling. I have tried it both ways myself. Just for the experience.

The grubs, no doubt a fair source of protein, are now appearing on the smartest of menus. They are even available from gourmet supermarkets in tinned soup form (from Vic Cherikoff Food Services). Chef Diane Holuigue once told *The Australian Magazine* how she served this up to a Florida dinner party in the USA, 'fluffed into cappucino-like consistency and dredged with wattle seed'.

Vic Cherikoff pioneered the integration of Australian bush foods and Aboriginal delicacies into mainstream cooking, as seen in his books *The Bushfood Handbook*, *Uniquely Australian* and *Dining Downunder*. The impact of his work can be seen in the rest of Diane Holuigue's Australiana menu, which included crocodile macadamia brochettes with bush tomato chutney; prawns fried in coconut with curried mayonnaise; quail and emu ham salad, among other more conventional items, such as Australian lamb. (Macadamia nuts, by the way, are another fine Australian native food, unfortunately known to some people abroad as 'Hawaiian nuts', since they were first commercially grown on Hawaii, but originally came from Queensland.)

Another of Diane's efforts produced baby wattle seed blini topped with cress, smoked emu, handmade agnolotti filled with yabbie mousseline, and baby Barramundi fish wrapped in the bark of the paperbark tree (the wrapping, she says, imparts a 'delicate earthy taste' to the food), served with Kakadu plum sauce.

The list of exotica is seemingly endless: the quandong and boab fruits, lemon myrtle, lilli-pilli berries, warragal greens, bunya nuts, the bogong moth, black nightshade, lemon-aspen lemon curd and wattle seed everything…

A great treat awaits the world when bush tucker at last hits international gourmet circles, as it surely will one day.

GROG

We spent a lot of time tramping supermarkets puzzling over where on earth the beer and wine could be, before we cottoned on to the Australian system which has separate 'bottle-shops' (what the British call 'the off-licence') to sell alcohol. If you're feeling lazy, there are plenty of drive-in bottle-shops, allowing you to order and collect through your car window.

Traditionally, Australia has been a beer-drinking nation. But annually, the Aussie today is only knocking back about 90 litres of the stuff, compared with the 1980s when he would have gargled 125 litres. As a result, Australia now barely scrapes into the world's top ten beer-drinking nations, sitting at ninth place in 2004, behind top beer-drinker, the Czech Republic, as well as Luxembourg. This is a steep fall from number three in the world, Australia's ranking in the early 1990s. Wine is the culprit: wine-sipping is shooting up, now standing at about 27 litres of wine per person, compared

The bottle shop, an Aussie institution.

with less than 3 litres in the late 1930s, one of the highest figures for any English-speaking nation.

Nonetheless, there is a host of beers to choose from, brewed by five major companies: Foster's lager from Victoria is best known abroad, but there are many others, such as Castlemaine's XXXX (Four-ex) from Queensland, VB (Victoria Bitter), Carlton, and Western Australia's Swan Lager and Redback (named after the spider), among others—and the very latest cold-filtered beers, such as Carlton Cold, or Tooheys' Hahn Ice.

Americans should be warned that the alcohol content in Australian beers is far higher than what they are used to—it is higher than in most British beers too. Some pubs offer in-house brews with extremely high levels (try a Fremantle 'Dog-Bolter'). And of course, Australian beer is always drunk ice-cold, hence the importance of the 'esky' thermos box on trips to the beach or into the bush.

Alcohol always has been an Australian social problem. While drunk driving, unfortunately, is a major hazard on Australian roads, especially at night and during weekends or holidays—one that the novice driver in Australia should be made keenly aware of—it is also a serious offence which can lose you your licence. There are random checks on the roads.

Many Australian pubs feature a 'do-it-yourself' breathalyser affixed to the wall, which will tell you whether you are over your limit or not; permitted alcohol limits vary from state to state. It is the custom in all responsible groups of friends, or among husbands and wives, to decide before going out for the night who will remain sober and within the alcohol limits in order to be the driver when the time comes to go home.

A variety of low-alcohol 'light' beers is now available to help moderate drinkers stay within the rules. If you are a woman, remember that female physiology is such that it takes fewer drinks to push your alcohol readings up than for a man.

THE GRAPEVINE

The availability, affordability and high quality of Australian wines are among many good reasons for living in Australia. Nowadays, wine-lovers outside of Australia too have a very good idea of the quality of Australian wines; gone are the days, thankfully, when the country was judged solely on its then outrageous invention, the cardboard-cask wine. Wine exports, at about 600 million litres in 2003–2004, are booming, as are domestic sales (over 400 million litres).

A clear indication of the quality is the fact that some 13 per cent of the Australian industry is now in the hands of French investors (names like Bollinger and Veuve Cliquot), with the Japanese also emerging as important players.

Although the big names—Wyndham Estate, Wolf Blass, Seppelt, Hardy Bros, Penfolds, Orlando, Lindemans and the like—dominate the market, there are also regional stars like Western Australia's Leeuwin Estate or Vasse Felix in Margaret River, besides many small independent 'boutique' vineyards, challenging the would-be connoisseur with one-off gems. I myself have much enjoyed bottles from the less well-known Evans and Tate, and Cullen's vineyards, in Western Australia.

Note that Australian wines, largely for obvious legal reasons, are named after the grape variety used, e.g. Shiraz, rather than a European counterpart based on location, such as Bordeaux or Beaujolais.

In Vino Veritas

Since the start of the 21st century, Australian wine-lovers have been delighted to find themselves in the midst of a wine glut, making it possible to get excellent wines for just A$ 10-12 a bottle. The 'clean-skins' phenomenon—unbranded bottles of wine stating only the region of provenance and grape type used—has become trendy and canny clean-skin buyers can now walk off with a premium vineyard bottle at a mere A$ 7. This is the result of top vineyards' desperation to clear surplus stock and keep their best bottle prices up. Their loss, our gain.

Australia has 60 wine regions, the major wine-growing states being Western Australia, New South Wales, Victoria and South Australia; the Northern Territory for example, has only one winery.

In Western Australia, you'd best opt for the Margaret River (south-west) and Swan Valley (close to Perth) regions, with newbie southern districts like Mount Barker coming along nicely. The state produces superb Cabernet Sauvignon and Merlot reds, as well as tasty Sauvignon Blanc and Semillon whites.

If you are a Chardonnay-buff, stick to the eastern states' wines. An interesting oddity is WA's oldest inland winery, Coorinja, outside the country town of Toodyay (a nice stop en route for the fascinating historic Benedictine monastery town of New Norcia, a couple of hours' drive from Perth, noted for its olive cultivation, home-baked bread and cakes, Spanish architecture and religious art collection), where you can pick up excellent sherries, ports and other fortified wines (try liqueur Shiraz) for bargain basement prices.

Victoria offers rarer fortified styles such as Muscat, in the Rutherglen region, and fine Chardonnay (white) as well as Pinot Noir (red) in the Yarra Valley.

In South Australia are found the famous German-style whites of the Barossa Valley, and other famous regions such as Coonawarra, Clare Valley and McLaren Vale, rich in reds. The jewel among the New South Wales regions is the Hunter Valley, with its exceptional Chardonnay and Shiraz (red).

Red Red Wine

What to try? First, be aware that the only wine that Australian vineyards do not seem to be very good at is champagne (which they are not allowed by the French to call champagne, so look for 'sparkling wine' instead); Australia is still a big importer of the original, French, champagne. But the Australian version (look for the Pinot Noir-Chardonnay grape blend to get that 'real' champagne taste) is getting better by the minute.

A distinctive feature of Australian wines is experimentation with blends of grapes. They are often fruity and soft, easier for novices to enjoy than some French wines. As a very crude guideline, you will probably like Hunter Valley reds (New South Wales) as well as Coonawarra reds (South Australia), Barossa Valley whites (South Australia) as well as Cabernet Sauvignon or Merlot from Margaret River (Western Australia) and Chardonnay whites from almost anywhere in the eastern states. The Cabernet Sauvignon-Merlot red blend is particularly in fashion at the moment. The Sauvignon Blanc-Semillon blend is a lovely sparkly white.

Pinot Noir refers to the red grape of Burgundy, best from the cooler areas of Victoria state. Shiraz, is another attractive red, particularly when matured in American oak barrels.

If you are looking for Australia's top, top wine, then there is no dispute: it is Penfold's Grange Hermitage, a South Australian shiraz, famous not quite since its birth in the 1950s, but certainly since the 1960s. And it costs an arm and a leg (or about A$ 200–400 a bottle, depending on the vintage). In fact, it is more often bought and laid down as an investment (cellaring for at least 15 years is recommended) than actually drunk. Collectors eagerly await each new vintage of this Australian classic.

I have found it a real joy after avoiding red wine for years while living in the tropics (it sends you to sleep in the heat of the afternoon and/or gives you a headache, is too expensive, travels badly and tastes so-so), to sample good red wine once again in an Australian winter. Cheers!

Trivia: in Australia, suave well-heeled left-wingers who frequent big-city boulevard cafes and conduct political debate over a glass of wine are often referred to contemptuously by their right-wing adversaries as 'Chardonnay socialists.'

THE PHILISTINE SLANDER

CHAPTER 7

'You're a brave man, but I don't think you can do it.'
—The sacked Danish architect for the Sydney Opera House,
Joern Utzon, to his replacement, Australian Peter Hall,
in the *Sydney Morning Herald*, 23 April 1966.

"AUSTRALIA? IT'S A CULTURAL DESERT!" snorted one of my acquaintances when I told her I had a home in Australia.

Only the very ignorant—perhaps also the blind and deaf—could possibly support such a slander about Australia. Especially with reference to any time after the 1960s. Even before that, there is a case for saying much was going on that the outside world simply did not know about. But the personal commitment to the arts of the 1970s Labor Prime Minister Gough Whitlam did act as an important catalyst to artistic activity.

One of the most stimulating things about the Australian artistic tradition is that, like the continent's ecology, it has often had to evolve in isolation, generating its own forms. At times, that has also been a problem, but more often, distance from the world's more acclaimed artistic centres has been a plus for Australia in terms of achieving a truly singular artistic identity.

Whether the home audience—Australians themselves—always appreciates or understands its own compatriots' artistic achievements is another issue. This is possibly because very few Australian artistic works really address or empathise with ordinary Australian lives as they are today—in a word, urban middle-class. Instead there has been a romantic obsession with the land, the environment and the past in which pioneer Australians battled with Nature to create their present. You can still see this at play in Australian director Sue Brooks' excellent 2003 movie *Japanese Story* starring Australian actress Toni Collette alongside Japan's Gotaro Tsunashima, a bicultural love story with a sting in its tail, set against the backdrop of the Australian wilderness.

Foreign Influences

A problem for Australian art forms, in terms of preserving their separate identity, is pervasive Americanisation, a trend much lamented by pundits and critics, but which apparently few know how to resist. Another problem has been the seeming inevitability of Australia's best and brightest departing for foreign shores to experience a broader cultural milieu with either the excitement of America or the glamour of older cultures, in England and continental Europe. And there to sit as expatriates, often publicly sneering at their homeland for good measure—literary and feminist critic Germaine Greer, comic raconteur Clive James and journalist John Pilger, all London-based, are among the examples most often cited.

In recent years, concerns like the environment, feminism and Aboriginal rights, as well as a strong stream of political satire, have been influential themes right across the board of the Australian arts. Development of the arts has been somewhat constrained since the 1990s, however, by the realities first of a national economic downturn, and then of a slightly less generous government. Licking the most painful wounds is the Australian film industry, somewhat in decline since the late 1990s, with government funding reduced in real terms and home-grown movies taking only 1.3 per cent of a record A\$ 907-million box office take in Australia during 2004, according to figures in the *The Age* newspaper.

But some of the liveliest and richest artistic endeavour can be seen 'on the fringe' or at the community-neighbourhood level, perhaps not as well publicised as the more formal events. You must seek it out for yourself; it is there, tucked away in obscure corners.

On the Australian art scene, small very often means even more beautiful—like the exquisite performance of one of Gilbert and Sullivan's ultra-British, Victorian-era operettas

Children from Goollelal Primrary School in Kinsgley, Western Australia dress up in vibrant costumes and have a parade on the streets.

that I stumbled upon one evening in a quiet suburb of Perth, or the laid-back exhibition by young artists in a converted Fremantle warehouse, against the backdrop of Moroccan and Malay drummers, or the Caribbean reggae gig in a Perth pub, or the bouncing Seychellois folk music another evening, the blues musicians in the bars of Fremantle, or…

There is no shortage of cultural things to do, see, hear and experience in Australia—all this in Perth, supposedly a backwater that isn't anywhere near the centre of all that is going on.

STILL PICTURES

The ancient and sacred tradition of Aboriginal art has already been dealt with in Chapter 3: The People (*pages 116–118*). It has taken a long time for this school of art to influence the

Charming mural on a wall in the Western Australian Wheat Belt town of Carnamah. It shows the typical farmer taking a break from a hard day's work, with his typical working farm dogs by his side.

work of white Australian artists; there was no sign of real interchange until after World War II. A turning point was the comprehensive exhibition of Aboriginal art displayed at the Australian National Gallery in 1989, seven years after the Gallery's foundation. Today, the understanding and the actual practice of Aboriginal art has expanded far beyond the 'dot paintings', 'X-ray' styles and bark or rock paintings that rightly first impressed white society, to include much more sophisticated and contemporary styles and materials, including new skills such as sculpture, weaving and Indonesian-style wax-resist *batik* fabric art. In 2005, a life-size reed-woven 4WD jeep sculpture produced by the women of a remote Aboriginal community caused quite a sensation with its innovative, witty style.

Painters of the 1850s gold rush at last abandoned earlier colonial artists' picturesque, Eurocentric distortions of the Australian landscape and began to record truly Australian scenes—painters like S T Gill on the goldfields or Tom Roberts on the Australian landscape and lifestyle.

The Australian art world remained for the most part resolutely conservative right through the 1920s and

1930s, taking only slight notice of the revolutions of impressionism, cubism, surrealism and so on, abroad. The social-realist depiction of immigrant and working-class suffering favoured by a group of artists led by Noel Counihan and Josi Bergner during the 1950s somehow seemed more 'Australian'.

One expatriate Australian artist who is particularly well known overseas is Sir Sidney Nolan (1917–1992). He developed a number of styles—abstract before World War II, more topic-oriented after the war, with famous works on Australian historical episodes, such as the World War I debacle at Gallipoli, and the ill-fated Burke and Wills expedition.

For the period immediately following World War II, names that leap to mind include Albert Namatjira (1902–1959), the Aboriginal watercolourist from Central Australia who switched with ease to European styles and techniques; Donald Friend, who lived and worked in Bali in 1967–80, producing complex, sensual works until he died in Australia in 1989; and Sir Russell Drysdale (1912–1981), whose landscapes dwelled on the harsh Australian terrain, on outback lifestyles and the Aboriginal people.

American avant-garde thinking began to influence Australian artists as the 1960s moved into the 1970s. However, there are several men-unto-themselves, like neo-expressionist Peter Booth, who specialises in the frightening, the doom-laden and the bizarre. Women artists have also begun to play a bigger role in cultural life in recent years.

It is interesting to note that the latent puritanism in Australian society could surface in the art world as late as 1982, when New South Wales police raided a Sydney gallery to seize Juan Davila's work, *Stupid as a Painter*, for being 'sexually explicit'. However, the painting was later returned to the gallery. In more recent years, controversy has tended to centre more on artistic works considered by some to be offensive to Christians, as with the exhibition by American photographer Andres Serrano at the National Gallery of Victoria in 1997 that included the image *Piss Christ* depicting a crucifix submerged in urine; the exhibition was quickly closed down.

Australian art today is vibrant and diverse, with a distinct character of its own and a much more realistic appreciation of the country's natural environment. From the funky graphics of designer Ken Done to the sometimes tortured explorations of Brett Whiteley (died 1992), Australian art has found its place on the international scene. And let us not forget that the most iconic Aussie expat of them all, the multi-talented Rolf Harris, now in England, donned his artist's beret-hat in 2005 to serve the throne when Queen Elizabeth II of England consented to let him produce a formal portrait of Her Majesty (also Queen of Australia, remember) for her 80th birthday celebrations.

Biggest 'Chook Raffle' of Them All

The Archibald Prize for portraiture is Australia's oldest, best-known and most controversy-stalked visual arts award. Its judgements are always eagerly awaited and debated by the arts world. This coveted prize offers the winner A$ 35,000 cash and a guaranteed national profile. Final judgement is delivered by the Trustees of the Art Gallery of New South Wales. It all started in 1921 with a bequest from Jules Francois Archibald, the editor of Australia's current affairs weekly *The Bulletin*, setting up the prize for the best portrait of a distinguished Australian produced over the past year by an artist resident in 'Australasia'. To make things more democratic, a 'People's Award' category was introduced in 1988—the gap between the expert judges' and the popular vote for the prize is often instructive. In 1991, yet another such category was created, the 'Packing Room Prize', where the behind-the-scenes workers who unpack and hang the Archibald entries, vote for their choice. This one is always awarded a couple of days before the Archibald Prize proper.

Sir William Dobell's much disputed win in 1943 gained the prize somewhat negative publicity when the subject of Dobell's painting, fellow artist Joshua Smith, took offence, and a lawsuit, against Dobell on the grounds that his work was not a portrait but a caricature. Smith lost the case, thus pushing the boundaries of what kind of art could be considered for the prize.

Just for the record, the 2005 Archibald went to established Australian artist John Olsen (1928–) for his dark-hued *Self Portrait Janus Faced*. Ironically, he himself is on record in the 1950s as having described the Archibald as a 'chook raffle', a dismissive term for a parochial, small-time Australian neighbourhood fund-raising event that raffles chickens, cooked or otherwise .

Located on Bennelong Point, the Sydney Opera House was officially opened by Queen Elizabeth II on 20 October 1973.

Tales of Two Cities

Melbourne and Sydney are old rivals and perhaps in no area more than the arts. Goldrush wealth in the 1850s made Victoria rich, hence the rise of its capital city Melbourne as a major cultural centre, well endowed with wealthy merchant patrons of the arts.

Melbourne established the country's first public art gallery, the National Gallery of Victoria, in 1861. Since the mid-1990s, this gallery has been housed in two buildings, the Ian Potter Centre at Federation Square for its important collection of Australian works, and NGV International at St Kilda Road for its equally impressive array of acquired European and international art.

The Art Gallery of New South Wales, founded in 1875, is housed in what was supposed to be a 'temporary' building back in 1895 and also features a good collection of colonial Australian art.

Canberra, too, has played a role in stimulating fine art. Australian painting got a big boost with the opening of the Australian National Gallery in Canberra in 1982, late though this was for such an institution to emerge for the first time. However, most states had galleries by the end of the 19th century.

MOVING PICTURES

There were Australian films made before World War II, some of them very good, but for the purpose of this book, what happened after the war is probably most interesting.

The Australian cinema virtually slumbered after the war, until the Labor government of Gough Whitlam set up the Australian Film Development Corporation, now the Australian Film Commission (AFC), in 1970. The AFC created the government's own film-making unit, Film Australia, and also funded other films. Naturally, this immediately stimulated a new rush of cinematic creativity. One of the most active participants was Phillip Adams, also known today as a newspaper columnist and advertising guru. Since then, Australian film-makers and directors have won an undoubted place in world cinema with their unique style.

Among the giants of the Australian industry are names like:

- Peter Weir—*Picnic at Hanging Rock* (1975), *Gallipoli* (1981), *Fearless* (1993), *Dead Poets Society* (1989), *The Truman Show* (1998) and *Master and Commander* (2003)
- Fred Schepisi—*The Chant of Jimmie Blacksmith* (1978), *Six Degrees of Separation* (1993), *It Runs in the Family* (2003)
- Bruce Beresford—*The Getting of Wisdom* (1977), *Breaker Morant* (1980), *Driving Miss Daisy* (1990) *Paradise Road* (1997), *Bride of the Wind* (2001)
- Rolf de Heer—*Bad Boy Bubby* (1993) and *The Tracker* (2004)
- Gillian Armstrong—*My Brilliant Career* (1978), *Little Women* (1995), *Oscar and Lucinda* (1997), *Charlotte Gray* (2001)
- Phillip Noyce – *Patriot Games* (1992), *Rabbit-Proof Fence* (2002), and *The Quiet American* (2002).

Weir, Schepisi, Beresford and Noyce have all long since removed themselves to the USA, where the substantial expat Aussie film-maker and movie star community is often tagged 'the Gum-Leaf Mafia.'

Many of the more interesting of these films, from the point of view of the non-Australian, are those which deal with the Australian landscape and Australian history or issues. I would rate *Picnic at Hanging Rock*, *Gallipoli*, *The Chant of Jimmie Blacksmith* (an indictment of white attitudes to Aboriginals) and *Evil Angels, Rabbit-Proof Fence,*

The Tracker, Japanese Story, The Dish and *The Castle* (see below) pretty high as routes to the understanding of the Australian psyche.

Early Australian cinema was somewhat slow-moving, melancholic even, and this tradition has survived into the 1990s with contributions like Gillian Armstrong's wistful dissection of a failing marriage, *The Last Days of Chez Nous*, and *The Sum of Us* by Geoff Burton and Kevin Dowling, a moving examination of a father's reconciliation with his son's homosexuality.

But more typical of the 1990s crop have been literally punchy works like *Romper Stomper*, a brutal stare at street warfare between Vietnamese gangs and white skinheads in a Melbourne suburb, and delightful comedies such as Baz Luhrmann's bitter-sweet *Strictly Ballroom* starring twinkletoes heart-throb Paul Mercurio, the romantic (straight) *Muriel's Wedding*, the glamorous (gay) *Priscilla, Queen of the Desert*, and the farcical *The Castle,* depicting a very ordinary family's battle to stop their home being compulsorily acquired. Following the trail blazed across the world and in the USA by *Crocodile Dundee* in 1986, starring archetypal bushman Paul Hogan, George Miller and Chris Noonan's animatronics triumph *Babe,* and Scott Hicks' *Shine* about mentally-ill Western-Australian concert pianist David Helfgott (played by Geoffrey Rush) won international accolades and box-office returns in the 1990s. Rush has gone on to play magnificently in *Elizabeth* and *Shakespeare in Love* (both in 1998), *The Tailor of Panama* (2001), *Pirates of the Caribbean: The Curse of the Black Pearl* (2003) and *The Life and Death of Peter Sellers* (2004).

New-Zealand-born Australian woman director Jane Campion took the coveted Palme d'Or best-film award with her dark drama *The Piano* at the Cannes Film Festival in 1993, and continues such quality, as in *Portrait of a Lady* in 1997, starring Australia's own Nicole Kidman, and the lighter *Holy Smoke* in 1999, with Kate Winslet and Harvey Keitel.

Notable Australian film actors not already mentioned include Judy Davis, Rachel Griffiths, Sam Neill, Jack

Thompson, Hugo Weaving, Hugh Jackman and Heath Ledger. And does anyone remember that the swashbuckling Errol Flynn, darling of the 1930s, was in fact a Tasmanian-Australian? Another bright Australian star, Cate Blanchett, has proved her talent in *Oscar and Lucinda* and *Elizabeth*, also playing the iconic Katharine Hepburn in director Martin Scorsese's 2004 movie *The Aviator.*

Australians in Hollywood

Some Aussie stars who have won coveted movie Oscars in recent times

- **1990**   Dean Semler, cinematography, *Dances with Wolves.*
- **1991**   Luciana Arrighi, art direction, *Howards End.*
- **1993**   Jane Campion, original screenplay, *The Piano.*
- **1994**   Lizzy Gardner & Tim Chappel, costume design, *The Adventures of Priscilla, Queen of the Desert.*
- **1995**   Bruce Davey & Mel Gibson, best picture, *Braveheart*
  Mel Gibson, director, *Braveheart*
  John Cox, visual effects, *Babe*
  Peter Frampton & Paul Pattison, makeup, *Braveheart.*
- **1996**   Geoffrey Rush, actor, *Shine*
  John Seale, cinematography, *The English Patient.*
- **1999**   David Lee, Sound, *The Matrix*
  Steve Courtley, visual effects, *The Matrix.*
- **2000**   Russell Crowe, actor, *Gladiator.*
- **2001**   Andrew Lesnie, cinematography, *Lord of the Rings*
  Catherine Martin, art/costumes, *Moulin Rouge.*
- **2002**   Nicole Kidman, actress, *The Hours.*
- **2003**   Russell Boyd, cinematography, *Master and Commander*
  Adam Elliot, animated short film, *Harvie Krumpet.*
- **2004**   Cate Blanchett, actress, *The Aviator.*

But perhaps the biggest Aussie names on the international scene today are Mel Gibson (his *The Passion of the Christ,* 2004, is among the world's top ten grossing movies ever, with about US$ 700,000) and Russell Crowe who, since *Romper Stomper* in 1992, has turned in stunning performances in a diversity of roles, for example in *LA Confidential* (1997), *The*

Insider (1999), in the philosophical epic *Gladiator* (2000), in *A Beautiful Mind* (2001) and in the swashbuckling *Master and Commander* (2003).

Australian movie-makers' quirky style has continued in the 21st century, with delicious contributions such as *The Dish* (2001), about Australia's contribution to America's 1969 moon-walk via a satellite dish in a boondocks place called Parkes, and the fantasy extravaganza, Baz Luhrmann's *Moulin Rouge* (2001). This has been accompanied by a trend to smaller, tighter, almost TV-screen size human dramas such as the murderous but clever *Chopper* (2000), the interior tale of a notorious Australian criminal, starring Australian Eric Bana (who moved on to play Hector alongside Brad Pitt's Achilles in the Hollywood epic *Troy* of 2004) and *Lantana* (2001), a tense psycho-drama disguised as a murder mystery, starring Australian luminaries Geoffrey Rush, Anthony LaPaglia (often cast as a New Yorker tough guy—did you know he is Australian?), Glenn Robbins and Kerry Armstrong.

The Australian documentary ('doco' in proper Strine) is also alive and very well. If you want a twisted giggle, get *Cane Toads* out of your friendly DVD library. This 1988 film details the menace of the advance of the alien Hawaiian sugar cane toad across Australia since it was unwisely introduced to the continent as a possible biological control agent; now it is doing more harm than good.

THESPIAN THINGS

In theatre as in other arts, government support in the past has been a stimulus, specifically the establishment in 1968 of what is now called the Australia Council, until recently headed by Donald Horne.

Two groups have been important catalysts in the development of indigenous drama—the now defunct Nimrod company (wound up in 1988) and the Australian Performing Group. The latter group advocated 'worker control of the theatre', operating as a co-operative, and based itself in a converted Melbourne press factory, but more or less gave up the ghost in 1979.

Women's theatre has enjoyed much attention during the 1980s and 1990s.

Aboriginal theatre, and dance, experienced similar growth during these decades. The name Jack Davis towers above all others in this niche, his *Sugar* of 1985 and *In Our Town* (1990) both still standards on countless theatre companies' repertoires. Davis, a Western Australian Aboriginal from the Noongar people of the south-west, died in 2000 at the age of 83. Western Australia continues a tradition of indigenous theatre, notably through the Yirra Yaakin Noongar Theatre group established since 1993.

Australia's most productive, best-known playwright now is David Williamson, with plays like *Don's Party* (1973) and *Travelling North* (1980), both also successfully rendered as movies. Williamson was also the screenwriter for major cinema hits *Gallipoli* and *The Year of Living Dangerously*. With a backlist of more than 35 plays now, he is among the few Australian artists to examine average middle-class Australian life. *Up for Grabs* (2001), a satire about greed in the art world, starred international pop-diva Madonna in its London premiere, while *Dead White Males* (2004) dealt with university ethics. The allegedly workaholic Williamson, born in 1942, is reputed to be slowing down at last. If so, his parting shot was *Influence* in 2005, a play that tilts at Australia's often right-wing rabble-rousing 'shock-jock' journalists and radio hosts.

But how to forget the richest and most successful of all Australian live stage acts? *The Wiggles'* well-crafted and cheeringly innocent onstage idiocies presented for tiny tots are a global hit, with parents too (especially with sexually deprived 'desperate housewives', claimed one journalist). The four-man Wiggles team—Jeff Fatt, Anthony Field, Greg Page and Murray Cook—are believed to earn a combined total of around A$ 45 million a year. They certainly work for it.

THE BOX

Television has also fostered Australian theatre, partly through its attempts to comply with rulings that set a minimum quota for Australian-origin television drama (although the big television story of the late 1990s was the rise of quality programming on the so-called 'ethnic' channel, SBS, now as much respected as ABC). *SeaChange*, about professionals seeking a simpler life outside the city, signalled big changes in audiences and in Australian society. The content was more sophisticated and the characters more diverse, often multicultural. Veteran actress Sigrid Thornton helped ABC score with this one.

In the 21st century, however, real drama has struggled to compete with a barrage of 'lifestyle' programmes such as the veteran *Gardening Australia* (whose resident garden gnome, Peter Cundall, is a treat to watch), *Burke's Backyard* (just recently defunct) hosted by Don Burke, and *Better Homes and Gardens,* besides the internationally franchised pestilence of 'reality TV' shows such as *Big Brother, Australian Idol* and *Outback House* (where the pitiable participants replicate the 19th century pioneer settlers' experience of Australia in the raw). Offbeat and sometimes off-colour live hosted shows such as *Rove Live,* fronted by the personable young Rove McManus, and the (to me) incomprehensible *Roy and HG* (actually John Doyle and Greg Pickhaver), a blend of crude foolery and sports trivia, are the only other formats currently cutting the mustard.

More enjoyable by far, to my mind, is the ABC's roaring success *Strictly Dancing,* a running ballroom and camp contemporary dance contest hosted by the witty and eloquent Paul McDermott.

Home-grown soap operas like *Neighbours* have always been hits (the theatrical cradle of mega-star Kylie Minogue in her role as 'Charlene' during the 1980s, and still going 18 years later, has not only riveted Australia to its living room chairs but has also been watched by more than 15 million British viewers). Aussie sitcoms and comedy shows are often excellent but for some reason always burn themselves out quickly, more on the *Fawlty Towers* model than the *Seinfeld* one, so you have to catch them while you can. One quintessentially Australian gem has been *Kath and Kim* (premiered 2002), a scary recital of all that is most mundane and banal in Australian suburban life, set in the fictional Fountain Lakes estate. If it isn't on the TV, go get the DVDs or whatever; it will be worth it for the deep probe into Australian manners and mores that the series offers. This is the natural, and in some ways more subtle yet more relaxed and comfortable, heir to Barry Humphries' acerbic observations of 'Moonee Ponds' (see below).

The Artistic Bottom Line

In 1999–2000, the value to the Australian economy of arts and related industry groups was around A$ 8 billion—bigger than the beer, wine and spirits industries combined; the arts are about half the size of the Australian banking sector. Australian Bureau of Statistics figures show that arts and leisure employ more than 800,000 Australians, including 300,000 full-time.

—Figures from an address by Australia Council
CEO Jennifer Bott, April 2004.

CABARET AND COMEDY

Australian performers seem particularly adept at cabaret comedy and satire, both of which translate well to the small screen.

King of the field—or should one say, Queen?—is Barry Humphries, who has so immortalised one of his roles, 'Dame Edna Everage' (Everage = Average, geddit?) that the Australian public now perceives her as an entirely real person. Book reviewers no longer tack on any helpful brackets like 'aka Barry Humphries', radio interviewers interview 'Edna Everage' straight-faced without ever referring to Barry Humphries. You need to know this, or else you may swallow Dame Edna hook, line and sinker without ever realising you have been experiencing satire, in drag.

It is very hard to describe to the non-Australian what it is about Dame Edna that so hypnotises Australians. She embodies all the most awful aspects of Australian suburban values, but she has also grown beyond this, to monstrous and mythic proportions, very much larger than life. 'Housewife-megastar', is how she describes herself. 'Moonee Ponds' is where she lives.

The queen of Ausralian surburbia, Dame Edna Everage (Barry Humphries), at her ghastly best.

Physically, the Dame is big-boned and Cartlandesque, and follows the grandest traditions of the English pantomime dame, plus quite a bit. 'She' specialises in huge horned spectacle frames, heavy make-up and a stridently high-pitched voice. She is almost bound to address you as 'Possums' and has a cruel way of probing for the secret hangups of her audience when she is live onstage. Reading the Dame's autobiography, *My Gorgeous Life*, will give you a feel for the character, seeing her on television a little more, but there is nothing quite like seeing her 'live'. Wicked, possums, wicked.

Barry Humphries became a household name in Britain in the 1960s with his creation of another great Australian character, the ultimate 'Ocker', cartoon-strip character Barry McKenzie. The McKenzie character, who spoke broad 'Strine', re-popularised old Australian slang-phrases like 'Point Percy at the porcelain' for the male act of urination.

Not content with all this, Humphries has also spawned the horrendous, drunken, buck-toothed Australian diplomat, Sir Leslie Paterson, and the quietly tragic hero of outdated, Gallipoli-conscious Melbournian suburbia, Sandy Stone, who usually appears onstage in his dressing gown and bedroom slippers. Sandy is, as reviewer John Doust said in 1990, 'racist, sexist, boring, self-indulgent, suburban and yes, dead'. The essence of Stone is also captured in a book, *The Life and Death of Sandy Stone*.

Television has been the perfect playground for other comedians. Paul Hogan first made his comic mark in this medium, as did other names of note like Steve Vizard, the creator of the now defunct satirical show *Fast Forward* (and now disgraced big businessman, censured for his stocks and shares dealings). In 1996, *Good News Week*, a quirky version of a quiz-panel show, was pretty much built around its star host Paul McDermott, and his companions— the rotund Mikey Robbins and sparky Julie McCrossin. Together with a star panel, they offer off-the-wall perspectives on the week's events. Fans of Shaun Micallef's bizarre sense of mischief wait with bated breath to see what will be his next move, following no follow-up to his *The Micallef Programme* of 2000. Even more one of a kind are the confronting topics addressed by two very special comedians, cerebral palsy victim and comedian 'Steady Eddy', and Vietnamese former 'boat-person' refugee Hung Le.

You can even make a study of the Australian sense of humour just by watching the TV ads, some of which are quite hilarious and utterly unlike ads you will see anywhere else. Recent examples were the one in 2002 where things kept going wrong, usually in a rural Australian setting and

> Another Aussie wit who made his name largely overseas is the urbane Clive James, well known to British television viewers.

centred on a Toyota Hilux 'ute' van, culminating with the harassed lead character, a farmer or even a sheep dog, venting his frustration by muttering under his breath, "Bugga!"; a 2005 ad, for Carlton beer, has an epic-scale cast of hundreds rushing around impressive open spaces to form a huge image of a human being drinking beer that can be seen clearly from the air—the operatically chanted captions for this ad run something like "This is a big ad... a very big ad... and expensive too... it's a bloody big ad... it had bloody well better sell some beer..." etc. It has joined the exclusive 'computer virus' club of ads that are spread like wildfire via the Internet just because people enjoy them.

FANCY FOOTWORK

Ballet has always—quite wrongly, of course—been derided by philistines as a 'sissy' art. In this context, it is intriguing that 'macho' Australia should have excelled in this very art form. There are something like 2,500 ballet schools in the country now.

The great dancer Sir Robert Helpmann, active in the 1920s–1930s, was Australian. Other great Australian dancers include Marilyn Jones (most active in the 1950s), Meryl Tankard of the Australian Dance Theatre, Paul Mercurio (known for his role in *Strictly Ballroom*) of the Sydney Dance Company and Lisa Bolte of The Australian Ballet (founded in 1962 with the eminent Dame Peggy Van Praagh as its first director, thereafter well-shepherded by Maina Gielgud, from 1983–1996). The 'AB' now enjoys an international reputation for excellence, today hosting names such as Nicole Rhodes, principal artist since 2000, David McAllister, artistic director since 2001, and Stanton Welch, a resident choreographer since 1995.

MUSIC
The Serious Stuff

The Australian Opera, established in 1970, is Australia's largest performing arts organisation, but is heavily dependent on government subsidies. Australia has particularly distinguished itself by producing more than its share of world-class operatic singers. Sopranos Dame Nellie Melba (1880s) and Dame Joan Sutherland (1950s–1980s) are among the most famous. Their male counterparts include world-famous baritones John Brownlee (1900–1969) and Peter Dawson (1882–1961).

Among composers, another Sutherland, Margaret, stands out. She died in 1984 after a lifetime of classical compositions based on Australian themes. Percy Grainger of *Country Garden* fame (circa 1907) was a well-known Australian name after World War II (see the film *Passion* for an account of his bizarre private life). Other cherished names are Eileen Joyce, an international concert pianist in the 1950s, and John Williams, one of the world's top classical guitarists.

The most important actor in Australian music development was Sir Bernard Heinze (1894–1982). As musical adviser to the ABC from its establishment in 1929, he helped create state symphony orchestras linked to the public by a radio and television concert network which continues today.

The Other Stuff

You must have heard of the Bee Gees and the Easy Beats. Perhaps also of INXS, Men At Work, Midnight Oil, Little River Band, AC/DC, Air Supply and The Black Sorrows. Almost certainly of Olivia Newton-John and Kylie Minogue (a whole crop of Kylies is growing all over Australia, thanks to her). And what better illustration of the Aussie sense of humour than Bjorn Again, the Abba look-alike-sound-alike that started in Melbourne in 1988? They are all Australian pop bands and singers of course. Men At Work are to be commended in particular for having given the world the song 'Down Under', containing the immortal words:

'I said, "Do you speak my language?"
He just smiled and gave me a Vegemite sandwich.'

Midnight Oil is a politically-motivated environmentalist band representing a new genre of popular protest music, which also championed Aboriginal rights. However, in 2002 the band lost the charismatic lead singer Peter Garrett who had helmed it through its heyday in the 1980s, to politics—he is now a Labor MP charged with environmental affairs. Another 1980s Melbourne rock group, Hunters & Collectors, one of Australia's many excellent 'pub bands' described by *The Australian's* Clinton Walker as 'a deliberately esoteric, sprawling, post-punk, tribal/industrial art-funk ensemble' turned 'populist', has also left its mark.

Among other groups that have been rated highly, either inside Australia or beyond, are Regurgitator, Savage Garden (split in 2001), Silverchair (still big), Mental as Anything and The Screaming Jets. On the rock and pop sólo vocalist scene, Jimmy Barnes and John Farnham go on for ever, seemingly indestructible monuments.

The white-Aboriginal fusion band Gondwanaland is excellent but seems relatively cerebral compared with the raw energy of Yothu Yindi, straight from the Aboriginal heartland of Arnhem Land, a band sprung from among the Yolngu people, demonstrating a stunning blend of traditional sound and Western technology. Listen to their song 'Treaty' on their *Tribal Voice* album, 'Super Highway' on the album *Bercuta*, and get their latest, sixth, album *Garma*. Much of their genius derives from the vision of schoolteacher and lead singer Mandawuy Yunupingu, voted 1992 'Australian of the Year', and the first Aboriginal from Arnhem Land to achieve a tertiary degree.

Kylie Minogue, of course, has become an international star, way outstripping her male counterpart Jason Donovan. (Kylie reached stardom through the part of Charlene, the girl-next-door in *Neighbours,* the role she first played in 1987 as an 18 year-old newbie).

Both Kylie and Jason projected an essentially wholesome, simple image, in itself quite Australian. Even international supermodel Elle MacPherson, with her high-flying jet-setting life, has retained the Aussie fresh-and-sweet-outdoors-girl image. Kylie, however, has gone the way of Madonna.

Somewhat dated—but still going strong—and undeniably Australian, is Rolf Harris of 'Tie Me Kangaroo Down, Sport' fame (1960s). ('Play your didgeridoo, Blue,' it went.) Another Aussie singer who left her mark on the international scene in a Germaine-Greer sort of way, is Helen Reddy, known internationally for her song 'I Am Woman'.

In bars, pubs and restaurants, you will find surprisingly good new groups cutting their teeth. You have to know your way around the scene to find them from one day to the next, however, for Australian bands rarely sit on long-stay contracts at the same venue. They move from spot to spot very frequently.

Be warned, showmanship of the sequins-and-lamé kind is not really part of the Australian performance style. Many a time, a nondescript band in the most unremarkable everyday gear will shuffle onstage, mumble a few inaudible words of introduction, perform brilliantly, then shrug, take a swig of beer and amble off. Only later do you discover by chance that this was one of Australia's top groups. That kind of understatement is very Australian: remember the tall poppy syndrome?

Bushed

Australian folk music is of great interest for its historic roots stretching back into Celtic, especially Irish, and English traditions, including old Victorian sea shanties. The early bush ballads are like libraries of memories about early pioneer life, on the goldfields and the cattle ranges, in the mines and in the outback deserts. Songs like that old favourite, 'Click Go The Shears', for example.

Australian themes have also been converted into the American country-and-western style, which is very popular in rural areas and among the Aboriginals in particular. Among the most famous songs in this genre are 'A Pub With No Beer' by Gordon Parsons (based on a poem by Queenslander Dan Sheehan) and another ode to beer and mateship, 'Duncan', both recorded by Australia's Slim Dusty, in 1958 and in 1980 respectively. (Slim Dusty, born David Gordon Kilpatrick, himself remains an Aussie icon even after his much lamented passing in 2003 at the age of 76, still working even then, on his 106th recording album.)

Beer-less in Oz

It's lonesome away from your kindred and all
By the camp fire at night where the wild dingoes call,
But there's nothing so lonesome, so morbid or drear
Than to stand in a bar of a pub with no beer.

—First verse of Gordon Parsons' 'A Pub With No Beer',
recorded as an Oz-country hit by the legendary Slim Dusty.

If you see a 'bush-dance' advertised, do go to sample the down-to-earth fun; among other things, you may catch sight of strange bush-band instruments like the 'lager-phone', constructed of beer-bottle caps. Among the better-known bush bands are the traditionalist Bushwackers and the more political Redgum, also the Mucky Duck Bush Band of Western Australia, while big-name singers include John Williamson and Eric Bogle. Two of Bogle's protest songs are 'And The Band Played Waltzing Matilda' (anti-war) and 'I Hate Wogs' (anti-racism).

Bush Balladeers

Closely allied with the country and folk music movements is the literary tradition of the folk poets of the past, chief among

Street musicians serenade passers-by with a variety of tunes.

them Henry Lawson (1867–1922), C J Dennis (1876–1938), hailed as 'Laureate of the Larrikin' and bush balladeer 'Banjo' Paterson (1864–1941). The bush poetry movement is very democratic and to some extent, every Australian is a potential bush poet. The tradition of homespun bush poetry is still strong and you may hear Aussies spontaneously break into verse over a campfire, or you may be able to attend specially arranged bush poetry events where wannabe poets will turn up to perform in the literary equivalent of a karaoke contest.

THE LITERARY TRADITION

Just as the AFC stimulated growth in the cinema, so the Literature Board of the Arts Council, set up in 1973, promoted Australian writing. Achievements in this field have been considerable, attracting world attention in some cases.

One of the greatest early novels was based on convict life, although published well after the days of transportation—*His Natural Life* by Marcus Clarke, 1874. The bush poets of the late 19th century represented a breakaway from English traditions, in search of a more Australian identity. Backing this trend energetically was the national news-and-views weekly magazine *Bulletin*, founded in 1880 and still going strong.

The novel gained strength from the 1920s onward, with major contributions like *Coonardoo* (1929) by Susannah Prichard, a novel of cattle-station life in the far north-west which, for the first time in Australia, dared to touch on black-white sexual relationships, and *Capricornia* (1938) on a similar theme, by Xavier Herbert. Herbert's very long *Poor Fellow My Country* (1975) is also well regarded.

A giant has been Patrick White (1912–1990), who won the Nobel Prize for Literature in 1973, the first Australian ever to do so, for his *The Eye of the Storm*. One reviewer, Greg Sheridan, however, wrote recently that reading White's work, *Riders in the Chariot*, was a 'dread and dire duty that hangs over every Australian'. I myself tend to fall into the Sheridan camp.

Today's giants of the Australian literary scene are probably the ocean-obsessed Tim Winton of Western

Australia, Peter Carey and Bryce Courtenay. Winton's *Cloudstreet* (1991) is possibly his defining work, but there are also *The Riders* (1995) and *Dirt Music* (2001), and quite a stable of children's books too. Winton has won the Miles Franklin Award three times and been shortlisted for the Booker Prize twice.

Peter Carey, a former advertising copywriter, produced his Booker Prize winner *Oscar and Lucinda* in 1988. His *True History of the Kelly Gang* (2000) is a superb introduction to Australia's folk history centering on the Robin Hood-like figure of Irish-Australian bandit Ned Kelly, written entirely in the authentic Irish working class voice of Kelly himself, missing punctuation and all.

Bryce Courtenay, like Carey, was also an advertising man before he wrote his first novel *The Power of One* at the late age of 55. Now he's more than 11 books away from that, with the best known titles including *April Fool's Day, Tommo & Hawk,* and *Jessica.*

Ex-priest Thomas Keneally is another Australian literary name to conjure with. *Bring Larks and Heroes* (1967) and *The Chant of Jimmie Blacksmith* (1972), also a film, are among his best-known titles, and his *Schindler's Ark* (the book of the movie, so to speak, 1993) won the Booker McConnell fiction prize in 1982.

Murray Bail's 1998 award-winning *Eucalyptus* is a must-read, with a strongly Australian setting.

Other notable contributions have been the short stories of David Malouf (try *An Imaginary Life*—1978).

Gigantic success came to Colleen McCulloch with her 1997 epic blockbuster novel *The Thorn Birds*, an Irish-Australian saga. Nor should we forget Nevil Shute, a Briton who migrated to Australia in 1950, and his famous Aussie boy-meets-Pommie girl romance *A Town Like Alice* (1950). Other classic Australian writers are Miles Franklin, Robert Drewe, Elizabeth Jolley and Judith Wright. Theirs is a distinctly Australian voice.

In poetry, the World War II poems of Kenneth Slessor, who died in 1971, and the passion of Aboriginal poet Kath Walker ('Oodgeroo Noonuccal', died 1993), stand out. High school students are also regularly exhorted to absorb the down-to-basics morality of poet Bruce Dawe (still with us).

On the non-fiction front, there is the massive six-volume *History of Australia* (1962–1987) by the late Manning Clark. This, read in conjunction with Geoffrey Blainey's *The Tyranny of Distance* (1966—on how Australia's geographical isolation shaped the country's history) and Robert Hughes' moving account of the early convict years, *Fatal Shore* (1987), makes for a near-perfect Australian history lesson.

Melbourne-born (expatriate in England) Germaine Greer's *The Female Eunuch* (1970) is one of the bibles of world feminism. I have mentioned Donald Horne's important study of Australian society, *The Lucky Country* (1964), before but it cannot be mentioned too often. Also on the non-fiction side, Blanche d'Alpuget's meaty, warts-and-all biography of Bob Hawke, 1982, is a fascinating read. Finally, she married him.

Where to Get Your Books

To get your own copies of any of these books, go browse in any Angus & Robertson book emporium, a homegrown bookseller established since 1886.

The fount of all wisdom, when it comes to publishing Australian reference books like dictionaries and encyclopaedias, is Macquarie.

Con Artists

Australian writers and artists unfortunately have recently brought a dubious art form to new heights: artistic fraud. Many believe the root cause is excessive political correctness in artistic circles favouring works by ethnic minorities, whether migrants or Aboriginals: white artists have been obliged to masquerade as minorities in order to get noticed. I myself think this flood of fraud, particularly evident in the 1990s, is as much an outgrowth of the Australian distaste for intellectual pretentiousness and the Australian sense of humour which delights in mocking the over-earnest. Making a bunch of professors awarding prizes for literature look very silly simply warms the cockles of any 'dinky-di' Australian.

Recent scandals of this ilk have ranged from Helen Darville's elaborate reinvention of herself as Ukrainian-origin Helen Demidenko (*The Hand That Signed The Paper*, 1995), through middle-age white male Leon Carmen's briefly successful pose as award-winning Aboriginal woman writer Wanda Koolmatrie (*My Own Sweet Time*, 1995), to eminent painter Elizabeth Durack's 1997 confession to painting under the guise of a highly-rated Aboriginal alter ego, *Eddie Burrup*. Sadly there are several others. But these incidents do illustrate liberal white Australia's '90s obsession with multiculturalism, and a new-found identity crisis.

BRICKS AND MORTAR

Finally, a word about architecture. Australian architects have excelled more in small-scale, detailed works, and especially in the area of heritage conservation. Only gold-mining and wool-industry money brought a degree of pomposity into public buildings, around the mid-19th century.

Among the more monumental buildings are the Queen Victoria Building in Sydney (foundation stone laid in 1893, officially opened in 1898), the National Art Gallery in

Sydney's old Queen Victoria Building was restored as a shopping arcade by Asian investment.

Charming and stylish architecture can be found tucked away even in the smallest and most remote farming towns, like this church in Carnamah, in Western Australia's Wheat Belt.

Canberra, which has touches of the style set by the famous Swiss architect Le Corbusier, the Victorian Arts Centre in Melbourne, and of course, the Sydney Opera House. The Opera House, opened in 1973, is the work of a Danish architect, however, although finally completed by Australian Peter Hall; it cost A$ 100 million.

Canberra in particular has been an architects' playground, as a planned city from the beginning, a fact which gives it something of an artificial look and feeling.

Another fine building far away from the eastern centres is the relatively new Maritime Museum of Fremantle in Western Australia, designed by Cox Howlett & Bailey Woodland. Built right into a working port (ships draw up to dock outside the museum windows and a permanent submarine exhibit is positioned in the water outside), it is striking example of a truly maritime building.

As noted elsewhere in this book, low-rise sprawl provoked by the bungalow on a quarter-acre block is characteristic of Australian cities. Australian nostalgia surfaces often with the use of rustic features and materials, from exposed brickwork to timber and rammed earth. Revivalist features such as stained-glass windows and panels, wrought-iron 'lace-work', ornamented porticos and verandahs, and elaborate ceiling mouldings, are also much favoured. The climate has also made possible the wholesale import of many Californian, Mediterranean and tropical Asian styles.

In recent times, architects have directed their attention to issues of energy conservation, recycling and so on. Heritage conservation is a particularly active field, with a very wide-ranging brief, including Aboriginal sacred sites and rock-art treasures.

National trust bodies have existed since 1945, but the real catalyst was the establishment of the Australian Heritage Commission in 1975. Australia's conservation work in areas like Sydney's Rocks, and parts of Adelaide, as well as Fremantle, Perth's port city, to name only three examples, has won world renown. On the other hand, the destruction of old Perth in the 1970s and 1980s has also been quite remarkable.

Barwill House (also known as Wilhelmsen House) in Fremantle, Western Australia is just one of the buildings in the Heritage Grants Programme. Comprehensive conservation plans are underway to see to its restoration and preservation.

STREET-WISE CULTURE

Culture, of course, does not reside solely in books, plays or impressive buildings. It can be found in a people's lifestyle. Australians remain some of the most hedonistic of any people, reflecting the many hours of sunshine that they are blessed with every year. In a way, the enjoyment of life is, for them, a serious matter that they regard almost as a cultural heritage. You will find Australian culture at the many festivals and carnivals that Australians just love to create, almost at the drop of a hat, whether at the school and neighbourhood level, or at the State or national level. There will always be locally made handicrafts and amateur artworks to view and buy, always some local band comprising cheerful volunteers, people selling things at the market, others cooking—civil society at street level is healthy, vigorously 'DIY' and completely spontaneous. Key opportunities for

Australia's vibrant street-life is showcased at weekends, at fairs and markets; this 'statue' posing on the sidewalk in Fremantle, Western Australia's port city, is in fact a live actor painted up to look like a sculpture and shocking passers-by as he springs to life every so often.

such grassroots culture are of course the various public opportunities, so you would be well advised to get out and about on such days, not relapse into couch potato mode, always supposing that you have not taken the alternative Australian lifestyle option, the much loved backyard barbecue party with good mates. Note, though, that some holidays vary from state to state, which can be a bit confusing; for example, the Queen's Birthday holiday is the second Monday of June everywhere in Australia except Western Australia, where it is 6 October (Don't ask me why)! Aussies skilfully engineer public holidays to be Mondays wherever possible, to ensure that much sought-after long weekend. Watch out, too, for the time-zone differences between the states, and for the slight shift in these caused by daylight saving every year.

A Selection of Public Holidays and Special Dates

January

1	New Year's Day
26	Australia Day (public holiday on the following Monday)
	Festival of Sydney

January–February

Festival of Perth

March

1st Monday	Labour Day, Western Australia
2nd Monday	Labour Day, Victoria, and Moomba Parade
	Labour Day, Australian Capital Territory (ACT)
	Canberra Day Festival
	Adelaide Festival of the Arts (even-numbered years)

April

	Easter holiday—from Good Friday until the following Monday, or Tuesday in some states
at Easter	Clare Valley Wine Festival, South Australia
	Barossa Valley Vintage Festival (odd-numbered years)
25	Anzac Day

(Continued on the next page)

(Continued from previous page)

May

1st Monday   Labour Day, Queensland

                     May Day Holiday, Northern Territory

June

2nd Monday   Queen's Birthday (except Western Australia)

                     Brisbane Festival of Creative Arts

                     Darwin Beer Can Regatta, Northern Territory.

August

1   Wattle Day (not all states)

1st Monday   New South Wales Bank Holiday

                     Broome Shinju Matsuri Festival (multicultural),

                     Western Australia

1st Monday   Henley-on-Todd Regatta, Alice Springs (yacht

                     race on the dry bed of Todd River).

September

1   Wattle Day (not all states)

3   National Australia Flag Day.

October

1st Monday   Labour Day, New South Wales, ACT

6   Queen's Birthday, Western Australia

2nd Monday   Labour Day, South Australia

2nd weekend   'Spring in the Valley' Wine Festival—Perth.

November

1st Tuesday   Melbourne Cup Day, Victoria

                     (nation closes down)

11   Remembrance Day.

December

25   Christmas Day

26   Boxing Day (not South Australia)

28   South Australia Proclamation Day

                     Sydney-Hobart and Melbourne-Hobart yacht

                     races/Tasmanian Fiesta (start)

                     Hobart-Salamanca Arts Festival, Tasmania.

Yet another way to indulge in cultural 'interface' with fellow Australians it to get out on the road and maybe join the 'grey nomads' as the armies of retirees determined to 'see Australia before we die' are called—the endless highway ribbons of the wild north and central interior are dotted with the 4WD vehicles and caravans belonging to this 'tribe' and Australia's well-organised camping sites and parklands, as well as the many roadhouses, are abuzz with these Australians getting to know each other. This traditional ritual of 'going walkabout' or rather, 'driveabout' to get to know each other and the land is also a central part of Australian culture. It's hard to resist the suspicion that it was the naturally nomadic Aboriginals who first gave white Australians this very good idea.

THE ART OF LEISURE

The tradition of home-based arts and crafts is still quite strong in Australia and those who want to take up hobbies other than the ubiquitous gardening craze that inhabits every Australian suburb, may well opt for something artistic. Every community centre and adult education college is replete with offerings of courses in everything from woodcarving and ceramics to stained-glass work and block printing, often at very affordable prices or even free of charge. Consult your local TAFE college or university adult extension course list.

Other hobbies that Australia is well suited to include many outdoors options such as bush-walking, bird-watching, horse-riding, rafting or rowing. Or you might fancy a tango or salsa class, ballroom dancing or belly-dancing (there's an awful lot of the latter!). Whatever, when you get really good at it, you can go back and pass it on, become a teacher yourself.

SPEAKING STRINE

CHAPTER 8

'To employ more than the most limited of vocabularies
is not only ostentatious but anti-democratic. If the
teachers are half right, little has changed since
I attended primary school in the 1940s, when to
show an interest in words was to damn yourself as
some sort of deviant. As a wimp, or worse.'
—Columnist Phillip Adams in *The Weekend Australian*,
27 July 1991, on the Australian attitude to words.

AN ENGLISH-SPEAKING COUNTRY?

Nothing distinguishes the Australian more sharply from the average Anglo-Saxon than his very special brand of English.

Many English-speaking newcomers to the country make the awful mistake of imagining that operating there will be a breeze because 'They speak English there, don't they?' Well, not quite. Like English in other former colonial outposts, from the West Indies to South Africa and Zimbabwe, from India to Singapore and Malaysia, the language has mutated in Australia's desert soils.

The extraordinary thing is that many of the central features of Australian English were well in place by the late 19th century, hiving off from the mother tongue very soon after the original convicts' and settlers' arrival in Australia. The language of a rebellious subculture.

Unfortunately, the lingo is extremely hard for the outsider to penetrate, or to imitate, (for practice, try saying 'Australia' the Strine way—'Orst-rai-ya', or else recite 'in moi aoun toime' for 'in my own time'—but these are not scientifically phonetic spellings, needless to say). If you are a new migrant, you may gain comfort (or despair, depending on your point of view) from the certain knowledge that your children will be fluent 'Strine' speakers within months of setting foot on Australian soil. ('Strine' is an approximation of how the word 'Australian' sounds, coming out of an Australian's mouth.) It's definitely catching.

So no point in giving you a formal pronunciation guide now—a forced attempt at speaking like the locals can sound quite awful and few Aussies will be taken in by it. When in doubt, better just be yourself. The chances are though, that the accent will just naturally 'grow' on you until one day, your Mum, your Dad and your best friends back home, all say, "Hey! What happened? Your accent has completely changed!" You won't even have noticed and this news will come as a shock to you.

There is still an older generation of Australians, particularly the more educated ones, which was brought up to speak 'English English', but this cohort is fast dwindling. There are also some distinctly well-moderated, gentler accents to be found among educated and well-travelled Australians and some Cabinet ministers, especially in the eastern states, in major cities such as Sydney, Melbourne and Adelaide.

Although the trend is definitely for a more earthy Australian accent to take over the airwaves, out of a sense of increasing national pride, there are still quite a few such moderated accents to be heard on 'Auntie', the Australian Broadcasting Corporation's radio programmes.

A headline from *The West Australian* newspaper. A 'rort' is sharp practice of some sort, a scam, dirty dealing or cheating, and 'fixing' or 'rigging', especially in business and financial matters. 'Rorting the system' is a frequently used phrase referring to 'bludgers' who take advantage of, say, welfare assistance payments etc.

No Plums Please, We're Australian

Generally speaking, though, you will be considered suspect and a bit 'up yourself' (an obscene but commonly heard reference to er, 'having your head up your own arse'; 'wanker' is another frequently heard insult of the same breeding, referring to masturbation) if your English comes with too 'plummy' an accent. ('Plummy' refers to the over-careful speech you would produce if you had a plum in your mouth.)

Not only does the majority of the nation favour 'Ozspeak' but there is now also a subgroup of youngsters whose dialect of choice is sarcastically alluded to by older journalists as 'Wayne-speak', this term being a reference to today's 'in' names for Australian children, Wayne (or Jason; female version, Kylie), rather than the good old Bruce (or Jan). (There was also a brief hippy interlude during the 1960s, which produced Amber, Jasmine, Jade and Sky for some.)

Much of Wayne-speak is plain old lousy pronunciation, rather than just dialect English. Examples are *heighth* for height and *esculator* for escalator, as noted by journalist Deborah Bogle in an article for *The Australian Magazine*. In the same category can be bagged the increasing tendency to pronounce 't' as 'd', thus, *qwordah* for quarter and *wor-dah* for water. Overlaid on this is the growing impact of American English.

Today or To Die?

True-blue Australian English differs from the 'mother tongue' both in terms of its accent and in terms of its vocabulary. The accent is best gauged from old jokes which run thus…

Wounded soldier to nurse in Australian hospital: "Have I come here to die?"

Nurse: "Now, love, yer came 'ere yesterdie!"

And a punning headline in *The West Australian* newspaper, 30 April 1993, would not have been possible were it not for the Aussie accent: referring to Princess Diana of England, the newspaper headlined 'Diana—Princess of Wiles' (should have been Princess of Wales, for those of you who do not already know).

... and the national form of greeting, 'G'day, mate!' (not common currency between the sexes or among women, it should be noted), which could be transcribed roughly as 'Ger-die, mite!' Woe indeed were my two migrant friends desperately looking for Hay Street—they would have been better understood if they had said 'High Street' like everybody else in Australia.

Be very careful whom you label an Australian on first hearing. It is difficult for the beginner to tell an Australian accent from a New Zealand one, but New Zealanders do not like to be taken for Australians, not one bit (the feeling is mutual). As a general guideline, Australians open their mouths wider, while New Zealanders are said to speak through their clenched teeth and semi-closed lips. Typically, a New Zealander will say 'yis' for 'yes', and 'fush n' chups' for 'fish and chips', somewhat like the Scots' accent.

The contortions that Australians can perform with diphthongs are a marvel to the ear. Often they are extended to double-diphthongs, to the point that a simple 'no' may well become more like 'nah-oh-oo-u'. For reasons I do not quite understand myself—probably sexist ones—the essentially nasal accent sits particularly uneasily with the female voice, which in Australia also seems to be higher-pitched than it would be in most of Western Europe (although not so much higher than is common among Asian females).

A commentator in the 1940s once surmised that the Australian accent was attributable to a permanent inflammation of the nose, due to the excessive pollen to be found in the air. Australian vocal delivery is most often slow and rather flat by outsiders' standards, without great light and shade contrasts, tending to a monotone in some cases. An Australian is capable of saying something extraordinarily interesting and lively in such a low-key manner that you may not notice he has said anything out of the way at all. It's a style of speech uniquely suited to deadpan humour. 'Bought the supermarket, 'av yer, luv?' might be the typical comment as you stagger to the checkout counter with a trolley laden to the top with goodies for the party you are holding tonight.

Dorothy dixers to rule, cries Labor

BEN RUSE
CANBERRA

The Government would field 66 fewer questions from the Opposition and minor parties after using its new Senate majority to change the rules for Senate question time, Labor claimed yesterday.

The Opposition is outraged by the changes, which will allow ministers to answer more soft questions from their own backbenchers, but the Government says they simply reflect the new make-up of the Senate.

Traditionally, the question roster has been worked out co-operatively between all Senate parties. Labor is angry that the Government did not discuss its changes with other parties.

Labor says the Government intends to use its control of the Senate to prevent scrutiny. It has already raised concerns that the Government will dominate Senate committees and prevent them from investigating issues that may embarrass the Government.

Under the new rules, out of every 14 questions, Government

> **'It was a farce when we were in Government, and a farce now.'**
>
> ALP SENATOR CHRIS EVANS

senators will get six, Labor will get six and senators from other parties will get two. Previously, Labor was able to ask seven, the Government four and the minor parties three. This gives Government senators, who now control the Senate, fewer questions per head than the Opposition.

Liberal Senate leader Rob Hill said the changes were f because they were based on t number of senators each party h and that Labor should not be co plaining. He said Labor would st be able to use supplementary que tions.

Questions from Governme backbenchers to Governme ministers are known as doroth dixers, after a newspaper advi columnist who was suspected writing both the questions and t answers in her columns.

Although the questions are su posed to be asked without notic generally ministers have a pr pared answer which makes fun the Opposition.

Labor's Senate leader Chr Evans admitted the truth yeste day when he said of dorothy di ers: "It was a farce when we we in Government, and a farce now.

Another headline from *The West Australian* newspaper. What's this? 'Dorothy Dix' was an American newspaper columnist in the 1950s who ran an agony aunt column in which many suspected she just made up the Q and A to suit her own purposes. In Australia, this memory has set in aspic and the term 'Dorothy Dixer' has now come to mean a completely pre-planned, unspontaneous 'planted' or 'fixed' question with a pre-prepared 'fixed' answer, usually in Parliament, by politicians.

Ups and Downs

For this reason alone, never mind the accent, you need to concentrate on what Australians are saying (try hard not to fall asleep), in case you miss something. Since the Australian also has a penchant for terse understatement, the risk of misunderstanding is great

Here is a guide on how you should converse with an Australian. Loud, assertive delivery will not go down well. Lower your voice and flatten it like his, erase all excitement or emotion, and you should be able to get your point across without too much offence. There is one interesting exception to this rule: the infectious Australian habit of lifting the voice at the end of the sentence as if asking a question or seeking your approval/understanding.

'And it was raining, really hard' (on 'hard', the voice goes sharply up as if '?' were there and '… you know what I mean?' were tacked on the end), 'but we had no umbrellas…' (up again on 'umbrellas'… 'you know what I mean?').

This verbal tic can be infuriating to the novice but it will insidiously creep into your own voice over time, sure as the sun shines. And when you think about it, it is really quite a friendly habit, this constant seeking of others' involvement in the conversation.

One aspect of Australian speech that breaks the 'don't get excited' rule is the 'full on' (another Australianism) argument. Australian arguments can get very loud and very public—often on the street—and will be laced with violent expletives of all kinds. More of this later.

Antique Hangovers

Some Australian English is, in fact, more original and 'pure' than the version spoken in Mother England today. Many Australian words were long ago discarded in England. Australians, as a rule, betray an innate conservatism by clinging on to old forms and idioms, while at the same time creating new ones. This makes Australian English quite a rich, 'dense' language.

You have to look back to white Australia's roots in 19th-century, Cockney London and Ireland to understand this. Quite apart from the accent, how else can you explain the extraordinary survival of Cockney rhyming slang in everyday Australian speech? It even gets printed in the daily newspapers as a matter of course—like the photo caption I once came across, reading 'Mr So-and-So on the dog and bone'. This photo showed Mr So-and-So using the telephone.

I might have passed this by and thought nothing of it, had not a young Aussie friend remarked to me over a coffee, "So you're all on your Al Capone, then?" when I said my husband was away. That of course translated as 'So you're all on your own, then?'

I must mention here, however, that at least one reputable dictionary lists 'Al Capone' as the rhyming slang for telephone (and not 'dog and bone'), but 'Pat Malone' as the rhyming slang for 'alone', so I am not quite sure where this leaves us. But the examples I have cited have come from my first-hand experience.

Rhyming SMS

The old cockney rhyming slang is alive and well even in the era of SMS or 'texting'. I was present at the Perth end when two older generation Aussies in Melbourne texted their grandson in Perth, about to attend his younger sister's 21st birthday party, with this message for his mobile:

'What time's the gay and hearty?
Don't get elephant trunk!'

Get it?

Translation: 'What time is the party? Don't get drunk!'

Thinking Little

An Australian idiosyncrasy is the strange obsession with reducing any word possible to its diminutive form. (Such words are known as 'hypocorisms' to academics but we could call them 'hypos' here.) This, too, is quite a catching disease for newcomers. Hence 'postie' refers to the postman, 'U-ie' for a motorist's U-turn, 'barbie' for barbecue, 'vegie' or 'veggie' for vegetable, 'prezzie' for present and 'Chrissie' for Christmas.

Other words are shortened with an '-o' at the end: 'reffo' for refugee, 'Freo' for the port of Fremantle in Western

An official campaign card for Australia Post, mailed out to all households in Western Australia, promoting safety for postmen 'using the typically Strine abbreviation 'Postie' for postman.

Australia, 'reggo' (soft 'g') for car registration, 'journo' for journalist, 'muso' for musician, and so on. The 'o' suffix more usually applies to people than things—for example, a 'veggo' (soft 'g') is a vegetarian, whereas a 'veggie meal' is a vegetable or vegetarian meal.

University of Queensland professor Roland Sussex has recently estimated that Australian English now showcases no fewer than 2,500 of these hypocorisms. As Sussex remarked in 2000, it looks like we now need a' dickie' of Aussie hypos.

Conversation Smoothers

Then, of course, there are the famous Australian catchphrases: 'No worries' and 'She'll be right,' epitomising the nation's fabled plucky optimism and laid-back style. These are by no means clichés and are still in common use, although 'Not a problem' seems to be gaining ground. 'She'll be apples' (from the rhyming slang 'apples and spice' for 'nice'?) belongs to the same family of phrases but increasingly is seen as archaic.

However, it must be said that the trials of economic hard times have of late strained even the most sanguine of Aussies and such phrases increasingly have a hollow ring to them, belying the desperation beneath.

'Just Popping into Manchester'

The way Australians have clung to very old language is yet another illustration of their innate conservatism and strongly traditionalist urges. We have seen how 19th century forms from East End London have survived in modern Australian English. Here's another example of this modern usage of 'linguistic fossils' in daily Australian life: the newcomer may at first be mystified by the word 'Manchester' to be seen on signs in many Australian department stores and over many shop windows. This refers back to the late 19th century, when the industrial town of Manchester in north-eastern England was the world's greatest centre of textiles and cotton manufacturing, exporting to the farthest corners of the British Empire, including Australia. Although Manchester's pre-eminence in the cotton trade had declined even before World War II, still, since the early 1900s at least, 'Manchester' in Australia has referred to all household linens, bedding, towels and cottons. You can quite confidently ask a shop assistant in a big Australian store like Myers 'Which way to the Manchester department, please?' and expect an immediate response.

(Continued on the next page)

(Continued from previous page)

> The *Australian National Dictionary* cites an article in a 1983 issue of Australia's national weekly *The Bulletin* which tells the comic tale of an Australian customer shopping in London who asks the shop assistant in the dress department to hold on to her purchase while she just 'goes over to Manchester,' assuring her 'I'll be back in a while.' The baffled English assistant points out to her that Manchester is really quite a long way from London. 'Only Australian shoppers buy their sheets and pillowcases from the 'Manchester department,' smiled *The Bulletin*.

Another, fairly newly arrived, phrase in this conversation-lubricating category is 'There you go'. This crops up all over the place and if you use it skilfully, it will help you blend into the Australian background nicely. As a shop assistant hands over your change, she may well say pleasantly, 'There you go', as may a waiter delivering your order.

The Americanised pleasantry 'Have a nice (or good) day' is rampant, with the variation 'Now you have a good weekend, won't you, dear?'.

THE ART OF ABUSE

When it comes to insults, the Australian suddenly springs to life and abandons his laid-backness with a vengeance. In general, Australians are quite free with abuse and obscenities, swearing liberally, so you need to discount this as much as possible.

If you should happen to become the butt of Aussie artistry in this department, try to take it all with a smile and a pinch of salt. Do not take it to heart. There is more bark than bite in it all. In Australia, you must always be a sport. Better still, once you have got the hang of things, give back as good as you get—it's expected, and accepted.

Australian English is particularly rich in invective (especially the obscene sexual variety), easily matching close rivals, such as Cantonese, for example. Four-letter swear words are used like punctuations by the man-in-the-street and even by politicians in Parliament. 'Bloody' hardly raises an Australian eyebrow. There is much worse to come.

If you come from a genteel background, it is best you prepare yourself for this and train yourself not to hear it. There will be no avoiding it. (The most painful experience is when your children start picking it up.) Relegate it to wallpaper status, for that is all it really is—wallpaper. Those 'bad' words have lost their violence and their meaning in Australian English, through over-frequent use.

'Bastard' is one word that leads to great misunderstanding. Learn that in Australia, more often than not, it is used affectionately, very rarely as an insult. Only when it is applied to a 'Pommy', an Englishman, is it really meant to hurt. (There are many other terms of racist abuse, but I shall deal with these in another chapter). Beware of using the word affectionately too early in a relationship; it must be reserved for fairly close friends or longstanding workmates, and normally is used only among men not across the genders. If you are visibly, physically foreign—Asian, for instance—you will need to take your time using such language, as some Australians will find you difficult to 'read' and will wonder whether you might mean these words literally.

Paradoxically, however, until quite recently such words as 'Fuck' were still considered fundamentally taboo in Australia, as elsewhere. It was only in 1985 that the Western Australian police charged the Sydney comedian Rodney Rude with obscenity for using the word to excess onstage (once every 3 minutes, during a 90-minute show). Western Australia has been one of the last bastions of a once uniformly puritanical Australian culture, yet this case was dismissed in the end with the following rationale, to quote *The West Australian* newspaper of 22 April 1986: 'Used in combination with the word 'off', the offending word was vulgar and quite impolite,

The Australian Labor Party's (ALP—note confused spelling of 'Labor') former Foreign Affairs and Trade Minister, Gareth Evans, had a reputation for foot-in-the-mouthers. Not only did he dismiss a local policeman as 'Fucking useless!' while on an official visit to South Africa in 1991, but he also used the 'F' word in Federal Parliament in 1990, the first to do so in 20 years, dutifully recorded by Hansard. But then, Evans was reported by Alan Attwood in The Australian Magazine to have said to a friend, "Fuck it, I'm not going to stand around being diplomatic and nice to everyone. If people had been less diplomatic about Hitler, we would not have had the fucking Second World War."

but well understood and not necessarily obscene. The word's primary meaning was 'to copulate' but more often than not it was used simply as a strong expletive, and repeated use had tended to lessen the impact.'

While the word remains taboo in really genteel circles, the fact is, it has become common currency, on the streets and in the arts, especially in the cinema, often on TV. In fact the 'F' word was deemed no longer offensive by an Australian magistrate in 1999 when in Dubbo, New South Wales, he dismissed charges against a man who allegedly told a police officer to 'Fuck off'. "The word 'Fuck' is extremely commonplace now and has lost much of its punch," said magistrate David Heilpern, citing the fact the word abounds on the youth radio station TripleJ and that he had heard it twice in a PG movie (Parental Guidance classification). Yet a survey by AustraliaSCAN in 2001 found that 69 per cent of Australians still believe sexually explicit language on TV is unacceptable, a statistic 10 per cent up on a 1997 finding.

Punchy Politicians

The master of Australian invective without sole recourse to swear words is generally agreed to have been the former ALP government's Prime Minister, Paul Keating. He would berate his political opponents in public as 'Boxhead', 'Pig', 'Clown', 'Sleazebag' and so on. To a vociferous leftwing delegate at the New South Wales state ALP conference in 1982, he remarked, "You could talk under wet cement."

Another former Labor Prime Minister, Bob Hawke, is also well known for once turning aside from the irritating heckling of an old-age pensioner to remark sotto voce, "Silly old bugger!" The remark unfortunately was overheard by the entire nation, courtesy of TV and radio.

To sum up, the standard Australian attitude to excessive politeness is that it is anathema in a truly democratic society. Being able to call a spade a bloody spade is a politically important Australian freedom.

With leaders like these using lingo like this, the man-in-the-street needs little further encouragement. After an upbringing soaked in English hypocrisy and a young adulthood saturated with Asian evasiveness, I personally have found this trait refreshing, once you get over the initial shock.

The simile is a dynamic living form. Of very recent coinage is one I myself heard: 'Yeah, he's as busy as a bricklayer in Baghdad!' Then there is 'He's as camp as a row of circus tents!' referring to a person's gay tendencies. 'This idea hasn't got a snowflake's chance in hell!' is a popular one right now. More on the scatological side is 'That's not worth a fart in a hurricane.'

In the same vein, Australians have concocted some extraordinary and often ingeniously insulting similes, making hyperbole a typically Australian vehicle. "Three old ladies dressed like Queen Elizabeth II in floral prints and sensible shoes tell me they think their premier Bob Hawke is as 'shady as a rat with a parasol'," reported Singaporean journalist Chai Kim Wah in the Sunday Times of Singapore, 26 November 1989.

MIS-SPEAK

Differences in vocabulary can sometimes lead to hilarious misunderstandings, or embarrassing double entendres. Take, for example, the experience of my Malaysian-Eurasian friend, a fresh migrant to Australia. Invited by some new Australian friends to their dinner party, she asked politely if she should bring anything along and was at first puzzled by their response: "Yes, bring along a plate, will you?" Poor things, she thought, they must be a bit short of crockery, and so she took along practically her entire dinner service, only to discover that a 'plate' referred to a dish of cooked food. This was what is known elsewhere as a 'pot-luck' dinner, where each guest brings a contribution of food, a very common variation on the 'Bring Your Own' or BYO theme in Australian life.

And then there was my other Malaysian friend, a timid new migrant in his early teens. He had made arrangements to meet someone on a particular street and so he was loitering there quite peaceably at the appointed time until he noticed a large sign which said, 'No Standing At Any Time'. Panicked, he proceeded to pace up and down wildly in the belief that so long as he kept moving, he would not be arrested. But this was in fact a traffic sign, which in other countries would probably have read something like 'No Parking' or 'No Waiting'.

Pity the Macedonian refugee lady who went on her first visit to an Australian doctor's clinic. At the end of her consultation with the doctor, the doctor bid her a warm farewell, saying "See you later then." The Macedonian woman sat down in the waiting room—and waited, and waited and waited, until the very last patient had left and the doctor emerged from his room with a puzzled look: "Goodness, what are you doing here still, is anything the matter?" he asked her. "No", said she, "but you said you would want to see me later, so I am waiting to see what it is that you want." The doctor laughed and said, "Oh dear! No, you see, that's just an Aussie way of saying 'Goodbye', like 'see you again some time, but I don't know when!'."

The Tender Tea-Trap

The classic in this genre is, of course, the Australian 'tea'. The worst case scenario is that you, an English or Asian migrant, have invited your Australian friend round for tea. The Australian will wait around hopefully—and hungrily—for a long time before he or she realises that 'tea' is just tea, and very little more.

For an Australian, tea is the full evening meal, known to most other cultures as 'dinner'. Beware of 'The Tea Trap'—it still catches out many a foreign visitor!

Subcultures as well as communities within multicultural Australia have spawned their own lexicons. The surfing subculture is one example: when they refer to 'a Margaret' in Western Australia, they mean a big wave of the type found around the popular surfing beaches of Margaret River in south-western Australia.

A Beer is a Beer is a Beer?

Besides the macro-differences between Australian English in general and other 'Englishes,' there are also interstate micro-differences to be considered.

You can see this particularly with measures of beer. 'Grog' in Australia is known as 'Jimmy' in 'Tazzie' or Tasmania, whereas it would be a 'Stubby' anywhere else (a small bottle holding 375 ml). A Western Australian 'Middy' measure brings you 7 oz, but 10 oz in New South Wales. And so on, ad nauseam. A pint, thank goodness, is just that.

In New South Wales, you may don a 'cozzie' (i.e. costume) to swim, but in Queensland it would be 'togs', and in Western Australia, 'bathers.' There is plenty more like this.

Budgies are Black

Influences from ancient Aboriginal cultures, not to mention many newer migrant minority ones, have further complicated Australian vocabulary. Northern, north-western and central Australia are the heartlands for these original tongues.

The Aboriginals once boasted some 250 separate languages, Australia-wide, but less than half of these are still alive today, although there is a movement to revive them. Many Aboriginal words, particularly place names and words referring to wildlife or natural phenomena, have entered white Australian English: 'wombat', 'kangaroo' and 'budgerigar', for example.

SPELLING BEE DAMNED?

The language is of course evolving, like any other living language. But that does not seem to be sufficient excuse for the sheer volume of misspellings on show in Australia.

I was charmed by the offer of 'Lovely Cheeries' outside a grocery shop and intrigued by the display of 'Laces and Brades' at a drapery shop. It was fascinating to learn in a leading television and entertainment magazine that the popular TV compere John Mangos has a beautiful 'Frency Penny' tree in his garden, but surely, this must have been a Frangipani?

Semi-literate shop signs and the like could perhaps be excused in the context of a multicultural nation full of 'NESBs' (Non-English Speaking Background persons). But what really is disturbing is the fact that very few official letters escape serious spelling mistakes. In 1996, 30 per cent of Year 9 students (14-year-olds) did not have basic literacy skills.

Add to this, uncertainty throughout the country as to whether to adopt English or American spelling and the whole situation spells, as it were, confusion. Even the ruling party of the 1980s–1990s, the ALP, spells itself the Australian Labor Party, rather than using the English 'Labour'. That would be OK if the nation used consistent American spelling, but it does not; it mixes the two forms almost at random.

JOKE FOR DEMOCRACY

Language, of course, is the foundation of any nation's sense of humour. And Australia's humour is special indeed. It is considered a sacred cow of sorts.

Significantly, when certain states decided in 1989 to legislate against public incitement of racial hatred, racial jokes were specifically excluded from the list of offences that could be penalised under the new laws. It is an article of faith in Australia that everybody must be able to take a joke. The

Sign demonstrating the Aussie sense of humour and love of fun.

freedom to pull tails, tweak noses and generally satirise all comers is considered fundamental to democracy. Probably the most internationally known of Australia's satirists is Barry Humphries, who has dissected Australian society far more cruelly than any outsider.

A great deal of non-satirical Australian humour is outrageous in some way, whether salacious or sacrilegious. There is almost nothing you cannot make fun of, from cripples to Christ on the Cross. Nothing is sacred, except the right to poke fun itself.

Celebrated TV comedy shows such as the late lamented *Fast Forward*, the recently deceased *Good News Week*, and the more recently departed *Micallef* and the new *Kath and Kim* amply demonstrate this quirky, irreverent Australian sense of humour.

Australian humour, when it's not just plain bawdy (which it often is) is above all as dry as the country itself, always understated, and if possible, mumbled out of the corner of the mouth. Listen carefully—there are some gems around.

YOUR VERBAL CAMOUFLAGE

Finally, a word of advice to those trying to acquire Australian camouflage: do not rush in too enthusiastically greeting everyone 'G'day, mate!' This phrase is so quintessentially Australian that if you don't have a 'full-on' accent, you cannot really pull it off.

A useful greeting, more easily adopted by foreigners than 'G'day,' is 'How're yer going?' (frequently followed by the rhetorical 'Orright?'). On the other hand, the phrase 'No worries' is quickly and effortlessly adopted by most new arrivals, with some success. Also, the casual dropping here and there of single words, such as 'reggo', 'dag' or phrases such as 'Good on yer!' (to indicate approval) can be achieved quite naturally.

BODY LANGUAGE

Like a lot of westerners, Aussies don't like you to intrude on their body space too much—don't get too close to them when you are talking to them.

You will observe a version of this respect for private space both in supermarket and other types of queues, and particularly in the queue to use an ATM banking machine on the street. The Australian will stand well away from the person actually being served at the counter, or using the ATM. Of course there are security reasons for this—not intimidating the person doing the banking with the fear that you might be about to snatch their cash, and not leaning over their shoulder to see what their PIN is, for example—but this innate respect for personal space is another factor behind this behaviour. It is not considered good manners to crowd up against the people in front of you in a queue.

A less attractive form of non-verbal communication you may encounter, particularly as a driver on Australian roads, is 'the finger'—it is unfortunately quite common to have a motorist overtake you or draw up alongside gesticulating and 'giving you the finger' in an obscene gesture to indicate their disgust at something you may or may not have done. Even more alarming, in such cases, the gesticulating driver may as well be a woman as a man. The only thing to do is to ignore it, keep your windows and doors locked and shut, and drive on calmly.

DOING BUSINESS
IN AUSTRALIA

CHAPTER 9

'It has been written and said by very incompetent
judges of human nature that Australians, by the
cultivation of and time devoted to outdoor sports, are
degenerating in mental ability. This is, however, not true.'
—Anon, Australian Etiquette, 1885.

THE LEISURE ETHIC
Work and Play

Times are changing. In 1989, being newly arrived from workaholic Asia, I made the awful mistake of asking an West Australian bank clerk innocently, on a Friday afternoon, 'And will you be open tomorrow morning?'

She stared at me as if I were raving mad and declared firmly, 'Oh no, I should think not! Certainly not!'

Well, now they are, and workers like her are muttering darkly about added stress, the evils of globalisation etc., etc.

But the facts speak for themselves. For example, between 1982 and 2002, the average weekly working hours for full time employees in Australia increased from 42 to 44, while the proportion of workers reporting more than 50 hours a week moved from 20 per cent to 30 per cent. Other surveys show that employees are experiencing enhanced stress and workload levels, complaining of unrealistic expectations and inadequate manpower to get jobs done.

There is a constant national debate, also playing out at the micro level inside most workplaces, about 'Family-Work Balance' and while the achievement of this ideal is a mantra for all parties involved, few seem able actually to achieve it.

In many ways, the world of work in Australia is split sharply into two separate worlds: the stressed environment of the conventional full-time worker and the drifting, insecure world of the casualised part-timer, representing some 60 per cent of the workforce.

But some things are still sacrosanct. Woe indeed is he who attempts to come between the Australian and his or her weekend. Or even he who attempts to push the weekday working clock beyond 5:00 pm. Australians put high value on their leisure time.

I have seen it suggested that this attitude is a carry-over from convict days, when work was an imposition on enslaved men. And so the attitude grew that one should never do more than one has to do. Emancipation from the chains of the convict automatically meant freedom not to work if one chose not to.

As Australia's veteran national analyst, writer Donald Horne, has said of his compatriots, 'To some they seem lazy. They are not really lazy but they don't always take their jobs seriously.'

Slowing Down

Once you have learned to calm down your New York, Singapore, Hong Kong or Tokyo pace, you can get used to Australia's slower pace of work, and even like it. After all, there is a lot to be said for being able to spend more quality time with your family over the weekend. And for being able to develop social life, hobbies or further studies in the evenings. And for watching your blood pressure slowly drop, thus prolonging your life.

The Australian 'leisure ethic' (as opposed to the work ethic) cuts two ways. While other people may not always want to work for or with you, it also means you may not have to work so hard yourself.

It seems more than possible that Australians have got this one right, especially when you watch the rest of the developed world struggling with the problem of excess leisure time in this automated, information technology age. Indeed, one of the underlying reasons for apparent 'laziness' in Australia, and for some of the unemployment or underemployment as well, is increasing computerisation and automation, replacing human labour, as is the case in many affluent post-industrial countries today.

Other times besides weekends when you might as well go whistle in the wind as get some action on the work front, are Christmas–New Year, with the wind-down starting fairly early in December, and the Great Exodus at the Easter holiday, in early April. Oh, and Melbourne Cup Day too (first Tuesday of November), for the few hours before, during and after this great horse race, plus the bibulous lunch that often ensues, whether to cry about lost bets or celebrate winnings. Well, make that the whole day, actually. Businessmen, take note.

Appearances Can Be Deceptive

Australian workers are deceptive. They look and sound extremely slow and casual. But in the majority of cases, they turn out to be meticulous workers, and nearly always specialists in their field.

You will rarely get that 'I don't know how it works, I only sell the things' style sadly found in many other countries. They really like to discuss their equipment and explain it to you. They will always service it and repair it, unlike the 'escape artists' often encountered elsewhere. If achieving this quality means slowing things down a bit, personally I still prefer it as a work attitude to the 'slam bang thank you ma'am' type of deal which leaves you with not the faintest idea of how to handle whatever it is that has just been delivered.

Perhaps that is one of the reasons the Australian worker costs so much more than others. But remember, costly workers means that you too are rewarded handsomely if you choose a so-called 'menial' or manual occupation—Australia has justifiably been called 'a working-man's paradise'.

The cost may be one reason you will get fewer workers on a job than you might see, say, in Asia, where labour costs are low. When my husband and I packed up our goods and chattels in Singapore, our apartment was swarming with at least six men looking very busy indeed, creating much sound and fury. It all looked very impressive.

When our huge 20-foot container arrived at our new home in Perth, there were only two Aussies to unload it. We helped a bit, of course (that is the sort of thing you are quietly expected to do in Australia, anyway), but they would have done fine without us.

Now which of the two teams could be called the more hardworking, more efficient, or more productive, I wonder?

Keep It Friendly, Mate

By 'casual', I mean that Australian workers expect you to be friendly. If you want to develop a productive relationship with an Aussie worker, make sure you offer him a cup of tea and a chat. You will be amazed at how much time (presumably, it's really his boss' time, but that doesn't seem to matter) he has to sit down with you. He will be quite happy to tell you his life story. And that can be quite fascinating sometimes, especially if you are new to the country.

> I recall one such contractor who told me of his boyhood in the countryside and how farmers used to pay him and his school friends to strangle emu chicks on their way to school, because they were seen as pest birds.

If you come from a country used to a more formal relationship between client and contractor, or between boss and employee, you would be well advised to adapt to Australia's more chatty mode as quickly as possible. Too much of an 'I'm the boss' or 'I'm paying you, aren't I?' type of attitude, or too formal a demeanour could well provoke hostility, or at best, only minimal co-operation. The job might not be done as well.

There is one particular category of worker that you have to look out for a bit: the Secretary/Personal Assistant/Receptionist person, usually a woman. Because there is an underlying thread in Australian society of 'I'm not your servant, I am a proud worker earning an honest crust, and besides I know what I am doing, I am in charge', this person may often seem offhand and rude on the phone if you come from a culture used to a more fawning style of service. Some of them are over-anxious to prove that their role is not to serve but is actually sort of pseudo-executive and please go away, they are busy with important things. Don't be fazed, just remain calm and be firm, insist on getting from them whatever you think is your due.

Tall Poppies

One of the reasons an Australian worker will sometimes look and sound much less competent or professional than in fact he really is, is the ingrained Australian fear of appearing too 'uppity'. This fear often prevents him from competing effectively and from demonstrating his maximum potential.

The Australian does not want to appear too good at what he or she does, lest this in some way offend or put down other people around him or her. Worse, to truly excel might put him or her in the category 'Tall Poppy'—and tall poppies exist only to be cut down.

Western societies are quite used to airings of this problem in the context of women's relationships with men: the phenomenon of intelligent women working hard at the 'dumb blonde' masquerade lest they be put on the shelf by insecure men, is well known in feminist circles. But a whole nation working hard to appear dumb?

You better believe it. But then again, you better not believe it—because, as I have said, appearances are deceptive.

Remember, you too must play the game if you are to get on with Australians. If you are working hard, try not to show it or talk about it. If you are successful or intelligent, hide it, or at least actively play it down. If you have money, look as poor as possible (besides, flashing it too much is only an advertisement that you may have some to spare and therefore available to steal).

The Tall Poppy Syndrome in Australia has been described by some observers as 'the psychology of envy'. Eminent academics such as psychologist Professor Norman Feather of Australia's Flinders University in 1989, and historian W K Hancock back in 1930, have noted this strong trait in the Australian character.

It is the Tall Poppy Syndrome that most sharply separates Australian psychology from that of the Americans, for whom individualistic achievement in contrast is almost a religion. In America, you aspire to achieve the same heights as some rags-to-riches role model; in Australia, you grudge him/her their success and aim to bring them down to your own level. Some say it's a trait inherited from the English.

Don't Judge This Book by Its Cover

One of the manifestations of the anti-tall poppy school of thought is sloppy dress. This is quite rife in Australia. Viewed benevolently, it looks pleasantly unpretentious, undemanding of others too. But a lot of the time, it just looks, well—sloppy.

In men, it takes the form of shorts for everything—often unpleasantly short and tight ones, too, in the case of older adults. In women, just poorly co-ordinated wardrobes. In both sexes, tatty jeans, and above all, the ubiquitous 'thongs', aka Japanese slippers, flip-flops, rubber sandals, etc.

Setting aside the fact that many Australians truly are strapped for cash, a factor likely to limit one's ability to run a snazzy wardrobe, considering the price of clothing in Australia, the real reason for this lack of attention to personal appearance is the strong desire not to stand out, and above all, never to look at all well off. In short, not to threaten others.

This makes it very easy to dress in Australia, since the trick really is either to un-dress or to down-dress, depending on the time of day. But it makes it very hard to dress up—with the notable exception of the 'special ball' or dinner dance type of event, usually no more than an annual thing and probably during the festive season, in which case absolutely everybody dresses to the nines, the women uniformly clad in very ritzy full-length ball gowns.

This anti-couture culture does mean that nobody can be classified by the way they dress or look. If you come from a country where dress really matters, particularly when negotiating business deals, try to throw your prejudices out of the window when in Australia.

Sickies, Overtime and Wages

Australian work attitudes are in transition right now, as a result of 'down-sizing' and a realisation that globalisation means business. It used to be commonplace for younger workers in particular to save on the job, then leave work for a year or two to travel the world, fully confident that they would be able to step straight into a job on their return. They still do it—but they are lot less confident, and rightly so. Many adults even avoid taking leave now, in case they return to find their job gone. Others stick to holidays in Australia and keep a watchful eye on the workplace. In 2002, only 39 per cent of full-time workers dared to take their full annual leave.

For many, the only occupation they will have for some time is regular visits to the job centre (Centrelink agency), looking for work or to register for unemployment benefits. But among those still at work, certain old habits still die hard. For one thing, the 'sickie' is commonplace. This refers to the institution of declaring yourself sick for the day when in fact you just do not much feel like going to work, or you have set your mind on shopping or picnicking instead; this is aided by the formal provision of a set entitlement of sick days per year in most worker's contracts. So if you don't 'use up' your sickies within the year, you're a bit of 'a mug' (stupid), since they represent potential extra leave you cannot get any other way than by declaring yourself unfit to work. This is a situation that the Liberal government under Prime Minister John Howard was trying to stamp out within the terms of unpopular new industrial relations laws, as this book went to press. Sickies cost the Australian public and private sectors dearly every year, as opportunity cost, man-hours lost and absolute cash losses.

'I Don't Feel Too Good, Won't Be Coming In Today'

An Australian National Audit Office survey covering 74 public sector agencies, about three-quarters of the total, and covering 99 per cent of public sector staff, calculated that for the year 2001–2002:

- total 'unscheduled absences' from work, such as sick leave ('sickies'), carer's leave, worker's compensation and miscellaneous leave, were some 1.36 million days, of which 73 per cent was sick leave.
- the average 'unscheduled absence' was 11.9 days per full-time employee.
- average sick leave taken was 8.7 days per full-time employee.
- the overall direct salary cost of 'unscheduled absences' was estimated to be A$ 295 million, or about A$ 2,600 per full-time employee. This did not include related costs such as the additional costs that can arise from the need for replacement staff, or any possible consequential costs associated with potentially reduced government services. Total costs may be up to three times the direct cost of the salaries of the absent staff.
- on any given working day, at least one in every 20 public sector employees will be absent on unscheduled leave.

Said the Audit: 'International and Australian research indicates that unscheduled absence rates in the public sector are commonly higher than in the private sector. Research has also found that organisations with lower sick leave entitlements have lower absence rates than those with higher entitlements. One conclusion often drawn is that, for some individuals, sick leave expands to fill the entitlement available, suggesting that not all sick leave taken is genuine. However, there is no conclusive evidence to support such a conclusion.'

A completely new variation on this theme in 2005 was the phenomenon of 'blue flu' (originally an American term), in which workers suddenly report sick en masse, thus paralysing worksites. This is a disguised strike, designed to circumvent tougher laws these days against 'wildcat' strikes. It's still a rare occurrence in Australia, but surfaced with a vengeance in Western Australia's construction industry during 2005.

Another high cost to the employer is payment for overtime work. Overtime comes on top of already high wages—the Australian Bureau of Statistics category of average weekly ordinary time earnings for full-time adult employee jobs in 2004 showed average earnings at about A$ 1,000 a week for men, A$ 851 for women.

There are other commonly encountered additional costs for employers, or goodies for workers, depending on your point of view: paid holiday leave ('leave loading'), and long service leave (usually three to six months, available after ten years' continuous employment in the same job) are two of the key provisions again under assault in the Howard government's proposed new industrial relations laws of 2005.

The concept of a legal right to long service leave is uniquely Australian, a throw-back to colonial days when officers needed time to travel back 'home' from the colonies to England. Since then it has been seen as a just reward for faithful service, a useful means of preventing labour turnover, and an opportunity for workers to 'recharge their batteries' that is also beneficial to the employer in terms of getting full value out of his/her employees.

Another feature of Australia's labour laws has been strong protection of the worker against 'unfair dismissal', making it quite difficult for employers to fire workers without making a cast-iron case via masses of paperwork and plenty of litigation. The Howard government's new industrial relations laws proposed in 2005 also intend to remove this provision in the case of small businesses with fewer than 100 workers (and some say this is just the thin end of the wedge, that the concept will be extended to all employers, big or small, eventually).

The accumulation of these 'perks' for employees is just one of the reasons that the Australian workforce is now significantly 'casualised', with around 64 per cent in some form of casual, part-time or short-contract employment (30 per cent in plain part-time work, with more women than men part-timing). Protection for such workers' conditions is far less structured than it is for those in conventional full-time employment, hence part-time workers are much cheaper for employers to run. The result is that a large part of the Australian workforce is underemployed and also financially insecure, while the overall unemployment rate appears healthy, at around five per cent in 2005.

The Dignity of Labour

Australian workers won their basic rights very early, and have defended them vigorously ever since—but again, times are changing. The eight-hour day was secured by striking stonemasons in 1855, the basic minimum wage in 1907, and the 40-hour week in 1946—working weeks nowadays are closer to 36 hours, or even less in the case of the many industries running on half-time because of the recession. The world's first legislation providing for paid sick leave and paid long-service leave was enacted in the state of New South Wales in 1951.

Australians are particularly hot on matters of industrial safety and health, to a degree that may take some more cavalier outsiders aback.

Without going into the detailed pros and cons, enormous fusses have been made in recent years about allegedly debilitating 'Repetitive Strain Injury' or 'RSI', incurred through repeated restricted movements of the hand and arm in particular—such as those made by high-speed typists and computer-keyboard operators—about workers in contact with asbestos (many of Australia's older homes are insulated and roofed with asbestos), and about the health dangers or otherwise of extended work at Visual Display Units (VDUs) such as computer monitor screens—in 1980, journalists won special cash 'hardship' allowances for operating VDUs, which are still in place.

Service, Civility and Servility

As already mentioned, the Australian style of service can be a problem, depending on where you are coming from. Possibly another hangover from the tribulations of a convict past and of the triumphant shaking off of those fetters, is the average Australian's determination never again to bow his head to any man, to serve no one—but to his credit, neither does he particularly wish to be served. Nothing embarrasses and confuses your average Australian, a natural socialist, more than being presented with a servant, as happens to him when travelling in Asia, for example. He simply don't know what to do with one.

Service industries like tourism do have a hard time in Australia. It is not that Australian workers are rude—far from it —but they are offhand, casual and familiar if you compare them with, say, the best available in the European capitals, or in many Asian capitals for that matter. To put it another way, they do not crawl. To put it the earthy Australian way, they do not 'brown-nose' (an unpleasant reference to being so much of an 'arse-licker' that you get a brown nose).

Columnist Ruth Ostrow once complained in *The Weekend Australian* how bad hotel and restaurant service was on Australia's premier tourist strip, the Gold Coast, concluding her diatribe with 'To be unable to serve is a testimony of our ever-present national insecurity complex'.

On the other hand, I surely cannot be the only person who has enjoyed the straight, eye-to-eye equality assumed by all Australian service personnel, and the candour that goes with it: the waiter who warns that you may not enjoy your order as 'it's not so fresh today', why don't you try something else? There are a lot of easy smiles around in the service industry, and that's always pleasant.

One of the glories of the Australian system is that the tip is still considered demeaning by most Australian workers—although admittedly, increasing tourism, migration and the pressures of recession are now all combining to create some cracks in that façade. But traditionally, the tip is seen as the thin end of the wedge towards making excuses for low wages; a man should be paid what he is worth in the form of a decent wage, no more, no less. No tips please, we're Australian.

Everybody Out!

The Australian worker's propensity to strike has become legend, but to be fair, this is indeed a legend, belonging more to a particular period of the 1970s than to the here and now. That said, it is easy to predict a stormy period during 2005 or so, as unions rally to fight the Howard government's much reviled new industrial law proposals. The tone is likely to become ever more desperate in the context of the government now having secured majority control of the Senate or Upper House for the first time, making passage of its new legislation much easier.

After the Australian Council of Trade Unions (ACTU) signed the so-called 'Accord' (the Prices and Incomes Accord) with the Australian Labor Party in 1983, the problem muted somewhat, with Labor in power until 1996, and the legendary Bob Hawke, a former ACTU president, prime minister for much of that time. Relations between the labour movement and the Labor Party traditionally have been close, although the unions have become increasingly uncomfortable with right-wing dominance of party policy in recent years. The unions have often shown their muscle over purely political, even foreign-policy issues, for example, against Japanese aggression in China during the 1930s, against Australian involvement in the Vietnam War in 1965, against foreign sailors' working conditions, and against Indonesian action in East Timor in more recent years. Even the Labor government saw the need to modernise the union movement: in 1987, it moved to restructure and rationalise the movement with the objective of reducing the number of unions from 215 (1987)—only nine of which were truly, numerically, powerful—to about 20 by the turn of the 20th century, by means of amalgamating some of the smaller unions.

Under Prime Minister John Howard since 1996 however, there have been even more concerted persistent attacks on the old Labor orthodoxy.

The old system of fixed 'awards'—benchmark payment rates set by a pact among government, employers and labour unions—has faded in recent years so that now about 80 per cent of wage agreements come in the form either of collective agreements or the newer idea of individual agreements ('enterprise bargaining') between each employee and employer. The collective agreement is in decline, surviving chiefly in the public sector, while the individual contract has already taken hold for more than half of private sector workers. This trend can be expected to accelerate, with or without the current pressure from the sitting Liberal government.

Not surprisingly then, with one of the main purposes of unions gradually pulled from under the unions' feet— i.e. the negotiation of collective agreements—during the decade of the 1980s, Australian labour unions saw their membership drop by 20 per cent, to less than 40 per cent of the workforce, and again during the 1990s, to the point where in most industries today, only a quarter of the workforce is unionised. In better times, the Australian rate of union membership, along with New Zealand's, was the highest of any democracy in the world.

The average number of working days lost in industrial disputes during the 1980s was about 1.5 million a year, much less than the 6.3 million of 1974. But by 2003, the figure had declined to fewer than half a million working days, through 642 separate disputes.

Caution, All Kiwis and Wannabe New Zealanders

New Zealanders used to get a cushy 'special relationship' type deal in Australia, on an automatically obtained 'Special Category Visa' (SCV) which automatically made them an Australian resident, with full access to social security and welfare. This was a convenient 'backdoor entry' too for migrants who failed in their application to move to Australia but succeeded with New Zealand. No longer.

The Australian Government changed this situation in 2001. New Zealanders can still live and work indefinitely in Australia but now they are not classified as Australian residents. They need to apply to become a citizen or permanent resident, and, like other new arrivals, wait for two years, before they can access social security.

The industry causing the most problems today is the coal mining industry, with a high 356 work days lost per 1,000 workers in 2003. These workers will not be any more pleased by recent indications of a shift in Australia's energy generation policies towards gas not coal, and possibly also nuclear power in the near future. Another sticky area for strikes is transport, including airports and airlines, but particularly the docks, manned by tough 'wharfies' or dock workers, still locked into many old-fashioned work practices.

Western Australia is the state registering the highest proportion of work days lost in strikes: 97 days per 1,000 workers in 2003.

Handout Heartbreak

Australia is fundamentally a welfare society. But unemployment benefits—'the dole', recently metamorphosed into the 'Job Search' and 'Newstart' allowances—are nowhere near as easy to get nowadays as they used to be, particularly if you are young and strong enough to work.

The ongoing restructuring of Australia's economy and labour market is already having real impact on the handout psychology of the dole.

Even the disabled are subjected to closer scrutiny these days, with a government policy declared in 2002 (but not yet officially implemented) that anybody deemed fit to work 15 hours or more a week would automatically be moved from the Disability Support Pension (DSP) welfare grant to the Newstart allowance (the 'dole'). Previously, the cutoff level has been set at 30 hours a week.

The dole payment ('Newstart allowance') is A$ 399.30 a fortnight, while the DSP is considerably higher, at A$ 476.30 a fortnight. It's interesting to note that about 74,000 people a year move onto the DSP, with total DSP recipients standing at 750,000 in 2005. Some observers feel that this DSP figure hides further unemployment or underemployment statistics.

Who Gets the Dole?

The 'Newstart ' allowance is available to the unemployed if they are Australian residents (present in Australia for two years or more), over 21 years old and under 62 (women) or 65 years old (men), and therefore cannot access the Age Pension. But you have to agree first to cooperate by actively seeking work and preparing yourself for work through whatever training courses are recommended to you by the Centrelink job search agency contracted by the government to handle such matters. You will be expected pretty much to accept whatever jobs you are offered, even if they don't seem to you to match your skills. You also have to prove that you don't have income or assets valued above a certain level. You will have to report to Centrelink any and every time you decide to travel, and such travel could cut off your allowance. You cannot access the dole if you are currently on strike from your usual job.

The key problem area is the 15–18 year-olds out of work who are no longer eligible for the dole.

Their unemployment rate is more than four times the national level, about 23 per cent, which means that close to one in four teenagers are without work. Some observers think the phenomenon of young people on the streets without work or money is contributing to a rising wave of juvenile crime.

Australia's high rates of income tax (for most people, close to 40 per cent) cover not only social security but also include a Medicare levy for the provision of almost-free medical care; your doctor bills the government ('bulk-billing'), or if he bills you, you claim a partial rebate from the government. This perhaps over-generous system, like the unions, is suffering nibbling erosion at present as the government struggles to prevent its costly abuse by the public. For one thing, it is virtually compulsory now (in view of strong disincentives if you don't do it) to pay for private medical coverage (among the big names, 'HBF', and Medibank)—the advantage of this for the consumer is assured medical attention when you want it (there is a long queue for non-emergency surgery under the Medicare system in public hospitals), with your choice of hospital and surgeon, but the disadvantage is, of course, the high premium to be paid and the frequent discovery of an awkward 'gap' between your coverage and the cost of your treatment, a gap which you largely have to cover with your own money. Needless to say, Medicare still takes care of emergencies immediately, whether a person has private coverage or not.

Tax Rates 2005–2006

Taxable income	Tax on this income
A$ 0–6,000	Nil
A$ 6,001–21,600	A$ 0.15 for each A$ 1 over A$ 6,000
A$21,601–63,000	A$ 2,340 plus A$ 0.30 for each A$ 1 over A$ 21,600
A$ 63,001–95,000	A$ 14,760 plus A$ 0.42 for each A$ 1 over A$ 63,000
Over A$ 95,000	A$ 28,200 plus A$ 0.47 for each A$ 1 over A$ 95,000

These rates do not include a further Medicare (health service) levy of 1.5 per cent.

If you earn below A$ 27,475 a year, you can often get a tax rebate or offset. Older Australians, 'seniors', also get special concessions.

Medicine prescription charges are already high, and a battle has recently been fought between the Labor government's right and left wings over the institution in late 1991 of a A$ 2.50 'co-operative charge' which doctors now charge anyone wishing to consult them for anything (the object being to discourage frivolous visits to the doctor).

But when the moan goes up about decent taxpayers forking out for layabouts on the dole ('dole-bludgers') or for fake 'sickies', as it often does, my thoughts go to two mercy cases I have encountered. One was my girlfriend whose little girl was born four months prematurely, with cerebral palsy which prevented her from walking properly. In the other case, another girlfriend's daughter, aged about eight, was quite suddenly diagnosed with a hole in her heart. Both stories had a happy ending, largely thanks to the Medicare welfare system. I was paying for it as a tax-payer, but why wouldn't I ?

YOUR PARTNER IN BUSINESS

The Australian businessman is strangely schizoid: superficially pally but really quite cagey, seemingly mild and undriven but in fact capable of unbridled aggression, apparently egalitarian and incorrupt but actually a lot more 'flexible' than that would imply, casual and relaxed on the surface but deep down, quite tense. Once again, avoid judging the book by its cover.

The best way to break the ice is to share a beer together at the pub, to talk about sport, or to meet at a barbie party and talk about anything but work.

The fundamentally anti-intellectual stance of the average Australian sometimes affects business too. People get things done in a makeshift, nonchalant 'She'll be right' fashion, without reference to any real expertise, whether published or in the person of a flesh-and-blood expert.

Getting To Know You...

The phenomenon of the use of the familiar first name, and a general reticence about handing out business cards, means that it is entirely possible to exit from even a business meeting in Australia, certainly from a social gathering, still not knowing the full names of anybody present, even less what their titles, functions or phone numbers are. You may have to impose yourself fairly aggressively on your business associates if you really want their details, by making the first move yourself. But be aware that you risk being thought of as a bit 'pushy.'

Be prepared, too, for the familiarity of official and business letters from complete strangers addressing you as 'Dear Bill' or 'Dear Susan', etc. Australia has never liked honorific titles of any kind and now it seems, even 'Mr', 'Mrs', 'Ms' and 'Miss' have been cast aside forever. And you can call your boss 'Bill' or 'Susan' to their face too. It's all part of the national egalitarian ethos, although one does doubt that these people would write to their Prime Minister in quite the same tone. I could be wrong, though. This is Australia. Certainly, at cocktail parties I myself have witnessed people bounding up to State ministers with a cheerful, "Hello, Judy, how yer goin'?" Asians in particular will be horrified by this.

But reverting to letters, in any case, you will have been very lucky indeed to get any kind of letter. Australians are notoriously reluctant to answer letters. Email response may be somewhat better, but, like the Americans, Australians respond better to phone calls, and also to faxes.

Keeping Up Appearances

Overall, dress standards in Australian offices are relaxed but conservative, if that makes any sense. You shouldn't dress to the nines, and women don't really need make-up, but on the other hand, men in suits and ties and women in long-skirted dress-suits are favoured. Young girls do sometimes ignore it, but it's fair to say that generally, flashing your cleavage and/or your belly button at work is not a good way to climb the career ladder. It's quite common for workers to arrive at work by bicycle in full cycling gear, helmet and all, but they will always go to the office social club changing rooms or gym to change into something formal before starting work. It all depends on your industry, really, as well as local weather conditions, and generally speaking, standards in the eastern states capitals like Sydney and Melbourne are more international, more 'hip-chic' than in far-flung parts like Western Australia or the Northern Territory. Public relations and media are, as elsewhere, notoriously eccentric. But the public sector is pretty stiff.

Sometimes, on the main business street of Perth, capital of Western Australia, I feel as though I am among a flock of Australian ravens, so uniform is the black-suit, black jacket and black skirt look adopted by men and women employees alike. Time was, back in the 1970s, when most Western Australian men went to work, even formal offices, in a short-sleeved shirt and tie, longish shorts, knee-high socks and lace-up shoes—honest, I saw it myself—but those days are long gone.

Some Do's and Don'ts in the Office

Don't

- turn down an invitation to go out for lunch, a drink, or to view the Melbourne Cup, least of all while saying, 'Sorry, I've got too much work to do.' You'll get a name as an unfriendly workaholic bore and too ambitious by half, a bit of a threat.
- treat secretaries, personal assistants or tea-ladies (if any) etc. as anything other than valued equals and intelligent comrades fully participating in the tasks of your office—that would be very un-Australian;
- express too many new ideas about good new things to do or ways to change established procedures in the office, until about a year after you arrive—take things slowly, and quietly.
- call up co-workers about work issues after 5:00 pm, or at weekends or when they are on holiday—urgency no excuse!
- (as a male) touch female workers, even in an affectionate platonic way, offer elaborate compliments on their looks or dress, or make off-colour jokes in their presence—sexism and harrassment charges lurk around the corner!

Do

- observe whether there is a roster for stocking the office fridge or making tea etc., and offer to participate accordingly.
- stop by the water dispenser, or while making coffee in the kitchen, for a quick but light chat with your co-workers, on the lines of 'So how was your weekend?', or 'Has your kid got better now?' Or better still, 'Mate, did you see that footy score on Saturday!?'.
- join office sports teams and leisure clubs.

After Hours

Australians draw a sharp line between work-time and play-time. And they work hard at play. Their favourite form of play is sport, whether spectator or participatory. Sport—the practice and the theoretical knowledge of it—is your surest and shortest route to the heart of Australians, your safest topic of conversation with the highest and lowest in the land.

Australian politicians scramble to be associated with sporting events and to be seen as such on the TV screen. Prime Minister John Howard himself pops up every so often on telly to offer his views on the current state of cricket and 'footy' (but chiefly cricket), and so bolster his popularity ratings. He is renowned for timing his official visits to England around the time of cricket Test Matches. Sport in any case has always played an important part in Australia's concept of foreign diplomacy.

Because so much of the population is concentrated around the coastline, water sports are important—swimming, sailing, surfboarding, windsurfing, water-skiing and rowing, as well as white-water rafting.

But partly because winters are usually short and mild, many other sports can be played almost the whole year

White-water rafting in Tasmania.

round. Cricket, Australian Rules football ('Footy') and horse-racing are three of the most important; with reference to the latter, take note that the Melbourne Cup races (first Tuesday in November) are a national happening of massive significance, albeit a public holiday only in Melbourne itself—do not try to talk to Australians (even overseas) about anything else on this day.

Tennis is popular, thanks to the stunning victories at major championships such as Wimbledon by top-calibre Australian players like Evonne Goolagong Cawley, Pat Cash and the World Number 2 of the moment, Leyton Hewitt.

Golf in Australia is not the preserve of the moneyed elite as it is in so many other societies, but is enjoyed by all, at minimal cost. Fine Australian golfers have emerged regularly, Greg Norman being one of the strongest 'brands' names to hit the international sports pages.

Australia has had an international sporting presence for almost a century, at first as part of the cricketing British Empire, later as an independent member of the world community—the 1956 Olympics were hosted in Australia (Melbourne), with Australian swimmers taking eight of the 14 available gold medals, as were the 2000 Olympics, in Sydney.

The annual Formula One Grand Prix motor race was staged in Adelaide from 1985 to 1996, when it moved to Melbourne.

Willow and Leather

The Melbourne Cricket Club was established as early as 1838, but cricket was played in Australia much earlier than that. It seems slightly odd that a sport so strongly associated with the British Empire and the British upper classes should have rooted so easily in convict-settled Australia, but the game is indeed a national passion.

If you do not come from a cricket-playing nation, my advice is that you read up on this puzzling game before attempting to relate with Australia.

The first 'Test' match between Australian and English cricketers was won by Australia, at the Melbourne Cricket

Ground in 1876. Thereafter, the Test trophy has always been the 'Ashes', supposedly the ashes of the dead English game at that 1876 match. Test matches were a sensitive topic for Australian sportsmen until quite recently, in 1989, when Allan Border's team won back the Ashes on tour in England—this was the first time the Australians had retrieved the Ashes in England since 1934, and they retained them right up to 2005.

Cricket pundits worldwide are familiar with great Australian cricketing names like Sir Donald Bradman (more than 28,000 runs against England in Test matches 1928–1948, and a record of 1,448 runs in one season unbeaten until 1971), Richie Benaud, Ian Chappell, Dennis Lillee, Jeff Thomson, Greg Chappell and Allan Border, to name but a few. Today, star bowler Shane Warne is the name to drop, whether in gossip about his lamentable off-field sexual exploits (numerous and painfully public) or in tribute to his extraordinary cricketing performances.

To get by with the sports small-talk that is essential to survival at the Australian dinner table, in the pub or at the neighbourhood barbie (outdoors barbecue party), you will also need to be familiar with two particularly famous cricketing incidents.

The first of these is the 'bodyline' incident in the 1932–1933 English tour of Australia, during which English bowlers were believed to have bowled directly to Bradman's body in a deliberately threatening manner. Several Australian batsmen were injured during this tour and Australian feeling against the English cricketers rose to fever pitch.

In the second incident, the boot was on the other foot, with Australia monopolising the infamy. This was the notorious 'underarm' tactic against New Zealand in 1981. Bowler Trevor Chappell, one of three famous cricketing brothers, was instructed by his captain, coincidentally also his brother Greg, to bowl underarm for the last ball of the limited-over final.

The New Zealand team at that point needed six runs from the last ball to level with Australia in this one-day match, but Chappell's stratagem effectively denied the opposition a tie with Australia—it would be impossible to hit the underarm-delivery ball hard or high enough to get time for runs while the fielders chased it. Australia's reputation for sportsmanship suffered a bashing and underarm bowling was subsequently banned, as underhand and not cricket.

Australian Rules Football

This virtual amalgam of rugby and soccer was invented in Melbourne in 1858. It is a lot rougher than soccer, with plenty of hand-ball, body contact, hand-passing and the like.

The good news does not seem to have spread outside Australia, but domestically, footy is the leading ball game and an authentic item of Australiana which all visitors should experience for themselves. Loyalties focus on local clubs, which compete in a relatively recently established national competition.

However, a fierce battle is brewing between the entrenched tradition of footy and the imported, more international, game of 'soccer' (which its devotees in Australia are trying hard to rebrand simply as 'football'). Unfortunately, this battle divides strongly on ethnic lines, since most of the soccer enthusiasts are first or second-generation migrants who hail from soccer-playing nations such as the former Yugoslavia, Greece, Italy, England and South America. Soccer has even rudely been referred to by footy-buffs as 'wogball' to emphasise this ethnic dimension.

There's been a lot of action in this sport since the publication in 2003 of the Report of the Independent Soccer Review Committee, also known as the 'Crawford Report' which delved into allegations of corruption and mismanagement in the former governing body, Soccer Australia. Since only 2005, the newly formed Football Federation Australia (FFA) or 'Football Australia' has been the governing body overseeing the game. There is a national men's team, the Socceroos, as well as a national women's team, the Matildas. The FFA launched a new national league in 2005, the 'A-League', replacing the National Soccer League that had existed since 1977. It's been agreed, not without some controversy, that the FFA should move from the Oceania

Football Confederation (of which Australia was a founding member) to the Asian Football Confederation as of 2006, on the premise that this should help to improve Australian football standards and raise the nation's chances of participating in the World Cup series in future.

The America's Cup

The America's Cup sailing event has been a national obsession ever since Australia won it in the USA, in 1983, a win not repeated since; Australia has competed for the Cup since 1962.

The victory of the 12-m (39.4 ft) yacht Australia II, owned by Western Australian business tycoon Alan Bond and captained by John Bertrand, made Australia the first nation to take the Cup away from America since the inaugural race in 1851. The yacht featured a controversial, revolutionary winged keel designed in Australia by Ben Lexcen (who died in 1988).

The nation went simply bananas in the delirium of this triumph. The return event in 1988 brought great prosperity to the host city, Fremantle in Western Australia, as well as to Perth, although unfortunately only very temporarily as it appears with hindsight, with New Zealand capturing the Cup n 1995 and 2000, to Australia's great chagrin.

All a Bluff?

Strangely enough, despite the strong sporting culture which permeates the macho-skewed Australian social ethos, statistics I have discussed in Chapter 6 on food (*page 250*), show that a large number of Australians are physically lazy, overweight and unfit. In the 1970s, the government launched a campaign featuring a slovenly, beer-bellied couch potato named 'Norm', who only watched sports on the small screen from his living room sofa, 'tinnie' in hand. He was berated into more physical activity with the slogan 'Life, Be In It.' But Norm remains a familiar sight today.

'Crikey, mate. You're far safer dealing with Crocodiles and
Western Diamondback Rattlesnakes than the executives and
the producers and all those sharks in the big MGM building.'
—Steve Irwin, Australia's iconic 'Crocodile Hunter'
and Director of the Australia Zoo in Queensland,
on his experiences with Hollywood movieland.

EVERY SOCIETY HAS A HIDDEN MENU OF TOPICS—people, events, things—with which all members of that society are supposed to be familiar. Such knowledge serves as a sort of password proving that you are indeed an insider, or almost, and so allows you to enter that society.

Australia is no exception. To help you get your foot past more than just the door, here is a grab-bag of information which once internalised, should allow you to bluff your way through dinner parties, cocktail party small talk and even job interviews, without asking the fatal questions 'Who?' or 'What?'

It's a kind of DIY kit for constructing 'Instant Australia', for storage in your mental filing cabinet.

I am deliberately excluding any names or events which have been adequately dealt with in earlier chapters, so exclusion from this chapter naturally does not imply that the missing name or event is somehow unimportant.

BASIC FACT-FILE ON AUSTRALIA
Official Name
Commonwealth of Australia

Capital
Canberra (*No, not Sydney, like you thought!*)

Flag

Blue background with the Union Jack (upper left hand corner) and a single star on the left, and the Southern Cross on the right

National Anthem

Advance Australia Fair

God Save The Queen!—the British National Anthem is played as 'the Royal Anthem' in Australia at any occasion at which members of the royal family or their representative, the Governor General of Australia or his state-based equivalent, is present.

Official Language

English

Time Zones

There are three time zones in Australia: Western, Central and Eastern.

Using Perth as a benchmark (apologies to easterners), the Western Australian capital is 8 hours ahead of Greenwich Mean Time in England, except during Summer Time, when it is 9 hours ahead.

Eastern Australia—New South Wales, Victoria, Queensland and Tasmania—is usually 2 hours ahead of Perth. The eastern states adopt Summer Time (daylight saving) from about November through to February and then become 3 hours ahead.

The Northern Territory and South Australia, in the Central zone, are 1½ hours ahead of Perth.

You can get an idea of how close Perth is to Asia by noting the fact that the time there (except during Eastern Summer Time) is the same as in Hong Kong, Bali (Indonesia), Singapore and Malaysia.

Telephone Codes

The international dialling code is 61 followed by one of the four regional codes; but note that when you are calling from outside the country, these codes do not have the '0' in front that they must have when calling from inside Australia. Hence '02' for the Sydney area becomes just '2' when calling from outside Australia. So to dial Sydney number 4444-5555 from abroad, you would dial 61-2-4444-5555. (Australian fixed line numbers are all 8-digit).

Note also that when calling an Australian mobile phone number from outside the country, you should again drop the first '0' of the number (most Australian mobiles begin with a '0'). Additionally, you do **not** need to use a regional code prefix for the mobile—so when dialling an Australian mobile, you will use a number such as 61-444-555-666, whereas from inside Australia, that number is 0444-555-666.

Regional Codes

- 02   New South Wales (e.g. Sydney–NSW) and Australian Capital Territory (e.g. Canberra–ACT)
- 03   Victoria (e.g. Melbourne–Vic) and Tasmania (e.g. Hobart–Tas)
- 07   Queensland (e.g. Brisbane–Qsld)
- 08   South Australia (e.g. Adelaide–SA), Western Australia (e.g. Perth–WA), and the Northern Territory (e.g. Darwin–NT) including the Broken Hill area.

Land

The island continent of Australia, comprising the two land masses of mainland Australia and the island state of Tasmania to its far south, sits in the southern hemisphere with the Indian Ocean to the west and the South Pacific Ocean to the east.

Area

total: 7,686,850 sq km (2,967, 909.4 sq miles)
land: 7,617, 930 sq km (2,941,299.2 sq miles)
water: 68,920 sq km (26,610.2 sq miles)

Highest Point

Mount Kosciuszko in New South Wales (2,229 m / 7,312.9 ft)

Lowest Point

Lake Eyre (16 m or 53 ft below sea level), in Central Australia, spread across parts of the states of South Australia, Northern Territory and Queensland.

Major Rivers

Murray River, Darling River, Murrumbidgee Rivers.

Climate

The climatic range is wide, from arid to semi-arid climates in the centre to tropical and monsoonal in the north, and 'Mediterranean' to temperate weather in the east and south. The highest temperature ever recorded was 53.1 °C (127°F) at Cloncurry, Queensland, in 1889, but in northern and central parts of the continent, temperatures such as 45°C (113°F) are quite common in the summer.

Natural Resources

Australia is 'filthy rich' when it comes to minerals, precious metals and gems: bauxite, coal, copper, diamonds, gold, opals, iron ore, lead, mineral sands, natural gas, nickel, petroleum, silver, tin, tungsten, uranium, zinc...

Population

On 25 August 2005, at 10:42:10 (Canberra time), the resident population of Australia was estimated at 20,388,210. The 20 million mark was reached at the end of 2003. The population is expected to reach about 30 million by 2045. But a decline is expected after 2069, when the number of deaths will begin to exceed gains both natural and as a result of immigration. When the colonial British First Fleet landed in Botany Bay in 1788, there were around 1,000 people on board. Australia's indigenous population at that time, the Aboriginals, has been estimated by some at 300,000, by others up to a million, but the real number will probably never be known.

Population Density

Population density in the vastness that is Australia is low, at only about two persons per square kilometre. About a quarter

The Sydney Harbour Bridge with the Opera House in the background.

of the population are first or second-generation settlers. And about 88 per cent are urban dwellers.

Population Centres

The largest cities, in order of population size, are Sydney (over 4 million), Melbourne (over 3m), Brisbane (over 1.5m), Perth (over 1.5m) and Adelaide (over 1.1m). About 60 per cent of the total population is clustered in the far south, around Sydney, Melbourne, Canberra and Hobart (Tasmania), with another 25 per cent in areas close to Adelaide or Brisbane.

Religion

Roman Catholic and Anglican Christianity dominate, together with other forms of Christianity. Almost 30 per cent practise religions other than Christianity or have no religion (2001 census), with Buddhism one of the fastest growing religions.

Administrative Divisions

Six states:
New South Wales, Queensland, South Australia, Tasmania, Victoria, and Western Australia

Two territories:
Australian Capital Territory and Northern Territory

There are also some external territories: Norfolk Island, the Cocos Islands, Christmas Island, Macquarie Island and Australian Antarctica (between 45° south and 160° east).

The Capital Cities

Canberra is the federal capital, in Australian Capital Territory. State capitals are:

- Sydney — New South Wales
- Melbourne — Victoria
- Brisbane — Queensland
- Perth — Western Australia
- Adelaide — South Australia
- Hobart — Tasmania
- Darwin — Northern Territory

Government Structure

Australia has a federal system of government, with a Commonwealth and six State parliaments, and representative councils in the Australian Capital Territory and Northern Territory (which are not states).

With the Queen of Australia and her representative, the Governor-General, at the top—and an Executive Council to advise the Governor-General—to give Cabinet decisions legal force, major political decisions and most real government are in the hands of the Federal Prime Minister and his Cabinet. The power of the Federal Government is limited by the Australian Constitution, which cannot be changed except by a referendum vote.

In current politics, the 'Westminster model' is more or less in force, with government faced by an Opposition in Parliament. Glossing over subtleties, there is at present in effect a two-party system, with the Liberal Party's coalition alliance with the National Party holding government, and the Australian Labor Party in opposition; powerful independent voices come from the two strongest minority parties, the Greens and the Democrats. Voting is compulsory for all Australians over 18 years old, except for the Aboriginals who may choose whether or not to register on the electoral roll.

The 150-seat federal House of Representatives is the equivalent of Britain's House of Commons, elected every three years, while the Senate acts as an 'upper house' representing State interests and reviewing legislation, elected every six years (ACT and NT, three years).

State government mirrors this structure, each state with its own royally-approved Governor, its own Premier and Cabinet, its own constitution, an upper house called the Legislative Council (elected for twice the period of the lower house) and a lower house called either the Legislative Assembly or the House of Assembly (elected for four years, except in Queensland).

The Northern Territory (self-governing since 1978) and Australian Capital Territory (a federal government territory, with self-government more or less imposed on it against the will of most residents) have a single house of parliament—the Legislative Assembly—which is elected for four years, and the head of the majority party is called the Chief Minister, while the Queen's representative is called the Administrator.

Head of State
Her Majesty Queen Elizabeth II, represented by the Governor-General (Major-General Michael Jeffery as of 2005).

Head of Government
The Prime Minister (John Winston Howard of the Liberal Party, since 1996).

Elections
Every three years—2007, 2010 etc.

Currency
The Australian dollar—decimal since 1966—consists of 100 cents. Denominations go right down to the small bronze one-cent coin. There are 1 and 2 dollar coins, and five notes of 5, 10, 20, 50 and 100 denominations, all polymer (plastic) since

1992—Australia is the first country in the world to produce all its currency notes in polymer rather than paper.

Gross Domestic Product (GDP)
US$ 611.7 billion (2004)

Products and Industries
Barley, wheat cattle, chemicals, food processing, fruit, industrial and transportation equipment, mining, poultry, sugar cane, sheep, steel, wheat

Exports
A$ 118 billion worth of goods, A$ 34 billion services (2004)—alumina, coal, gold, iron ore, machinery and transport equipment, wool.

Imports
A$ 141 billion worth of goods, A$ 36 billion services (2004)—cars and other passenger vehicles, computers and office machines, crude oil and petroleum products, medicaments (including veterinary), telecommunication equipment and parts.

Current Account Balance
US$ 40 billion deficit (2004)

Foreign Investment in Australia
A$ 1,139,217 million

NAME-DROPPING
Phillip Adams
Urbane liberal columnist, arts-world personality and pioneer of Australian cinema, Adams presides over ABC Radio National's *Late Night Live* programme, writes for *The Australian* newspaper, and makes little secret of his opposition to the Howard government, recently celebrating publicly the fact that Australia's 'secret service' ASIO has a fat file on his 'suspicious' left-wing activities.

Barlow and Chambers

Brian Chambers, 28, and Kevin Barlow, 28, became the first Australians to be hanged for drug trafficking (in heroin) in Malaysia, despite appeals from the Australian government, in 1986. (*See Schapelle Corby, below.*)

Kim Beazley

Leader of the Australian Labor Party (ALP) party now in Opposition following Paul Keating's defeat by John Howard and the Liberal Party in 1996.

Geoffrey Blainey

A distinguished historian and columnist who provoked controversy with his steady criticism of Labor's Asian immigration drive during the 1980s.

Alan Bond

Former national hero as English migrant rags-to-riches business tycoon, declared bankrupt in 1992.

Don Bradman

Australian-born cricketer, a brilliant batsman whose record of 452 runs not out in 1930 survived until 1994. He was knighted in 1979.

Martin Bryant

The disturbed lone gunman who massacred 35 innocents at Port Arthur in Tasmania on 28 April 1996, provoking the government to sweeping gun-control law reforms. He got 35 life-terms in jail.

Brian Burke

Former premier of Western Australia, 1983–1987, he is now generally discredited and was jailed for his role in the 'W.A. Inc.' scandal in Western Australia. His stamp-collecting hobby was a particular point of interest during these investigations. Even today, you will hear constant references to the free-wheeling greed of this period, with its heyday in the 1980s.

The Chamberlains

In 1980, Seventh Day Adventists Michael and Lindy Chamberlain claimed that their baby daughter Azaria had been taken by a desert dingo near remote Ayers Rock. No body was found. All Australia debated the case then, and even now. Lindy was convicted of Azaria's murder in 1982, released in 1987 and pardoned in 1990. See Fred Schepisi's 1988 movie *Evil Angels* starring Meryl Streep as Lindy Chamberlain.

Schapelle Corby

In 2005, 'the shit hit the fan' as some South-east Asian governments, notably Thailand, Vietnam, Cambodia and Indonesia, announced a crackdown on drug users and traffickers, and several Australians were arrested, with stiff prison sentences, and even potential death sentences, pending, some for simple possession charges. The case most in the headlines was and at the time of writing still is, that of pretty 27-year-old beautician Schapelle Corby, allegedly caught with 4.1 kg of marijuana in her unlocked baggage on landing at Ngurah Rai airport, Bali in Indonesia. The majority of Australians believed she was innocent, despite the lack of evidence to support her story that the drugs had been planted in her bags by someone else.

Major General Peter Cosgrove

A real-life Aussie hero who rose to fame in 1999 as commander of the UN-backed Interfet peacekeeping force that restored order to a chaotic East Timor fighting for independence from Indonesia. He distinguished himself as a soldier—and a politically competent one too—and won Australian hearts with his modest demeanour laced with compassion. He retired as Australia's Defence Force Chief in 2005.

Janet Holmes à Court

Widow of multi-millionaire business deal-maker Robert Holmes à Court, she inherited his mantle after his death in 1990 and proved to be his equal as a businesswoman to be reckoned with, presiding over a highly diversified business empire as chairperson of Heytesbury Pty. She is Australia's richest woman.

Ruth Cracknell

Former grand dame of Australian theatre, Ruth Cracknell is a commanding presence. She died in 2002 at the age of 76, but is still fondly and often remembered.

Paul Davies

Australian (English-born) physicist and author of stirring books on the interface of science and religion—e.g. *God and the New Physics*, *The Big Questions*.

Graham Farmer

Arguably Australia's most famous 'footy' player, this Western Australian Aboriginal star was at his peak in the 1950s. Perth's newest freeway is named the Graham Farmer Freeway after him.

Peter Garrett

The charismatic, bald, vertically challenged and highly intelligent lead singer of the rock band Midnight Oil. Many regard him as a prophet more than as a rock musician because of his political and spiritual commitment to the environment (he is a former president of the Australian Conservation Foundation). In 2004, he took the plunge into politics and became Labor MP for the division of Kingsford Smith in New South Wales, and now argues for environmental issues from that standpoint.

Harold Holt

Australia's Prime Minister in 1966, believed drowned while swimming off Victoria in 1967. As his body was never recovered, some mystery lingers—and articles about 'what really happened' crop up every so often. Colourful theories include Holt being whisked away by a foreign power in a submarine because he had served as their spy in Australia all along.

Steve Irwin is the tough 'bushie bloke' who has taken the place of the former 'Crocodile Dundee' (Paul Hogan) in recent years, representing the Australian image overseas in his extraordinary TV programmes and films about his life as a wildlife expert and zoo director at Queensland's Australia Zoo. He is seen here catching crocodiles to relocate them by helicopter.

Fred Hollows

A national hero though New Zealand-born. As an ophthalmologist, he worked to introduce eye-surgery techniques to the developing world, including Aboriginal Australia, Africa, Vietnam and Nepal. He died of cancer in 1993, but the Fred Hollows Foundation and his wife Gaby carry on his work.

Steve Irwin

Famous for lots of things, Queensland zoo director (the Australia Zoo) and wildlife enthusiast Irwin is the natural successor to former 'typical Aussie' Paul Hogan alias 'Crocodile Dundee'. He is internationally known for his hyperactive TV shows on animals, and notorious within Australia for apparently endangering his baby son by publicly dangling him over a crocodile pool at his zoo.

Kamahl

Extremely popular with 'middle Australia', from tiny tots to grandmas, this very successful Indian-descent singer who came originally from Malaysia is an Australian institution, although now somewhat passé.

Paul John Keating

Australia's Labor Prime Minister 1991–1996, notable for his determination to bring Australia closer to Asia (and Indonesia in particular), for his commitment to the cause of Aboriginal land rights and reconciliation, and for his transformation of the Australian economy, although a self-taught economist who left school in his teens. A brilliant and vicious parliamentary street-fighter with a talent for abusive language, his 'big picture' vision, his sheer sense of style (e.g. a liking for posh suits and collectible French clocks) and his penchant for the international stage eventually undid him, as the ordinary Australian apparently was more concerned with the 'small picture' in his own backyard.

The story of Tasmania-born Mary Donaldson's fairy-tale romance with Crown Prince Frederik of Denmark since they met in a pub at the Sydney Olympics in 2001 has entranced Australians; her grace and beauty as the new Crown Princess of Denmark has totally supplanted any former Aussie affection for the British Royal Family. She is seen here on her state visit to Australia in 2005.

Crown Princess Mary of Denmark

Born in Tasmania as plain and simple Mary Donaldson, this charming and stylish woman struck lucky when she fell in love with a handsome Danish yachtsman whom she met in a Sydney bar during the Sydney Olympics of 2001. Little did she realise—until a little later—that he was none other than Crown Prince Frederik of Denmark. The wedding was in May 2004. And so they lived happily ever after. Aussies are totally 'rapt' with Mary, who has achieved 'Princess Diana' status with them, and virtually displaced any Australian interest in the jug-eared Prince Charles of Wales from the British Royal Family.

Ned Kelly

Legendary 'bushranger' (bandit) of Victoria in the 1870s, famous for his 40-kg home-made suit of armour. In 1880, he was hanged for murder. Lionised in Australian folklore as a kind of Robin Hood, he stands for the ancient Irish hatred of the English and for the generally uneasy relationship between Australians and policemen or other authority figures. Do read Peter Carey's *The True Story of the Kelly Gang* (2001).

Paul Kelly

Celebrated middle-aged Australian singer-songwriter; his work is diversely original, often with strong Australian references in the lyrics. He collaborated with the iconic Aboriginal band Yothu Yindi on their 1990s hit song 'Treaty Now'.

Tirath Hassaram Khemlani

Mysterious Sindhi middleman said to have brokered an A$ 4-billion Middle Eastern loan for Prime Minister Gough Whitlam's government. Revelation of the loan provoked a constitutional crisis, which led to the Queen's representative Governor-General Sir John Kerr's dismissing Whitlam's government in 1975. Many Republican Australians have since used this incident to illustrate how the British monarch can undermine Australia's independence.

Carmen Lawrence

Australia's first woman Premier, 1990–1993, in Western Australia, now in Federal (Labor) politics. Dogged by political 'accidents', she is thought to have been Prime Minister material.

Elle Macpherson

Delectable top international model 'made in Australia'.

Ray Martin

Currently host of the *A Current Affair* TV programme on the Nine Network, he is a well known TV personality, sometimes mocked for his over-earnest and moral style. But his moderate and even-handed style, and campaigning for causes, is appreciated by much of 'middle Australia.'

Robert Gordon Menzies

Australia's longest-serving Prime Minister 1939–1941 and 1949-1966 and the founder of the Liberal Party. A symbol of the old 'Anglo' Australia and some detractors say, a model for the world according to John Howard, Prime Minister since 1996.

Rupert Murdoch

Melbourne-born, Murdoch took American citizenship in 1985 to expand his US media investments. The world's most powerful, and richest, press baron, he is owner of *The Times* in London, *The Australian* in Australia, and others worldwide under his News Corporation banner.

George Negus

Author, journalist and TV presenter (currently with SBS TV's *Dateline*), Negus is a highly respected and skilled commentator on current affairs, foreign and domestic.

Lee Lin Chin

One of the now numerous non-white faces, with non-standard accents, on Australian television and a popular presenter, this Hongkong-born 'fashionista' is almost a cult figure, partly for her whackiness in dress sense and weird spectacles. Another popular TV news presenter, of Greek heritage, is Mary Kostakidis. Both appear on SBS TV.

Ian MacNamara

Known to Australians as 'Macca', he hosts ABC Radio's folksy *All Over Australia* programme (particularly popular in rural Australia) and is known for his dedication to Australia's 'core values'.

Kerry Packer

Another media baron through his Consolidated Press empire, and Australia's wealthiest man. In the 1970s, he transformed cricket with his World Series of one-day matches and unorthodox coloured clothing, etc.

Phar Lap

A race-horse known to almost every Australian. A consistent winner, notably in the 1930 Melbourne Cup event, he was found dead in April 1932. Speculation on the causes continues.

Rose Porteous

Formerly Hancock, as the Filipina widow of Western Australian iron-ore tycoon Lang Hancock, whom she met when working as his housekeeper. She is now married to American Willie Porteous and, when not engaged in legal strife with Hancock's children, lives either in the US or in Perth. In 2005, she axed her A$ 30-million fantasy palace 'Prix D'Amour' in Perth in favour of developing the site. She boasts a total property portfolio worth at least A$ 20 million.

The Poseidon Incident

A feverish Australian share market swallowed over-optimistic reports of a nickel strike in Western Australia, shooting Poseidon shares from A$ 1 in October 1969 to A$ 280 in February 1970, and ending with a market crash later attributed to malpractice.

Recent Federal Prime Ministers	
Sir Robert Gordon Menzies	1939–1941/1949–1966
Harold Edward Holt	1966–1967
Sir John McEwen	1967–1968
Sir John Grey Gorton	1968–1971
Sir William McMahon	1971–1972
Edward Gough Whitlam	1972–1975
John Malcolm Fraser	1975–1983
Robert James Lee Hawke	1983–1991
Paul John Keating	1991–1996
John Winston Howard	1996–

Geoffrey Robertson

Impressive Australian-born but Oxford-educated (England) barrister dedicated to defending human rights issues in particular, both at home and abroad, and one of the leaders of the republican movement.

Ralph Sarich

Great Australian inventor best known for his development of the orbital combustion process engine.

Greg Sheridan

One of Australia's most influential commentators on Asian affairs, Sheridan writes chiefly for *The Australian* newspaper, where he serves as Foreign Editor.

Peter Singer

Controversial Australian philosopher and committed vegetarian known internationally for his radical views on euthanasia and as the 'Father of Animal Liberation' (see his 1975 book *Animal Liberation*).

Christopher Skase

Media and resort billionaire who came unstuck in the 1987 stock-market crash and then 'went walkabout' to Majorca, evading trial; he died there in 2001. A satirical film *Let's Get Skase* was directed by Mathew George in 2001.

Dick Smith

A successful entrepreneur, founder of a thriving electronic goods chain, Smith uses his money to fund a series of hobbies, from publishing to aviation and exploration, or for plain philanthropy. In 1983, he was the first person to circumnavigate the world in a helicopter and in 1987, the first to fly a helicopter to the North Pole, and has been trying out ballooning since.

Joan Sutherland

Sydney-born, internationally recognised soprano opera singer, born in 1926.

Shane Warne

Hailed as the greatest leg spin bowler of all time, this Aussie cricketer holds the record for taking wickets in the Test series and is a favourite of the gossip columnists since he apparently has no control over his rampaging sex drive.

SELECTED ACRONYMS

ABN Australian Business Number. If you are working for yourself, things can get nasty if you don't register for one of these. But having one exposes you to the trials of the BAS, GST and PAYG (see below).

ACTU The Australian Council of Trade Unions, a power in the land.

AFL Australian Football League (Aussie Rules football).

ALP Australian Labor Party.

ASIO Australian Security Intelligence Organisation (pronounce like a real word, 'Ayzeeoh'). Australia's official intelligence outfit (like the British MI5 and American CIA, etc.)

ASX   Australian Stock Exchange.

ATO   Australian Taxation Office, not exactly everyone's favourite, in the context of recent complications such as the quarterly BAS (see above) and PAYG tax paperwork (see below).

BAS   Business Activity Statement, already semi-affectionately referred to by Aussies as 'the Bazz.' This demanding statement of GST (see below) collections and liabilities must be rendered to government quarterly, with payment for the liabilities of course.

BSB   Bank-State-Branch number. You will need this number for bank transactions such as electronic funds transfer. It is the number which clearly identifies exactly which bank/branch your account is with. You will find it, a six-digit number expressed in two separated sets of three numbers, printed immediately to the left of your account number, and to the right of the cheque number, at the bottom of your cheques, just about in the centre.

EST   Eastern Standard Time in the eastern states, i.e. 10 hours ahead of Greenwich Mean Time (and 2 hours ahead of Western Australia's time zone), except in summer, when daylight saving moves it ahead another hour.

GST   Goods and Services Tax. A new tax on consumption imposed for the first time in 2000, supposedly to free up income tax rigidities, but not everyone is cheering.

PAYG   Pay As You Go income tax. For the first time, in 2001, small businesses and the self-employed were asked to pay their tax in advance, quarterly, based on income estimates from the previous year. Not as popular as a single annual payment based on full and actual annual income assessment.

RSL   Returned Services League, an ex-servicemen's association, synonymous (justly or unjustly) with crusty old conservatives, usually anti-migrant and anti- just about everything about New Australia.

SBS   The Special Broadcasting Service, established to serve ethnic minorities. SBS TV now does far more than this, offering excellent world news coverage and quality documentaries and movies.

TAFE   Technical and Further Education—say as a real word, 'Tayfe'. TAFE colleges are an important avenue for tertiary education and self-advancement in a wide range of disciplines and skills, for students of any age or level who are not going to a university.

CULTURE QUIZ

Can you be Australian enough to merge into the background? Here are a few test situations to try yourself out.

SITUATION 1

The Australian office you work with is having some problems with a document in French which needs translating. You have a post-graduate degree in French language and literature. Do you:

ⓐ Announce the fact loud and clear and proceed to do the translation?

ⓑ Keep quiet until some else says, "Hey, Bill knows a bit of French, doesn't he?" and asks you to do it?

ⓒ Offer rather tentatively to do the translation , saying, "Look, I'm not sure I can handle it, but let me take a look at it," and then translate, but deliberately take a little more time that you really need, and include a few mistakes which the boss can spot, to make him feel proud?

Comments

Of the three options, **ⓒ** is definitely the most Australian. The idea is not to stand out too much, not to excel too obviously—not to risk becoming a tall poppy asking to be mown down. However, **ⓑ** is a good alternative, while **ⓐ** is definitely not on. Oh, and if by any chance you get a promotion as a result of this performance, remember not to throw a party to celebrate it—that would be crowing too much.

SITUATION 2

You've landed a date with this gorgeous Australian blonde at last. Do you:

ⓐ Take her to the most expensive restaurant in town to wine and dine her, opening the car door and the restaurant door for her, as well as pulling out her chair for her, and pay the whole bill before escorting her right to her front door?

🅑 Take her to a medium or low-budget restaurant, let her largely fend for herself and split the bill with her before seeing her to her own car or taxi so that she can drive herself home?

🅒 Take her to the local footy match after a quick fish-and-chips snack at the neighbourhood takeaway?

Comments

Choice **🅑** is probably right for the first date. Falling over yourself to charm her as in **🅐** will probably alarm her and convince her you 'want to get into her knickers' as the saying goes. On the other hand, choice **🅒** is just too Aussie male for a real date, although it is an option by no means unheard of or untried among Aussie males. You can step up the charm on subsequent dates if you like, once she gets used to your foreign ways.

SITUATION 3

The chairman of an important business associate company in Australia, whom you have never met, has written to you for some information which he says he needs 'soonish'. Do you:

A Compose a letter beginning, 'Dear Sir, with reference to yours of the 18th inst, re data required...' etc., and fax it forthwith, mailing the original by express airmail?

B Put it in your KIV tray for a few days and then answer it by ordinary airmail, writing, 'Dear Joe, it's been a bit of a problem finding what you need, but no worries, this should be about right...'?

C Forget about it?

Comments

Option **A** will do you little good, maybe some harm, while **B** is correct and non-threatening in terms of over-efficiency. It is quite essential that you address your correspondent by his first, given name to get the right Australian tone. If possible, do remember to include a few spelling mistakes. Option **C**, while it does occur, is just too unfriendly for an Australian.

SITUATION 4

Just to prove you can speak the lingo, now translate this short passage (courtesy of writer Frank Devine's 'That's Language' column in *The Australian Magazine*, 28–29 May 1994, which is circulated nationally with *The Weekend Australian* newspaper, a marvellous source of information for all Australia-watchers):

'At Chrissie, me and my sister went to Brizzie to see our rellies. I got an eleckie blankie for a prezzy and she got some lippy. We both got sunnies and pushies. For brekky, we had muchies and chocky bikkies.'

Answer

'At Christmas, me and my sister went to Brisbane to see our relatives. I got an electric blanket for a present and she got some lipstick. We both got sunglasses and pushbikes. For breakfast, we had mushrooms and chocolate biscuits.'

DO'S AND DON'TS

DO

- Respond in like manner to friendly comments made to you in passing by strangers—it is quite normal for Aussies to talk to people they don't know. It's rude to cold shoulder them.

- Accept that strangers and new acquaintances will use your first name, and do likewise yourself—it's a subtle signal of equality.

- Take seriously and obey all warning signs on beaches and if local experts or lifeguards say get out of the water, get out!

- Apply full lane discipline and signalling etiquette when driving—no zig-zagging without signalling—and give way graciously, while minimising the use of the horn.

- Take the local drink-driving blood alcohol limit seriously and get someone else to drive on that night out.

- Talk about sport and learn to enjoy a beer with the boys in the pub if you are male.

- Pay your share of the bill at restaurants and bars.

- Bring a bottle of booze or some food with you when you are invited to a party or dinner.

- Refer to anyone who does not appear to be married to their companion, but is obviously living with them, (whether heterosexual or homosexual) as that person's 'partner.'

- Rein in any prejudices you may harbour about homosexuals, women in society and feminists, or the unemployed—it is definitely not done in polite Australian circles to display public animosity to any of these (although you may hear plenty in other circles).

- Acquire knowledge of a few 'Strine' phrases to get you through daily life with some understanding of what is going on (but note a 'Don't' below that also applies to this knowledge).

- Learn to do things for yourself; Australia is a do-it-yourself society, and labour is costly.

- Equip yourself immediately with outdoors gear such as a picnic blanket, 'esky' (cooler-box), folding chairs, folding parasol, picnic basket and plastic table-ware and cutlery—you're not an Aussie if you don't picnic during summer; likewise for the backyard 'barbie' (barbecue)—better buy one now.
- Hand over your parking coupon with unused but already paid time on it to a fellow motorist about to park; that's the sharing Australian spirit, and it also indicates in true Aussie style that you are not about to let the authorities get away with taking the common man's hard-earned cash.

DON'T

- Even try to be smart or funny or to hoodwink Australian Customs and Immigration officers; especially, do NOT try to smuggle in food or plants.
- Overreact to bad language, insults or rude gestures, just return them in kind and in good humour and then forget it.
- Take disagreement personally. Don't hold grudges or brood after a healthy Aussie argument; it's all part and parcel of the normal rough and tumble of Australian life.
- Raise over-serious issues such race or religion at relaxed social functions.
- Launch into discussions or jokes about cultural or racial differences before checking who is who in any social gathering—Australia is multi-cultural and multi-racial so you can't always be sure exactly what everyone's background may be nor how you may offend. Remember for example that many Aboriginals can look almost white.
- Talk about money, particularly your own money, on social occasions .
- Throw money around, buying everyone in sight dinner or beers; Aussies hate to feel indebted.
- Assume you should tip, at the hairdresser's, in a restaurant etc.—it's often offensive outside of the tourism industry context.

- Dress too sharply at relaxed social functions—learn to be creatively shabby sometimes.
- Assume that throwing lots of Strine phrases like 'G'day, mate!' around will bring you instant love; some Aussies resent outsiders appropriating their lingo like this—you have to win your right to use the language over time.
- Expect Aussies to be impressed by big flashy cars, opulent homes and career success; they are not impressed by that, all they want to know is, are you a good bloke at a party or a pleasant woman with heart.
- Publicly compare things in Australia negatively with things 'back home'.
- Complain—about the heat, about people, about Australia—since 'whingeing' is a cardinal sin in get-on-with-it Australia.
- Ask personal questions such as 'What's your salary like?', 'Why aren't you married?'
- Expect Australian-reared children and teenagers to be quiet and deferential to you as an older person or even as their teacher or parent.
- Try to bargain prices down at most retail establishments.
- Go into the deep countryside/outback on a driving or trekking trip without studying local conditions, taking a map and basic supplies (especially water and spare petrol), and informing local police or rangers of your itinerary. Outside of the suburbs, it can be tough territory.
- Flatter people excessively or offer to serve them too much—Aussies detest obsequiousness.
- Smoke anywhere without asking permission. Most Aussies assume it is impolite to smoke inside someone else's house and automatically step out into the backyard to smoke even without asking.
- Cast aspersions on, or engage in over objective analysis of, those who have served in wars such as World Wars I and II, and certainly not sacred cows such as the defeat at Gallipoli in 1915.
- Use politically incorrect phrases such as 'cripple' or 'handicapped' for the disabled, 'abo' for Aboriginals etc,

in polite company. Learn as quickly as possible which are the no-nos.

- Attempt to jump queues or blatantly use connections/position in any way to influence outcomes in your favour—the egalitarian Aussie will slap you down even harder. (The operative word here is 'blatantly,' however. A lot of this goes on behind closed doors, but you mustn't be caught out.)
- Invite people, or accept invitations, to 'tea' or 'dinner' without checking carefully what they mean by that term. Many Aussies refer to the main evening meal when they say 'tea' and lunch when they say 'dinner'.
- Talk about yourself too much, unless asked.
- Be too much of a goody-goody when it comes to obeying government and other rules and regulations or, at least, don't reveal that you are. Cheat a little on your bus tickets or something. Aussies admire rebels.
- Underestimate the Australian sun and risk of skin cancer. Don't bake in the sun for more than 30 minutes maximum. Hats, UV-protected 'sunnies' (sunglasses), cover-ups and the highest possible sun protection factor sunscreen lotion (e.g. SPF 30) are musts, even in winter sun.
- Start any fires anywhere, including at home, without first studying current fire warnings and wind conditions and checking for permission to do so. Avoid lighting fires in the summer.

GLOSSARY

Akubra	The classic broad-brimmed Aussieman's hat, now very chic, once the headgear of rural folk.
Arvo	Afternoon. 'See you this arvo.'
Barbie	The barbecue pit in your back garden, the centre of all social action during the Australian summer. Barbies are also barbecue parties serving charcoal-cooked meats and salads, always in the open air.
Bathers	Bathing costume, swimming costume.
Battler	A quintessentially Aussie concept, fronting a philosophy of life. The battler is the little man, the underdog struggling to survive, often in conflict with the top dog. He or she is always a hero.
Beaut	Great! Also common is 'Beauty!', pronounced 'Bewdy!'.
Bell	'Give us a bell tomorrow'—please phone tomorrow.
Bickies	Bucks, money. 'I reckon I could earn big bickies on this deal, mate.'
Bludger	Usually used in the term 'dole-bludger'. A bludger is anyone who sponges off anyone else, someone who never buys his round of drinks, and in the case of dole-bludging, someone living off the state's unemployment benefits.
Blue	A quarrel, a row, or else, a blunder.

Bodgie	The Australian equivalent of a Teddy Boy in the 1950s. Former Prime Minister Bob Hawke has been dubbed 'The Silver Bodgie' for looking like a leftover Teddy Boy at times earlier in his political career, complete with loud jackets and sideburns, albeit silvering ones.
Bonzer	Like 'cobber' (see below), this is another word which outsiders think is quintessential Strine but it too is obsolete now. It used to mean 'excellent'.
Bucketing	To get or 'cop' a bucketing, is to be reviled, strongly criticised. The phrase recalls the pre-flush toilet days when human excreta were collected in buckets; in other words, when you get 'bucketed', you get a bucket of shit poured over you.
Buckley's Chance	No chance. Origins of this phrase are obscure, but certainly of early 19th century date and Buckley clearly was a very unlucky man. This is also used more concisely, as 'You've got Buckley's of winning this bet, mate!'
Cark it	To die.
Chook	A chicken.
Chuck a wobbly	Have a fit, lose your temper.
Chunder	To vomit, the word deriving from a warning on board ship to those unfortunates happening to stand below the seasick, 'Watch under!'
Clayton's	A Clayton's thing is a false or 'bluff' thing, not the real thing. From a non-alcoholic drink of the same name—a drink that's not a drink.

Cobber	Fondly believed by many to be one of the most typical Aussie slang words, referring to a friend, this word is in fact just about dead in the Australian dialect.
Cocky	Originally, a smallholder farmer from the smallholder's propensity to grow crops, only to have them eaten up by pest cockatoos. Used "for cockatoos as well.
Crook	Sick or ill, badly done or formed, not right.
Crust	Your bread and butter, livelihood. The question 'What does he do for a crust?' is quite common.
Dag	Derogatory. A dag (the word being derived from the filthy matted wool at the hind end of a sheep) is someone who's awful in some way, whether badly dressed, pretentious or boring.
Daks/Strides	Men's trousers. 'Daks' originates from a brand-name.
Dingbat	A weirdo, someone eccentric or deranged.
Dinkum	Most famously used in the fuller expression 'Fair dinkum', meaning 'Honest, it's the truth!' It refers to the 'real thing.' 'Dinky-di' is a more intense version of this.
Dob In	To inform on someone, to betray, especially a friend, workmate or neighbour. Dobbing in, even to the police for a crime, is not considered admirable behaviour in the Australian value system.

Drongo	A hopeless loser, a stupid or clumsy person. After a horse in the 1920s which persistently failed to win a single race.
Drum	Information, the latest news, the inside story. 'What's the drum on that takeover proposal, Pete?'
Dunny	A legendary item of Australiana, the outdoors WC (toilet, lavatory) shed, pretty rarely encountered in cities nowadays, but in the countryside, still, anything goes.
Esky	Portable cooling box used to carry food and drink (more importantly, beer) to picnics on the beach or in the park, etc. Derived from the original trade name, 'Eskimo'.
Full Bottle	Fully informed, well up in. 'Henry's not full bottle on this issue, so let's call Reggie instead.'
Furphy	A rumour or false report. It arose from soldiers' tall-tale telling while sitting around water carts (servicing the latrines) branded with the manufacturer's name, 'Furphy'.
Get on your bike	Better hurry up, then.
Globe	Where other English-speakers might buy a bulb or a light-bulb, Aussies always ask for a 'globe'.
Gong	Medal or badge of authority. 'He looked important alright, all covered in gongs, he was.'
Good Oil	All the latest news, the gossip, the low-down.
Grog	Booze, liquor. Any alcoholic drink, but usually beer.

Guernsey	A symbol of acceptance, from a type of sweater, and the team jersey you get on selection for a footy team.
Gutser	Come a gutser, meaning to come a cropper, to fail dramatically.
Jackaroo/ Jackeroo	Usually a young city-slicker working on a sheep or cattle station in the rough outback to get first-hand experience of farming. A jackeroo's life is almost synonymous with toughing it out.
Jammies	Pyjamas (Pajamas).
Lakkies	Rubber bands (from 'elastics').
Larrikin	A rowdy no-gooder, a hooligan, a mischievous youth, a trouble-maker. But also a scallywag with a golden heart.
Lolly/Lollies	An abbreviation from 'Lollipop', it means any sweet or candy, especially brightly coloured ones.
Nong	A fool or simpleton.
Ocker	The ultimate, uncultured Australian boor. He is almost certain to be found wearing shorts and thongs, as the Aussies call what others call flip-flops, Japanese sandals, etc, and clutching a can of beer over a protruding belly. He is also characteristically jingoistic and insular when confronted with other races, creeds or cultures or indeed, any culture at all. Thankfully, his tribe is dwindling very quickly.
Pokey	Poker machines, or more rarely, a jail.

Poofter	A derogatory term for male homosexuals, very commonly used, probably to reaffirm what Australian men see as their central macho identity.
Pooh	Shit. 'Oh, the cat's just done a pooh on the carpet,' or 'Oh dear, looks like I'm in the pooh with my boss again!'
Prang	As in 'My son went and pranged the car again.' Only for minor car accidents, dents and so on.
Rack Off	Push off, get lost.
Rage	This has very recently acquired the meaning of 'to party wildly'. Hence, an all-night rock-video TV programme on Saturdays is titled *Rage*. You may well be invited to 'go rageing' at the weekend; do not be alarmed, this is probably an invitation to visit a few discos. It may have its origins in a farming term referring to over-excited cattle.
Ratbag	An eccentric or stupid person. Gradually coming to have a very general derogatory meaning.
Ringer	An outstanding performer. Originally the best shearer in the sheep-shearing shed. But in northern Australia, it usually only refers to a cattle muster.
Ripper	Similar to 'beaut', this means 'terrific!' 'What a ripper night we had!'.

Roo-bar	A large and solid structure made of metal bars attached to the front of Australian cars. Any car driving out of the city needs this fixture to cope with kangaroos bounding into the headlights on country roads at twilight or night. A collision with a kangaroo will otherwise result in far more serious damage to you and your car than to the 'roo itself!
Root	A dangerous one for Americans, this one. Americans may use it to mean cheering on their favourite sports team—'I was rooting for the Mets'—but in Strine it refers only to sexual intercourse, being the equivalent of 'screw'. You have been warned.
Rort	What the Americans and British know as a 'scam'—a fraudulent scheme or stunt; to con or cheat.
Sandgropers	Natives of Western Australia, because their state is largely desert sand.

Sangers	Sandwiches.
Shonky	Dubious, fraudulent, charlatan.
Shout	Both a noun and a verb. A shout is a round of drinks, for which someone has to pay. 'When my shout came round, I did the honours. But the whole evening, he never shouted one drink!'.
Smoko	Short for a 'smoke', it has come to mean all features of a break from work, for a smoke, for tea and sandwiches.
Snags	Sausages.
Spruik (verb) / Spruiker (noun)	A weird one, this, apparently of unknown origin but used as far back as 1902. It looks South-African-Dutch, doesn't it? It means (verb), to advertise something loudly and vigorously as if selling on a street market and canvassing for customers. 'She used the child's school report to spruik the child's genius all over town.'
Sticky Beak	A graphic word for the nosey parker, he or she who sticks his or her nose into things. It can also be used as a verb.
Stubby	When not a small beer bottle, a pair of tight, short shorts for men. Rarely an attractive sight.
Swag	In the past, the ill-gotten goods carried by a thief or vagabond, but today used of any traveller's quite legitimate bags and baggage. 'Here, you can rest your swag here while you come inside.'

Tart	This sounds most offensive to English ears, since in modern English outside of Australia, it would normally refer only to a prostitute. But in Australia, it just refers to any young, and usually pretty, woman. 'Eh, that new tart he's dating is a bit of alright!' It is actually a contraction of the affectionate 'sweetheart'.
Technicolor Yawn	Coined by Barry Humphries' comic-strip anti-hero, Barry McKenzie, this lurid phrase refers to a particularly violent bout of throwing-up, usually induced by an excessive intake of alcohol.
Too right!	I couldn't agree more.
Tube	A can of beer, another word popularised by the Barry McKenzie comic strip of the 1970s.
Two-up	A traditional Australian gambling game based on spinning two coins and betting whether they will fall as two heads or two tails. A two-up gambling den is often referred to as a 'Two-up School', but even Australia's most respectable casinos feature this game, which originated in the pioneer outback.
Wag	To skip something, drop out or play truant. 'My daughter's been wagging school for weeks, the head teacher just told me.'
Whinger	Anyone who complains too much instead of getting on stoically with being a battler like the rest of Australia. 'Poms'—the British—are supposed by Australians to have developed whingeing into a fine art.

Women's Business	Those rituals and secrets within an Aboriginal group that are taboo to men.
Wowser	A killjoy, one who lectures, a puritan. The wowsers would like everything to close on Sundays.
Yakker	Not to be confused with 'yacker' (a talker), this word means 'work'. 'Did a bit of hard yakker in the garden the other day, pulled me back, mate.'
Yard	A general term used for the land at the back of your house, whether it is in fact a garden or a paved area.
Youse	Probably of Irish origin, substitutes for 'you'. 'Youse blokes is OK,' or 'One of youse, come over here.'

SOME IDIOMATIC PHRASES

I'll give it a go; I'll give it a burl.
- I'll try, never mind if it doesn't work, but I'm sure it will... This mindset, while optimistic, can however lead to amateurism when it comes to the more precise technologies.

I don't know her from a bar of soap.
- I haven't the faintest idea who she is.

I suppose it's better than a poke in the eye with a burnt stick.
- It's better than nothing. As *The Bulletin* weekly magazine put it in 1974, this is the Australian way of expressing ecstasy.

I'll just pencil it in for Monday, then.
- By this, the Aussie speaker means he will tentatively jot this appointment down in his diary for Monday. But it's tentative: remember, you can erase pencil easily! But it does mean you have some sort of a prior claim, a reservation on his/her time. It's also typically old-technology for an Aussie to refer to (and even to use) pencils—you won't catch him/her 'inputting'!

If it was raining palaces, I'd get hit on the head by the dunny door.
- I never have any luck.

Don't come the raw prawn with me.
- Don't try to bluff me, to put one over me.

Good on yer!
- Good for you, well done!

In like Flynn.
- To seize an opportunity with enthusiasm, especially a sexual one. It derives from the energetic romantic exploits of the Australian-born (Tasmanian) Hollywood hero of 1930s movies, Errol Flynn.

A cut lunch and a water-bag.
- An old bushman's way of saying 'It's a long way.' 'You're going there? Well, it's a cut lunch and a water-bag for sure.'

I'll be in that; I'm up for that.
- I'm pretty keen to do that, alright.

SOME COMMON ABORIGINAL WORDS

Billabong	A waterhole.
Boomerang	The curved Aboriginal hunting weapon that returns to its owner after hitting its target, making sophisticated use of aerodynamics.
Corroboree	A festive gathering, a get-together, usually with music and dance.
Humpy	An Aboriginal bark hut, now any rough hut or shelter.
Walkabout	The habit ingrained in Aboriginal culture, of temporary migration from one's home base, for an unplanned period of time and often without a specific goal in mind. Used now of anyone who disappears mysteriously for a while to be alone or to escape something. 'Can't find Bill anywhere, musta gone walkabout.'

SOME COMMON DIMINUTIVES

Brickie	Bricklayer.
Chrissie	Christmas.
Cozzie	Swimming costume.
Deli	Delicatessen shop or counter.
Divvie	Dividend.
Footy, Footie	Australian Rules Football.
Journo	Journalist.
Muso	Musician.
Pokie	Poker machines, in casinos, etc.
Prezzie	Present, gift.
Sickie	Taking sick leave off work. Often used jokingly, on the understanding that it is just a way of getting off work. 'Your party's on Thursday morning? No worries, I'll just take a sickie and I'll be there.'
Spit the Dummy	Completely lose your temper.
Super	Superannuation—savings achieved for old-age pension and retirement income, usually by putting away a (small, compulsory) proportion of their salary in a selected superannuation fund (with another contribution from their employer). Many opt to enhance the compulsory contribution by adding 'salary sacrifice,' which is useful in more ways than one since such voluntary contributions to the super are tax-deductible.
Tazzie	Tasmania.
Tinnie	A tin can of beer.
U-ie	A U-turn, when driving a vehicle.

Uni	Where others might say 'varsity' (antique British) or 'U', the Aussies say 'Uni' for University.

SELECTED RHYMING SLANG

Bag of Fruit	Suit.
Butcher's	For Butcher's Hook = Look ('I'll just take a butcher's at the baby for a minute').
Chevy Chase	Face. (An interesting potential source of confusion for Americans, this one, as a well-known comic film actor in the USA is also named Chevy Chase.)
Dog and Bone	Telephone.
Khyber Pass	Arse.
Plates	For Plates of Meat = Feet.
Pot	For Pot and Pan = Old Man = Dad.
Steak and Kidney	Sydney.
Titfer	For Tit for Tat = Hat.
Trouble and Strife	Wife.

RESOURCE GUIDE

Australia is very good at providing information: every library, health clinic and tourist centre seems to be crammed with helpful brochures and leaflets. The federal structure of the country means that many services have a single central reference point, such as a phone number, often in Canberra or Sydney, which then directs you on to the exact information point in the state where you are; or else services are replicated in each state. There are also plenty of dial-in phone help lines.

Use Your Phone Directory

Do not neglect to consult your local phone directory which you will find is full of useful information, some of it very helpfully indexed. Local tourism authority information lines and websites are also useful.

- International call access code: **0011**
  Put this before the country/area codes for the foreign number you are contacting.
- If you want to have the duration and cost of your call played back to you, dial **0012** instead.
- From outside Australia, dial 61 for Australia, followed by the area code. Do not use the '0' in the area code, which applies only when you are inside Australia. For example, to dial Perth in Western Australia from Singapore or London, you dial 61-8-Perth phone number.

Area Codes

• Australian Capital Territory	02
• New South Wales	02
• Northern Territory	08
• Queensland	07
• South Australia	08
• Tasmania	03
• Victoria	03
• Western Australia	08

- Phone numbers with the **1800** prefix offer free calls, while calls to a **13** or **1300**-prefix number entail only the cost of a local call. These numbers cannot be called from outside Australia.
- Mobile phone numbers are prefixed with **04**, followed by two digits and the subscriber's number, dialled in full, e.g. **0412-xxx-xxx**.
- The **190** prefix on indicates an information service incurring a special charge, usually anything from A$ 0.38–5.50 a minute.

Abbreviated Form

You will find that most Australians list telephone numbers under the abbreviation 'Ph.' for "Phone", rather than 'Tel' for 'Telephone'.

- Directory Enquiries
  Tel: **12455** or **1223** for local numbers
  1225 for international numbers

IMPORTANT TELEPHONE NUMBERS

- **Emergencies (Police/Fire/Ambulance)**
  Australia-wide—for life-threatening or time-critical emergencies only:
  - **000**   from a land line
  - **112**   from a mobile

  If you have hearing difficulties, dial **1800-555-677** *to get a relay to 000.*

- For less urgent police matters
  Tel: **13-1444**

- **Crime Stoppers** line
  Tel: **1800-333-000**
  To report anything you know that could help the police solve a crime that has already been committed.

Crisis

For all kinds of crises and distress, including fire, flood, storm damage etc, your local State Emergency Service (SES) or Fire & Emergency Service will provide sterling assistance—find them in the local *White Pages* phone directory.

'Lifeline' provides crisis counselling on
Tel: **13-1114**, Australia-wide, particularly re suicide.
- In Perth, there are also the
  - **Samaritans**
    Tel: **(08) 9381-5555**
  - **Crisis Care** help-line
    Tel: **(08) 9223-1111, 1800-199-008**
- In Melbourne
  - **Crisis Care**
    Tel: **1800-177-135**

Search & Rescue

Tel: **1800-641-792** (maritime)
   1800-815-257 (aviation)
This should be reserved for major emergencies—for example, your friends have disappeared while hiking wilderness, rock-climbing or sailing the high seas.

National Security Hotline (report suspicious activity that may relate to terrorism): **1800-123-400.**

Telephone Services

Australian telephone services are de-regulated for competition, but still with essentially a duopoly split between:
- **Telstra**, the original government server
  WebsiteL http://www.telstra.com
- **Optus**
  Website: http://www.optus.com.au

Other phone companies such as AAPT, DigiPlus and others also operate. Small charges apply to most telephone services. Telstra, up to 2006 partially publicly owned, is slated for full privatisation and fragmentation into separate retail and wholesaling ventures etc.

General Information
- National Time
  Tel: **1900-931-240**
- Wake Up/Reminder
  Tel: **1902-247-019**
  Rate: A$ 2.75
- Weather
  Tel: **1902-241-677**
  Rate: A$ 1.05 per minute

Search the:
- *White Pages* for residential numbers
  Website: http://www.whitepages.com.au
- *Yellow Pages* for business numbers
  Website: http://www.yellowpages.com.au

WEB TIPS
A few starting points on the Internet, with information on Australia:

Government
- Federal Government gateway
  Website: http://www.fed.gov.au
- Prime Minister of Australia
  Website: http://www.pm.gov.au
- Austrade (trade & investment)
  Website: http://www.austrade.gov.au

Natural Environment & Science
- Environment Australia (Department of the Environment)
  Website: http://www.dest.gov.au
- Commonwealth Scientific & Industrial Research Organisation (CSIRO)
  Website: http://www.csiro.au

Migration, Citizenship & Travel

- Department of Immigration & Multicultural & Indigenous Affairs
  Website: http://www.immi.gov.au
- Australian Customs Service
  Website: http://www.customs.gov.au
- Tourism Australia (Australian Tourist Commission)
  Website: http:// www.australia.com

Aboriginal Australia

- Australians for Native Title and Reconciliation (ANTaR)
  Website: http://www.antar.org.au
- Aboriginal Australia
  Website: http://www.aboriginalaustralia.com
  See also, Department of Immigration & Multicultural & Indigenous Affairs, above

Culture & The Arts

- Australia Council
  Website: http://www.ozco.gov.au
- Australian government culture and recreation portal
  Website: http://www.cultureandrecreation.gov.au

Reference/General Information

- For a wide range of more general information on Australia, as well as tourism, visit the Australian Tourist Commission
  Website: http://www.australia.com
- National Library of Australia
  Website: http:www.nla.gov.au
- Australian National University (ANU), Canberra
  Website: http://www.anu.edu.au

MEDIA

- *The Australian* newspaper
  Website: http://www.theaustralian.com.au
- *The Age* newspaper
  Website: http://www.theage.com.au
- *Sydney Morning Herald* newspaper
  Website: http://www.smh.com.au

- *Australian Financial Review* newspaper
  Website: http://afr.com
- *The Bulletin* weekly, see Australian Consolidated Press (ACP)
  Website: http://www.acp.com.au
- *Australian Broadcasting Corporation* (ABC) radio/TV
  Website: http://www.abc.gov.au
- *Special Broadcasting Service* (SBS) radio/TV
  Website: http://www20.sbs.com.au

HEALTH EMERGENCIES

- 24-hour Health Advice
  Tel: **1800-022-222**
- Medicines Line
  Tel: **1300-888-763**

- For a full list of hospitals, state-by-state, and other useful information:
  Website: http:// www.drsref.com.au

Medical Services

The Online Medical Dictionary is full of information about medicine in general and the Australian medical scene in particular:
Website: http://www.mydr.com.au/tools/dictionary.asp

For quick medical treatment, especially overnight or on holidays or weekends, you need an on-call Locum doctor. Here are some contacts:

- **Australian Capital Territory/Canberra**
  Tel: (02) 6288-1711
- **New South Wales/Sydney**
  24-hour Hotel Doctor Service
  Tel: (02) 9962-6000
- **Northern Territory/Darwin**:
  24-hour medical crisis counselling
  Tel: (08) 8922-7156
- **Queensland/Brisbane**
  Tel: 1800-80-2622

- **South Australia/Adelaide**
  State Emergency Service
  Tel: 13-25008
- **Western Australia/Perth**
  Tel: (08) 9328-7111

First Aid Online

- If you have time, there is some excellent Australian first aid briefing at:
  Website: http://www.parasolemt.com.au

- St John Ambulance
  Tel: **1300-360-455**

Hospitals

- **Brisbane**
  Royal Brisbane Hospital (University of Queensland)
  Tel: (07) 336-5111
- **Canberra**
  - Canberra Hospital
    Tel: (02) 6244-2222
  - Calvary Hospital
    Tel: (02) 6201-6111
- **Melbourne**
  Royal Melbourne Hospital
  Tel: (03) 9342-7000
- **Perth**
  - Royal Perth Hospital
    Tel: (08) 9224-2244;
  - Princess Margaret Hospital for Children
    Tel: (08) 9340-8222
- **Sydney**
  - Royal North Shore Hospital
    Tel: (02) 9926-7111
  - Sydney Children's Hospital
    Tel: (02) 9382-1111
  - St Vincent's (public) Hospital
    Tel: (02) 9382-1111

Dental Emergencies

- **Melbourne**
  Tel: (03) 9341-0222, (07) 9341-1040
- **Perth**
  Tel: (08) 9220-5777, (08) 9325-3452
- **Sydney**
  Tel: (02) 9906-1660, (08) 9369-7050

Poisons Information Centre

Tel: **13-1126** Australia-wide.
You can use this number for serious bites (by snakes, for instance) or stings (e.g. by jelly-fish, known to Aussies as 'stingers')

Other Medical Helplines

- **Asthma Australia**
  Tel: 1800-645-130
- **Diabetes Australia**
  Tel: 1300-136-588

Medical Insurance & Treatment

Visitors from Finland, Norway Italy, Malta, the Netherlands, New Zealand, Sweden, the UK and the Republic of Ireland have reciprocal health rights with Australia's Medicare authority and can register with any Medicare office.
Tel: **13-2011** (information line)

Pharmacies

24-hour or 7-day pharmacies are plentiful in Australia:

Perth

- Beaufort St Pharmacy, Mt Lawley
  Tel: (08) 9328-7775
- Bell's Drive-In
  Tel: (08) 9328-5762
- Fremantle Drive-in Pharmacy
  Tel: (08) 9335-9633
- Forrest Chase
  Tel: (08) 9221-1691

Sydney

Try the Kings Cross & Oxford Street night-life areas, e.g.
- Darlinghurst Prescription Pharmacy
  Tel: (02) 9361-5882
- Wu's Pharmacy
  Tel: (02) 9211-1805
- Pharmacy Guild's Emergency Prescription Service
  Tel: (02) 9235-0333 (5:00–9:00 pm)

Translating & Interpreting Service (TIS)

Tel: 13-1450, Australia-wide.
If you cannot speak English well, you can get help in your chosen language.

Legal Aid Information

Tel: 1300-650-579, Australia-wide

Lost Property Services

At the airport:
- **Melbourne,**
  - Arrivals information desk
    Tel: (03) 9297-1805
  - Departures information desk
    Tel: (03) 9297-1814
- **Perth**
  Tel: (08) 9478-8503
- **Sydney**
  Tel: (02) 9667-9111. (02) 9667-9583

Otherwise contact the local police.

Resources for the Disabled

Australia is exceptionally sensitive to the needs of the disabled and almost every website or information service provides targeted information for the disabled user. Even websites for national parks and nature reserves offer trail guides etc. for disabled trekkers. So never be afraid to ask.

- Information lines: equipment, access and services, Australia-wide
  Tel: **1800-330-066**, **1800-068-424**, **1800-808-981**
- To solve transport problems, call the Commonwealth Carelink Centres
  Tel: **1800-052-222**
- Assistance with disability, sickness and carers enquiries
  Tel: **13-2717**
- **Spinal Cord Injuries Australia** (formerly The Australian Quadriplegic Association)
  Tel: 1800-819-775 if outside Sydney
       (02) 9661-8855 in Sydney
  Email: office@spinalcordinjuries.com.au
  Website: http://www.spinalcordinjuries.com.au/home
- ***Easy Access Australia*** is a travel guide for disabled travellers by wheelchair-bound Bruce Cameron that offers good state-specific information (512 pp, A$ 27.45), first published 1995 and updated since. Available at bookshops or via email: bruceeaa@vicnet.net.au or through the post at PO Box 218 Kew, Vic 3101, Australia.

News and Business Information

- **News**
  Tel: 1902-241-691 (includes stocks, business, sport)
  Rate: A$ 1.05 per minute
- **Sports News**
  Tel: 1902-241-694
  Rate: A$ 1.05 per minute
- **Financial News**
  Tel: 1900-937-012
  Rate: A$ 1.05 per minute
- **Legal Advice**
  Tel: 1902-243-736
  Rate: A$ 3.30 per minute
- **Stocks and Shares news**
  Tel: 1902-241-682
  Rate: A$ 1.05 per minute

EMBASSIES

The key diplomatic posts are located at full embassies, in Canberra, Australian Capital Territory. Other locations, including state capitals, mostly host only consulates.

Australian Capital Territory (Canberra)

- Canada (High Commission)
  Tel: (02) 6270-4000
- China
  Tel: (02) 6273-4780
- France
  Tel: (02) 6216-0100
- Germany
  Tel: (02) 6270-1911
- India (High Commission)
  Tel: (02) 6273-3999, (02) 6273-3774
- Indonesia
  Tel: (02) 6250-8600
- Japan
  Tel: (02) 6273-3244
- Malaysia (High Commission)
  Tel: (02) 6273-1543
- New Zealand (High Commission)
  Tel: (02) 6270-4211
- Singapore (High Commission)
  Tel: (02) 6273-3944
- United Kingdom (High Commission)
  Tel: (02) 6270-6666
- United States of America
  Tel: (02) 6214-5600

AIRLINES

- **American Airlines**
  Tel: 1300-650-747
- **British Airways**
  Tel: 1300-767-177
- **Qantas Airways**
  Tel: 13-1313

- **Singapore Airlines**
  Tel: 13-1011
- **Virgin Blue Airlines**
  Tel: 13-6789

FURTHER READING

THE 'HARD CORE'

Here is the minimum reading and reference list of key titles, to achieve that 'Instant Australia' confidence:

The Lucky Country. Donald Horne. Australia: Penguin Books Australia, 1988 (revised).
- This is the definitive study and should be your 'Bible' on Australia; it hardly seems outdated to me, even today.

Down Under ('In A Sunburned Country' in the US). Bill Bryson. London, UK: Black Swan, 2001; New York, USA: Broadway, 2001
- Lighthearted, witty, readable account of the Australia and why it is the way it is.

Reinventing Australia: the Mind and Mood of Australia in the 90s. Hugh Mackay. Sydney, Australia: Angus & Robertson, 1993 (revised edition).
- There also several others by Hugh Mackay, such as *Generations* on baby-boomers in Australia, 1997.

A Short History of Australia. Manning Clark, Australia: Penguin Books Australia, 1996 (4th edition).
- The big historical picture, right up to the 1980s. (The full version, *A History of Australia,* comes in six volumes.)

The Fatal Shore. Robert Hughes, London, UK: Vintage, 2003; New York, USA: Vintage, 1998.
- Sobering detail on the terrible years of convict transportation to Australia.

The Australians: In Search of an Identity. Ross Terrill. London, UK: Bantam,1987; New York, USA: Simon & Schuster, 1987.

Some relax while other partake of Western Australia's vibrant street life.

A Secret Country. John Pilger. London, UK: Vintage, 2004; New York, USA: Knopf Publishing, 1991.
- A thought-provoking assessment of the darker side of contemporary Australia, touching on politics, business, sociology and the environment.

The Future Eaters: An Ecological History of the Australasian Lands and People. Tim Flannery. New York, USA: Grove Press 2002.
- A distinguished Sydney-based research scientist looks at the human relationship with the land of Australia and the impact on its unique ecology.

The Little Aussie Fact Book. Margaret Nicholson. Australia: Penguin Books Australia, 2002. (21st century edition)
- Everything you could ever want to know about anything Australian, in neat concise form, pocket-sized.

A Dictionary of Australian Colloquialisms. G A Wilkes. Sydney, Australia: Sydney University Press, 1978/1985.
- A flashlight in the maze of 'Strine'.

The Australian National Dictionary: A Dictionary of Australianisms on Historical Principles. Ed. W S Ramson. Melbourne, Australia: Oxford University Press, 1989.

The Macquarie Dictionary of Australian Quotations. Eds. Stephen Torre & Peter Kirkpatrick. Sydney, Australia: The Macquarie Library, 1990.

The Penguin Australian Encyclopaedia. Ed. Sarah Dawson, Melbourne, Australia: Viking/Penguin Books, 1990.
- A crash course in Australia.

The Book of Australia, an almanac. Hodder & Stoughton, Sydney 1990/reprinted.

The Macquarie Book of Events. Ed. Bryce Fraser. Sydney, Australia: The Macquarie Library, 1990.

ON ABORIGINAL AUSTRALIA

My Place. Sally Morgan. Western Australia: Fremantle Arts Centre Press, 2000.
- A personal search for lost Aboriginal 'roots'

The Other Side of the Frontier: Aboriginal Resistance to the European Invasion of Australia. Henry Reynolds. Victoria, Australia: Penguin Books Australia, 1990.
- White settlement of Australia seen from the other side, by the Aboriginals.

Seeing the First Australians. Eds. Ian Donaldson and Tamsin Donaldson. New South Wales., Australia: Allen & Unwin, 1985.
- A well illustrated and researched account of how the first European settlers and later Australians have viewed the Aboriginals of Australia.

The Chant of Jimmie Blacksmith. Thomas Keneally. Sydney, Australia: Angus & Robertson, 2002; New York, USA: Penguin Books, 1989.
- A novel dramatically depicting the Aboriginal plight.

The Songlines. Bruce Chatwin. London, UK: Vintage, 1998; New York, USA: Penguin, 1988
- This mystical work tells of the ancient paths travelled by the Aboriginals while singing the songs of their ancestors.

My People. Kath Walker. Australia: Jacaranda Wiley, 1981.
- Collected verse by this established, campaigning Aboriginal poet.

Charles Perkins: A Biography. Peter Read. Australia: Penguin Books Australia, 2001; New York, USA: Viking, Australia 1990.

Being Whitefella. Ed. Duncan Graham. Western Australia: Fremantle Arts Centre Press, 2001.
- Essays by thinking whites on their relationships with the Aboriginals.

MORE HISTORY AND CURRENT AFFAIRS

The Tyranny of Distance. Geoffrey Blainey. New South Wales, Australia: Pan Macmillan Australia, 2001.
- How the geography and sheer vastness of Australia have shaped the country's history. For more historical insight, try also Blainey's *Triumph of the Nomads*, a history of ancient Australia, *The Rush That Never Ended* and *A Land Half Won.*

A Fortunate Life. A B Facey. Victoria, Australia: Penguin Books Australia, 1985.
- The moving autobiography of a completely ordinary white Australian, born in 1894, who helped pioneer the harsh West, survived Gallipoli, saw and experienced the lot.

For the Term of His Natural Life. Marcus Clarke. Gloucerstershire, UK: Nonsuch Publishing, 2005; New York, USA: HarperCollins Publishers, 2002
- A pioneering novel of colonial times depicting the horrors of Australia as a penal colony.

The Horne Trilogy: *The Education of Young Donald; Confessions of a New Boy; Portrait of an Optimist.* Donald Horne. Victoria, Australia: Penguin Books Australia, 1988.
- An intellectual autobiography and indirectly an intellectual history of three decades in Australia.

Robert J Hawke: A Biography. Blanche d'Alpuget. New York, USA: Penguin Books, 1985.
- This substantial warts-and-all biography of Australia's second-longest-serving prime minister, up to his first election victory in 1983, paints a revealing picture of Australian political life.

WOMEN IN AUSTRALIA

Damned Whores and God's Police. Ann Summers. Victoria, Australia: Penguin Books Australia, 1975.
- A startling and revealing feminist history of Australia.

Tracks. Robyn Davidson. London, UK: Picador, 1998; New York, USA: Vintage, 1995
- An incredibly brave desert solo trek in which the camels star as much as this intrepid female explorer.

Pioneer Women of the Bush and Outback. Jennifer Isaacs. Australia: Lansdowne, 1990.
- The women pioneers' story—European, Chinese, Aboriginal—as researched through archival records.

No Place for a Nervous Lady. Ed. Lucy Frost. Australia: University of Queensland Press, 1999
- The letters and diaries of 13 white women struggling with 19th century Australia.

FICTION

Power Without Glory. Frank Hardy. Australia: Angus & Robertson, 1982.
- A novel based on the true story of a businessman's life, this book gave rise to an unsuccessful suit for criminal libel.

Voss. Patrick White. London, UK: Vintage, 1994
- A novel of exploration, dwelling on the landscape. Difficult, dense reading. The author was a Nobel prize winner in 1973. If you like it, try also White's *The Tree of Man, The Aunt's Story* and *Riders in the Chariot*.

Don's Party. David Williamson, New South Wales, Australia: Currency Press, 1978.
- A novel of rumbustious postwar, pre-Whitlam Australia in the raw.

Oscar & Lucinda. Peter Carey. London, UK: Faber & Faber, 2004; New York. USA: Vintage, 1997.

- Like White's works, a difficult, dense piece of writing which yields magic if you concentrate. This novel won the Booker McConnell prize for fiction. Carey's complex narrative has epic shape and surrealistic, nightmarish qualities. His characters are very strange indeed. If you like this one, try also his *Bliss* and *Illywhacker*. His *True History of the Kelly Gang* (Random House, 2000) account of the 19th century Irish bandit, Ned Kelly, written in Ned Kelly's own (somewhat illiterate) voice, is a masterpiece.

A Town Like Alice. Nevil Shute. London, UK: House of Stratus, 2000; New York, USA: Ballantine, 1987.

- This wartime romance of an Englishwoman and an Aussie soldier tells much about Australia.

The Thorn Birds. Colleen McCulloch. New York, USA: Avon Trade, 2005.

- An epic family 'dynasty' romance, through the generations of an Irish-Australian family. Some 20 million copies of the book have been sold.

Kangaroo. D H Lawrence. Cambridge, UK: Cambridge University Press, 2004.

Cloudstreet. Tim Winton. New York, USA: Scribner, 2002.

- Like many Australians, this West Australian novelist is in love with beaches and the sea, and it shows. An award-winner, this one.

Dirt Music. Tim Winton. London, UK: Picador, 2003; NEw York, USA: Scribner, 2003.

- A love story set among fishermen and the wild coastline of Western Australia. A Booker Prize shortlist nominee.

AUSTRALIANA: BUSH BALLADS AND SATIRE

The Best of Henry Lawson. Henry Lawson. Australia: Angus & Robertson, 1981.
- Favourite bush ballads and poetry.

The Prose Works of Henry Lawson. Australia: Angus & Robertson, 1948/1980s.

Collected Verse. A B 'Banjo' Paterson. Australia: Angus & Robertson, 1993.

The Songs of a Sentimental Bloke. C J Dennis. UK: Kessinger Publishing Co, 2004.

Australian Bush Ballads. Eds. Douglas Stewart & Nancy Keesing. Australia: Angus & Robertson, 1986.

Great Australian Legends. Frank Hardy (in association with Truthful Jones). Australia: Hutchinson, 1988.

My Gorgeous Life, An Adventure. Dame Edna Everage (alias Barry Humphries). London, UK: Mandarin, 1995.
- To quote a W*eekend Australian* review: 'Scorned at school for her mauve hair, little Edna eventually triumphs as an international megastar.' A spoof, of course.

The Life and Death of Sandy Stone. Barry Humphries. London, UK: Penguin Book Ltd, 1991.
- Moribund suburban Australia captured with lugubrious accuracy.

Keating: 'Shut Up and Listen and You Might Learn Something!' Compiler Edna Carew, New Endeavour Press, Sydney 1990.
- True sayings of the former Treasurer. It was a toss-up whether to categorise this book under Humour, Current Affairs, or what …

CULTURE SHOCK HUMOUR

How to Survive Australia. Robert Treborlang. Sydney, Australia: Major Mitchell Press, 2005 (9th edition).

How to be Normal in Australia. Robert Treborlang. Sydney: Major Mitchell Press, 1999 (8th edition).

They're a Weird Mob. Nino Culotta (John O'Grady), Sydney 1957.
- A big hit at the time, this is a lighthearted account of early migrants' lives.

AT HOME AND OUTDOORS

Traditional Australian Cooking. Shirley Constantine, McPhee Gribble/Penguin Books Australia, 1991.
- Replete with fascinating social history, this is more than a cookery book, but it is also that.

Australian Bushcraft : A Guide to Survival and Camping. Richard Graves. Australia: New Holland Publishers, 1989 (3rd edition).

Stay Alive, A Handbook on Survival. Maurice Dunlevy, Canberra: Australian Government Publishing Service, 1997.

Bushwalking in Australia. John Chapman and Monica Chapman. Melbourne, Australia: Lonely Planet Publications, 1997.

What Bird Is That?: Classic Guide to the Birds of Australia. Neville W. Cayley. Ed. Alec H Chisholm. Australia: HarperCollins, 1991.
- The classic birdwatcher's field guide.

The Slater Field Guide to Australian Birds. Peter Slater, Pat Slater and Raoul Slater. Australia: New Holland Publishers, 2003.
- Very clear colour illustrations in this handy small-and-tall guidebook.

ABOUT THE AUTHOR

Ilsa Sharp is uniquely well positioned to explain culture shock in Australia. She comes to the subject from many different directions: British-born, she has worked as a journalist in South-east Asia, chiefly in Singapore, since 1968. She holds a degree in Chinese Studies from Leeds University, England, and is married to a Singaporean-Tamil. In 1989, she and her husband became migrants to Western Australia, and a new love affair with Australia began.

Ilsa is the author of several books ranging from histories of Raffles Hotel (1982/1986), the Singapore Cricket Club (1986/1993), the national lottery, Singapore Pools (1998) and Land Transport (2005), in Singapore, and a privately commissioned Indonesian family history (1992), to wildlife/nature books such as *Green Indonesia* (Oxford University Press, 1994) and the story of the Singapore Zoological Gardens (1994). An active environmentalist since the 1970s, she was manager of public relations and marketing (1998–2000) for Greening Australia (Western Australia), a non-governmental organisation dedicated to the conservation and renewal of native vegetation. She is now a freelance writer.

INDEX

Titles in the CULTURE**SHOCK**! series:

Argentina	Hong Kong	Paris
Australia	Hungary	Philippines
Austria	India	Portugal
Bahrain	Indonesia	San Francisco
Barcelona	Iran	Saudi Arabia
Beijing	Ireland	Scotland
Belgium	Israel	Sri Lanka
Bolivia	Italy	Shanghai
Borneo	Jakarta	Singapore
Brazil	Japan	South Africa
Britain	Korea	Spain
Cambodia	Laos	Sweden
Canada	London	Switzerland
Chicago	Malaysia	Syria
Chile	Mauritius	Taiwan
China	Mexico	Thailand
Costa Rica	Morocco	Tokyo
Cuba	Moscow	Turkey
Czech Republic	Munich	Ukraine
Denmark	Myanmar	United Arab
Ecuador	Nepal	Emirates
Egypt	Netherlands	USA
Finland	New York	Vancouver
France	New Zealand	Venezuela
Germany	Norway	Vietnam
Greece	Pakistan	

For more information about any of these titles, please contact any of our Marshall Cavendish offices around the world (listed on page ii) or visit our website at:

www.marshallcavendish.com/genref